DISCARD

W9-ARG-656

COLLECTED POEMS

1950-2012

BY ADRIENNE RICH

Later Poems: Selected and New, 1971–2012

Tonight No Poetry Will Serve: Poems 2007–2010

A Human Eye: Essays on Art and Society, 1997–2008

Poetry & Commitment: An Essay

Telephone Ringing in the Labyrinth: Poems 2004–2006

The School Among the Ruins: Poems 2000–2004

What Is Found There: Notebooks on Poetry and Politics

The Fact of a Doorframe: Poems 1950–2001

Fox: Poems 1998–2000

Arts of the Possible: Essays and Conversations

Midnight Salvage: Poems 1995–1998

Dark Fields of the Republic: Poems 1991–1995

Collected Early Poems 1950–1970

An Atlas of the Difficult World: Poems 1988–1991

Time's Power: Poems 1985–1988

Blood, Bread, and Poetry: Selected Prose 1979–1985

Your Native Land, Your Life: Poems

Sources

A Wild Patience Has Taken Me This Far: Poems 1978–1981

On Lies, Secrets, and Silence: Selected Prose, 1966–1978

The Dream of a Common Language: Poems 1974–1977

Twenty-One Love Poems

Of Woman Born: Motherhood as Experience and Institution

Poems: Selected and New, 1950–1974

Diving into the Wreck: Poems 1971–1972

The Will to Change: Poems 1968–1970

Leaflets: Poems 1965–1968

Necessities of Life

Snapshots of a Daughter-in-Law: Poems 1954–1962

The Diamond Cutters and Other Poems

A Change of World

COLLECTED POEMS

1950-2012

ADRIENNE RICH

W. W. Norton & Company

Independent Publishers Since 1923

New York | London

Copyright © 2016, 2013 by the Adrienne Rich Literary Trust.
Copyright © 2011, 2007, 2004, 2001, 1999, 1995, 1991, 1989, 1986,
1984, 1981, 1967, 1963, 1962, 1961, 1960, 1959, 1958, 1957, 1956,
1955, 1954, 1953, 1952, 1951 by Adrienne Rich.
Copyright © 1984, 1978, 1975, 1973, 1971, 1969, 1966
by W. W. Norton & Company, Inc.

Introduction © 2016 by Claudia Rankine

All rights reserved
Printed in the United States of America
First Edition

Lines from "The Panther" by Rainer Maria Rilke from *Translations from the Poetry of Rainer Maria Rilke*, translated by M. D. Herter Norton. Copyright 1938 by W. W. Norton & Company, Inc., renewed © 1966 by M. D. Herter Norton. Used by permission of W. W. Norton & Company, Inc. Lines from "Bird on the Wire" excerpted from *Stranger Music* by Leonard Cohen. Copyright © 1993 Leonard Cohen. Reprinted by permission of McClelland & Stewart, a division of Penguin Random House Canada Limited. Lines from "The Flowering of the Rod" by H. D. (Hilda Doolittle), from *Trilogy*, edited by Norman Holmes Pearson. Copyright © 1997 by Carcanet Press. Reprinted by permission of Carcanet Press. Lines from "The Flowering of the Rod" by H. D. (Hilda Doolittle), from *Collected Poems, 1912–1944*, copyright © 1944, 1945, 1946 by Oxford University Press, renewed 1973 by Norman Holmes Pearson. Reprinted by permission of New Directions Publishing Corp. Lines from "Como Presentación, Como Disculpa" by Georgina Herrera (and English translation) by permission of Margaret Randall. Lines from "Elogio de la Dialectica" by Nancy Morejón reprinted with permission from the author. Lines from "U.S. 1" by Muriel Rukeyser from *The Collected Poems of Muriel Rukeyser*, University of Pittsburgh Press, 2005, used by permission of William L. Rukeyser.

For information about permission to reproduce selections from this book, write to Permissions, W. W. Norton & Company, Inc.,
500 Fifth Avenue, New York, NY 10110

For information about special discounts for bulk purchases, please contact W. W. Norton Special Sales at specialsales@wwnorton.com or 800-233-4830

Manufacturing by LSC Crawfordsville
Production manager: Julia Druskin

Library of Congress Cataloging-in-Publication Data

Names: Rich, Adrienne, 1929–2012, author.
Title: Collected poems : 1950–2012 / Adrienne Rich.
Other titles: Poems
Description: First edition. | New York : W. W. Norton & Company, [2016] |
Includes bibliographical references and index.
Identifiers: LCCN 2016009163 | ISBN 9780393285116 (hardcover)
Classification: LCC PS3535 .I233 2016 | DDC 811/.54—dc23
LC record available at https://lccn.loc.gov/2016009163

W. W. Norton & Company, Inc.
500 Fifth Avenue, New York, N.Y. 10110
www.wwnorton.com

W. W. Norton & Company Ltd.
15 Carlisle Street, London W1D 3BS

2 3 4 5 6 7 8 9 0

CONTENTS

POEMS (1950–1951)

THE DIAMOND CUTTERS (1955)

SNAPSHOTS OF A DAUGHTER-IN-LAW (1963)

POEMS (1955–1957)

NECESSITIES OF LIFE (1966)

PART ONE: POEMS 1962–1965

DIVING INTO THE WRECK (1971–1972)

POEMS (1973–1974)

THE DREAM OF A COMMON LANGUAGE
(1974–1977)

A WILD PATIENCE HAS TAKEN ME THIS FAR
(1978–1981)

YOUR NATIVE LAND, YOUR LIFE (1981–1985)

TIME'S POWER (1985–1988)

AN ATLAS OF THE DIFFICULT WORLD (1988–1991)

DARK FIELDS OF THE REPUBLIC (1991–1995)

MIDNIGHT SALVAGE (1995–1998)

FOX (1998–2000)

THE SCHOOL AMONG THE RUINS (2000–2004)

I.

TELEPHONE RINGING IN THE LABYRINTH
(2004–2006)

TONIGHT NO POETRY WILL SERVE (2007–2010)

LATER POEMS (2010–2012)

INTRODUCTION

BY CLAUDIA RANKINE

In answer to the question "Does poetry play a role in social change?" Adrienne Rich once answered:

> Yes, where poetry is liberative language, connecting the fragments within us, connecting us to others like and unlike ourselves, replenishing our desire. . . . [I]n poetry words can say more than they mean and mean more than they say. In a time of frontal assaults both on language and on human solidarity, poetry can remind us of all we are in danger of losing—disturb us, embolden us out of resignation.

There are many great poets, but not all of them alter the ways in which we understand the world we live in; not all of them suggest that words can be held responsible. Remarkably, Adrienne Rich did this and continues to do this for generations of readers. In her *Collected Poems 1950–2012* we have a chronicle of over a half century of what it means to risk the self in order to give the self.

Rich's desire for a transformative writing that would invent new ways to be, to see, and to speak drew me to her work in the early 1980s while I was a student at Williams College. Midway through a cold and snowy semester in the Berkshires, I read for the first time James Baldwin's 1962 *The Fire Next Time* and two collections by Rich, her 1969 *Leaflets* and her 1971–1972 *Diving into the Wreck*. In Baldwin's text I underlined the following: "Most people guard and keep; they suppose that it is they themselves and what they identify with themselves that they are guarding and keeping, whereas what they are actually guarding and keeping is their system of reality and what they assume themselves to be. One can give nothing whatever without giving oneself—that is to say, risking oneself."

Rich's interrogation of the "guarding" of systems was the subject of everything she wrote in the years leading up to my first encounter with her work. *Leaflets, Diving into the Wreck*, and *The Dream of a Common Language* were all examples of her interrogation, as were her other works, all the way to her final poems in 2012. And though I did not have the critic Helen Vendler's experience upon encountering Rich—"Four years after she published her first book, I read it in almost disbelieving wonder; someone my age was writing down my life. . . . Here was a poet who seemed, by a miracle, a twin: I had not known till then how much I had wanted a contemporary and a woman as a speaking voice of life"—I was immediately drawn to Rich's interest in what echoes past the silences in a life that wasn't necessarily my life.

In my copy of Rich's essay "When We Dead Awaken," the faded yellow highlighter still remains recognizable on pages after more than thirty years: "Both the victimization and the anger experienced by women are real, and have real sources, everywhere in the environment, built into society, language, the structures of thought." As a nineteen-year-old, I read in both Rich and Baldwin a twinned dissatisfaction with systems invested in a single, dominant, oppressive narrative. My initial understanding of feminism and racism came from these two writers in the same weeks and months.

Rich claimed that Baldwin was the "first writer I read who suggested that racism was poisonous to white as well as destructive to Black people" ("Blood, Bread, and Poetry: The Location of the Poet" [1984]). It was Rich who suggested to me that silence, too, was poisonous and destructive to our social interactions and self-knowledge. Her understanding that the ethicacy of our personal relationships was dependent on the ethics of our political and cultural systems was demonstrated not only in her poetry but also in her essays, interviews, and in conversations like the extended one she conducted with the poet and essayist Audre Lorde.

Despite the vital friendship between Lorde and Rich, or perhaps because of it, both poets were able to question their own everyday practices of collusion with the very systems that oppressed them. As self-identified lesbian feminists, they openly negotiated the difficulties of their very different racial and economic realities. Stunningly, they showed us that, if you listen closely enough, language "is no longer personal," as Rich writes in "Meditations for a Savage Child," but stains and is stained by the political.

In the poem "Hunger" (1974–1975), which is dedicated to Audre Lorde, Rich writes, "I'm wondering / whether we even have what we think we have / . . . even our intimacies are rigged with terror. / Quantify suffering? My guilt at least is open, / I stand convicted by all my convictions—you, too . . ." And as if in the form of an answer, Lorde wrote in "The Uses Of Anger: Women Responding to Racism," an essay published in 1981, "I cannot hide my anger to spare your guilt, nor hurt feelings, nor answering anger; for to do so insults and trivializes all our efforts. Guilt is not a response to anger; it is a response to one's own actions or lack of action."

By my late twenties, the early 1990s, I was in graduate school at Columbia University and came across Rich's recently published *An Atlas of the Difficult World*. I approached the volume thinking I knew what it would hold but found myself transported by Rich's profound exploration of ethical loneliness. Rich called forward voices created in a precarious world. And though the term "ethical loneliness" would come to me years later from the work of the critic Jill Stauffer, I understood Rich to be drawing into her stanzas the voices of those who have been, in the words of Stauffer, "abandoned by humanity compounded by the experience of not being heard."

Perhaps because of its pithy, if riddling, directness, the opening stanza of the last poem in *An Atlas of the Difficult World*, "Final Notations," willed its way into my memory like a popular song. This shadow sonnet, with its intricate and entangled complexity, seemed to have come a far distance from the tidiness of the often-anthologized "Aunt Jennifer's Tigers," a poem that appeared in her first collection. The open-ended pronoun "it" seemed as likely to land in "change" as in "poetry" or "life" or "childbirth":

> It will not be simple, it will not be long
> it will take little time, it will take all your thought
> it will take all your heart, it will take all your breath
> it will be short, it will not be simple

As readers, when we are lucky, we can experience a poet's changes through language over a lifetime. For me, these lines enacted Rich's statement in "Images for Godard" (1970) that "the moment of change is the only poem." Rich's own transformations brought her closer to the ethical lives of her readers even as she wrote poems that at times lost patience with our culture's inability to change with her.

Arriving at Radcliffe, the daughter of a Southern Protestant pianist mother and a Jewish doctor father, Rich initially excelled at being exceptional in accepted ways. Often working in traditional form in her early writing, she, even in these nascent poems, was already addressing the frustration of being constrained by forces that traditionally were not inclusive. Consequently, Rich was never primarily invested in traditional meter and form, though she employed them early on. Some of her earliest poems suggest she was already grasping toward what could not yet be described as "liberative language." Her poems often found ways to critique existing expectations for one's femininity and sexuality, and a decorum that did not include speaking her truth to power.

Rich began her public poetic career as the 1951 winner of the Yale Younger Poets Prize for her first collection, *A Change of World*. W. H. Auden selected Rich's volume and brought to the world's attention Rich's first thorny questions, embedded in lyrics, addressing a culture's disengagement with its embattled selves. A poem like "A Clock in the Square," published in that volume, finds its inspiration in a "handless clock" that refuses, rather than is unable, "to acknowledge the hour":

> This handless clock stares blindly from its tower,
> Refusing to acknowledge any hour,
> But what can one clock do to stop the game
> When others go on striking just the same?
> Whatever mite of truth the gesture held,
> Time may be silenced but will not be stilled,
> Nor we absolved by any one's withdrawing
> From all the restless ways we must be going
> And all the rings in which we're spun and swirled,
> Whether around a clockface or a world.

The clock appears initially to be broken, but its handlessness proves an ineffective strategy against the "game." Silence as a form of rebellion proves inadequate to the moment.

Auden praised *A Change of World* for, among other things, its "detachment from the self and its emotions," as is demonstrated in "Aunt Jennifer's Tigers," a poem that has always been coupled in my mind with Rainer Maria Rilke's "The Panther." "Aunt Jennifer's Tigers" projects freedom onto the image of the tigers the poem's protagonist stitches into her needlework. This is in contrast to Rilke's portrayal of the panther as imprisoned and behind bars. Rilke depicts the panther's very will as having been paralyzed:

> The padding gait of flexibly strong strides,
> that in the very smallest circle turns,
> is like a dance of strength around a center
> in which stupefied a great will stands

Rich's dialectical use of the tigers to contrast with the paralysis intrinsic to Aunt Jennifer's domestic life speaks gently to her early "absolutist approach to the universe," as she herself observed in a 1964 essay. She would come to understand society's limits as touching all our lives. "Aunt Jennifer's Tigers" ends with the quatrain:

> When Aunt is dead, her terrified hands will lie
> Still ringed with ordeals she was mastered by.
> The tigers in the panel that she made
> Will go on prancing, proud and unafraid.

Those "terrified hands," "ringed" and "mastered," also could imagine and create a fantastical reflection of life, *those tigers*, that were "proud and unafraid."

Rich came of age in a postwar America where civil rights and antiwar movements were either getting started or were on the horizon. Poets like Robert Lowell, Allen Ginsberg, James Wright, and LeRoi Jones/Amiri Baraka, among others, were abandoning the illusionary position of objectivity and finding their way to the use of the first person and gaining access to their emotional as well as political lives on the page. Rich's reach for objectivity would be similarly short-lived.

Rich joined poets engaged in political-poetic resistance to the Vietnam War, as can be seen in "The Burning of Paper Instead of Children" (1968), which includes lines like "Frederick Douglass wrote an English purer than Milton's." She began to elide traditions in order to speak from a more integrated history. "Even before I called myself a feminist or a lesbian," Rich wrote in "Blood, Bread, and Poetry," "I felt driven—for my own sanity—to bring together in my poems the political world 'out there'—the world of children dynamited or napalmed, of the urban ghetto and militarist violence—and the supposedly private, lyrical world of sex and of male/female relationships."

With Rich came the formulation of an alternate poetic tradition that distrusted and questioned paternalistic, hetero-normative, and hierarchical notions of what it meant to have a voice, especially for female writers. All of culture found its way into Rich's poems, and as her work evolved, she made it almost impossible for any writers mentored by her poetry and essays to experience their own work as "spo-radic, errant, orphaned of any tradition of its own," to quote from her foreword to the 1979 *On Lies, Secrets, and Silence.*

A dozen years after *A Change of World* was published, Rich would look back on her earlier work—which includes her second volume, *The Diamond Cutters,* and its metrical and imagistic tidiness—and admit that "in many cases I had suppressed, omitted, falsified even, certain disturbing elements, to gain that perfection of order." This understanding that disruption seen and negotiated inside the poem might be closer to her actual experience of the world changed the content, form, and voice of her poetics. In her third collection, *Snap-shots of a Daughter-in-Law* (1963), a restlessness settles into the poems that explore marriage and childrearing. It's here the exasperation of a "thinking woman" begins the fight "with what she partly understood. / Few men about her would or could do more, / hence she was labeled harpy, shrew and whore," as Rich writes in the title poem.

The 1970s saw the publication of some of Rich's most memorable and powerful poems. She developed in her writing the appearance of the unadorned simplicity of a mind in rigorous thought. In a 1971 conversation with Stanley Plumly, Rich said she was "interested in the possibilities of the 'plainest statement' at times, the kind of things that people say to each other at moments of stress." In poems like the groundbreaking "Diving into the Wreck," Rich clearly chooses reality over myth in order to create room within the poems to confront what was broken in our common lives:

> I came to explore the wreck.
> The words are purposes.
> The words are maps.
> I came to see the damage that was done
> and the treasures that prevail.
> I stroke the beam of my lamp
> slowly along the flank
> of something more permanent
> than fish or weed

the thing I came for:
the wreck and not the story of the wreck
the thing itself and not the myth
the drowned face always staring
toward the sun
the evidence of damage
worn by salt and sway into this threadbare beauty
the ribs of the disaster

When *Diving into the Wreck* won the National Book Award in 1974, Rich accepted the prize in solidarity with fellow nominees Alice Walker and Audre Lorde:

The statement I am going to read was prepared by three of the women nominated for the National Book Award for poetry, with the agreement that it would be read by whichever of us, if any, was chosen.

We, Audre Lorde, Adrienne Rich, and Alice Walker, together accept this award in the name of all the women whose voices have gone and still go unheard in a patriarchal world, and in the name of those who, like us, have been tolerated as token women in this culture, often at great cost and in great pain. We believe that we can enrich ourselves more in supporting and giving to each other than by competing against each other; and that poetry—if it is poetry—exists in a realm beyond ranking and comparison. We symbolically join together here in refusing the terms of patriarchal competition and declaring that we will share this prize among us, to be used as best we can for women. We appreciate the good faith of the judges for this award, but none of us could accept this money for herself, nor could she let go unquestioned the terms on which poets are given or denied honor and livelihood in this world, especially when they are women. We dedicate this occasion to the struggle for self-determination of all women, of every color, identification, or derived class: the poet, the housewife, the lesbian, the mathematician, the mother, the dishwasher, the pregnant teenager, the teacher, the grandmother, the prostitute, the philosopher, the waitress, the women who will understand what we are doing here and those who will not understand yet; the silent women whose voices have been denied us, the articulate women who have given us strength to do our work.

In 1997, over twenty years later, Rich declined the National Medal for the Arts, this country's highest artistic honor, because she believed "the very meaning of art, as I understand it, is incompatible with the cynical politics of this administration." In her July 3 letter to the Clinton administration and Jane Alexander, the chairwoman of the National Endowment for the Arts, she wrote:

> I want to clarify to you what I meant by my refusal. Anyone familiar with my work from the early sixties on knows that I believe in art's social presence—as breaker of official silences, as voice for those whose voices are disregarded, and as a human birthright. In my lifetime I have seen the space for the arts opened by movements for social justice, the power of art to break despair. Over the past two decades I have witnessed the increasingly brutal impact of racial and economic injustice in our country.
>
> There is no simple formula for the relationship of art to justice. But I do know that art—in my own case the art of poetry—means nothing if it simply decorates the dinner table of power which holds it hostage.

Positioned as a teacher, as I often am now, at the front of a classroom, I was struck by reading a line in "Draft #2006" from *Telephone Ringing in the Labyrinth*. The line—"Maybe I couldn't write fast enough.   Maybe it was too soon."—reminded me that this urgency, apprehension, and questioning has characterized all of Rich's poems. Still it seems she responds in time, as she will always be once and future, and her work always relevant.

They asked me, is this time worse than another.

I said for whom?

Wanted to show them something.   While I wrote on the
chalkboard they drifted out. I turned back to an empty room.

Maybe I couldn't write fast enough.   Maybe it was too soon.

In her *Collected Poems 1950—2012* we have a chronicle of over a half century
of what it means to risk the self in order to give the self, to refer back to Bald-
win. As the poet Marilyn Hacker has written,

> Rich's body of work establishes, among other things, an intellectual
> autobiography, which is interesting not as the narrative of one life
> (which it's not) and still less as intimate divulgence, but as the evo-
> lution and revolutions of an exceptional mind, with all its curiosity,
> outreaching, exasperation and even its errors.

One of our best minds writes her way through the changes that have
brought us here, in all the places that continue to entangle our liber-
ties in the twenty-first century. And here is not "somewhere else but
here," Rich writes. We remain in "our country moving closer to its own
truth and dread, / its own way of making people disappear."

What Kind of Times Are These

There's a place between two stands of trees where the grass grows
            uphill
and the old revolutionary road breaks off into shadows
near a meeting-house abandoned by the persecuted
who disappeared into those shadows.

I've walked there picking mushrooms at the edge of dread, but
            don't be fooled
this isn't a Russian poem, this is not somewhere else but here,
our country moving closer to its own truth and dread,
its own ways of making people disappear.

I won't tell you where the place is, the dark mesh of the woods
meeting the unmarked strip of light—
ghost-ridden crossroads, leafmold paradise:
I know already who wants to buy it, sell it, make it disappear.

And I won't tell you where it is, so why do I tell you
anything? Because you still listen, because in times like these
to have you listen at all, it's necessary
to talk about trees.

EDITOR'S NOTE

This is the first collection of Adrienne Rich's poetry to be published without her active involvement. However, in certain ways it is based on similar collected works that she edited at intervals over the course of her career. She undertook the last of these in the year leading up to her death in 2012—going through all the work she'd published since *The Will to Change* in 1971 and adding ten new poems to create *Later Poems: Selected and New, 1971–2012.*

Rich had already gone through this process several times during the previous fifty years: looking through the books of poetry she had published up to that point to choose representative work for a volume of "selected" poems. In 1975, just a year after her pivotal book *Diving into the Wreck*, W. W. Norton published the first such volume, *Poems: Selected and New, 1950–1974.* Nearly ten years later, in 1984, she repeated the process with *The Fact of a Doorframe*, followed in 1993 by *Collected Early Poems 1950–1970*, which consists of the full text of her first six books.

In each case, along with selections from earlier books, she chose what she called "uncollected" work: poems that she had previously held back or had only published in magazines but never included in a book. She also added new work; important poems like "The Fact of a Doorframe" and "From an Old House in America" first appeared in *Poems: Selected and New.* In the foreword to that book, she described her selection as "the graph of a process still going on," a statement equally true of *The*

Fact of a Doorframe when it was first published in 1984 and also when she updated it for W. W. Norton more than fifteen years later.

Those books are the basis for the present collection, except that now nothing has been omitted: all of Rich's published poetry appears here in one volume, including all of the uncollected poems. Explanatory notes that she provided for some of her poems are compiled and appear here in a single section at the back. There were a few instances where she changed words or lines in an earlier poem when preparing to include it in one of the "selected" books. These alterations were described in her notes, and this collection preserves the later versions.

Except for *Later Poems: Selected and New, 1971–2012*, she also wrote short forewords for each of the "selected" volumes, describing how she made her selections and offering an account of her experience as the person who wrote those poems and of the world in which she found herself at work. The forewords are often self-critical, and they emphasize her place in a wider current of language, poetry, and events. These short essays aren't included in the present book, but some information from them, specific to individual poems, is incorporated into the endnotes of the present collection.

In omitting any appendix of drafts or discarded poems, this volume respects Rich's own directions regarding the papers she donated to Radcliffe's Arthur and Elizabeth Schlesinger Library on the History of Women. There she notes that over the years, in collecting poems for her books, she had "weeded out work I felt was not to my own standards or was repetitive," and specifies that those discards and drafts are not for publication.

However, the otherwise "uncollected" poems that appeared only in *Poems: Selected and New, The Fact of a Doorframe*, and *Collected Early Poems* are all here. Likewise, the major poems from the late 1970s and early 1980s that she left out of her final selected volume—"From an Old House in America," "Transcendental Etude," and "Natural Resources"—can now be read in their fullest possible context.

Elements of typography and page design varied over the years from one book to another and are here made uniform. But I have tried to preserve as nearly as possible the structure of each book as it appeared for the first time, including all dedications and epigraphs, as well as the division of poems into separate numbered sections.

Even after she submitted her book manuscripts, Rich continued to work with tremendous care and precision, collaborating with her editors, book designers, proofreaders, and everyone else at W. W. Norton associated with her work over thirty-one volumes of poetry and prose. In assembling *Collected Poems*, I benefited from her example and from the collaboration of a publisher with a deep connection to this body of work.

I grew up hearing the keystrokes and carriage returns of my mother's typewriter as she worked on some of these poems. Some I saw for the first time when they arrived enclosed with her letters and some I first heard in her own voice at public readings. In editing this collection, I was struck over and over by how these poems change in sound and meaning when read at different times and in different settings. This is Adrienne Rich's poetry from over sixty years, and although it's now gathered under one cover, the poems continue to breathe, reaching forward to find new and different readers.

—PABLO CONRAD

A CHANGE
OF WORLD
(1951)

For Theodore Morrison

STORM WARNINGS

The glass has been falling all the afternoon,
And knowing better than the instrument
What winds are walking overhead, what zone
Of gray unrest is moving across the land,
I leave the book upon a pillowed chair
And walk from window to closed window, watching
Boughs strain against the sky

And think again, as often when the air
Moves inward toward a silent core of waiting,
How with a single purpose time has traveled
By secret currents of the undiscerned
Into this polar realm. Weather abroad
And weather in the heart alike come on
Regardless of prediction.

Between foreseeing and averting change
Lies all the mastery of elements
Which clocks and weatherglasses cannot alter.
Time in the hand is not control of time,
Nor shattered fragments of an instrument
A proof against the wind; the wind will rise,
We can only close the shutters.

I draw the curtains as the sky goes black
And set a match to candles sheathed in glass
Against the keyhole draught, the insistent whine
Of weather through the unsealed aperture.
This is our sole defense against the season;
These are the things that we have learned to do
Who live in troubled regions.

AUNT JENNIFER'S TIGERS

Aunt Jennifer's tigers prance across a screen,
Bright topaz denizens of a world of green.
They do not fear the men beneath the tree;
They pace in sleek chivalric certainty.

Aunt Jennifer's fingers fluttering through her wool
Find even the ivory needle hard to pull.
The massive weight of Uncle's wedding band
Sits heavily upon Aunt Jennifer's hand.

When Aunt is dead, her terrified hands will lie
Still ringed with ordeals she was mastered by.
The tigers in the panel that she made
Will go on prancing, proud and unafraid.

VERTIGO

As for me, I distrust the commonplace;
Demand and am receiving marvels, signs,
Miracles wrought in air, acted in space
After imagination's own designs.
The lion and the tiger pace this way
As often as I call; the flight of wings
Surprises empty air, while out of clay
The golden-gourded vine unwatered springs.
I have inhaled impossibility,
And walk at such an angle, all the stars
Have hung their carnival chains of light for me:
There is a streetcar runs from here to Mars.
I shall be seeing you, my darling, there,
Or at the burning bush in Harvard Square.

THE ULTIMATE ACT

What if the world's corruption nears,
The consequence they dare not name?
We shall but realize our fears
And having tasted them go on,
Neither from hope of grace nor fame,
Delivered from remorse and shame,
And do the things left to be done
For no sake other than their own.
The quarry shall be stalked and won,
The bed invaded, and the game
Played till the roof comes tumbling down
And win or lose are all the same.
Action at such a pitch shall flame
Only beneath a final sun.

WHAT GHOSTS CAN SAY

When Harry Wylie saw his father's ghost,
As bearded and immense as once in life,
Bending above his bed long after midnight,
He screamed and gripped the corner of the pillow
Till aunts came hurrying white in dressing gowns
To say it was a dream. He knew they lied.
The smell of his father's leather riding crop
And stale tobacco stayed to prove it to him.
Why should there stay such tokens of a ghost
If not to prove it came on serious business?
His father always had meant serious business,
But never so wholly in his look and gesture
As when he beat the boy's uncovered thighs
Calmly and resolutely, at an hour

When Harry never had been awake before.
The man who could choose that single hour of night
Had in him the ingredients of a ghost;
Mortality would quail at such a man.

An older Harry lost his childish notion
And only sometimes wondered if events
Could echo thus long after in a dream.
If so, it surely meant they had a meaning.
But why the actual punishment had fallen,
For what offense of boyhood, he could try
For years and not unearth. What ghosts can say—
Even the ghosts of fathers—comes obscurely.
What if the terror stays without the meaning?

THE KURSAAL AT INTERLAKEN

Here among tables lit with bottled tapers
The violins are tuning for the evening
Against the measured *"Faites vos jeux,"* the murmur,
Rising and falling, from the gaming rooms.
The waiters skim beneath the ornate rafters
Where lanterns swing like tissue-paper bubbles.
The tables fill, the bottled candles drip,
The gaming wheels spin in the long salon,
And operetta waltzes gild the air
With the capricious lilt of costume music.

You will perhaps make love to me this evening,
Dancing among the circular green tables
Or where the clockwork tinkle of the fountain
Sounds in the garden's primly pebbled arbors.
Reality is no stronger than a waltz,

A painted lake stippled with boats and swans,
A glass of gold-brown beer, a phrase in German
Or French, or any language but our own.
Reality would call us less than friends,
And therefore more adept at making love.

What is the world, the violins seem to say,
But windows full of bears and music boxes,
Chocolate gnomes and water-color mountains,
And calendars of French and German days—
Sonntag and *vendredi,* unreal dimensions,
Days where we speak all languages but our own?
So in this evening of a mythical summer
We shall believe all flowers are edelweiss,
All bears hand-carved, all kisses out of time,
Caught in the spinning vertigo of a waltz.

The fringe of foam clings lacelike to your glass,
And now that midnight draws with Swiss perfection
The clock's two hands into a single gesture,
Shall we pursue this mood into the night,
Play this charade out in the silver street
Where moonlight pours a theme by Berlioz?
If far from breath of ours, indifferent, frozen,
The mountain like a sword against the night
Catches a colder silver, draws our sight,
What is she but a local tour de force?

The air is bright with after-images.
The lanterns and the twinkling glasses dwindle,
The waltzes and the croupiers' voices crumble,
The evening folds like a kaleidoscope.
Against the splinters of a reeling landscape
This image still pursues us into time:
Jungfrau, the legendary virgin spire,
Consumes the mind with mingled snow and fire.

RELIQUARY

The bones of saints are praised above their flesh,
That pale rejected garment of their lives
In which they walked despised, uncanonized.

Brooding upon the marble bones of time
Men read strange sanctity in lost events,
Hold requiem mass for murdered yesterdays,
And in the dust of actions once reviled
Find symbols traced, and freeze them into stone.

PURELY LOCAL

Beside this door a January tree
Answers a few days' warmth with shoots of green;
And knowing what the winds must do, I see
A hint of something human in the scene.
No matter how the almanacs have said
Hold back, distrust a purely local May,
When did we ever learn to be afraid?
Why are we scarred with winter's thrust today?

A VIEW OF THE TERRACE

Under the green umbrellas
Drinking golden tea,
There sit the porcelain people
Who care for you but little
And not at all for me.

The afternoon in crinkles
Lies stiffly on the lawn
And we, two furtive exiles,
Watch from an upper window
With shutters not quite drawn.

The gilt and scalloped laughter
Reaches us through a glaze,
And almost we imagine
That if we threw a pebble
The shining scene would craze.

But stones are thrown by children,
And we by now too wise
To try again to splinter
The bright enamel people
Impervious to surprise.

BY NO MEANS NATIVE

"Yonder," they told him, "things are not the same."
He found it understated when he came.
His tongue, in hopes to find itself at home,
Caught up the twist of every idiom.
He learned the accent and the turn of phrase,
Studied like Latin texts the local ways.
He tasted till his palate knew their shape
The country's proudest bean, its master grape.
He never talked of fields remembered green,
Or seasons in his land of origin.

And still he felt there lay a bridgeless space
Between himself and natives of the place.

Their laughter came when his had long abated;
He struggled in allusions never stated.
The truth at last cried out to be confessed:
He must remain eternally a guest,
Never to wear the birthmark of their ways.
He could be studying native all his days
And die a kind of minor alien still.
He might deceive himself by force of will,
Feel all the sentiments and give the sign,
Yet never overstep that tenuous line.

What else then? Wear the old identity,
The mark of other birth, and when you die,
Die as an exile? it has done for some.
Others surrender, book their passage home,
Only to seek their exile soon again,
No greater strangers than their countrymen.
Yet man will have his bondage to some place;
If not, he seeks an Order, or a race.
Some join the Masons, some embrace the Church,
And if they do, it does not matter much.

As for himself, he joined the band of those
Who pick their fruit no matter where it grows,
And learn to like it sweet or like it sour
Depending on the orchard or the hour.
By no means native, yet somewhat in love
With things a native is enamored of—
Except the sense of being held and owned
By one ancestral patch of local ground.

AIR WITHOUT INCENSE

We eat this body and remain ourselves.
We drink this liquor, tasting wine, not blood.
Among these triple icons, rites of seven,
We know the feast to be of earth, not heaven:
Here man is wounded, yet we speak of God.
More than the Nazarene with him was laid
Into the tomb, and in the tomb has stayed.

Communion of no saints, mass without bell,
Air without incense, we implore at need.
There are questions to be answered, and the sky
Answers no questions, hears no litany.
We breathe the vapors of a sickened creed.
Ours are assassins deadlier than sin;
Deeper disorders starve the soul within.

If any writ could tell us, we would read.
If any ghost dared lay on us a claim,
Our fibers would respond, our nerves obey;
But revelation moves apart today
From gestures of a tired pontifical game.
We seek, where lamp and kyrie expire,
A site unscourged by wasting tongues of fire.

FOR THE FELLING OF AN ELM
IN THE HARVARD YARD

They say the ground precisely swept
No longer feeds with rich decay
The roots enormous in their age
That long and deep beneath have slept.

So the great spire is overthrown,
And sharp saws have gone hurtling through
The rings that three slow centuries wore;
The second oldest elm is down.

The shade where James and Whitehead strolled
Becomes a litter on the green.
The young men pause along the paths
To see the axes glinting bold.

Watching the hewn trunk dragged away,
Some turn the symbol to their own,
And some admire the clean dispatch
With which the aged elm came down.

A CLOCK IN THE SQUARE

This handless clock stares blindly from its tower,
Refusing to acknowledge any hour.
But what can one clock do to stop the game
When others go on striking just the same?
Whatever mite of truth the gesture held,
Time may be silenced but will not be stilled,
Nor we absolved by any one's withdrawing
From all the restless ways we must be going
And all the rings in which we're spun and swirled,
Whether around a clockface or a world.

WHY ELSE BUT TO FORESTALL THIS HOUR

Why else but to forestall this hour, I stayed
Out of the noonday sun, kept from the rain,
Swam only in familiar depths, and played
No hand where caution signaled to refrain?

For fourteen friends I walked behind the bier;
A score of cousins wilted in my sight.
I heard the steeples clang for each new year,
Then drew my shutters close against the night.

Bankruptcy fell on others like a dew;
Spendthrifts of life, they all succumbed and fled.
I did not chide them with the things I knew:
Smiling, I passed the almshouse of the dead.

I am the man who has outmisered death,
In pains and cunning laid my seasons by.
Now I must toil to win each hour and breath;
I am too full of years to reason why.

THIS BEAST, THIS ANGEL

No: this, my love, is neither you nor I.
This is the beast or angel, changing form,
The will that we are scourged and nourished by.

The golden fangs, the tall seraphic sword,
Alike unsheathed, await the midnight cry,
Blazon their answer to the stammered word.

Beneath this gaze our powers are fused as one;
We meet these eyes under the curve of night.
This is the transformation that is done

Where mortal forces slay mortality
And, towering at terrible full height,
This beast, this angel is both you and I.

EASTPORT TO BLOCK ISLAND

Along the coastal waters, signals run
In waves of caution and anxiety.
We'll try the catboat out another day.
So Danny stands in sea-grass by the porch
To watch a heeling dinghy, lone on grey,
Grapple with moods of wind that take the bay.

One year we walked among the shipwrecked shingles
Of storm-crazed cottages along the dune.
Rosa Morelli found her husband's boat
Ruined on the rocks; she never saw him dead,
And after seven years of stubborn hope
Began to curse the sight of things afloat.

The mother of the Kennedy boys is out
Stripping the Monday burden from the line
And looking for a rowboat round the headland.
Wonder if they stopped for bait at Mory's
And if the old man made them understand
This is a day for boys to stay on land?

Small craft, small craft, stay in and wait for tidings.
The word comes in with every hour of wind.
News of a local violence pricks the air,
And we who have seen the kitchen blown away,
Or Harper's children washed from sight, prepare
As usual in these parts for foul, not fair.

AT A DEATHBED IN THE YEAR TWO THOUSAND

I bid you cast out pity.
No more of that: let be
Impotent grief and mourning.
How shall a man break free
From this deathwatch of earth,
This world estranged from mirth?

Show me gay faces only.
I call for pride and wit—
Men who remember laughter,
Brave jesters to befit
An age that would destroy
Its last outpost of joy.

No longer condolence
And wailing on the tongue.
An old man bids you laugh;
This text I leave the young:
Your rage and loud despair
But shake a crumbling stair.

Laughter is what men learn
At seventy years or more,
Weary of being stern
Or violent as before.
Laughter to us is left
To light that darkening rift

Where little time is with us,
Let us enact again
Not *Oedipus* but *The Clouds*.
Summon the players in.
Be proud on a sorry earth:
Bring on the men of mirth.

AFTERWARD

Now that your hopes are shamed, you stand
At last believing and resigned,
And none of us who touch your hand
Know how to give you back in kind
The words you flung when hopes were proud:
Being born to happiness
Above the asking of the crowd,
You would not take a finger less.
We who know limits now give room
To one who grows to fit her doom.

THE UNCLE SPEAKS IN THE DRAWING ROOM

I have seen the mob of late
Standing sullen in the square,
Gazing with a sullen stare
At window, balcony, and gate.
Some have talked in bitter tones,
Some have held and fingered stones.

These are follies that subside.
Let us consider, none the less,
Certain frailties of glass
Which, it cannot be denied,
Lead in times like these to fear
For crystal vase and chandelier.

Not that missiles will be cast;
None as yet dare lift an arm.
But the scene recalls a storm
When our grandsire stood aghast
To see his antique ruby bowl
Shivered in a thunder-roll.

Let us only bear in mind
How these treasures handed down
From a calmer age passed on
Are in the keeping of our kind.
We stand between the dead glass-blowers
And murmurings of missile-throwers.

BOUNDARY

What has happened here will do
To bite the living world in two,
Half for me and half for you.
Here at last I fix a line
Severing the world's design
Too small to hold both yours and mine.
There's enormity in a hair
Enough to lead men not to share
Narrow confines of a sphere
But put an ocean or a fence
Between two opposite intents.
A hair would span the difference.

FIVE O'CLOCK, BEACON HILL

Curtis and I sit drinking auburn sherry
In the receptive twilight of the vines
And potted exile shrubs with sensitive spines
Greening the glass of the conservatory.

Curtis, in sand-grey coat and tie of madder,
Meets elder values with polite negation.
I, between yew and lily, in resignation
Watch lime-green shade across his left cheek spatter.

Gazing beyond my elbow, he allows
Significance of sorts to Baudelaire.
His phrases float across the lucent air
Like exotic leaves detached from waxy boughs.

I drink old sherry and look at Curtis' nose—
Intelligent Puritan feature, grave, discreet,
Unquestionably a nose that one might meet
In portraits of antique generalissimos.

The study seems sufficient recompense
For Curtis' dissertations upon Gide.
What rebel breathes beneath his mask, indeed?
Avant-garde in tradition's lineaments!

FROM A CHAPTER ON LITERATURE

After the sunlight and the fiery vision
Leading us to a place of running water,
We came into a place by water altered.
Dew ribboned from those trees, the grasses wept
And drowned in their own weeping; vacant mist
Crawled like a snail across the land, and left
A snail's moist trace; and everything there thriving
Stared through an aqueous half-light, without mirth
And bred by languid cycles, without ardor.

There passion mildewed and corrupted slowly,
Till, feeding hourly on its own corruption,
It had forgotten fire and aspiration,
Becoming sodden with appetite alone.
There in the green-grey thickness of the air
Lived and begat cold spores of intellect,
Till giant mosses of a rimelike aspect
Hung heavily from the boughs to testify
Against all simple sensualities,
Turning them by a touch gross and discolored,
Swelling the warm taut flesh to bloated symbol
By unrelenting watery permeations.

So from promethean hopes we came this far,
This far from lands of sun and racing blood.
Behind us lay the blazing apple tree,
Behind us too the vulture and the rock—
The tragic labor and the heroic doom—
For without passion the rock also crumbles
And the wet twilight scares the bird away.

AN UNSAID WORD

She who has power to call her man
From that estranged intensity
Where his mind forages alone,
Yet keeps her peace and leaves him free,
And when his thoughts to her return
Stands where he left her, still his own,
Knows this the hardest thing to learn.

MATHILDE IN NORMANDY

From the archaic ships the green and red
Invaders woven in their colored hosts
Descend to conquer. Here is the threaded headland,
The warp and woof of a tideless beach, the flight,
Recounted by slow shuttles, of swift arrows,
And the outlandish attitudes of death
In the stitched soldiery. That this should prove
More than the personal episode, more than all
The little lives sketched on the teeming loom
Was then withheld from you; self-conscious history

That writes deliberate footnotes to its action
Was not of your young epoch. For a pastime
The patient handiwork of long-sleeved ladies
Was esteemed proper when their lords abandoned
The fields and apple trees of Normandy
For harsher hunting on the opposite coast.
Yours was a time when women sat at home
To the pleasing minor airs of lute and hautbois,
While the bright sun on the expensive threads
Glowed in the long windless afternoons.

Say what you will, anxiety there too
Played havoc with the skein, and the knots came
When fingers' occupation and mind's attention
Grew too divergent, at the keen remembrance
Of wooden ships putting out from a long beach,
And the grey ocean dimming to a void,
And the sick strained farewells, too sharp for speech.

AT A BACH CONCERT

Coming by evening through the wintry city
We said that art is out of love with life.
Here we approach a love that is not pity.

This antique discipline, tenderly severe,
Renews belief in love yet masters feeling,
Asking of us a grace in what we bear.

Form is the ultimate gift that love can offer—
The vital union of necessity
With all that we desire, all that we suffer.

A too-compassionate art is half an art.
Only such proud restraining purity
Restores the else-betrayed, too-human heart.

THE RAIN OF BLOOD

In the dark year an angry rain came down
Blood-red upon the hot stones of the town.
Beneath the pelting of that liquid drought
No garden stood, no shattered stalk could sprout,
As from a sunless sky all day it rained
And men came in from streets of terror stained
With that unnatural ichor. Under night
Impatient lovers did not quench the light,
But listening heard above each other's breath
That sound the dying heard in rooms of death.
Each loudly asked abroad, and none dared tell
What omen in that burning torrent fell.
And all night long we lay, while overhead
The drops rained down as if the heavens bled;
And every dawn we woke to hear the sound,
And all men knew that they could stanch the wound,
But each looked out and cursed the stricken town,
The guilty roofs on which the rain came down.

STEPPING BACKWARD

Good-by to you whom I shall see tomorrow,
Next year and when I'm fifty; still good-by.
This is the leave we never really take.
If you were dead or gone to live in China
The event might draw your stature in my mind.
I should be forced to look upon you whole
The way we look upon the things we lose.
We see each other daily and in segments;
Parting might make us meet anew, entire.

You asked me once, and I could give no answer,
How far dare we throw off the daily ruse,
Official treacheries of face and name,
Have out our true identity? I could hazard
An answer now, if you are asking still.
We are a small and lonely human race
Showing no sign of mastering solitude
Out on this stony planet that we farm.
The most that we can do for one another
Is let our blunders and our blind mischances
Argue a certain brusque abrupt compassion.
We might as well be truthful. I should say
They're luckiest who know they're not unique;
But only art or common interchange
Can teach that kindest truth. And even art
Can only hint at what disturbed a Melville
Or calmed a Mahler's frenzy; you and I
Still look from separate windows every morning
Upon the same white daylight in the square.

And when we come into each other's rooms
Once in awhile, encumbered and self-conscious,
We hover awkwardly about the threshold
And usually regret the visit later.

Perhaps the harshest fact is, only lovers—
And once in a while two with the grace of lovers—
Unlearn that clumsiness of rare intrusion
And let each other freely come and go.
Most of us shut too quickly into cupboards
The margin-scribbled books, the dried geranium,
The penny horoscope, letters never mailed.
The door may open, but the room is altered;
Not the same room we look from night and day.

It takes a late and slowly blooming wisdom
To learn that those we marked infallible
Are tragic-comic stumblers like ourselves.
The knowledge breeds reserve. We walk on tiptoe,
Demanding more than we know how to render.
Two-edged discovery hunts us finally down;
The human act will make us real again,
And then perhaps we come to know each other.

Let us return to imperfection's school.
No longer wandering after Plato's ghost,
Seeking the garden where all fruit is flawless,
We must at last renounce that ultimate blue
And take a walk in other kinds of weather.
The sourest apple makes its wry announcement
That imperfection has a certain tang.
Maybe we shouldn't turn our pockets out
To the last crumb or lingering bit of fluff,
But all we can confess of what we are
Has in it the defeat of isolation—
If not our own, then someone's anyway.

So I come back to saying this good-by,
A sort of ceremony of my own,
This stepping backward for another glance.
Perhaps you'll say we need no ceremony,

Because we know each other, crack and flaw,
Like two irregular stones that fit together.
Yet still good-by, because we live by inches
And only sometimes see the full dimension.
Your stature's one I want to memorize—
Your whole level of being, to impose
On any other comers, man or woman.
I'd ask them that they carry what they are
With your particular bearing, as you wear
The flaws that make you both yourself and human.

ITINERARY

The guidebooks play deception; oceans are
A property of mind. All maps are fiction,
All travelers come to separate frontiers.

The coast, they said, is barren; birds go over
Unlighting, in search of richer inland gardens.
No green weed thrusts its tendril from the rock face.

Visit it if you must; then turn again
To the warm pleasing air of colored towns
Where rivers wind to lace the summer valleys.

The coast is naked, sharp with cliffs, unkind,
They said; scrub-bitten. Inland there are groves
And fêtes of light and music.

But I have seen

Such denizens of enchantment print these sands
As seldom prowl the margins of old charts:
Stallions of verd antique and wild brown children
And tails of mermaids glittering through the sea!

A REVIVALIST IN BOSTON

But you shall walk the golden street,
And you unhouse and house the Lord.

—Gerard Manley Hopkins

Going home by lamplight across Boston Common,
We heard him tell how God had entered in him,
And now he had the Word, and nothing other
Would do but he must cry it to his brother.

We stood and listened there—to nothing new.
Yet something loosed his tongue and drove him shouting.
Compulsion's not play-acted in a face,
And he was telling us the way to grace.

Somehow we saw the youth that he had been,
Not one to notice; an ordinary boy—
Hardly the one the Lord would make His tool—
Shuffling his feet in Baptist Sunday school.

And then transfiguration came his way;
He knew the secret all the rest were seeking.
He made the tale of Christendom his own,
And hoarsely called his brethren to the throne.

The same old way; and yet we knew he saw
The angelic hosts whose names he stumbled over.
He made us hear the ranks of shining feet
Treading to glory's throne up Tremont Street.

THE RETURN OF THE
EVENING GROSBEAKS

The birds about the house pretend to be
Penates of our domesticity.
And when the cardinal wants to play at prophet
We never tell his eminence to come off it.

The crows, too, in the dawn prognosticate
Like ministers at a funeral of state.
The pigeons in their surplices of white
Assemble for some careful Anglican rite.

Only these guests who rarely come our way
Dictate no oracles for us while they stay.
No matter what we try to make them mean
Their coming lends no answer to our scene.

We scatter seed and call them by their name,
Remembering what has changed since last they came.

THE SPRINGBOARD

Like divers, we ourselves must make the jump
That sets the taut board bounding underfoot
Clean as an axe blade driven in a stump;
But afterward what makes the body shoot
Into its pure and irresistible curve
Is of a force beyond all bodily powers.
So action takes velocity with a verve
Swifter, more sure than any will of ours.

A CHANGE OF WORLD

Fashions are changing in the sphere.
Oceans are asking wave by wave
What new shapes will be worn next year;
And the mountains, stooped and grave,
Are wondering silently range by range
What if they prove too old for the change.

The little tailors busily sitting
Flashing their shears in rival haste
Won't spare time for a prior fitting—
In with the stitches, too late to baste.
They say the season for doubt has passed:
The changes coming are due to last.

UNSOUNDED

Mariner unpracticed,
In this chartless zone
Every navigator
Fares unwarned, alone.
Each his own Magellan
In tropics of sensation:
Not a fire-scorched stone
From prior habitation,
Not an archaic hull
Splintered on the beach.
These are latitudes revealed
Separate to each.

DESIGN IN LIVING COLORS

Embroidered in a tapestry of green
Among the textures of a threaded garden,
The gesturing lady and her paladin
Walk in a path where shade and sunlight harden
Upon the formal attitudes of trees
By no wind bent, and birds without a tune,
Against the background of a figured frieze
In an eternal summer afternoon.

So you and I in our accepted frame
Believe a casual world of bricks and flowers
And scarcely guess what symbols wander tame
Among the panels of familiar hours.
Yet should the parting boughs of green reveal
A slender unicorn with jeweled feet,
Could I persuade him at my touch to kneel
And from my fingers take what unicorns eat?

If you should pick me at my whim a rose,
Setting the birds upon the bush in flight,
How should I know what crimson meaning grows
Deep in this garden, where such birds alight?
And how should I believe, the meaning clear,
That we are children of disordered days?
That fragmentary world is mended here,
And in this air a clearer sunlight plays.

The fleeing hare, the wings that brush the tree,
All images once separate and alone,
Become the creatures of a tapestry
Miraculously stirred and made our own.
We are the denizens of a living wood
Where insight blooms anew on every bough,
And every flower emerges understood
Out of a pattern unperceived till now.

WALDEN 1950

Thoreau, lank ghost, comes back to visit Concord,
Finds the town like all towns, much the same—
A little less remote, less independent.
The cars hurl through from dawn to dawn toward Boston
Paying out speed like a lifeline between towns.
Some of them pause to look at Alcott's house.
No farmer studies Latin now; the language
Of soil and market would confound a scholar;
And any Yankee son with lonesome notions
Would find life harder in the town today.

Under the trees by Walden Pond, the stalls
Where summer pilgrims pause beside the road,
Drown resinous night in busy rivalry
While the young make boisterous love along the shores.

He used to hear the locomotive whistle
Sound through the woods like a hawk's restless cry.
Now the trains run through Concord night and day,
And nobody stops to listen. The ghost might smile—
The way a man in solitude would smile—
Remembering all the sounds that passed for sound
A century ago.
                    He would remain
Away from houses other ghosts might visit,
Not having come to tell a thing or two
Or lay a curse (what curse could frighten now?)
No tapping on the windowpane for him
Or twilight conversation in the streets
With some bewildered townsman going home.
If he had any errand, it would be
More likely curiosity of his own
About the human race, at least in Concord.
He would not come so far from distant woods
Merely to set them wondering again.

SUNDAY EVENING

We are two acquaintances on a train,
Rattling back through darkening twilight suburbs
From a weekend in the country, into town.
The station lights flare past us, and we glance
Furtively at our watches, sit upright
On leather benches in the smoke-dim car
And try to make appropriate conversation.

We come from similar streets in the same city
And have spent this same hiatus of three days
Escaping streets and lives that we have chosen.
Escape by deck chairs sprawled on evening lawns,
By citronella and by visitant moths;
Escape by sand and water in the eyes,
And sea-noise drowned in weekend conversation.

Uneasy, almost, that we meet again,
Impatient for this rattling ride to end,
We still are stricken with a dread of passing
Time, the coming loneliness of travelers
Parting in hollow stations, going home
To silent rooms in too-familiar streets
With unknown footsteps pacing overhead.

For there are things we might have talked about,
And there are signs we might have shared in common.
We look out vainly at the passing stations
As if some lamplit shed or gleaming roof
Might reawake the sign in both of us.
But this is only Rye or Darien,
And whoever we both knew there has moved away.

And I suppose there never will be time
To speak of more than this—the change in weather,
The lateness of the train on Sunday evenings—
Never enough or always too much time.
Life lurches past us like a windowed twilight
Seen from a train that halts at little junctions
Where weekend half-acquaintances say good-by.

THE INNOCENTS

They said to us, or tried to say, and failed:

With dust implicit in the uncurled green
First leaf, and all the early garden knowing
That after rose-red petals comes the bleak
Impoverished stalk, the black dejected leaf
Crumpled and dank, we should at Maytime be
Less childlike in delight, a little reserved,
A little cognizant of rooted death.

And yet beneath the flecked leaf-gilded boughs
Along the paths fern-fringed and delicate,
We supple children played at golden age,
And knelt upon the curving steps to snare
The whisking emerald lizards, or to coax
The ancestral tortoise from his onyx shell
In lemon sunlight on the balcony.
And only pedagogues and the brittle old
Existed to declare mortality,
And they were beings removed in walk and speech.

For apprehension feeds on intellect:
Uneasy ghosts in libraries are bred—
While innocent sensuality abides
In charmed perception of an hour, a day,
Ingenuous and unafraid of time.

So in the garden we were free of fear,
And what the saffron roses or the green
Imperial dragonflies above the lake
Knew about altered seasons, boughs despoiled,
They never murmured; and to us no matter
How in the drawing room the elders sat

Balancing teacups behind curtained glass,
While rare miraculous clocks in crystal domes
Impaled the air with splintered chips of time
Forever sounding through the tea-thin talk,
An organpoint to desperate animation.

They knew, and tried to say to us, but failed;
They knew what we would never have believed.

"HE REMEMBERETH THAT WE ARE DUST"

And when was dust a thing so rash?
Or when could dust support the lash
And stand as arrogant as stone?
And where has revelation shown
Conceit and rage so interfused
In dust, that suns have stood bemused
To watch the reckless consequence?
And when did dust break reticence

To sing aloud with all its might
In egotistical delight?
Yet when the tale is told of wind
That lifted dust and drove behind
To scoop the valleys from their sleep
And bury landscapes inches deep
Till there must follow years of rain
Before the earth could breathe again—
Or when the appetite of fire
Blazes beyond control and higher,
Then sinks into the sullen waste
Of what, devouring, it effaced,
And thinly in my palm I hold
The dust of ash grown wan and cold,
I know what element I chose
To build such anger, mould such woes.

LIFE AND LETTERS

An old man's wasting brain; a ruined city
Where here and there against the febrile sky
The shaft of an unbroken column rises,
And in the sands indifferent lizards keep
The shattered traces of old monuments.
Here where the death of the imagination
Trances the mind with shadow, here the shapes
Of tumbled arch and pediment stand out
In their last violence of illumination.

By day his valet rules him, forcing him
With milk and medicines, a deference
Cloaking the bully. "Signora X was here
During your nap; I told her doctor's orders,

You must stay quiet and rest, keep up your strength."
He leaves the pasteboard rectangle, engraved,
Scrawled in regretful haste, and goes his way
To join a lounging crony belowstairs.
("The old man's not so wide awake today.")

The ivory body in the dressing gown
(Not the silk robe the Countess sent; he spills
His milk sometimes, and that would be a pity)
Stirs in the sinking warmth that bathes his chair
And looks on summer sunlight in the square.
Below, the fat concierge points out his window
With half-drawn blinds, to tourists who inquire.
There are a few who make the pilgrimage;
They stand and gaze and go away again.
Something to say that one has stood beneath
His window, though they never see himself.
The post brings letters stamped in foreign countries.
He holds them in his fingers, turns them over.
"He always says he means to read them later,
But I should say his reading days are finished.
All he does now is watch the square below.
He seems content enough; and I've no trouble.
An easy life, to watch him to his grave."

The letters still arrive from universities,
Occasionally a charitable cause,
A favor-seeker, or an aged friend.
But now it seems no answers are expected
From one whose correspondence is collected
In two large volumes, edited with notes.
What should that timid hand beneath its sleeve
Warmed by the rich Italian sun, indite
To vindicate its final quarter-decade?
No; he has written all that can be known.

If anything, too much; his greedy art
Left no domain unpillaged, grew its breadth
From fastening on every life he touched.
(Some went to law, some smiled, some never guessed.)
But now the art has left the man to rest.

The failing searchlight of his mind remains
To throw its wavering cone of recognition
Backward upon those teeming images.
New York invades the memory again:
A million jewels crowd the boyish brain
With apprehension of an unmastered world.
The red-haired girl waves from the Brooklyn ferry,
The bridges leap like fountains into noon.
Again the train goes rocking across-country
Past midnight platforms where the reddish light
Plays on a game of checkers through the window,
Till dawn spells snow on emptiness of plains.
Once more in San Francisco Margaret wakes
Beside him in the heat of August dark,
Still weeping from a nightmare.
                      So by day
He looks on summer sunlight in the square.

The grinning Bacchus trickles from his gourd
A thin bright spume of water in the basin,
While the hot tiles grow cool as evening drops
Deep cobalt from white buildings. Far in air
Buonarroti's dome delays the gold.
The old man who has come to Rome to die
Ignores the death of still another day.
So many days have died and come to life
That time and place seem ordered by his valet;
He puts them on and off as he is told.

Now he is standing bareheaded in dusk
While fireworks rain into the sea at Biarritz,
And at his shoulder Louis Scarapin
Quotes La Fontaine. The giddy winds of fortune
Make love to him that night; and he recalls
Toasts drunk by rocketlight, and Louis' voice
With its perpetual drawl: *"Mon bon monsieur . . ."*
Louis, who could have made the world more sane,
But killed himself instead, a Pierrot-gesture,
His face a whiteness in the dark apartment.

The bitter coffee drunk on early mornings
With Sandra's straw hat hanging from the bedpost,
Red roses, like a bonnet by Renoir.
And the incessant tapping of her heels
Late evenings on the cobbles as they stroll:
Splinters to tingle in an old man's brain.
Again the consumptive neighbor through the wall
Begins his evening agony of coughing
Till one is ready to scream him into silence.
And the accordion on the river steamer
Plays something from last season, foolish, gay;
Deaf ears preserve the music of a day.

Life has the final word; he cannot rule
Those floating pictures as he ruled them once,
Forcing them into form; the violent gardener,
The two-edged heart that cuts into every wound,
Reciprocates experience with art.
No more of that for now; the boughs grow wild,
The willful stems put forth undisciplined blooms,
And winds sweep through and shatter. Here at last
Anarchy of a thousand roses tangles
The fallen architecture of the mind.

FOR THE CONJUNCTION OF
TWO PLANETS

We smile at astrological hopes
And leave the sky to expert men
Who do not reckon horoscopes
But painfully extend their ken
In mathematical debate
With slide and photographic plate.

And yet, protest it if we will,
Some corner of the mind retains
The medieval man, who still
Keeps watch upon those starry skeins
And drives us out of doors at night
To gaze at anagrams of light.

Whatever register or law
Is drawn in digits for these two,
Venus and Jupiter keep their awe,
Wardens of brilliance, as they do
Their dual circuit of the west—
The brightest planet and her guest.

Is any light so proudly thrust
From darkness on our lifted faces
A sign of something we can trust,
Or is it that in starry places
We see the things we long to see
In fiery iconography?

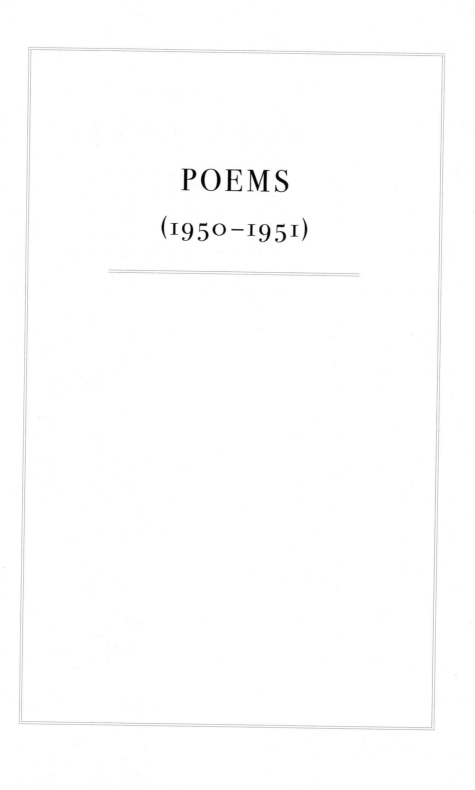

POEMS
(1950–1951)

THE PRISONERS

Enclosed in this disturbing mutual wood,
Wounded alike by thorns of the same tree,
We seek in hopeless war each other's blood
Though suffering in one identity.
Each to the other prey and huntsman known,
Still driven together, lonelier that alone.

Strange mating of the loser and the lost!
With faces stiff as mourners', we intrude
Forever on the one each turns from most,
Each wandering in a double solitude.
The unpurged ghosts of passion bound by pride
Who wake in isolation, side by side.

1950

NIGHT

The motes that still disturbed her lidded calm
Were these: the tick and whisper of a shade
Against the sill; a cobweb-film that hung
Aslant a corner moulding, too elusive
For any but the gaze of straitened eyes;
The nimbus of the night-lamp, where a moth
Uneasily explored the edge of light
Through hours of fractured darkness. She alone
Knew that the room contained these things; she lay
Hearing the almost imperceptible sound
(As if a live thing shivered behind the curtains)
Watching the thread that frayed in gusts of air
More delicate than her breathing, or by night

Sharing a moth's perplexity at light
Too frail to drive out dark: minutiae
Held in the vise of sense about to die.

1950

THE HOUSE AT THE CASCADES

All changed now through neglect. The steps dismantled
By infantries of ants, by roots and storms,
The pillars tugged by vines, the porte-cochère
A passageway for winds, the solemn porches
Warped into caricatures.
                              We came at evening
After the rain, when every drunken leaf
Was straining, swelling in a riot of green.
Only the house was dying in all that life,
As if a triumph of emerald energy
Had fixed its mouth upon the walls and stones.
The tamest shrub remembered anarchy
And joined in appetite with the demagogue weed
That springs where order falls; together there
They stormed the defenseless handiwork of man
Whose empire wars against him when he turns
A moment from the yoke. So, turning back,
He sees his rooftree fall to furious green,
His yard despoiled, and out of innocent noon
The insect-cloud like thunder on the land.

1951

THE DIAMOND
CUTTERS
(1955)

For A.H.C.

THE ROADWAY

When the footbridge washes away,
And the lights along the bank
Accost each other no longer,
But the wild grass grows up rank,
And no one comes to stand
Where neighbor and neighbor stood,
And each house is drawn in to itself
And shuttered against the road,

Under each separate roof
The familiar life goes on:
The hearth is swept up at night,
The table laid in the dawn,
And man and woman and child
Eat their accustomed meal,
Give thanks and turn to their day
As if by an act of will.

Nowhere is evil spoken,
Though something deep in the heart
Refuses to mend the bridge
And can never make a start
Along the abandoned path
To the house at left or at right,
Where neighbor and neighbor's children
Awake to the same daylight.

Good men grown long accustomed
To inflexible ways of mind—
Which of them could say clearly
What first drove kind from kind?
Courteous to any stranger,
Forbearing with wife and child—
Yet along the common roadway
The wild grass still grows wild.

PICTURES BY VUILLARD

Now we remember all: the wild pear-tree,
The broken ribbons of the green-and-gold
Portfolio, with sketches from an old
Algerian campaign; the placid three
Women at coffee by the window, fates
Of nothing ominous, waiting for the ring
Of the postman's bell; we harbor everything—
The cores of fruit left on the luncheon plates.
We are led back where we have never been,
Midday where nothing's tragic, all's delayed
As it should have been for us as well—that shade
Of summer always, Neuilly dappled green!

But we, the destined readers of Stendhal,
In monstrous change such consolations find
As restless mockery sets before the mind
To deal with what must anger and appall.
Much of the time we scarcely think of sighing
For afternoons that found us born too late.
Our prudent envy rarely paces spying
Under those walls, that lilac-shadowed gate.
Yet at this moment, in our private view,
A breath of common peace, like memory,
Rustles the branches of the wild pear-tree—
Air that we should have known, and cannot know.

ORIENT WHEAT

Our fathers in their books and speech
Have made the matter plain:
The green fields they walked in once
Will never grow again.
The corn lies under the locust's tooth
Or blistered in the sun;
The faces of the old proud stock
Are gone where their years are gone.

The park where stags lay down at noon
Under the great trees
Is shrill with Sunday strollers now,
Littered with their lees.
Poachers have trampled down the maze
And choked the fountains dry;
The last swan of a score and ten
Goes among reeds to die.

We were born to smells of plague,
Chalk-marks on every door;
We never have heard the hunting-horn
Or feet on the gallery floor—
The high-arched feet of dancers
Who knew how to step and stand.
We were born of a leaning house
In a changed, uneasy land.

Our fathers curse the crooked time
And go to their graves at last;
While some of us laugh at doting men,
And others sigh for the past.
And the dazzled lovers lie
Where summer burns blue and green,
In the green fields they'll be saying
Can never grow again.

VERSAILLES

(Petit Trianon)

Merely the landscape of a vanished whim,
An artifice that lasts beyond the wish:
The grotto by the pond, the gulping fish
That round and round pretended islands swim,
The creamery abandoned to its doves,
The empty shrine the guidebooks say is love's.

What wind can bleaken this, what weather chasten
Those balustrades of stone, that sky stone-pale?
A fountain triton idly soaks his tail
In the last puddle of a drying basin;
A leisure that no human will can hasten
Drips from the hollow of his lifted shell.

When we were younger gardens were for games,
But now across the sungilt lawn of kings
We drift, consulting catalogues for names
Of postured gods: the cry of closing rings
For us and for the couples in the wood
And all good children who are all too good.

O children, next year, children, you will play
With only half your hearts; be wild today.
And lovers, take one long and fast embrace
Before the sun that tarnished queens goes down,
And evening finds you in a restless town
Where each has back his old restricted face.

ANNOTATION FOR AN EPITAPH

> A fairer person lost not heaven.
>
> —*Paradise Lost*

These are the sins for which they cast out angels,
The bagatelles by which the lovely fall:
A hand that disappoints, an eye dissembling—
These and a few besides: you had them all.

Beneath this cherubed stone reclines the beauty
That cherubs at the Chair will never see,
Shut out forever by the gold battalions
Stern to forgive, more rigorous than we.

Oh, we were quick to hide our eyes from foible
And call such beauty truth; what though we knew?
Never was truth so sweet and so outrageous;
We loved you all the more because untrue.

But in the baroque corridors of heaven
Your lively coming is a hope destroyed.
Squadrons of seraphs pass the news and ponder,
And all their luxury glitters grand and void.

IDEAL LANDSCAPE

We had to take the world as it was given:
The nursemaid sitting passive in the park
Was rarely by a changeling prince accosted.
The mornings happened similar and stark
In rooms of selfhood where we woke and lay
Watching today unfold like yesterday.

Our friends were not unearthly beautiful,
Nor spoke with tongues of gold; our lovers blundered
Now and again when most we sought perfection,
Or hid in cupboards when the heavens thundered.
The human rose to haunt us everywhere,
Raw, flawed, and asking more than we could bear.

And always time was rushing like a tram
Through streets of a foreign city, streets we saw
Opening into great and sunny squares
We could not find again, no map could show—
Never those fountains tossed in that same light,
Those gilded trees, those statues green and white.

THE CELEBRATION
IN THE PLAZA

The sentimentalist sends his mauve balloon
Meandering into air. The crowd applauds.
The mayor eats ices with a cardboard spoon.

See how that color charms the sunset air;
A touch of lavender is what was needed.—
Then, pop! no floating lavender anywhere.

Hurrah, the pyrotechnic engineer
Comes with his sparkling tricks, consults the sky,
Waits for the perfect instant to appear.

Bouquets of gold splash into bloom and pour
Their hissing pollen downward on the dusk.
Nothing like this was ever seen before.

The viceroy of fireworks goes his way,
Leaving us with a sky so dull and bare
The crowd thins out: what conjures them to stay?

The road is cold with dew, and by and by
We see the constellations overhead.
But is that all? some little children cry.

All we have left, their pedagogues reply.

THE TOURIST AND THE TOWN

(San Miniato al Monte)

Those clarities detached us, gave us form,
Made us like architecture. Now no more
Bemused by local mist, our edges blurred,
We knew where we began and ended. There
We were the campanile and the dome,
Alive and separate in that bell-struck air,
Climate whose light reformed our random line,
Edged our intent and sharpened our desire.

Could it be always so—a week of sunlight,
Walks with a guidebook, picking out our way
Through verbs and ruins, yet finding after all
The promised vista, once!—The light has changed
Before we can make it ours. We have no choice:
We are only tourists under that blue sky,
Reading the posters on the station wall—
Come, take a walking-trip through happiness.

There is a mystery that floats between
The tourist and the town. Imagination
Estranges it from her. She need not suffer
Or die here. It is none of her affair,
Its calm heroic vistas make no claim.
Her bargains with disaster have been sealed
In another country. Here she goes untouched,
And this is alienation. Only sometimes
In certain towns she opens certain letters
Forwarded on from bitter origins,
That send her walking, sick and haunted, through
Mysterious and ordinary streets
That are no more than streets to walk and walk—
And then the tourist and the town are one.

To work and suffer is to be at home.
All else is scenery: the Rathaus fountain,
The skaters in the sunset on the lake
At Salzburg, or, emerging after snow,
The singular clear stars at Castellane.
To work and suffer is to come to know
The angles of a room, light in a square,
As convalescents know the face of one
Who has watched beside them. Yours now, every street,
The noonday swarm across the bridge, the bells
Bruising the air above the crowded roofs,
The avenue of chestnut-trees, the road
To the post-office. Once upon a time
All these for you were fiction. Now, made free
You live among them. Your breath is on this air,
And you are theirs and of their mystery.

BEARS

Wonderful bears that walked my room all night,
Where are you gone, your sleek and fairy fur,
Your eyes' veiled imperious light?

Brown bears as rich as mocha or as musk,
White opalescent bears whose fur stood out
Electric in the deepening dusk,

And great black bears who seemed more blue than black,
More violet than blue against the dark—
Where are you now? upon what track

Mutter your muffled paws, that used to tread
So softly, surely, up the creakless stair
While I lay listening in bed?

When did I lose you? whose have you become?
Why do I wait and wait and never hear
Your thick nocturnal pacing in my room?
My bears, who keeps you now, in pride and fear?

THE INSUSCEPTIBLES

Then the long sunlight lying on the sea
Fell, folded gold on gold; and slowly we
Took up our decks of cards, our parasols,
The picnic hamper and the sandblown shawls
And climbed the dunes in silence. There were two
Who lagged behind as lovers sometimes do,
And took a different road. For us the night
Was final, and by artificial light

We came indoors to sleep. No envy there
Of those who might be watching anywhere
The lustres of the summer dark, to trace
Some vagrant splinter blazing out of space.
No thought of them, save in a lower room
To leave a light for them when they should come.

LUCIFER IN THE TRAIN

Riding the black express from heaven to hell
He bit his fingers, watched the countryside,
Vernal and crystalline, forever slide
Beyond his gaze: the long cascades that fell
Ribboned in sunshine from their sparkling height,
The fishers fastened to their pools of green
By silver lines; the birds in sudden flight—
All things the diabolic eye had seen
Since heaven's cockcrow. Imperceptibly
That landscape altered: now in paler air
Tree, hill and rock stood out resigned, severe,
Beside the strangled field, the stream run dry.

Lucifer, we are yours who stiff and mute
Ride out of worlds we shall not see again,
And watch from windows of a smoking train
The ashen prairies of the absolute.
Once out of heaven, to an angel's eye
Where is the bush or cloud without a flaw?
What bird but feeds upon mortality,
Flies to its young with carrion in its claw?
O foundered angel, first and loneliest

To turn this bitter sand beneath your hoe,
Teach us, the newly-landed, what you know;
After our weary transit, find us rest.

RECORDERS IN ITALY

It was amusing on that antique grass,
Seated halfway between the green and blue,
To waken music gentle and extinct

Under the old walls where the daisies grew
Sprinkled in cinquecento style, as though
Archangels might have stepped there yesterday.

But it was we, mortal and young, who strolled
And fluted quavering music, for a day
Casual heirs of all we looked upon.

Such pipers of the emerald afternoon
Could only be the heirs of perfect time
When every leaf distinctly brushed with gold

Listened to Primavera speaking flowers.
Those scherzos stumble now; our journeys run
To harsher hillsides, rockier declensions.

Obligatory climates call us home.
And so shall clarity of cypresses,
Unfingered by necessity, become

Merely the ghost of half-remembered trees,
A trick of sunlight flattering the mind?—
There were four recorders sweet upon the wind.

AT HERTFORD HOUSE

Perfection now is tended and observed,
Not used; we hire the spawn of Caliban
For daily service. In our careful world
Inlay of purple-wood and tulip, curved
To mime the sheen of plumes and peacocks' eyes,
Exists for inspection only. And the jars
Of apple-green and white, where wooing's done
In panels after Boucher—such we prize
Too well to fill with roses. Chocolate, too,
Will not again be frothed in cups like these;
We move meticulously, ill at ease
Amid perfections. Why should a porcelain plaque
Where Venus pulls her pouting Adon on
Through beds of blushing flowers, seem unfit
For casual thumbprint? Ease is what we lack.
There's a division nothing can make sweet
Between the clods of usage and the toys
We strum our senses with. But Antoinette
Ran her long tortoise-shell and silver comb
Through powdered yellow hair, and would have laughed
To think that use too mean for art or craft.

THE WILD SKY

Here from the corridor of an English train,
I see the landscape slide through glancing rain,
A land so personal that every leaf
Unfolds as if to witness human life,
And every aging milestone seems to know
That human hands inscribed it, long ago.

Oasthouse and garden, narrow bridge and hill—
Landscape with figures, where a change of style
Comes softened in a water-colour light
By Constable; and always, shire on shire,
The low-pitched sky sags like a tent of air
Beneath its ancient immaterial weight.

The weather in these gentle provinces
Moves like the shift of daylight in a house,
Subdued by time and custom. Sun and rain
Are intimate, complaisant to routine,
Guests in the garden. Year on country year
Has worn the edge of wildness from this air.

And I remember that unblunted light
Poured out all day from a prodigious height—
My country, where the blue is miles too high
For minds of men to graze the leaning sky.
The telegraph may rise or timber fall,
That last frontier remains, the vertical.

Men there are beanstalk climbers, all day long
Haunted by stilts they clattered on when young.
Giants no longer, now at mortal size
They stare into that upward wilderness.
The vertical reminds them what they are,
And I remember I am native there.

THE PROSPECT

You promise me when certain things are done
We'll close these rooms above a city square,
And stealing out by half-light, will be gone
When next the telephone breaks the waiting air.
Before they send to find us, we shall be
Aboard a blunt-nosed steamer, at whose rail
We'll watch the loading of the last brown bale
And feel the channel roughening into sea.

And after many sunlit days we'll sight
The coast you tell me of. Along that shore
Rare shells lie tumbled, and the seas of light
Dip past the golden rocks to crash and pour
Upon the bowl-shaped beach. In that clear bay
We'll scoop for pebbles till our feet and hands
Are gilded by the wash of blending sands;
And though the boat lift anchor, we shall stay.

You will discover in the woods beyond
The creatures you have loved on Chinese silk:
The shell-gray fox, gazelles that at your sound
Will lift their eyes as calm as golden milk.
The leaves and grasses feathered into plumes
Will shadow-edge their pale calligraphy;
And in the evening you will come to me
To tell of honey thick in silver combs.

Yet in the drift of moments unendeared
By sameness, when the cracks of morning show
Only a replica of days we've marred
With still the same old penances to do,
In furnished rooms above a city square,
Eating the rind of fact, I sometimes dread
The promise of that honey-breeding air,
Those unapportioned clusters overhead.

EPILOGUE FOR A
MASQUE OF PURCELL

Beast and bird must bow aside,
Grimbald limp into the wings.
All that's lovely and absurd,
All that dances, all that sings

Folded into trunks again—
The haunted grove, the starlit air—
All turns workaday and plain,
Even the happy, happy pair.

Harpsichord and trumpet go
Trundling down the dusty hall.
That airy joy, that postured woe
Like the black magician's spell

Fall in pieces round us now,
While the dancer goes to lie
With the king, and need not know
He will jilt her by and by.

We were young once and are old;
Have seen the dragon die before;
Knew the innocent and bold,
Saw them through the cardboard door

Kiss the guilty and afraid,
Turning human soon enough.
We have wept with the betrayed,
Never known them die for love.

Yet, since nothing's done by halves
While illusion's yet to do,
May we still forgive ourselves,
And dance again when trumpets blow.

VILLA ADRIANA

When the colossus of the will's dominion
Wavers and shrinks upon a dying eye,
Enormous shadows sit like birds of prey,
Waiting to fall where blistered marbles lie.

But in its open pools the place already
Lay ruined, before the old king left it free.
Shattered in waters of each marble basin
He might have seen it as today we see.

Dying in discontent, he must have known
How, once mere consciousness had turned its back,
The frescoes of his appetite would crumble,
The fountains of his longing yawn and crack.

And all his genius would become a riddle,
His perfect colonnades at last attain
The incompleteness of a natural thing;
His impulse turn to mystery again.

Who sleeps, and dreams, and wakes, and sleeps again
May dream again; so in the end we come
Back to the cherished and consuming scene
As if for once the stones will not be dumb.

We come like dreamers searching for an answer,
Passionately in need to reconstruct
The columned roofs under the blazing sky,
The courts so open, so forever locked.

And some of us, as dreamers, excavate
Under the blanching light of sleep's high noon,
The artifacts of thought, the site of love,
Whose Hadrian has given the slip, and gone.

THE EXPLORERS

Beside the Mare Crisium, that sea
Where water never was, sit down with me,
And let us talk of Earth, where long ago
We drank the air and saw the rivers flow
Like comets through the green estates of man,
And fruit the colour of Aldebaran
Weighted the curving boughs. The route of stars
Was our diversion, and the fate of Mars
Our grave concern; we stared throughout the night
On these uncolonized demesnes of light.
We read of stars escaping Newton's chain
Till only autographs of fire remain;
We aimed our mortal searchlights into space
As if in hopes to find a mortal face.

O little Earth, our village, where the day
Seemed all too brief, and starlight would not stay,
We were provincials on the grand express
That whirled us into dark and loneliness.
We thought to bring you wonder with a tale
Huger than those that turned our fathers pale.
Here in this lunar night we watch alone
Longer than ever men have watched for dawn.
Beyond this meteor-bitten plain we see
More starry systems than you dream to be,
And while their clockwork blazes overhead,
We speak the names we learned as we were bred,
We tell of places seen each day from birth—
Obscure and local, patois of the Earth!
O race of farmers, plowing year by year
The same few fields, I sometimes seem to hear

The far-off echo of a cattle-bell
Against the cratered cliff of Arzachel,
And weep to think no sound can ever come
Across that outer desert, from my home.

LANDSCAPE OF THE STAR

The silence of the year. This hour the streets
Lie empty, and the clash of bells is scattered
Out to the edge of stars. I heard them tell
Morning's first change and clang the people home
From crèche and scented aisle. Come home, come home,
I heard the bells of Christmas call and die.

This Christmas morning, in the stony streets
Of an unaccustomed city, where the gas
Quivers against the darkly-shuttered walls,
I walk, my breath a veil upon the cold,
No longer sick for home nor hunted down
By faces loved, by gate or sill or tree
That once I used to wreathe in red and silver
Under the splintered incense of the fir.

I think of those inscrutables who toiled,
Heavy and brooding in their camel-train,
Across the blue-wrapped stretches. Home behind,
Kingdoms departed from, the solemn journey
Their only residence: the starlit hour,
The landscape of the star, their time and place.

O to be one of them, and feel the sway
Of rocking camel through the Judaean sand,—
Ride, wrapped in swathes of damask and of silk,
Hear the faint ring of jewel in silver mesh
Starring the silence of the plain; and hold
With rigid fingers curved as in oblation
The golden jar of myrrh against the knees.

To ride thus, bearing gifts to a strange land,
To a strange King; nor think of fear and envy,
Being so bemused by starlight of one star,
The long unbroken journey, that all questions
Sink like the lesser lights behind the hills;
Think neither of the end in sight, nor all
That lies behind, but dreamlessly to ride,
Traveller at one with travelled countryside.

How else, since for those Magi and their train
The palaces behind have ceased to be
Home, and the home they travel toward is still
But rumor stoking fear in Herod's brain?
What else for them but this, since never more
Can courts and states receive them as they were,
Nor have the trampled earth, the roof of straw
Received the kings as they are yet to be?

The bells are silent, silenced in my mind
As on the dark. I walk, a foreigner,
Upon this night that calls all travellers home,
The prodigal forgiven, and the breach
Mended for this one feast. Yet all are strange
To their own ends, and their beginnings now
Cannot contain them. Once-familiar speech
Babbles in wayward dialect of a dream.

Our gifts shall bring us home: not to beginnings
Nor always to the destination named
Upon our setting-forth. Our gifts compel,
Master our ways and lead us in the end
Where we are most ourselves; whether at last
To Solomon's gaze or Sheba's silken knees
Or winter pastures underneath a star,
Where angels spring like starlight in the trees.

LETTER FROM THE LAND OF SINNERS

I write you this out of another province
That you may never see:
Country of rivers, its topography
Mutable in detail, yet always one,
Blasted in certain places, here by glaciers,
There by the work of man.

The fishers by the water have no boast
Save of their freedom; here
A man may cast a dozen kinds of lure
And think his days rewarded if he sight
Now and again the prize, unnetted, flicking
Its prism-gleams of light.

The old lord lived secluded in his park
Until the hall was burned
Years ago, by his tenants; both have learned
Better since then, and now our children run
To greet him. Quail and hunter have forgotten
The echo of the gun.

I said there are blasted places: we have kept
Their nakedness intact—
No marble to commemorate an act
Superhuman or merely rash; we know
Why they are there and why the seed that falls there
Is certain not to grow.

We keep these places as we keep the time
Scarred on our recollection
When some we loved broke from us in defection,
Or we ourselves harried to death too soon
What we could least forgo. Our memories
Recur like the old moon.

But we have made another kind of peace,
And walk where boughs are green,
Forgiven by the selves that we have been,
And learning to forgive. Our apples taste
Sweeter this year; our gates are falling down,
And need not be replaced.

CONCORD RIVER

The turtles on the ledges of July
Heard our approach and splashed. Now in the mud
Lie like the memory of fecund summer
Their buried eggs. The river, colder now,
Has other, autumn tales to carry on
Between the banks where lovers used to lie.

Lovers, or boys escaped from yard and farm
To drown in sensual purities of sun—
No matter which; for single fisherman
Casting into the shade, or those absorbed
In human ardor, summer was the same,
Impervious to weariness or alarm.

The fisherman, by craft and love removed
From meanness, has an almanac at home
Saying the season will be brief this year
And ice strike early; yet upon its shelf
The book is no despoiler of this day
In which he moves and ponders, most himself.

That boy, watching for turtles by the shore,
Steeped in his satisfactory loneliness,
If asked could tell us that the sun would set,
Or autumn drive him back to games and school—
Tell us at second-hand, believing then
Only midsummer and the noonstruck pool.

And we, who floated through the sunlit green,
Indolent, voluntary as the dance
Of dragon-flies above the skimming leaves—
For us the landscape and the hour became
A single element, where our drifting silence
Fell twofold, like our shadows on the water.

This is the Concord River, where the ice
Will hold till April: this is the willowed stream
Much threaded by the native cogitators
Who wrote their journals calmly by its shore,
Observing weather and the swing of seasons
Along with personal cosmologies.

Henry Thoreau most nearly learned to live
Within a world his soul could recognize—
Unshaken by accounts of any country
He could not touch with both his hands. He saw
The river moving past the provincial town
And knew each curve of shoreline for his own.

He travelled much, he said—his wayward speech
Sounding always a little insolent,
Yet surer than the rest; they, like ourselves,
Ran off to dabble in a world beyond,
While he exalted the geography
He lived each day: a river and a pond.

For him there was no turning of the ear
To rumored urgencies that sought to rouse
The fisher from his pool, the serious child
From his unconscious wandering: the sound
Of desperate enterprises rang to him
Fictive as ghosts upon old Indian ground.

Lover and child and fisherman, alike
Have in their time been native to this shore
As he would have it peopled: all entranced
By such concerns in their perfected hour
That in their lives the river and the tree
Are absolutes, no longer scenery.

APOLOGY

You, invincibly yourself,
Have nothing left to say.
The stones upon the mountainside
Are not more free,
Bearing all question, all reproach
Without reply.

The dead, who keep their peace intact,
Although they know
Much we might be gainers by,
Are proud like you—
Or, if they spoke, might sound as you
Sounded just now.

For every angry, simple man
The word is but
A shadow, and his motive grows
More still and great
While the world hums around him, wild
That he should explicate.

And Socrates, whose crystal tongue
Perturbs us now,
Left all unsatisfied; the word
Can never show
Reason enough for what a man
Knows he must do.

You told us little, and are done.
So might the dead
Begin to speak of dying, then
Leave half unsaid.
Silence like thunder bears its own
Excuse for dread.

LIVING IN SIN

She had thought the studio would keep itself;
no dust upon the furniture of love.
Half heresy, to wish the taps less vocal,
the panes relieved of grime. A plate of pears,
a piano with a Persian shawl, a cat
stalking the picturesque amusing mouse
had risen at his urging.
Not that at five each separate stair would writhe
under the milkman's tramp; that morning light
so coldly would delineate the scraps
of last night's cheese and three sepulchral bottles;
that on the kitchen shelf among the saucers
a pair of beetle-eyes would fix her own—
envoy from some village in the moldings . . .
Meanwhile, he, with a yawn,
sounded a dozen notes upon the keyboard,
declared it out of tune, shrugged at the mirror,
rubbed at his beard, went out for cigarettes;
while she, jeered by the minor demons,
pulled back the sheets and made the bed and found
a towel to dust the table-top,
and let the coffee-pot boil over on the stove.
By evening she was back in love again,
though not so wholly but throughout the night
she woke sometimes to feel the daylight coming
like a relentless milkman up the stairs.

AUTUMN EQUINOX

The leaves that shifted overhead all summer
Are marked for earth now, and I bring the baskets
Still dark with clingings of another season
Up from the cellar. All the house is still,
Now that I've left it. Lyman in his study
Peers on a page of Dryden by the window,
Eyes alone moving, like a mended quaint
Piece of old clockwork. When the afternoon
Trails into half-light, he will never notice
Until I come indoors to light the lamps
And rouse him blinking from the brownish type,
The gilt and tarnished spine of volume five
Out of the glass-doored cabinet in the hall.
Why Satires, I have wondered? For I've seen
The title-page, and riffled through the volume,
When he was gone. I thought that growing old
Returned one to a vague Arcadian longing,
To Ovid, Spenser, something golden-aged,
Some incorruptible myth that tinged the years
With pastoral flavours. Lyman, too, as gentle
As an old shepherd, half-apologetic
When I come bustling to disturb his dreams—
What in that bitterness can speak to him
Or help him down these final sloping decades
With kindly arm? I've never been a scholar—
Reader, perhaps at times, but not a scholar,
Not in the way that Lyman used to be—
And yet I know there's acid on the page
He pores—that least acidulous of men.
While I, who spent my youth and middle-age
In stubbornness and railing, pass the time
Now, after fifty, raking in the sun
The leaves that sprinkle slowly on the grass,
And feel their gold like firelight at my back,
In slow preoccupation with September.

Sometimes I call across to Alice Hume
And meet her at the fence as women meet
To say the weather's seasonably fine,
Talk husbands, bargains, or philosophize—
The dry philosophy of neighborhood.
She thinks perhaps how sharp of tongue and quick
I used to be, and how I've quieted down,
Without those airs because I'd married Lyman,
Professor at the college, while her husband
Was just another farmer. That was pride
As raw and silly as the girl I was—
Reading too much, sneering at other girls
Whose learning was of cookery and flirtation.
Father would have me clever, sometimes said
He'd let me train for medicine, like a son,
To come into his practice. So I studied
German and botany, and hated both.
What good for me to know the Latin name
For huckleberry, while the others climbed
To pick the fruit and kissed across the bushes?
I never was a scholar, but I had
A woman's love for men of intellect,
A woman's need for love of any kind.

So Lyman came to ask me of my father:
Stiff-collared, shy, not quite the man I'd dreamed—
(Byron and Matthew Arnold vaguely mingled
Without the disadvantages of either.)
And yet he seemed superb in his refusal
To read aloud from Bryant to the ladies
Assembled on the boarding-house piazza
Among the moth-wings of a summer evening.
His quick withdrawal won my heart. I smile
Sometimes to think what quirks of vanity
Propel us toward our choices in the end.

The wedding-picture in the bureau drawer
Has on the back in Lyman's measured writing:
"September twenty-second, nineteen-twelve."
I keep it in its folder, deckle-edged
And yellowing. I see myself again,
Correct and terrified on our wedding-day,
Wearing the lace my mother wore before me
And buttoned shoes that pinched. I feel again
The trembling of my hand in Lyman's fingers,
Awkwardly held in that ungainly pose
While aunts around us nodded like the Fates
That nemesis was accomplished. Lyman stood
So thin and ministerial in his black,
I thought he looked a stranger. In the picture
We are the semblance of a bride and groom
Static as figures on a mantelpiece,
As if that moment out of time existed
Then and forever in a dome of glass,
Where neither dust nor the exploring fly
Could speck its dry immutability.

Thus I became his partner in a life
Annual, academic; we observed
Events momentous as the ceremony
To dedicate the chapel carillon
(Memorial to Edward Stephens Hodge,
Class of nineteen-fourteen). There we heard
Those sounds converge upon the rural air
That soon became familiar as a hinge
Creaking and never silenced. In our meadow
The angular young took up their bats and shouted
Throughout the afternoon, while I was pouring
Tea for the dean's arthritic wife. For Lyman
The world was all the distance he pursued
From home to lecture-room, and home again,
Exchanging nods with colleagues, smiling vaguely

Upon a shirtsleeved trio, tanned and jostling,
Who grinned and gave him room upon the path.
I bit my fingers, changed the parlor curtains
To ones the like of which were never seen
Along our grave and academic street.
I brought them home from Springfield in a bundle
And hung them in defiance. I took a walk
Across the fields one heavy summer night
Until the college from a mile away
Looked sallow, insignificant in the moonlight.
It seemed the moon must shine on finer things
I had not seen, things that could show with pride
Beneath that silver globe. Along the walls
Of Lyman's study there were steel engravings
Framed in black oak: the crazy tower of Pisa,
The Pyramids, rooted in desert sand,
Cologne Cathedral with its dangerous spires
Piercing the atmosphere. I hated them
For priggishly enclosing in a room
The marvels of the world, as if declaring
Such was the right and fitting rôle of marvels.

Night, and I wept aloud; half in my sleep,
Half feeling Lyman's wonder as he leaned
Above to shake me. "Are you ill, unhappy?
Tell me what I can do."

                "I'm sick, I guess—
I thought that life was different than it is."
"Tell me what's wrong. Why can't you ever say?
I'm here, you know."

                     Half shamed, I turned to see
The lines of grievous love upon his face,
The love that gropes and cannot understand.
"I must be crazy, Lyman—or a dream
Has made me babble things I never thought.
Go back to sleep—I won't be so again."

Young lovers talk of giving all the heart
Into each others' trust: their rhetoric
Won't stand for analyzing, I'm aware,
But have they thought of this: that each must know
Beyond a doubt what's given, what received?

Now we are old like Nature; patient, staid,
Unhurried from the year's wellworn routine,
We wake and take the day for what it is,
And sleep as calmly as the dead who know
They'll wake to their reward. We have become
As unselfconscious as a pair of trees,
Not questioning, but living. Even autumn
Can only carry through what spring began.
What else could happen now but loss of leaf
And rain upon the boughs? So I have thought,
And wondered faintly where the thought began,
And when the irritable gust of youth
Stopped turning every blade of grass to find
A new dissatisfaction. Meanwhile Lyman
Reads satire in the falling afternoon—
A change for him as well. We finish off
Not quite as we began. I hear the bells
Wandering through the air across the fields.
I've raked three bushel baskets full of leaves—
Enough for one September afternoon.

THE STRAYED VILLAGE

He had come nearly half a thousand miles,
And then to find it gone . . . He knew too well
Ever to be mistaken, where the hills
Dipped to reveal it first: the line of chimneys
Reflected in the unimportant stream,
The monument, worth half a line in guidebooks—
"Tower of a church that Cromwell's army burned,
Fine early Perpendicular"—itself
Subservient neither to theologies
Nor changing styles of architecture, still
A cipher on the landscape, something clear
In that unostentatious scenery.

Well, if the tower was gone—and who should say,
Depend on any landmark to remain?
He had been too far and known too many losses
Not to be reconciled that even landmarks
Go out like matches when you need them most.
So it could be with this. But not a house,
Not anything reflected in the river
But willows that could grow by any river,
Feminine, non-committal in their postures.
Willows: a bridge then? But the bridge was gone,
The piles had left no trace, no signature
Of stones beside the water. If, indeed,
There ever had been bridge or tower or house.
That was the question that enforeigned him,
Brushed forty years of memory aside
And made of him another obtuse tripper
Staring at signposts to be reassured:
This *is* the place—where I grew into manhood,
The place I had to leave when I was grown?
So often he had thought a man's whole life
Most rightly could be written, like his own,

In terms of places he was forced to leave
Because their meaning, passing that of persons,
Became too much for him.

                    "This *is* the place?"
He heard himself demand; and heard the other—
A youthful rector, by the look of him,
Pausing upon his evening stroll—reply,
"Oh, yes, this is the *place*. . . . The village went,
As I should reckon, twenty years ago.
Across the hill, in our town, there was once
Talk and conjecture; now you might suppose
Only the antiquarians breathe its name.
The memory of man, my friend, is short."
"Shorter and longer than it's credited,"
He answered; "but you say the village went?
I hardly care to ask, and yet I ask—
By flood? by fire? There used to be a tower
That Cromwell's zealots failed to bully down.
But there's no mark. It *went*? How did it go?"

"It went away. You've heard of men who went,
Suddenly, without partings or annulments,
Not carried off by accident or death,
But simply strayed? That was the way it went.
We went to bed on Thursday and could hear
The bells, as usual on a quiet night,
Across the hill between. On Friday morning
There were no bells. There wasn't anything.
The landscape stood as if since Magna Carta,
Empty, as it stands now. The village had gone,
Quite without taking leave. Strayed, is the word
We found ourselves as if by acquiescence
Using to speak of it, as if we thought
Someday to come upon it somewhere else

And greet our former neighbors as before.
No one has ever found it, though. One can't
Advertise for a village that has strayed:
'Lost, with one early Perpendicular tower,
A village numbering four hundred souls,
With stone and wooden footbridge.' And, as I say,
Men's memories grow short like winter daylight.
So much gets strayed that has to be replaced—
Dogs, wits, affections . . ."

                    "Yes, so much gets strayed;
But one of all the things a man can lose
I thought would keep till I could come again.
It almost seems it went lest I should come,
Because I always promised I would come,
And had this latest penalty in store,
The last of losses."

                    So he said goodbye,
And watched the little rector climb the hill
Back to his parish town. The stream ran on,
And all that walking was to do again.

THE PERENNIAL ANSWER

The way the world came swinging round my ears
I knew what Doctor meant the day he said,
"Take care, unless you want to join your dead;
It's time to end this battling with your years."
He knew I'd have the blackest word told straight,
Whether it was my child that couldn't live,
Or Joel's mind, thick-riddled like a sieve
With all that loving festered into hate.
Better to know the ways you are accurst,
And stand up fierce and glad to hear the worst.
The blood is charged, the back is stiffened so.

Well, on that day that was a day ago,
And yet so many hours and years ago
Numbered in seizures of a darkening brain,
I started up the attic stairs again—
The fifth time in the hour—not thinking then
That it was hot, but knowing the air sat stiller
Under the eaves than when the idiot killer
Hid in the Matthews barn among the hay
And all the neighbors through one August day
Waited outside with pitchforks in the sun.
Joel waited too, and when they heard the gun
Resound so flatly in the loft above
He was the one to give the door a shove
And climb the ladder. A man not made for love,
But built for things of violence; he would stand
Where lightning flashed and watch with eyes so wide
You thought the prongs of fire would strike inside;
Or sit with some decaying book in hand,
Reading of spirits and the evil-eyed,
And witches' Sabbaths in a poisoned land.

So it was Joel that brought the fellow out,
Tarnished with hay and blood. I still can see
The eyes that Joel turned and fixed on me
When it was done—as if by rights his wife
Should go to him for having risked his life
And say—I hardly knew what thing he wanted.
I know it was a thing I never granted,
And what his mind became, from all that woe,
Those violent concerns he lived among,
Was on my head as well. I couldn't go,
I never went to him, I never clung
One moment on his breast. But I was young.

And I was cruel, a girl-bride seeing only
Her marriage as a room so strange and lonely
She looked outside for warmth. And in what fashion
Could I be vessel for that somber passion—
For Joel, decreed till death to have me all?
The tortured grandsire hanging in the hall
Depicted by a limner's crabbed hand
Seemed more a being that I could understand.
How could I help but look beyond that wall
And probe the lawful stones that built it strong
With questions sharper than a pitchfork's prong?
If Joel knew, he kept his silence long.

But Evans and I were hopeless from the start:
He, collared early by a rigorous creed,
Not man of men but man of God indeed,
Whose eye had seen damnation, and whose heart
Thrust all it knew of passion into one
Chamber of iron inscribed *Thy will be done.*
Yet sense will have revenge on one who tries
To down his senses with the brand of lies.

The road was empty from the village home,
Empty of all but us and that dark third,
The sudden Northern spring. There must be some
For whom the thrusting blood, so long deferred
In alder-stem and elm, is not the rise
Of flood in their own veins; some who can see
That green unholy dance without surprise.
I only say it has been this for me:
The time of thinnest ice, of casualty
More swift and deadly than the skater's danger.
The end of March could make me stand a stranger
On my own doorstep, and the daily shapes
Of teapot, ladle, or the china grapes
I kept in winter on the dresser shelf
Rebuked me, made me foreign to myself.

Evans beside me on that moonless road
Walked hard as if he thought behind us strode
Pursuers he had fled through weary ways.
He only said: "Where I was born and grew,
You felt the spring come on you like a daze
Slow out of February, and you knew
The thing you were contending with. But here—"

"Spring is a bolt of lightning on the year,"
I said, "it strikes before you feel it near."

"The change of seasons is another thing
God put on earth to try us, I believe.
As if the breaking-out of green could bring
Escape from frozen discipline, give us leave
To taste of things by will and law forbidden."

"Maybe it was the weather lost us Eden,"
I said, but faltering, and the words went by
Like flights of moths under that star-soaked sky.

And that was all. He brought me to the door;
The house was dark, but on the upper floor
A light burned in the hallway. "Joel's asleep,"
I told him, and put out my hand. His touch
Was cold as candles kept unlit in church,
And yet I felt his seeking fingers creep
About my wrist and seize it in their grip
Until they hurt me.
                          "Neither you nor I
Have lived in Eden, but they say we die
To gain that day at last. We have to live
Believing it—what else can we believe?"

"Why not believe in life?" I said, but heard
Only the sanctioned automatic word
"*Eternal* life—" perennial answer given
To those who ask on earth a taste of heaven.

The penalty you pay for dying last
Is facing those transactions from the past
That would detain you when you try to go.
All night last night I lay and seemed to hear
The to-and-fro of callers down below,
Even the knocker rattling on the door.
I thought the dead had heard my time was near
To meet them, and had come to tell me so;
But not a footstep sounded on the stair.
If they are gone it means a few days more
Are left, or they would wait. Joel would wait
Down by the dark old clock that told me late
That night from Boston. "Evans walked me home;
We sat together in the train by chance."
But not a word; only his burning glance.
"We stopped to have some coffee in the station.
Why do you stand like that? What if I come
An hour or so after the time I said?

The house all dark, I thought you'd gone to bed."
But still that gaze, not anger, indignation,
Nor anything so easy, but a look
As fixed as when he stared upon his book.
No matter if my tale was false or true,
I was a woodcut figure on the page,
On trial for a nameless sin. Then rage
Took him like fire where lightning dives. I knew
That he could kill me then, but what he did
Was wrench me up the stairs, onto the bed.

The night of Joel's death I slept alone
In this same room. A neighbor said she'd stay,
Thinking the dead man lying down below
Might keep the living from rest. She told me so:
"Those hours before the dawn can lie like stone
Upon the heart—I've lain awake—I know."
At last I had to take the only way,
And said, "The nights he was alive and walking
From room to room and hearing spirits talking,
What sleep I had was likelier to be broken."
Her face was shocked but I was glad I'd spoken.
"Well, if you feel so—:" She would tell the tale
Next morning, but at last I was alone
In an existence finally my own.

And yet I knew that Evans would find reason
Why we were not our own, nor had our will
Unhindered; that disturbance of a season
So long removed was something he would kill
Yet, if he had not killed it. When I stood
Beside the churchyard fence and felt his glance
Reluctantly compelling mine, the blood
Soared to my face, the tombstones seemed to dance
Dizzily, till I turned. The eyes I met
Accused as they implored me to forget,

As if my shape had risen to destroy
Salvation's rampart with a hope of joy.
My lips betrayed their *Why?* but then his face
Turned from me, and I saw him leave the place.
Now Joel and Evans are neighbors, down beneath.

I wonder what we're bound to after death?
I wonder what's exacted of the dead,
How many debts of conscience still are good?
Not Evans or his Bible ever said
That spirit must complete what flesh and blood
Contracted in their term. What creditors
Will wait and knock for us at marble doors?

I'd like to know which stays when life is past:
The marriage kept in fear, the love deferred,
The footstep waited for and never heard,
The pressure of five fingers round the wrist
Stopping its beat with pain, the mouth unkissed,
The dream whose waking startles into sight
A figure mumbling by the bed at night,
The hopeless promise of eternal life—
Take now your Scripture, Evans, if you will,
And see how flimsily the pages spill
From spines reduced to dust. What have they said
Of us, to what will they pronounce me wife?
My debt is paid: the rest is on your head.

THE INSOMNIACS

The mystic finishes in time,
The actor finds himself in space;
And each, wherever he has been,
Must know his hand before his face,
Must crawl back into his own skin
As in the darkness after crime
The thief can hear his breath again,
Resume the knowledge of his limbs
And how the spasm goes and comes
Under the bones that cage his heart.

So: we are fairly met, grave friend—
The meeting of two wounds in man.
I, gesturing with practiced hand,
I, in my great brocaded gown,
And you, the fixed and patient one,
Enduring all the world can do.
I, with my shifting masks, the gold,
The awful scarlet, laughing blue,
Maker of many worlds; and you,
Worldless, the pure receptacle.

And yet your floating eyes reveal
What saint or mummer groans to feel:
That finite creatures finally know
The damp of stone beneath the knees,
The stiffness in the folded hands
A duller ache than holy wounds,
The draught that never stirs the sleeve
Of glazed evangelists above,
But drives men out from sacred calm
Into the violent, wayward sun.

My voice commands the formal stage;
A jungle thrives beyond the wings—
All formless and benighted things
That rhetoric cannot assuage.
I speak a dream and turn to see
The sleepness night outstaring me.
My pillow sweats; I wake in space.
This is my hand before my face.
This is the headboard of my bed
Whose splinters stuff my nightmare mouth;

This is the unconquerable drouth
I carry in my burning head.
Not my words nor your visions mend
Such infamous knowledge. We are split,
Done into bits, undone, pale friend,
As ecstasy begets its end;
As we are spun of rawest thread—
The flaw is in us; we will break.
O dare you of this fracture make
Hosannas plain and tragical,

Or dare I let each cadence fall
Awkward as learning newly learned,
Simple as children's cradle songs,
As untranslatable and true,
We someday might conceive a way
To do the thing we long to do—
To do what men have always done—
To live in time, to act in space
Yet find a ritual to embrace
Raw towns of man, the pockmarked sun.

THE SNOW QUEEN

Child with a chip of mirror in his eye
Saw the world ugly, fled to plains of ice
Where beauty was the Snow Queen's promises.
Under my lids a splinter sharp as his
Has made me wish you lying dead
Whose image digs the needle deeper still.

In the deceptive province of my birth
I had seen yes turn no, the saints descend,
Their sacred faces twisted into smiles,
The stars gone lechering, the village spring
Gush mud and toads—all miracles
Befitting an incalculable age.

To love a human face was to discover
The cracks of paint and varnish on the brow;
Soon to distrust all impulses of flesh
That strews its sawdust on the chamber floor,
While at the window peer two crones
Who once were Juliet and Jessica.

No matter, since I kept a little while
One thing intact from that perversity—
Though landscapes bloomed in monstrous cubes and coils.
In you belonged simplicities of light
To mend distraction, teach the air
To shine, the stars to find their way again.

Yet here the Snow Queen's cold prodigious will
Commands me, and your face has lost its power,
Dissolving to its opposite like the rest.
Under my ribs a diamond splinter now
Sticks, and has taken root; I know
Only this frozen spear that drives me through.

LOVE IN THE MUSEUM

Now will you stand for me, in this cool light,
Infanta reared in ancient etiquette,
A point-lace queen of manners. At your feet
The doll-like royal dog demurely set
Upon a chequered floor of black and white.

Or be a Louis' mistress, by Boucher,
Lounging on cushions, silken feet asprawl
Upon a couch where casual cupids play
While on your arms and shoulders seems to fall
The tired extravagance of a sunset day.

Or let me think I pause beside a door
And see you in a bodice by Vermeer,
Where light falls quartered on the polished floor
And rims the line of water tilting clear
Out of an earthen pitcher as you pour.

But art requires a distance: let me be
Always the connoisseur of your perfection.
Stay where the spaces of the gallery
Flow calm between your pose and my inspection,
Lest one imperfect gesture make demands
As troubling as the touch of human hands.

I HEARD A HERMIT SPEAK

Upon the mountain of the young
I heard a hermit speak:
"Purity is the serpent's eye
That murders with a look.

Purity's king of poisons
And duke of deadly night.
Abhor the single-minded man,
The woman lily-white.

Go cold under the heavens,
Run naked through the day,
But never wear the armored shirt
Of total Yea or Nay.

Stare into the looking-glass:
Your enemy stares you back.
Yet never cringe and hide your face;
Hear all that he will speak.

The day that glass dissolves to show
Your own reflection there,
Then change your mirror for the world,
The teeming, streaming air.

O let your human memory end
Heavy with thought and act.
Claim every joy of paradox
That time would keep intact.

Be rich as you are human,"
I heard that hermit cry
To the young men and women
All walking out to die.

COLOPHON

In this long room, upon each western pane
The sunset wreaks its final savage stain;
And we, like masquers costumed in an air
Outcrimsoning the gaudiest cock that crows,
Parade as torches and diabolos
Along the blood-red spiral of the stair.

An imminent amazement of the heart
Constricts our greeting as we meet and part.
A gesture or a word can make us turn
Ready to cry a sudden sharp goodnight;
Yet still delays the dark, still cockerel-bright
Smoulder the dyes in which we wade and burn.

Not tragical, the faces that we wear:
A modern gaiety, fitting as despair
Shall pass the hour till domes and sunsets fall.
Extravagant and ceremonious words
Rise on the air like flights of Chinese birds
Uncaged upon a fiery carnival.

What's left us in this violent spectacle
But kisses on the mouth, or works of will—
The imagination's form so sternly wrought,
The flashes of the brain so boldly penned
That when the sunset gutters to its end
The world's last thought will be our flaring thought?

A WALK BY THE CHARLES

Finality broods upon the things that pass:
Persuaded by this air, the trump of doom
Might hang unsounded while the autumn gloom
Darkens the leaf and smokes the river's glass.
For nothing so susceptible to death
But on this forenoon seems to hold its breath:
The silent single oarsmen on the stream
Are always young, are rowers in a dream.
The lovers underneath the chestnut tree,
Though love is over, stand bemused to see
The season falling where no fall could be.

You oarsmen, when you row beyond the bend,
Will see the river winding to its end.
Lovers that hold the chestnut burr in hand
Will speak at last of death, will understand,
Foot-deep amid the ruinage of the year,
What smell it is that stings the gathering air.

From our evasion we are brought at last,
From all our hopes of constancy, to cast
One look of recognition at the sky,
The unimportant leaves that flutter by.
Why else upon this bank are we so still?
What lends us anchor but the mutable?

O lovers, let the bridge of your two hands
Be broken, like the mirrored bridge that bends
And shivers on the surface of the stream.
Young oarsmen, who in timeless gesture seem
Continuous, united with the tide,
Leave off your bending to the oar, and glide
Past innocence, beyond these aging bricks
To where the Charles flows in to join the Styx.

NEW YEAR MORNING

The bells have quit their clanging; here beneath
The coldly furious streaks of morning stars
We hear the scraping of the last few cars,
And on the doorstep by the frozen wreath
Return goodnights to night. Dear friends, once more
We've held our strength against a straining door,

Again the siege is past, another year
Has lost the battle. You can leave us now.
The hours are done that must be clamored through
Lest darkness think us sleeping, lest we hear
Secret police engendered out of night
Advancing on our little zone of light.

Now each of us can dare to be alone,
His room no longer populous with spies
Bending above the pillow where he lies
To sow his dreams with fear that all is done,
That there's no more reprieve, no leaf to tear
And find another January there.

So we are safe again. Goodnight, brave friends.
So may beginnings always follow ends.
Though time is treasonable, may we stand
Gathered each year, a stubborn-hearted band
Whose gaiety rises like a litany
Under the dying ornamental tree.

IN TIME OF CARNIVAL

Those lights, that plaza—I should know them all:
The impotent blind beggar shouting his songs
Of lovers, while the headlong populace
Drinks, tramples, immolates itself in action;
The bloody light of braziers on the faces
Of women who are action's means and end,
Each a laughing Fury; the towering glass
Of those cathedral saints, whose stiffened forms,
Ruby in passing torchlight, stoop to dark
And flare again as puppets of disorder,
Lifeless without its light, but in that rout
Illumined and empowered. There's no crowd
In nave or playhouse any more; for all
Are actors where mere pasteboard roars to heaven
Under the dropped match, and the streets alone,
The amphitheatre of great night itself,
Suffice to contain their scene. Nothing will do
But action of the senses, total seizure
Of what's to hand. And through the swaying streets
That beggar, impotent since youth, sings on,
Ignorant of the scene, blind to his power,
The songs that send those lovers wild to bed.

THE MIDDLE-AGED

Their faces, safe as an interior
Of Holland tiles and Oriental carpet,
Where the fruit-bowl, always filled, stood in a light
Of placid afternoon—their voices' measure,
Their figures moving in the Sunday garden
To lay the tea outdoors or trim the borders,

Afflicted, haunted us. For to be young
Was always to live in other people's houses
Whose peace, if we sought it, had been made by others,
Was ours at second-hand and not for long.
The custom of the house, not ours, the sun
Fading the silver-blue Fortuny curtains,
The reminiscence of a Christmas party
Of fourteen years ago—all memory,
Signs of possession and of being possessed,
We tasted, tense with envy. They were so kind,
Would have given us anything; the bowl of fruit
Was filled for us, there was a room upstairs
We must call ours: but twenty years of living
They could not give. Nor did they ever speak
Of the coarse stain on that polished balustrade,
The crack in the study window, or the letters
Locked in a drawer and the key destroyed.
All to be understood by us, returning
Late, in our own time—how that peace was made,
Upon what terms, with how much left unsaid.

THE MARRIAGE PORTION

From commissars of daylight
Love cannot make us free.
Nights of ungracious darkness
Hang over you and me.
We lie awake together
And hear the clocks strike three.

Our loving cannot exile
The felons *but* and *if;*
Yet being undivided

Some ways we can contrive
To hold off those besiegers
Who batter round our life:

The thieves of our completeness
Who steal us stone by stone,
The patronage that scowls upon
Our need to be alone,
And all the clever people
Who want us for their own.

The telephone is ringing,
And planes and trains depart.
The cocktail party's forming,
The cruise about to start.
To stay behind is fatal—
Act now, the time is short.

If we refuse the summons
And stand at last alone,
We walk intact and certain,
As man and woman grown
In the deserted playground
When all the rest have gone.

THE TREE

Long ago I found a seed,
And kept it in a glass of water,
And half forgot my dim intent
Until I saw it start to reach

For life with one blind, fragile root.
And then I pressed it into earth
And saw its tendrils seek the air,
So slowly that I hardly knew
Of any change till it had grown
A stalk, a leaf; and seemed to be
No more a thing in need of me,
But living by some sapience
I had not given, could not withdraw.
So it grew on, and days went by,
And seasons with their common gifts,
Till at the leafage of the year
I felt the sun cut off from me
By something thick outside my room—
Not yet a tree grown to the full,
Yet so endowed with need and will
It took the warmth and left me cold.
And first I climbed with hook and shears
To prune the boughs that darkened me,
But the tree was stubborner than I,
And where I clipped it grew again,
Brutal in purpose as a weed.
Nor did it give of fruit or flower,
Though seasons brought their common gifts,
And years went by. It only grew
Darker and denser to my view,
Taking whatever I would yield—
The homage of a troubled mind—
Requiring nothing, yet accepting
My willingness to guard its life
By the endurance of my own.
It gives me nothing; yet I see
Sometimes in dreams my enemy
Hanged by the hair upon that tree.

LOVERS ARE LIKE CHILDREN

Chagall's sweet lovers mounting into blue
Remind me that discovery by two
Of any world the mind can wander through

Is like the time when young and left alone,
We touched the secret fringe of being one,
Back of the playground full of Everyone.

Love is like childhood, caught in trust and fear.
The statues point to omens in the air,
And yet the fountains bubble bright and clear.

Lost in the garden rank with contradiction,
We see the fences sprout for our affliction,
And the red-rose-tree curtly labelled Fiction.

Nothing to tell us whether what they mean
Is true of this or any other scene.
We only know the summer leaves are green,

Alive and dense for two to penetrate—
An exploration difficult and great
As when one day beside the schoolyard gate,

Straggling behind to glean a sunlit stone,
One first perceived and knew itself as one.
Now add this pebble to that early one.

WHEN THIS CLANGOR IN THE BRAIN

Say a master of the track
Lightly leaped and lightly ran,
Knew his powers of chest and thigh
Clean outstripped the thought of man—
Would it not be pill and patch
And worse than queasy cripples know,
If on a day the rheum should catch
And lay that master leaper low?

Say that into certain minds
A Merlin dances, in and out,
And what he chooses, must obey
And sway the thought it thinks about—
Would it not be old folks' home
And the dry end of the year
For the mind he left again
Unmastered, lock and stock and gear?

When this clangor in the brain
Grows perfunctory, or worse,
Put me down a sick old woman
Propped for sleep, hire me a nurse;
Till then, all things I look upon
Beat on my brain to hail and bless,
And every last and wayward power
I claim till then, and nothing less.

A VIEW OF MERTON COLLEGE

An interval: the view across the fields
Perfect and insusceptible as seen
In printshops of the High Street—sun on stone
Worn like old needlework, the sheen of grass,
Minute and ageless figures moving down
The Broad Walk under tinted trees. Awhile
Mind's local jangling lightens, ear is eased,
Eye's flaw is mended in such gazing, healed
By separation as through glass. Until
Sun shifts, air turns harsher, paler, rooks
Flap in the rising wind. The wind has found you,
The mortal light of day, whose envy, waste,
Irresolution tread you as you go
Guilty and human. Here as anywhere,
Peace of the mind lies through an arch of stone,
The limitations posted strict and clear:
Not to be littered or presumed upon.

HOLIDAY

Summer was another country, where the birds
Woke us at dawn among the dripping leaves
And lent to all our fêtes their sweet approval.
The touch of air on flesh was lighter, keener,
The senses flourished like a laden tree
Whose every gesture finishes in a flower.
In those unwardened provinces we dined
From wicker baskets by a green canal,
Staining our lips with peach and nectarine,

Slapping at golden wasps. And when we kissed,
Tasting that sunlit juice, the landscape folded
Into our clasp, and not a breath recalled
The long walk back to winter, leagues away.

THE CAPITAL

Under that summer asphalt, under vistas
Aspiring to a neo-classic calm,
The steaming burgeon of Potomac's swamp
Has never quite been laid to rest. The eye
Winces in sunlight off a marble dome.

But cannot fix the face of Jefferson
Through haze of an outrageous atmosphere
By diplomats called tropic; nor can the ear
Hold to the lifeline of a single voice
Through jettisoned rumors jamming all the air.

The dollar in that city of inscriptions
Is minted among pediments and columns
Purer than newmade coin. The afternoon
Steams with the drip of departmental fountains
And humid branches breathing overhead

Down avenues where the siren's nervous shriek
Pursues the murderer or the foreign guest
Through those indifferent noonday crowds who never
Ask, till history tells them, what they do
In that metropolis anything but Greek.

THE PLATFORM

The railway stations of our daily plight
See every hour love's threatened overthrow.
Each afternoon at five the buses go
Laden with those who shall be false by night.
We say goodbye in rooms too bright with noise
To catch the shades of a receding voice;
We turn at the revolving door and see
Love's face already changed, indelibly.

Not to admit we may not meet again—
This was the parting treason of our thought.
Battering down our cowardly "till then,"
Time's traffic hems the seeker from the sought.
We take too sudden leave; the platform reels
With thunder of a thousand pounding heels,
And at the gate where one remains behind,
Though most we strain to see, we most are blind.

Dear loves, dear friends, I take my leave all day
In practice for a time that need not come.
I turn and move from you a little way,
As men walk out beyond the fields of home
In troubled days, to view what they love well—
Distance confirming for a moment's spell,
Meeting or going, that when we embrace
We know the heart beyond the transient face.

LAST SONG

All in the day that I was born,
I walked across the shouting corn;
I saw the sunlight flash and hail
From every spire and every sail,
But most I leaned against the sky
To hear the eagles racing by,
And all the safety of the womb
Could not betray me, lure me home.

All in the day that I was wed
I saw them strew my bridal bed.
I smelled the wind across the sheets
Breathing of lavender and sweets
That neither sea nor meadow knew;
And when my bride was brought to view
I kept a hundred candles lit
All for light and the joy of it.

All in the day that I was old
I felt the wind blow salt and cold
Like seaspray on my shaking thighs
Or sand flung up to blind my eyes.
I cried for sun and the eagles flying,
But felt those fingers spying, prying,
The same that wrenched me into life
And cut my safety with a knife.

Soon they will bind me dark and warm
And impotent to suffer harm.

I shall be exiled to the womb
Where once I lay and thought it home.
The sun that flashed my first delight
Shall never learn to cleave that night;
And all the swords of danger fly
Far from the caul in which I lie.

THE DIAMOND CUTTERS

However legendary,
The stone is still a stone,
Though it had once resisted
The weight of Africa,
The hammer-blows of time
That wear to bits of rubble
The mountain and the pebble—
But not this coldest one.

Now, you intelligence
So late dredged up from dark
Upon whose smoky walls
Bison took fumbling form
Or flint was edged on flint—
Now, careful arriviste,
Delineate at will
Incisions in the ice.

Be serious, because
The stone may have contempt
For too-familiar hands,
And because all you do
Loses or gains by this:
Respect the adversary,
Meet it with tools refined,
And thereby set your price.

Be hard of heart, because
The stone must leave your hand.
Although you liberate
Pure and expensive fires
Fit to enamor Shebas,
Keep your desire apart.
Love only what you do,
And not what you have done.

Be proud, when you have set
The final spoke of flame
In that prismatic wheel,
And nothing's left this day
Except to see the sun
Shine on the false and the true,
And know that Africa
Will yield you more to do.

SNAPSHOTS

OF A

DAUGHTER-

IN-LAW

(1963)

AT MAJORITY

For C.

When you are old and beautiful,
And things most difficult are done,
There will be few who can recall
Your face that I see ravaged now
By youth and its oppressive work.

Your look will hold their wondering looks
Grave as Cordelia's at the last,
Neither with rancor at the past
Nor to upbraid the coming time.
For you will be at peace with time.

But now, a daily warfare takes
Its toll of tenderness in you,
And you must live like captains who
Wait out the hour before the charge—
Fearful, and yet impatient too.

Yet someday this will have an end,
All choices made or choice resigned,
And in your face the literal eye
Trace little of your history,
Nor ever piece the tale entire

Of villages that had to burn
And playgrounds of the will destroyed
Before you could be safe from time
And gather in your brow and air
The stillness of antiquity.

1954

FROM MORNING-GLORY TO PETERSBURG

(*The World Book*, 1928)

"Organized knowledge in story and picture"
    confronts through dusty glass
    an eye grown dubious.
I can recall when knowledge still was pure,
    not contradictory, pleasurable
    as cutting out a paper doll.
You opened up a book and there it was:
    everything just as promised, from
    Kurdistan to Mormons, Gum
Arabic to Kumquat, neither more nor less.
    Facts could be kept separate
    by a convention; that was what
made childhood possible. Now knowledge finds me out;
    in all its risible untidiness
    it traces me to each address,
dragging in things I never thought about.
    I don't invite what facts can be
    held at arm's length; a family
of jeering irresponsibles always
    comes along gypsy-style
    and there you have them all
forever on your hands. It never pays.
    If I could still extrapolate
    the morning-glory on the gate
from Petersburg in history—but it's too late.

1954

RURAL REFLECTIONS

This is the grass your feet are planted on.
You paint it orange or you sing it green,
    But you have never found
A way to make the grass mean what you mean.

A cloud can be whatever you intend:
Ostrich or leaning tower or staring eye.
    But you have never found
A cloud sufficient to express the sky.

Get out there with your splendid expertise;
Raymond who cuts the meadow does no less.
    Inhuman nature says:
Inhuman patience is the true success.

Human impatience trips you as you run;
    Stand still and you must lie.
It is the grass that cuts the mower down;
It is the cloud that swallows up the sky.

1956

THE KNIGHT

A knight rides into the noon,
and his helmet points to the sun,
and a thousand splintered suns
are the gaiety of his mail.
The soles of his feet glitter
and his palms flash in reply,
and under his crackling banner
he rides like a ship in sail.

A knight rides into the noon,
and only his eye is living,
a lump of bitter jelly
set in a metal mask,
betraying rags and tatters
that cling to the flesh beneath
and wear his nerves to ribbons
under the radiant casque.

Who will unhorse this rider
and free him from between
the walls of iron, the emblems
crushing his chest with their weight?
Will they defeat him gently,
or leave him hurled on the green,
his rags and wounds still hidden
under the great breastplate?

1957

THE LOSER

> A man thinks of the woman he once loved:
> first, after her wedding, and then nearly a decade later.

I.

I kissed you, bride and lost, and went
home from that bourgeois sacrament,
your cheek still tasting cold upon
my lips that gave you benison
with all the swagger that they knew—
as losers somehow learn to do.

Your wedding made my eyes ache; soon
the world would be worse off for one
more golden apple dropped to ground
without the least protesting sound,
and you would windfall lie, and we
forget your shimmer on the tree.

Beauty is always wasted: if
not Mignon's song sung to the deaf,
at all events to the unmoved.
A face like yours cannot be loved
long or seriously enough.
Almost, we seem to hold it off.

II.

Well, you are tougher than I thought.
Now when the wash with ice hangs taut
this morning of St. Valentine,
I see you strip the squeaking line,
your body weighed against the load,
and all my groans can do no good.

Because you still are beautiful,
though squared and stiffened by the pull
of what nine windy years have done.
You have three daughters, lost a son.
I see all your intelligence
flung into that unwearied stance.

My envy is of no avail.
I turn my head and wish him well
who chafed your beauty into use
and lives forever in a house
lit by the friction of your mind.
You stagger in against the wind.

1958

THE ABSENT-MINDED
ARE ALWAYS TO BLAME

What do you look for down there
in the cracks of the pavement? Or up there
between the pineapple and the acanthus leaf
in that uninspired ornament? Odysseus
wading half-naked out of the shrubbery
like a god, dead serious among those at play,
could hardly be more out of it. In school
we striped your back with chalk, you all oblivious,
your eyes harnessed by a transparent strand
reaching the other side of things, or down
like a wellchain to the center of earth.
Now with those same eyes you pull the
pavements up like old linoleum,
arches of triumph start to liquefy
minutes after you slowly turn away.

1958

EURYCLEA'S TALE

I have to weep when I see it, the grown boy fretting
for a father dawdling among the isles,
and the seascape hollowed out by that boy's edged gaze
to receive one speck, one only, for years and years withheld.

And that speck, that curious man, has kept from home
till home would seem the forbidden place, till blood
and the tears of an old woman must run down
to satisfy the genius of place. Even then, what
can they do together, father and son?
the driftwood stranger and the rooted boy
whose eyes will have nothing then to ask the sea.

But all the time and everywhere
lies in ambush for the distracted eyeball
light: light on the ship racked up in port,
the chimney-stones, the scar whiter than smoke,
than her flanks, her hair, that true but aging bride.

1958

SEPTEMBER 21

Wear the weight of equinoctial evening,
light like melons bruised on all the porches.
Feel the houses tenderly appraise you,
hold you in the watchfulness of mothers.

Once the nighttime was a milky river
washing past the swimmers in the sunset,
rinsing over sleepers of the morning.
Soon the night will be an eyeless quarry

where the shrunken daylight and its rebels,
loosened,   dive like stones in perfect silence,
names and voices drown without reflection.

Then the houses draw you. Then they have you.

1958

AFTER A SENTENCE
IN "MALTE LAURIDS BRIGGE"

The month's eye blurs.
The winter's lungs are cracked.
Along bloated gutters race,
shredded, your injured legions,
the waste of our remorseless search.
Your old, unuttered names are holes
worn in our skins
through which we feel from time to time
abrasive wind.

Those who are loved live poorly and in danger.
We who were loved will never
unlive that crippling fever.
A day returns, a certain weather
splatters the panes, and we
once more stare in the eye of our first failure.

1958

SNAPSHOTS OF A DAUGHTER-IN-LAW

1.

You, once a belle in Shreveport,
with henna-colored hair, skin like a peachbud,
still have your dresses copied from that time,
and play a Chopin prelude
called by Cortot: *"Delicious recollections*
float like perfume through the memory."

Your mind now, mouldering like wedding-cake,
heavy with useless experience, rich
with suspicion, rumor, fantasy,
crumbling to pieces under the knife-edge
of mere fact. In the prime of your life.

Nervy, glowering, your daughter
wipes the teaspoons, grows another way.

2.

Banging the coffee-pot into the sink
she hears the angels chiding, and looks out
past the raked gardens to the sloppy sky.
Only a week since They said: *Have no patience.*

The next time it was: *Be insatiable.*
Then: *Save yourself; others you cannot save.*
Sometimes she's let the tapstream scald her arm,
a match burn to her thumbnail,

or held her hand above the kettle's snout
right in the woolly steam. They are probably angels,
since nothing hurts her any more, except
each morning's grit blowing into her eyes.

3.

A thinking woman sleeps with monsters.
The beak that grips her, she becomes. And Nature,
that sprung-lidded, still commodious
steamer-trunk of *tempora* and *mores*
gets stuffed with it all: the mildewed orange-flowers,
the female pills, the terrible breasts
of Boadicea beneath flat foxes' heads and orchids.

Two handsome women, gripped in argument,
each proud, acute, subtle, I hear scream
across the cut glass and majolica
like Furies cornered from their prey:
The argument *ad feminam*, all the old knives
that have rusted in my back, I drive in yours,
ma semblable, ma soeur!

4.

Knowing themselves too well in one another:
their gifts no pure fruition, but a thorn,
the prick filed sharp against a hint of scorn . . .
Reading while waiting
for the iron to heat,
writing, *My Life had stood—a Loaded Gun—*
in that Amherst pantry while the jellies boil and scum,
or, more often,
iron-eyed and beaked and purposed as a bird,
dusting everything on the whatnot every day of life.

5.

Dulce ridens, dulce loquens,
she shaves her legs until they gleam
like petrified mammoth-tusk.

6.

When to her lute Corinna sings
neither words nor music are her own;
only the long hair dipping
over her cheek, only the song
of silk against her knees
and these
adjusted in reflections of an eye.

Poised, trembling and unsatisfied, before
an unlocked door, that cage of cages,
tell us, you bird, you tragical machine—
is this *fertilisante douleur?* Pinned down
by love, for you the only natural action,
are you edged more keen
to prise the secrets of the vault? has Nature shown
her household books to you, daughter-in-law,
that her sons never saw?

7.

"To have in this uncertain world some stay
which cannot be undermined, is
of the utmost consequence."
       Thus wrote
a woman, partly brave and partly good,
who fought with what she partly understood.
Few men about her would or could do more,
hence she was labelled harpy, shrew and whore.

8.

"You all die at fifteen," said Diderot,
and turn part legend, part convention.
Still, eyes inaccurately dream
behind closed windows blankening with steam.
Deliciously, all that we might have been,
all that we were—fire, tears,
wit, taste, martyred ambition—
stirs like the memory of refused adultery
the drained and flagging bosom of our middle years.

9.

Not that it is done well, but
that it is done at all? Yes, think
of the odds! or shrug them off forever.
This luxury of the precocious child,
Time's precious chronic invalid,—
would we, darlings, resign it if we could?
Our blight has been our sinecure:
mere talent was enough for us—
glitter in fragments and rough drafts.

Sigh no more, ladies.

Time is male
and in his cups drinks to the fair.
Bemused by gallantry, we hear
our mediocrities over-praised,
indolence read as abnegation,
slattern thought styled intuition,
every lapse forgiven, our crime
only to cast too bold a shadow
or smash the mould straight off.

For that, solitary confinement,
tear gas, attrition shelling.
Few applicants for that honor.

10.

Well,
she's long about her coming, who must be
more merciless to herself than history.
Her mind full to the wind, I see her plunge
breasted and glancing through the currents,
taking the light upon her
at least as beautiful as any boy
or helicopter,

poised, still coming,
her fine blades making the air wince
but her cargo
no promise then:
delivered
palpable
ours.

1958–1960

PASSING ON

The landlord's hammer in the yard
patches a porch where your shirts swing
brashly against May's creamy blue.
This year the forsythia ran wild,
chrome splashed on the spring evenings,
every bush a pile of sulphur.
Now, ragged, they bend
under the late wind's onslaught, tousled
as my head beneath the clotheslines.

Soon we'll be off. I'll pack us into parcels,
stuff us in barrels, shroud us in newspapers,
pausing to marvel at old bargain sales:
Oh, all the chances we never seized!
Emptiness round the stoop of the house
minces, catwise, waiting for an in.

1959

THE RAVEN

If, antique hateful bird,
flapping through dawngagged streets
of metal shopfronts grated down
on pedestrian nerve-ends,

if, as on old film,
my features blurred and grained like cereal,
you find me walking up and down
waiting for my first dream,

don't try to sully my head
with vengeful squirtings. Fly on,
ratfooted cautionary of my dark,
till we meet further along.

You are no dream, old genius.
I smell you, get my teeth on edge,
stand in my sweat—in mercury—
even as you prime your feathers and set sail.

1959

MERELY TO KNOW

I.

Wedged in by earthworks
thrown up by snouters before me,
I kick and snuffle, breathing in
cobwebs of beetle-cuirass:
vainglory of polished green,
infallible pincer, resonant nerve,
a thickening on the air now,
confusion to my lungs, no more.
My predecessors blind me—
their zeal exhausted among roots and tunnels,
they gasped and looked up once or twice
into the beechtree's nightblack glitter.

II.

Let me take you by the hair
and drag you backward to the light,
there spongelike press my gaze
patiently upon your eyes,
hold like a photographic plate
against you my enormous question.
What if you cringe, what if you weep?
Suffer this and you need suffer
nothing more. I'll give you back
yourself at last to the last part.
I take nothing, only look.
Change nothing. Have no need to change.
Merely to know and let you go.

1959

III.

Spirit like water
molded by unseen stone
and sandbar, pleats and funnels
according to its own
submerged necessity—
to the indolent eye
pure willfulness, to the stray
pine-needle boiling
in that cascade-bent pool
a random fury: Law,
if that's what's wanted, lies
asking to be read
in the dried brook-bed.

1961

ANTINOÜS: THE DIARIES

Autumn torture. The old signs
smeared on the pavement, sopping leaves
rubbed into the landscape as unguent on a bruise,
brought indoors, even, as they bring flowers, enormous,
with the colors of the body's secret parts.
All this. And then, evenings, needing to be out,
walking fast, fighting the fire
that must die, light that sets my teeth on edge with joy,
till on the black embankment
I'm a cart stopped in the ruts of time.

Then at some house the rumor of truth and beauty
saturates a room like lilac-water
in the stream of a bath, fires snap, heads are high,
gold hair at napes of necks, gold in glasses,
gold in the throat, poetry of furs and manners.
Why do I shiver then? Haven't I seen,
over and over, before the end of an evening,
the three opened coffins carried in and left in a corner?
Haven't I watched as somebody cracked his shin
on one of them, winced and hopped and limped
laughing to lay his hand on a beautiful arm
striated with hairs of gold, like an almond-shell?

The old, needless story. For if I'm here
it is by choice and when at last
I smell my own rising nausea, feel the air
tighten around my stomach like a surgical bandage,
I can't pretend surprise. What is it I so miscarry?
If what I spew on the tiles at last,
helpless, disgraced, alone,
is in part what I've swallowed from glasses, eyes,
motions of hands, opening and closing mouths,
Isn't it also dead gobbets of myself,
abortive, murdered, or never willed?

1959

JUVENILIA

Your Ibsen volumes, violet-spined,
each flaking its gold arabesque!
Again I sit, under duress, hands washed,
at your inkstained oaken desk,
by the goose-neck lamp in the tropic of your books,
stabbing the blotting-pad, doodling loop upon loop,
peering one-eyed in the dusty reflecting mirror
of your student microscope,
craning my neck to spell above me

A DOLLS HOUSE   LITTLE EYOLF
     WHEN WE DEAD AWAKEN

Unspeakable fairy tales ebb like blood through my head
as I dip the pen and for aunts, for admiring friends,
for you above all to read,
copy my praised and sedulous lines.

Behind the two of us, thirsty spines
quiver in semi-shadow, huge leaves uncurl and thicken.

1960

DOUBLE MONOLOGUE

To live illusionless, in the abandoned mine-
    shaft of doubt, and still
mime illusions for others? A puzzle
    for the maker who has thought
once too often too coldly.

Since I was more than a child
    trying on a thousand faces
I have wanted one thing: to know
    simply as I know my name
at any given moment, where I stand.

How much expense of time and skill
    which might have set itself
to angelic fabrications! All merely
    to chart one needle in the haymow?
Find yourself and you find the world?

Solemn presumption! Mighty Object
    no one but itself has missed,
what's lost, if you stay lost? Someone
    ignorantly loves you—will that serve?
Shrug that off, and presto!—

the needle drowns in the haydust.
    Think of the whole haystack—
a composition so fortuitous
    it only looks monumental.
There's always a straw twitching somewhere.

Wait out the long chance, and
    your needle too could get nudged up
to the apex of that bristling calm.
    Rusted, possibly. You might not want
to swear it was the Object, after all.

Time wears us old utopians.
    I now no longer think
"truth" is the most beautiful of words.
    Today, when I see "truthful"
written somewhere, it flares

like a white orchid in wet woods,
    rare and grief-delighting, up from the page.
Sometimes, unwittingly even,
    we have been truthful.
In a random universe, what more

exact and starry consolation?
    Don't think I think
facts serve better than ignorant love.
    Both serve, and still
our need mocks our gear.

1960

A WOMAN MOURNED BY DAUGHTERS

Now, not a tear begun,
we sit here in your kitchen,
spent, you see, already.
You are swollen till you strain
this house and the whole sky.
You, whom we so often
succeeded in ignoring!
You, are puffed up in death
like a corpse pulled from the sea;
we groan beneath your weight.
And yet you were a leaf,
a straw blown on the bed,
you had long since become
crisp as a dead insect.
What is it, if not you,
that settles on us now
like satin you pulled down
over our bridal heads?
What rises in our throats
like food you prodded in?
Nothing could be enough.
You breathe upon us now
through solid assertions
of yourself: teaspoons, goblets,
seas of carpet, a forest
of old plants to be watered,
an old man in an adjoining
room to be touched and fed.
And all this universe
dares us to lay a finger
anywhere, save exactly
as you would wish it done.

1960

READINGS OF HISTORY

> He delighted in relating the fact that he had been born
> near Girgenti in a place called Chaos during a raging
> cholera epidemic.
>
> —Domenico Vittorini, *The Drama of Luigi Pirandello*

I. *The Evil Eye*

Last night we sat with the stereopticon,
laughing at genre views of 1906,
till suddenly, gazing straight into
that fringed and tasseled parlor, where the vestal
spurns an unlikely suitor
with hairy-crested plants to right and left,
my heart sank. It was terrible.
I smelled the mildew in those swags of plush,
dust on the eyepiece bloomed to freaks of mold.
I knew beyond all doubt how dead that couple was.

Today, a fresh clean morning.
Your camera stabs me unawares,
right in my mortal part.
A womb of celluloid already
contains my dotage and my total absence.

II. *The Confrontation*

Luigi Pirandello
looked like an old historian
(oval head, tufted white beard,
not least the hunger
for reconciliation in his eye).
For fourteen years, facing

his criminal reflection
in his wife's Grand Guignol mind,
he built over and over
that hall of mirrors
in which to be appears
to be perceived.

The present holds you like a raving wife,
clever as the mad are clever,
digging up your secret truths
from her disabled genius.
She knows what you hope
and dare not hope:
remembers
what you're sick
of forgetting.
What are you now
but what you know together, you and she?

She will not let you think.
It is important
to make connections. Everything
happens very fast in the minds
of the insane. Even you
aren't up to that, yet.
Go out, walk,
think of selves long past.

III. *Memorabilia*

I recall
Civil War letters of a great-grand-uncle,
fifteen at Chancellorsville,

                    no raconteur,
no speller, either; nor to put it squarely,

much of a mind;

                the most we gather
is that he did write home:

                I am well,
how are my sisters, hope you are the same.
Did Spartan battle-echoes rack his head?
Dying, he turned into his father's memory.

History's queerly strong perfumes
rise from the crook of this day's elbow:
Seduction fantasies of the public mind,
or Dilthey's dream from which he roused to see
the cosmos glaring through his windowpane?
Prisoners of what we think occurred,
or dreamers dreaming toward a final word?

What, in fact, happened in these woods
on some obliterated afternoon?

IV. *Consanguinity*

Can history show us nothing
but pieces of ourselves, detached,
set to a kind of poetry,
a kind of music, even?
Seated today on Grandmamma's
plush sofa with the grapes
bursting so ripely from the curved mahogany,
we read the great Victorians
weeping, almost, as if
some family breach were healed.
Those angry giantesses and giants,
lately our kith and kin!
We stare into their faces, hear
at last what they were saying

(or some version not bruited
by filial irritation).

The cat-tails wither in the reading-room.
Tobacco-colored dust
drifts on the newest magazines.
I loaf here leafing ancient copies
of LIFE from World War II.
We look so poor and honest there:
girls with long hair badly combed
and unbecoming dresses—
where are you now?
                    You sail
to shop in Europe, ignorantly freed
for you, an age ago.
Your nylon luggage matches
                              eyelids
expertly azured.
I, too, have lived in history.

V. *The Mirror*

Is it in hopes
to find or lose myself
that I
fill up my table now
with Michelet and Motley?
To "know how it was"
or to forget how it is—
what else?
Split at the root, neither Gentile nor Jew,
Yankee nor Rebel, born
in the face of two ancient cults,
I'm a good reader of histories.
And you,

Morris Cohen, dear to me as a brother,
when you sit at night
tracing your way through your volumes
of Josephus, or any
of the old Judaic chronicles,
do you find yourself there, a simpler,
more eloquent Jew?

                  or do you read
to shut out the tick-tock of self,
the questions and their routine answers?

VI. *The Covenant*

The present breaks our hearts. We lie and freeze,
our fingers icy as a bunch of keys.
Nothing will thaw these bones except
memory like an ancient blanket wrapped
about us when we sleep at home again,
smelling of picnics, closets, sicknesses,
old nightmare,

                and insomnia's spreading stain.

Or say I sit with what I halfway know
as with a dying man who heaves the true
version at last, now that it hardly matters,
or gropes a hand to where the letters
sewn in the mattress can be plucked and read.
Here's water.   Sleep.   No more is asked of you.
I take your life into my living head.

1960

TO THE AIRPORT

Death's taxi crackles through the mist. The cheeks
of diamond battlements flush high and cold.
Alarm clocks strike a million sparks of will.
Weeping: all night we've wept and watched the hours
that never will be ours again: Now
weeping, we roll through unforgettable
Zion, that rears its golden head from sleep
to act, and does not need us as we weep.

You dreamed us, City, and you let us be.
Grandiloquence, improvidence, ordure, light,
hours that seemed years, and ours—and over all
the endless wing of possibility,
that mackerel heaven of yours, fretted with all
our wits could leap for, envy batten on.
Our flights take off from you into the sea;
nothing you need wastes, though we think we do.

You are Canaan now and we are lifted high
to see all we were promised, never knew.

1960

THE AFTERWAKE

Nursing your nerves
to rest, I've roused my own; well,
now for a few bad hours!
Sleep sees you behind closed doors.
Alone, I slump in his front parlor.
You're safe inside. Good. But I'm
like a midwife who at dawn

has all in order: bloodstains
washed up, teapot on the stove,
and starts her five miles home
walking, the birthyell still
exploding in her head.

Yes, I'm with her now: here's
the streaked, livid road
edged with shut houses
breathing night out and in.
Legs tight with fatigue,
we move under morning's coal-blue star,
colossal as this load
of unexpired purpose, which drains
slowly, till scissors of cockcrow snip the air.

1961

ARTIFICIAL INTELLIGENCE
To GPS

Over the chessboard now,
Your Artificiality concludes
a final check; rests; broods—
      no—sorts and stacks a file of memories,
while I
concede the victory, bow,
and slouch among my free associations.

You never had a mother,
let's say? no digital Gertrude
whom you'd as lief have seen
Kingless? So your White Queen

was just an "operator."
(My Red had incandescence,
ire, aura, flare,
and trapped me several moments in her stare.)

I'm sulking, clearly, in the great tradition
of human waste. Why not
dump the whole reeking snarl
and let you solve me once for all?
(*Parameter:* a black-faced Luddite
itching for ecstasies of sabotage.)

Still, when
they make you write your poems, later on,
who'd envy you, force-fed
on all those variorum
editions of our primitive endeavors,
those frozen pemmican language-rations
they'll cram you with? denied
our luxury of nausea, you
forget nothing, have no dreams.

1961

A MARRIAGE IN THE 'SIXTIES

As solid-seeming as antiquity,
you frown above
the *New York Sunday Times*
where Castro, like a walk-on out of *Carmen,*
mutters into a bearded henchman's ear.

They say the second's getting shorter—
I knew it in my bones—
and pieces of the universe are missing.
I feel the gears of this late afternoon
slip, cog by cog, even as I read.
"I'm old," we both complain,
half-laughing, oftener now.

Time serves you well. That face—
part Roman emperor, part Raimu—
nothing this side of Absence can undo.
Bliss, revulsion, your rare angers can
only carry through what's well begun.

When
I read your letters long ago
in that half-defunct
hotel in Magdalen Street
every word primed my nerves.
A geographical misery
composed of oceans, fogbound planes
and misdelivered cablegrams
lay round me, a Nova Zembla
only your live breath could unfreeze.
Today we stalk
in the raging desert of our thought
whose single drop of mercy is
each knows the other there.
Two strangers, thrust for life upon a rock,
may have at last the perfect hour of talk
that language aches for; still—
two minds, two messages.

Your brows knit into flourishes. Some piece
of mere time has you tangled there.
Some mote of history has flown into your eye.
Will nothing ever be the same,
even our quarrels take a different key,
our dreams exhume new metaphors?
The world breathes underneath our bed.
Don't look. We're at each other's mercy too.

Dear fellow-particle, electric dust
I'm blown with—ancestor
to what euphoric cluster—
see how particularity dissolves
in all that hints of chaos. Let one finger
hover toward you from There
and see this furious grain
suspend its dance to hang
beside you like your twin.

1961

FIRST THINGS

I can't name love now
without naming its object—
this the final measure
of those flintspark years
when one believed
one's flash innate.
Today I swear
Only in the sun's eye
Do I take fire.

1961

ATTENTION

The ice age is here.
I sit burning cigarettes,
burning my brain.
A micro-Tibet,
deadly, frivolous, complete,
blinds the four panes.
Veils of dumb air
unwind like bandages
from my lips
half-parted, steady as the mouths
of antique statues.

1961

END OF AN ERA

This morning, flakes of sun
peel down to the last snowholds,
the barbed-wire leavings of a war
lost, won, in these dead-end alleys.
Stale as a written-out journalist,
I sort my gear.—Nothing is happening.—City,
dumb as a pack of thumbed cards, you
once had snap and glare
and secret life; now, trembling
under my five grey senses' weight,
you flatten
onto the table.

Baudelaire, I think of you . . . Nothing changes,
rude and self-absorbed the current
dashes past, reflecting nothing, poetry
extends its unsought amnesty,
the roots of the great grove
atrophy underground.
Some voices, though, shake in the air like heat.

The neighborhood is changing,
even the neighbors are grown, methinks, peculiar.
I walk into my house and see
tourists fingering this and that.
My mirrors, my bric-à-brac
don't suit their style.

Those old friends, though,
alive and dead,
for whom things don't come easy—
Certain forests are sawdust,
from now on have to be described?
Nothing changes.   The bones of the mammoths
are still in the earth.

1961

RUSTICATION

In a gigantic *pot de chambre,* scrolled
with roses, purchased dearly at auction,
goldenrod and asters spill
toward the inevitable sunset.
The houseguests trail from swimming

under huge towels.
Marianne dangles barefoot in the hammock
reading about Martin Luther King.
Vivaldi rattles on the phonograph,
flutes ricocheting off the birchtrees.
Flies buzz and are gaily murdered.

Still out of it, and guilty,
I glue the distance-glasses to my eyes
ostrich-like, hoping
you'll think me in that clearing half a mile away.
Offstage I hear
the old time-killers dressing, banging doors,
your voice, a timbre or two too rich for love,
cheering them on.
A kestrel sails into my field of vision,
clear as a rising star.

Why should I need to quarrel
with another's consolations?
Why, in your mortal skin,
vigorously smashing ice and smoking,
a graying pigtail down your back,
should you seem infamous to me?

1961

APOLOGY

I've said: I wouldn't ever
keep a cat, a dog,
a bird—
chiefly because

I'd rather love my equals.
Today, turning
in the fog of my mind,
I knew, the thing I really
couldn't stand in the house
is a woman
with a mindful of fog
and bloodletting claws
and the nerves of a bird
and the nightmares of a dog.

1961

SISTERS

Can I easily say,
I know you of course now,
no longer the fellow-victim,
reader of my diaries, heir
to my outgrown dresses,
ear for my poems and invectives?
Do I know you better
than that blue-eyed stranger
self-absorbed as myself
raptly knitting or sleeping
through a thirdclass winter journey?
Face to face all night
her dreams and whimpers
tangled with mine,
sleeping but not asleep
behind the engine drilling
into dark Germany,

her eyes, mouth, head
reconstructed by dawn
as we nodded farewell.
Her I should recognize
years later, anywhere.

1961

IN THE NORTH

Mulish, unregenerate,
    not "as all men are"
    but more than most

you sit up there in the sunset;
    there are only three
    hours of dark

in your night. You are
    alone as an old king
    with his white-gold beard

when in summer the ships
    sail out, the heroes
    singing, push off

for other lands. Only
    in winter when
    trapped in the ice

your kingdom flashes
    under the northern lights
    and the bees dream

in their hives, the young
    men like the bees
    hang near you

for lack of another,
    remembering too, with some
    remorseful tenderness

you are their king.

1962

THE CLASSMATE

One year, you gave us
all names, hudibrastic
titles, skywrote
our gaudy histories.
We were all sparks
struck in your head,
we mocked but listened.
You filled a whole
zoological notebook
with sly generations
of should-have-beens,
were disgraced, not distressed.
Our howls died away.

Your poetry was in
paper-dart ballads
sailing beyond our noses,
in blackboard lyrics
scrawled in our own patois,

spirals of chalkdust,
inkblot manifestos
who could read today?
You less than any.
Because later you turned
to admiration of the classics
and a sedulous ear.

Still if I hear
the slash of feet
through gutters full of oakleaves
and see the boys
still unprized, unprizing,
dancing along, tossing
books and dusty leaves
into the sun,
they chant, it would seem,
your momentary quatrains,
nose-thumbing, free-lancing
poet of the schoolyard—
prize-giver and taker
now, a pillar
swaddled in laurels—
lost classmate, look!
your glory was here.

1962

PEELING ONIONS

Only to have a grief
equal to all these tears!

There's not a sob in my chest.
Dry-hearted as Peer Gynt
I pare away, no hero,
merely a cook.

Crying was labor, once
when I'd good cause.
Walking, I felt my eyes like wounds
raw in my head,
so postal-clerks, I thought, must stare.
A dog's look, a cat's, burnt to my brain—
yet all that stayed
stuffed in my lungs like smog.

These old tears in the chopping-bowl.

1961

GHOST OF A CHANCE

You see a man
trying to think.

You want to say
to everything:
Keep off! Give him room!
But you only watch,
terrified
the old consolations

will get him at last
like a fish
half-dead from flopping
and almost crawling
across the shingle,
almost breathing
the raw, agonizing
air
till a wave
pulls it back blind into the triumphant
sea.

1962

THE WELL

Down this old well
what leaves have fallen,
what cores of eaten apples,
what scraps of paper!
An old trash barrel.
November, no one comes.

But I come, trying
to breathe that word
into the well's ear
which could make the leaves fly up
like a green jet
to clothe the naked tree,
the whole fruit leap to the bough,
the scraps like fleets of letters
sail up into my hands.

Leiden, 1961

NOVELLA

Two people in a room, speaking harshly.
One gets up, goes out to walk.
(That is the man.)
The other goes into the next room
and washes the dishes, cracking one.
(That is the woman.)
It gets dark outside.
The children quarrel in the attic.
She has no blood left in her heart.
The man comes back to a dark house.
The only light is in the attic.
He has forgotten his key.
He rings at his own door
and hears sobbing on the stairs.
The lights go on in the house.
The door closes behind him.
Outside, separate as minds,
the stars too come alight.

1962

FACE

I could look at you a long time,
man of red and blue;
your eye glows mockingly
from the rainbow-colored flesh
Karel Appel clothed you in.
You are a fish,
drawn up dripping hugely
from the sea of paint,
laid on the canvas

to glower and flash
out of the blackness
that is your true element

1962

PROSPECTIVE
IMMIGRANTS
PLEASE NOTE

Either you will
go through this door
or you will not go through.

If you go through
there is always the risk
of remembering your name.

Things look at you doubly
and you must look back
and let them happen.

If you do not go through
it is possible
to live worthily

to maintain your attitudes
to hold your position
to die bravely

but much will blind you,
much will evade you,
at what cost who knows?

The door itself
makes no promises.
It is only a door.

1962

LIKENESS

A good man
   is an odd thing:
    hard to find
as the song says,

he is anarchic
   as a mountain freshet
   and unprotected
by the protectors.

1962

THE LAG

With you it is still the middle of the night.
Nothing I know will make you know
what birds cried me awake
or how the wet light leaked
into my sky.
Day came as no clear victory,
it's raining still, but light
washes the menace from obscure forms

and in the shaving mirror there's
a face I recognize.
With you it is still the middle of the night.

You hug yourself, tightened as in a berth
suspended over the Grand Banks
where time is already American
and hanging fire.
I'm older now than you.
I feel your black dreams struggling at a porthole
stuffed full of night. I feel you choking
in that thick place. My words
reach you as through a telephone
where some submarine echo of my voice
blurts knowledge you can't use.

1962

ALWAYS THE SAME

Slowly, Prometheus
bleeds to life
in his huge loneliness.

You, for whom
his bowels are exposed,
go about your affairs

dying a little every day
from the inside out
almost imperceptibly

till the late decades when
women go hysterical
and men are dumbly frightened

and far away, like the sea
Prometheus sings on
"like a battle-song after a battle."

1962

PEACE

Lashes of white light
binding another hailcloud—
the whole onset all over
bursting against our faces,
sputtering like dead holly
fired in a grate:
And the birds go mad
potted by grapeshot
while the sun shines
in one quarter of heaven
and the rainbow
breaks out its enormous flag—
oily, unnegotiable—
over the sack-draped backs
of the cattle in their kingdom.

1961

THE ROOFWALKER

For Denise Levertov

Over the half-finished houses
night comes. The builders
stand on the roof. It is
quiet after the hammers,
the pulleys hang slack.
Giants, the roofwalkers,
on a listing deck, the wave
of darkness about to break
on their heads. The sky
is a torn sail where figures
pass magnified, shadows
on a burning deck.

I feel like them up there:
exposed, larger than life,
and due to break my neck.

Was it worth while to lay—
with infinite exertion—
a roof I can't live under?
—All those blueprints,
closings of gaps,
measurings, calculations?
A life I didn't choose
chose me: even
my tools are the wrong ones
for what I have to do.
I'm naked, ignorant,
a naked man fleeing
across the roofs
who could with a shade of difference
be sitting in the lamplight

against the cream wallpaper
reading—not with indifference—
about a naked man
fleeing across the roofs.

1961

POEMS
(1955–1957)

AT THE JEWISH NEW YEAR

For more than five thousand years
This calm September day
With yellow in the leaf
Has lain in the kernel of Time
While the world outside the walls
Has had its turbulent say
And history like a long
Snake has crawled on its way
And is crawling onward still.
And we have little to tell
On this or any feast
Except of the terrible past.
Five thousand years are cast
Down before the wondering child
Who must expiate them all.

Some of us have replied
In the bitterness of youth
Or the qualms of middle-age:
"If Time is unsatisfied,
And all our fathers have suffered
Can never be enough,
Why, then, we choose to forget.
Let our forgetting begin
With those age-old arguments
In which their minds were wound
Like musty phylacteries;
And we choose to forget as well
Those cherished histories
That made our old men fond,
And already are strange to us.

"Or let us, being today
Too rational to cry out,
Or trample underfoot
What after all preserves
A certain savor yet—
Though torn up by the roots—
Let us make our compromise
With the terror and the guilt
And view as curious relics
Once found in daily use
The mythology, the names
That, however Time has corrupted
Their ancient purity
Still burn like yellow flames,
But their fire is not for us."

And yet, however we choose
To deny or to remember,
Though on the calendars
We wake and suffer by,
This day is merely one
Of thirty in September—
In the kernel of the mind
The new year must renew
This day, as for our kind
Over five thousand years,
The task of being ourselves.
Whatever we strain to forget,
Our memory must be long.

May the taste of honey linger
Under the bitterest tongue.

1955

MOVING IN WINTER

Their life, collapsed like unplayed cards,
is carried piecemeal through the snow:
Headboard and footboard now, the bed
where she has lain desiring him
where overhead his sleep will build
its canopy to smother her once more;
their table, by four elbows worn
evening after evening while the wax runs down;
mirrors grey with reflecting them,
bureaus coffining from the cold
things that can shuffle in a drawer,
carpets rolled up around those echoes
which, shaken out, take wing and breed
new altercations, the old silences.

1957

NECESSITIES
OF LIFE
(1966)

I

Poems

1962–1965

Changeray-je pas pour vous cette belle
contexture des choses? C'est la condition
de vostre creation, c'est une partie de
vous que la mort: vous vous fuyez vous-mesmes.

—Montaigne

NECESSITIES OF LIFE

Piece by piece I seem
to re-enter the world: I first began

a small, fixed dot, still see
that old myself, a dark-blue thumbtack

pushed into the scene,
a hard little head protruding

from the pointillist's buzz and bloom.
After a time the dot

begins to ooze. Certain heats
melt it.
   Now I was hurriedly

blurring into ranges
of burnt red, burning green,

whole biographies swam up and
swallowed me like Jonah.

Jonah! I was Wittgenstein,
Mary Wollstonecraft, the soul

of Louis Jouvet, dead
in a blown-up photograph.

Till, wolfed almost to shreds,
I learned to make myself

unappetizing. Scaly as a dry bulb
thrown into a cellar

I used myself, let nothing use me.
Like being on a private dole,

sometimes more like kneading bricks in Egypt.
What life was there, was mine,

now and again to lay
one hand on a warm brick

and touch the sun's ghost
with economical joy,

now and again to name
over the bare necessities.

So much for those days. Soon
practice may make me middling-perfect, I'll

dare inhabit the world
trenchant in motion as an eel, solid

as a cabbage-head. I have invitations:
a curl of mist steams upward

from a field, visible as my breath,
houses along a road stand waiting

like old women knitting, breathless
to tell their tales.

1962

IN THE WOODS

"Difficult ordinary happiness,"
no one nowadays believes in you.
I shift, full-length on the blanket,
to fix the sun precisely

behind the pine-tree's crest
so light spreads through the needles
alive as water just
where a snake has surfaced,

unreal as water in green crystal.
Bad news is always arriving.
"We're hiders, hiding from something bad,"
sings the little boy.

Writing these words in the woods,
I feel like a traitor to my friends,
even to my enemies.
The common lot's to die

a stranger's death and lie
rouged in the coffin, in a dress
chosen by the funeral director.
Perhaps that's why we never

see clocks on public buildings any more.
A fact no architect will mention.
We're hiders, hiding from something bad
most of the time.

Yet, and outrageously, something good
finds us, found me this morning
lying on a dusty blanket
among the burnt-out Indian pipes

and bursting-open lady's-slippers.
My soul, my helicopter, whirred
distantly, by habit, over
the old pond with the half-drowned boat

toward which it always veers
for consolation: ego's Arcady:
leaving the body stuck
like a leaf against a screen.—

Happiness! how many times
I've stranded on that word,
at the edge of that pond; seen
as if through tears, the dragon-fly—

only to find it all
going differently for once
this time: my soul wheeled back
and burst into my body.

Found! ready or not.
If I move now, the sun
naked between the trees
will melt me as I lie.

1963

THE CORPSE-PLANT

How dare a sick man, or an obedient man, write poems?

—Whitman

A milk-glass bowl hanging by three chains
from the discolored ceiling
is beautiful tonight. On the floor, leaves, crayons,
innocent dust foregather.

Neither obedient nor sick, I turn my head,
feeling the weight of a thick gold ring
in either lobe. I see the corpse-plants
clustered in a hobnailed tumbler

at my elbow, white as death, I'd say,
if I'd ever seen death;
whiter than life
next to my summer-stained hand.

Is it in the sun that truth begins?
Lying under that battering light
the first few hours of summer
I felt scraped clean, washed down

to ignorance. The gold in my ears,
souvenir of a shrewd old city,
might have been wearing thin as wires
found in the bones of a woman's head

miraculously kept in its essentials
in some hot cradle-tomb of time.
I felt my body slipping through
the fingers of its mind.

Later, I slid on wet rocks,
threw my shoes across a brook,
waded on algae-furred stones
to join them. That day I found

the corpse-plants, growing like
shadows on a negative
in the chill of fern and lichen-rust.
That day for the first time

I gave them their deathly names—
or did they name themselves?—
not "Indian pipes" as once
we children knew them.

Tonight, I think of winter,
winters of mind, of flesh,
sickness of the rot-smell of leaves
turned silt-black, heavy as tarpaulin,

obedience of the elevator cage
lowering itself, crank by crank
into the mine-pit,
forced labor forcibly renewed—

but the horror is dimmed:
like the negative of one
intolerable photograph
it barely sorts itself out

under the radiance of the milk-glass shade.
Only death's insect whiteness
crooks its neck in a tumbler
where I placed its sign by choice.

1963

THE TREES

The trees inside are moving out into the forest,
the forest that was empty all these days
where no bird could sit
no insect hide
no sun bury its feet in shadow
the forest that was empty all these nights
will be full of trees by morning.

All night the roots work
to disengage themselves from the cracks
in the veranda floor.
The leaves strain toward the glass
small twigs stiff with exertion
long-cramped boughs shuffling under the roof
like newly discharged patients
half-dazed, moving
to the clinic doors.

I sit inside, doors open to the veranda
writing long letters
in which I scarcely mention the departure
of the forest from the house.
The night is fresh, the whole moon shines
in a sky still open
the smell of leaves and lichen
still reaches like a voice into the rooms.
My head is full of whispers
which tomorrow will be silent.

Listen. The glass is breaking.
The trees are stumbling forward
into the night. Winds rush to meet them.
The moon is broken like a mirror,
its pieces flash now in the crown
of the tallest oak.

1963

LIKE THIS TOGETHER
For A.H.C.

1.

Wind rocks the car.
We sit parked by the river,
silence between our teeth.
Birds scatter across islands
of broken ice. Another time
I'd have said "Canada geese,"
knowing you love them.
A year, ten years from now
I'll remember this—
this sitting like drugged birds
in a glass case—
not why, only that we
were here like this together.

2.

They're tearing down, tearing up
this city, block by block.
Rooms cut in half
hang like flayed carcasses,
their old roses in rags,
famous streets have forgotten
where they were going. Only
a fact could be so dreamlike.
They're tearing down the houses
we met and lived in,
soon our two bodies will be all
left standing from that era.

3.

We have, as they say,
certain things in common.
I mean: a view
from a bathroom window
over slate to stiff pigeons
huddled every morning; the way
water tastes from our tap,
which you marvel at, letting
it splash into the glass.
Because of you I notice
the taste of water,
a luxury I might
otherwise have missed.

4.

Our words misunderstand us.
Sometimes at night
you are my mother:
old detailed griefs
twitch at my dreams, and I
crawl against you, fighting
for shelter, making you
my cave. Sometimes
you're the wave of birth
that drowns me in my first
nightmare. I suck the air.
Miscarried knowledge twists us
like hot sheets thrown askew.

5.

Dead winter doesn't die,
it wears away, a piece of carrion
picked clean at last,
rained away or burnt dry.
Our desiring does this,
make no mistake, I'm speaking
of fact: through mere indifference
we could prevent it.
Only our fierce attention
gets hyacinths out of those
hard cerebral lumps,
unwraps the wet buds down
the whole length of a stem.

1963

BREAKFAST IN A
BOWLING ALLEY IN
UTICA, NEW YORK

Smudged eyeballs,
mouth stale as air,
I'm newly dead, a corpse

so fresh the grave unnerves me.
Nobody here but me
and Hermes behind the counter

defrosting sandwich steaks.
Paeans of *vox humana*
sob from the walls. THIS LAND

IS MY LAND. . . . It sounds
mummified. Has no sex,
no liquor license.

I chew meat and bread
thinking of wheatfields—
a gold-beige ceinture—

and cattle like ghosts
of the buffalo, running
across plains, nearing

the abbatoir. Houses
dream old-fashionedly
in backwoods townships

while the land glitters
with temporary life
stuck fast by choice:

trailers put out taproots
of sewage pipe, suckers
of TV aerial—

but in one of them,
perhaps, a man
alone with his girl

for the first time.

1963

OPEN-AIR MUSEUM

Ailanthus, goldenrod, scrapiron, what makes you flower?
What burns in the dump today?

Thick flames in a grey field, tended
by two men: one derelict ghost,
one clearly apter at nursing destruction,
two priests in a grey field, tending the flames
of stripped-off rockwool, split
mattresses, a caved-in chickenhouse,
mad Lou's last stack of paintings, each a perfect black lozenge

seen from a train, stopped
as by design, to bring us
face to face with the flag of our true country:
violet-yellow, black-violet,
its heart sucked by slow fire
O my America
this then was your desire?

but you cannot burn fast enough:
in the photograph the white
skirts of the Harlem bride
are lashed by blown scraps, tabloid sheets,
and her beauty a scrap of flickering light
licked by a greater darkness

This then was your desire!
those trucked-off bad dreams
outside the city limits
crawl back in search of you, eyes
missing, skins missing, intenser in decay
the carriage that wheeled the defective baby
rolls up on three wheels

and the baby is still inside,
you cannot burn fast enough
Blue sparks of the chicory flower
flash from embers of the dump
inside the rose-rust carcass of a slaughtered Chevrolet
crouches the young ailanthus

and the two guardians go raking the sacred field, raking
slowly, to what endless end
Cry of truth among so many lies
at your heart burns on
a languid fire

1964

TWO SONGS

1.

Sex, as they harshly call it,
I fell into this morning
at ten o'clock, a drizzling hour
of traffic and wet newspapers.
I thought of him who yesterday
clearly didn't
turn me to a hot field
ready for plowing,
and longing for that young man
piercéd me to the roots
bathing every vein, etc.
All day he appears to me
touchingly desirable,
a prize one could wreck one's peace for.
I'd call it love if love
didn't take so many years
but lust too is a jewel
a sweet flower and what
pure happiness to know
all our high-toned questions
breed in a lively animal.

2.

That "old last act"!
And yet sometimes
all seems post coitum triste
and I a mere bystander.
Somebody else is going off,
getting shot to the moon.

Or, a moon-race!
Split seconds after my opposite number
lands
I make it—
we lie fainting together
at a crater-edge
heavy as mercury in our moonsuits
till he speaks—
in a different language
yet one I've picked up
through cultural exchanges . . .
we murmur the first moonwords:
Spasibo. Thanks. O.K.

1964

THE PARTING

The ocean twanging away there
and the islands like scattered laundry—

You can feel so free, so free,
standing on the headland

where the wild rose never stands still,
the petals blown off

before they fall
and the chicory nodding

blue, blue, in the all-day wind.
Barbed wire, dead at your feet,

is a kind of dune-vine,
the only one without movement.

Every knot is a knife
where two strands tangle to rust.

1963

NIGHT-PIECES: FOR A CHILD

THE CRIB

You sleeping I bend to cover.
Your eyelids work. I see
your dream, cloudy as a negative,
swimming underneath.
You blurt a cry. Your eyes
spring open, still filmed in dream.
Wider, they fix me—
—death's head, sphinx, medusa?
You scream.
Tears lick my cheeks, my knees
droop at your fear.
Mother I no more am,
but woman, and nightmare.

HER WAKING

Tonight I jerk astart in a dark
hourless as Hiroshima,
almost hearing you breathe
in a cot three doors away.

You still breathe, yes—
and my dream with its gift of knives,
its murderous hider and seeker,
ebbs away, recoils

back into the egg of dreams,
the vanishing point of mind.
All gone.

But you and I—
swaddled in a dumb dark
old as sickheartedness,
modern as pure annihilation—

we drift in ignorance.
If I could hear you now
mutter some gentle animal sound!
If milk flowed from my breast again. . . .

1964

THE STRANGER

Fond credos, plaster ecstasies!
We arrange a prison-temple

for the weak-legged little god
who might stamp the world to bits

or pull the sky in like a muslin curtain.
We hang his shrine with bells,

aeolian harps, paper windmills,
line it with biscuits and swansdown.

His lack of culture we expected,
scarcely his disdain however—

that wild hauteur, as if
it were we who blundered.

Wildness we fret to avenge!
Eye that hasn't yet blinked

on the unblinking gold archways
of its trance—*that* we know

must be trained away:
that aloof, selective stare.

Otherness that affronts us
as cats and dogs do not—

once this was original sin
beaten away with staves of holy writ.

Old simplemindedness. But the primal fault
of the little god still baffles.

All other strangers are forgiven
Their strangeness, but he—

how save the eggshell world from his
reaching hands, how shield

ourselves from the disintegrating
blaze of his wide pure eye?

1964

AFTER DARK

I.

You are falling asleep and I sit looking at you
old tree of life
old man whose death I wanted
I can't stir you up now.

Faintly a phonograph needle
Whirs round in the last groove
eating my heart to dust.
That terrible record! how it played

down years, wherever I was
in foreign languages even
over and over, *I know you better*
than you know yourself   I know

you better than you know
yourself   I know
you   until, self-maimed,
I limped off, torn at the roots,

stopped singing a whole year,
got a new body, new breath,
got children, croaked for words,
forgot to listen

or read your *mene tekel* fading on the wall,
woke up one morning
and knew myself your daughter.
Blood is a sacred poison.

Now, unasked, you give ground.
We only want to stifle
what's stifling us already.
Alive now, root to crown, I'd give

—oh,—something—not to know
our struggles now are ended.
I seem to hold you, cupped
in my hands, and disappearing.

When your memory fails—
no more to scourge my inconsistencies—
the sashcords of the world fly loose.
A window crashes

suddenly down. I go to the woodbox
and take a stick of kindling
to prop the sash again.
I grow protective toward the world.

II.

Now let's away from prison—
Underground seizures!
I used to huddle in the grave
I'd dug for you and bite

my tongue for fear it would babble
—Darling—
I thought they'd find me there
someday, sitting upright, shrunken,

my hair like roots and in my lap
a mess of broken pottery—
wasted libation—
and you embalmed beside me.

No, let's away. Even now
there's a walk between doomed elms
(whose like we shall not see much longer)
and something—grass and water—

an old dream-photograph.
I'll sit with you there and tease you
for wisdom, if you like,
waiting till the blunt barge

bumps along the shore.
Poppies burn in the twilight
like smudge pots.
I think you hardly see me

but—this is the dream now—
your fears blow out,
off, over the water.
At the last, your hand feels steady.

1964

MOURNING PICTURE

The picture is by Edwin Romanzo Elmer, 1850–1923.

They have carried the mahogany chair and the cane rocker
out under the lilac bush,
and my father and mother darkly sit there, in black clothes.
Our clapboard house stands fast on its hill,
my doll lies in her wicker pram
gazing at western Massachusetts.
This was our world.
I could remake each shaft of grass
feeling its rasp on my fingers,
draw out the map of every lilac leaf
or the net of veins on my father's
grief-tranced hand.

Out of my head, half-bursting,
still filling, the dream condenses—
shadows, crystals, ceilings, meadows, globes of dew.
Under the dull green of the lilacs, out in the light
carving each spoke of the pram, the turned porch-pillars,
under high early-summer clouds,
I am Effie, visible and invisible,
remembering and remembered.

They will move from the house,
give the toys and the pets away.
Mute and rigid with loss my mother
will ride the train to Baptist Corner,
the silk-spool will run bare.
I tell you, the thread that bound us lies
faint as a web in the dew.
Should I make you, world, again,
could I give back the leaf its skeleton, the air
its early-summer cloud, the house
its noonday presence, shadowless,
and leave *this* out? I am Effie, you were my dream.

1965

"I AM IN DANGER—SIR—"

"Half-cracked" to Higginson, living,
afterward famous in garbled versions,
your hoard of dazzling scraps a battlefield,
now your old snood

mothballed at Harvard
and you in your variorum monument
equivocal to the end—
who are you?

Gardening the day-lily,
wiping the wine-glass stems,
your thought pulsed on behind
a forehead battered paper-thin,

you, woman, masculine
in single-mindedness,
for whom the word was more
than a symptom—

a condition of being.
Till the air buzzing with spoiled language
sang in your ears
of Perjury

and in your half-cracked way you chose
silence for entertainment,
chose to have it out at last
on your own premises.

1964

HALFWAY
In Memory: M.G.J.

In the field the air writhes, a heat-pocket.
Masses of birds revolve, blades
of a harvester.
The sky is getting milkily white,
a sac of light is ready to burst open.

Time of hailstones and rainbow.
My life flows North. At last I understand.
A young girl, thought sleeping, is certified dead.
A tray of expensive waxen fruit,
she lies arranged on the spare-room coverlid.

To sit by the fire is to become another woman,
red hair charring to grey,
green eyes grappling with the printed page,
voice flailing, flailing, the uncomprehending.
My days lie open, listening, grandmother.

1965

AUTUMN SEQUENCE

1.

An old shoe, an old pot, an old skin,
and dreams of the subtly tyrannical.
Thirst in the morning; waking into the blue

drought of another October
to read the familiar message nailed
to some burning bush or maple.

Breakfast under the pines, late yellow-
jackets fumbling for manna on the rim
of the stone crock of marmalade,

and shed pine-needles drifting
in the half-empty cup.
Generosity is drying out,

it's an act of will to remember
May's sticky-mouthed buds
on the provoked magnolias.

2.

Still, a sweetness hardly earned
by virtue or craft, belonging
by no desperate right to me

(as the marmalade to the wasp
who risked all in a last euphoria
of hunger)

washes the horizon. A quiet
after weeping, salt still on the tongue
is like this, when the autumn planet

looks me straight in the eye
and straight into the mind
plunges its impersonal spear:

Fill and flow over, think
till you weep, then sleep
to drink again.

3.

Your flag is dried-blood, turkey-comb
flayed stiff in the wind,
half-mast on the day of victory,

anarchist prince of evening marshes!
Your eye blurs in a wet smoke,
the stubble freezes under your heel,

the cornsilk *Mädchen* all hags now,
their gold teeth drawn,
the milkweeds gutted and rifled,

but not by you, foundering hero!
The future reconnoiters in dirty boots
along the cranberry-dark horizon.

Stars swim like grease-flecks
in that sky, night pulls a long knife.
Your empire drops to its knees in the dark.

4.

Skin of wet leaves on asphalt.
Charcoal slabs pitted with gold.
The reason for cities comes clear.

There must be a place, there has come a time—
where so many nerves are fusing—
for a purely moral loneliness.

Behind bloodsoaked lights of the avenues,
in the crystal grit of flying snow,
in this water-drop bulging at the taphead,

forced by dynamos three hundred miles
from the wild duck's landing and the otter's dive,
for three seconds of quivering identity.

There must be a place. But the eyeball stiffens
as night tightens and my hero passes out
with a film of stale gossip coating his tongue.

1964

NOON

Light pulses through underground chambers.
I have to tell myself: my eyes are not blue.
Two dark holes
Feed at the sky.

It swirls through them, raging
in azure spirals.
Nothing changes them:
two black tubes, draining off

a lake of iris.
Cleave open my skull:
The gouts of blue
Leap from the black grotto.

1965

NOT LIKE THAT

It's so pure in the cemetery.
The children love to play up here.
It's a little town, a game of blocks,
a village packed in a box,
a pre-war German toy.
The turf is a bedroom carpet:
heal-all, strawberry flower
and hillocks of moss.
To come and sit here forever,
a cup of tea on one's lap

and one's eyes closed lightly, lightly,
perfectly still
in a nineteenth-century sleep!
it seems so normal to die.

Nobody sleeps here, children.
The little beds of white wrought iron
and the tall, kind, faceless nurse
are somewhere else, in a hospital
or the dreams of prisoners of war.
The drawers of this trunk are empty,
not even a snapshot
curls in a corner.

In Pullmans of childhood we lay
enthralled behind dark-green curtains,
and a little lamp burned blue
all night, for us. The day
was a dream too, even the oatmeal
under its silver lid, dream-cereal
spooned out in forests of spruce
skirting the green-black gorges,
thick woods of sleep, half prickle,
half lakes of fern.
To stay here forever
is not like that, nor even
simply to lie quite still,
the warm trickle of dream
staining the thick quiet.
The drawers of this trunk are empty.
They are all out of sleep up here.

1965

THE KNOT

In the heart of the queen anne's lace, a knot of blood.
For years I never saw it,

years of metallic vision,
spears glancing off a bright eyeball,

suns off a Swiss lake.
A foaming meadow; the Milky Way;

and there, all along, the tiny dark-red spider
sitting in the whiteness of the bridal web,

waiting to plunge his crimson knifepoint
into the white apparencies.

Little wonder the eye, healing, sees
for a long time through a mist of blood.

1965

ANY HUSBAND TO ANY WIFE

"Might I die last and show thee!"

I know: you are glycerine,
old quills, rose velvet,
tearstains in *Middlemarch*,
a style of getting into cabs, of eating fruit,
a drawer of stones, chains, seeds, shells, little mirrors:
Darling, you will outlive yourself, and me.

Sometimes the sea backs up against a lashed pier,
grinding and twisting,
a turmoil of wrecked stuff
alive and dead. And the pier stands groaning
as if the land depended on it.
We say it is the moon that draws these tides,
then glazes in aftercalm
the black, blurred face to something we can love.

1965

SIDE BY SIDE

Ho! in the dawn
how light we lie

stirring faintly as laundry
left all night on the lines.

You, a lemon-gold pyjama,
I, a trousseau-sheet, fine

linen worn paper-thin in places,
worked with the maiden monogram.

Lassitude drapes our folds.
We're slowly bleaching

with the days, the hours, and the years.
We are getting finer than ever,

time is wearing us to silk,
to sheer spiderweb.

The eye of the sun, rising, looks in
to ascertain how we are coming on.

1965

SPRING THUNDER

1.

Thunder is all it is, and yet
my street becomes a crack in the western hemisphere,
my house a fragile nest of grasses.

The radiotelescope flings its nets
at random; a child is crying,
not from hunger, not from pain,
more likely impotence. The generals are sweltering

in the room with a thousand eyes.
Red-hot lights flash off and on
inside air-conditioned skulls.

Underfoot, a land-mass
puffed-up with bad faith and fatigue
goes lumbering onward,

old raft in the swollen waters,
unreformed Huck and Jim
watching the tangled yellow shores
rush by.

2.

Whatever you are that weeps
over the blistered riverbeds
and the cracked skin of cities,
you are not on our side,

eye never seeking our eyes,
shedding its griefs like stars
over our hectic indifference,
whispered monologue

subverting space with its tears,
mourning the mournable,
nailing the pale-grey woolly flower
back to its ledge.

3.

The power of the dinosaur
is ours, to die
inflicting death,
trampling the nested grasses:

power of dead grass
to catch fire
power of ash
to whirl off the burnt heap
in the wind's own time.

4.

A soldier is here, an ancient figure,
generalized as a basalt mask.

Breathes like a rabbit, an Eskimo,
strips to an older and simpler thing.

No criminal, no hero; merely a shadow
cast by the conflagration

that here burns down or there leaps higher
but always in the shape of fire,

always the method of fire, casting
automatically, these shadows.

5.

Over him, over you, a great roof is rising,
a great wall: no temporary shelter.
Did you tell yourself these beams would melt,

these fiery blocs dissolve?
Did you choose to build this thing?
Have you stepped back to see what it is?

It is immense; it has porches, catacombs.
It is provisioned like the Pyramids, for eternity.
Its buttresses beat back the air with iron tendons.

It is the first flying cathedral,
eating its parishes by the light of the moon.
It is the refinery of pure abstraction,

a total logic, rising
obscurely between one man
and the old, affective clouds.

1965

MOTH HOUR

Space mildews at our touch.
The leaves of the poplar, slowly moving—
aren't they moth-white, there in the moonbeams?
A million insects die every twilight,
no one even finds their corpses.
Death, slowly moving among the bleached clouds,
knows us better than we know ourselves.

I am gliding backward away from those who knew me
as the moon grows thinner and finally shuts its lantern.
I can be replaced a thousand times,
a box containing death.
When you put out your hand to touch me
you are already reaching toward an empty space.

1965

FOCUS

For Bert Dreyfus

Obscurity has its tale to tell.
Like the figure on the studio-bed in the corner,

out of range, smoking, watching and waiting.
Sun pours through the skylight onto the worktable

making of a jar of pencils, a typewriter keyboard
more than they were. Veridical light . . .

Earth budges. Now an empty coffee-cup,
a whetstone, a handkerchief, take on

their sacramental clarity, fixed by the wand
of light as the thinker thinks to fix them in the mind.

O secret in the core of the whetstone, in the five
pencils splayed out like fingers of a hand!

The mind's passion is all for singling out.
Obscurity has another tale to tell.

1965

FACE TO FACE

Never to be lonely like that—
the Early American figure on the beach
in black coat and knee-breeches
scanning the didactic storm in privacy,

never to hear the prairie wolves
in their lunar hilarity
circling one's little all, one's claim
to be Law and Prophets

for all that lawlessness,
never to whet the appetite
weeks early, for a face, a hand
longed-for and dreaded—

How people used to meet!
starved, intense, the old
Christmas gifts saved up till spring,
and the old plain words,

and each with his God-given secret,
spelled out through months of snow and silence,
burning under the bleached scalp; behind dry lips
a loaded gun.

1965

II

*Translations from
the Dutch*

MARTINUS NIJHOFF

THE SONG OF THE FOOLISH BEES

A smell of further honey
embittered nearer flowers,
a smell of further honey
sirened us from our meadow.

That smell and a soft humming
crystallized in the azure,
that smell and a soft humming,
a wordless repetition,

called upon us, the reckless,
to leave our usual gardens,
called upon us, the reckless,
to seek mysterious roses.

Far from our folk and kindred
joyous we went careering,
far from our folk and kindred
exhuberantly driven.

No one can by nature
break off the course of passion,
no one can by nature
endure death in his body.

Always more fiercely yielding,
more lucently transfigured,
always more fiercely yielding
to that elusive token,

we rose and staggered upward,
kidnapped, disembodied,
we rose and vanished upward,
dissolving into glitter.

It's snowing; we are dying,
homeward, downward whirled.
It's snowing; we are dying;
it snows among the hives.

HENDRIK DE VRIES

MY BROTHER

My brother, nobody knows
the end you suffered.
Often you lie beside me, dim, and I
grow confused, grope, and startle.

You walked along that path through the elms.
Birds cried late. Something wrong
was following us both. But you
wanted to go alone through the waste.

Last night we slept again together.
Your heart jerked next to me. I spoke your name
and asked where you were going.
Your answer came:
"The horror! . . . there's no telling . . .
See: the grass
lies dense again, the elms
press round."

HENDRIK DE VRIES

FEVER

Listen! It's never sung like that! Listen!
The wallpaper stirred,
and the hairs of the heavy-fringed eye.
What flew
Through the rooms?

Tomorrow it will be
as if all night the whips hadn't lashed so.—

See, through the blinds,
The spirits in their cold ships!

Boughs graze the frame
of the window. Far off, a whistle
sounds, always clearly, along the fields.
The beasts on the walls
fade away. The light goes out.

GERRIT ACHTERBERG

EBEN HAËZER

(Hebrew for "Stone of Help"; a common old name
for farmhouses in Holland.)

Sabbath evening privacy at home.
Mist-footsteps, prowling past the shed.
At that hour, not another soul abroad;
the blue farmhouse a closed hermitage.

There we lived together, man and mouse.
Through cowstall windows an eternal fire
fell ridged from gold lamps on the threshing-floor,
stillness of linseed cakes and hay in house.

There my father celebrated mass:
serving the cows, priestlike at their heads.
Their tongues curled along his hands like fish.

A shadow, diagonal to the rafters.
Worship hung heavy from the loftbeams.
His arteries begin to calcify.

GERRIT ACHTERBERG

ACCOUNTABILITY

Old oblivion-book, that I lay open.
White eye-corner rounding the page.

Gold lace slips out under the evening,
Green animals creep backwards.

Lifelessness of the experimental station.
Added-up, subtracted sum.

Black night. Over the starlight skims
God's index finger, turning the page.

Death comes walking on all fours
past the room, a crystal egg,

with the lamp, the books, the bread,
where you are living and life-size.

GERRIT ACHTERBERG

STATUE

A body, blind with sleep,
stands up in my arms.
Its heaviness weighs on me.
Death-doll.
I'm an eternity too late.
And where's your heartbeat?

The thick night glues us together,
makes us compact with each other.
"For God's sake go on holding me—
my knees are broken,"
you mumble against my heart.

It's as if I held up the earth.
And slowly, moss is creeping
all over our two figures.

LEO VROMAN

OUR FAMILY

My father, who since his death
no longer speaks audibly
lies sometimes, a great walrus
from nightfall to daybreak
his muzzle in my lap
in the street from his chin down.

The light of morning feeds
through his hide, thinned to parchment,
and his slackened features dwindle
to a line creeping off among the chairs;
if I rise to peer at him
he winces away to a dot

In the daytime there's nothing to see
but an emphatically vanished
absence where moments ago
the sun too was just shining.

Where my father has stood
it now just quivers,
rippling by handfuls through
my little daughter's light hair
while on the sunny grass
she slowly scampers forward.

Her little snoot is so open
you could easily spread it out
with a teaspoon or your finger
on a slice of fresh white bread
or, if need be,
you could mold it into a pudding.

Her little voice itches like a fleece;
it wriggles gaily into my ear
and can't get out when it laughs;
with plopping fishfins
it folds itself struggling up
into my head. Where it spends the night.

And here, this taller child
is Tineke, my wife.
She hums a nursery rhyme

to the hair on her third breast,
which whimpers, being a baby,
and a thirsty baby at that.

I have such a gentle family,
it kisses, goes on eight legs,
but it has no moustache:
my father has vanished,

and they too are all going to die:
too soft, if they turn into air,
to swing a weathercock;
if turned into water, too slight
to fill a gutter; if into light
to make one live cock crow.

CHR. J. VAN GEEL

HOMECOMING

The sea, a body of mysterious calls
is almost motionless.
I know a beach, a tree stands there
in which women are singing,
voluptuous, languid.

In harbors ships are steaming
full of honey from the sea. Drizzle hangs
like eyelashes over the landscape.

Behind the seadike, breathing invisibly
in the mist, sleep the cows.
The hobble of a horse drags along the fence,
holding still where I stand with sweet words.

Listen, the sea calls,
claps her hands.
The ships running out in the wet
come like children—one drags
a sled into the garden.

CHR. J. VAN GEEL

SLEEPWALKING

(next to death.)

Sleep, horns of a snail

Out of the black and white bed, floors of red glaze,
mornings in the careful garden
on paths suitable rubbish slowly buried
and without urgency overgrown with grass
with ivy and sometimes a flower
just as we dream
to see unseen, to listen unattended.

The twigs of the moon
in indifferent white,
horns upright, wood with-
out leaf and seeking bees
sadness down to the ground.

Like silence always and from afar
lisps the water
never, by no one possessed.

Dead trees in green leaf.
What to do but among bushes,
what to see but underbrush.

On this sun time sharpens itself
to brilliance.

A stone of untouchable fire
on which time breaks its tooth.

Time caught no hour: loafing next to
a blaze.

                In the darkened town the old groped
                        with their sticks.
                The rays of the sun are tired,
                the beetles rot in the wood,
                only the sea. . . .
                In the earth of the dead
                earth covers leaf, leaf covers leaf.

Heartbeat of the wild creeper,
hammer between wing-lashes,
butterflies hammer at the sun.

                Now you must get to the institution
                with a mask on, your little feet
                tarred, an iron crown on your head.

                You awake there a python,
                a boa constrictor,
                after seven-and-twenty years,
                after six-and-twenty years,
                fair sleep, fair sleepers.

                You strike the prince twice
                a youth wasted with waiting
                for your serpent eyes and
                you unfold your scaly tail.

Now you must get to the institution
with a mask on, your little feet
tarred, an iron crown on your head.

Night blows away from the sun,
sky in fresh wind,
the sea kicks off its surf.

The moon scorches, a cloud of steam.
Driving water torn to shreds,
sunny twilight, fruitless field.

Tamed sea, muscular
to the temples, stoop where no coast
is, under the familiar blows,
stand where you cannot stand,
night is embraced on the sun.

A scared hind in a wood of one tree.

Whether the dead live, how they rest or
decay, leaves me cold, for cold for good and all
is death.

Poor is the frontier of life, to die blossoms
away over the graves.

Every existence competes in every
lost chance of life for death.

Of always fewer chances, one moved
and drove over her, naked standing by her child
death.

Residing in a thunderstorm,
sky hoists sun, night cuts light.
The wind's wings are at home.

Whistle now out of the nights
sparks of burnt paper.
Whisper fire in the days
dried by the sun, your desires
are lightened, curled to ash.

Flowers for hunger,

the darkest, the blue,
of ash, of grey granite,
black ice,
room without window,
abacus without beads,
room without a person,
the eaten past
gnaws,
the teeth out of the comb,
the funeral wreath emptily devoured,
a stone.

Whatever I may contrive—
and I contrive it—death's
private roads are the coldest night.

That I shall not be with her—
not with her—
that nothing shall glimmer
except danger.

Trees of ash, trees of ice,
the light frozen.
Summer and winter are
constructed of one emptiness.
The boughs of the wind are dead.

Must I dejected and contemplating death
now that above the sea a cloudless night
empties the sky, let treason and false laughter
prudently ring out until the morning?

the threshold of the horizon shifts—
and think with the thinkers of this earth:
"Life is thus"—then am I crazed
because my heart encloses what it held?

Morning has broken and the sea
is wide, I go back home to sleep.
Path, dune, trees and sheep
are rosy from the east, a rosy gull
flies up under the rash sky.
What's silent speaks aloud buried in sleep.

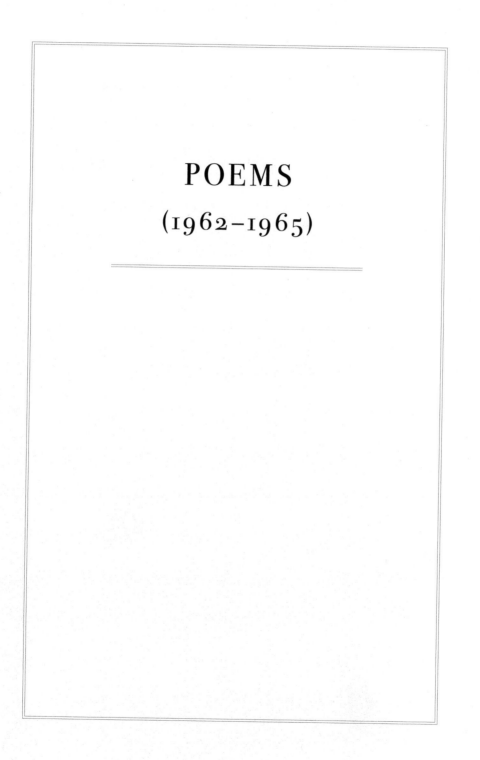

POEMS
(1962–1965)

TO JUDITH, TAKING LEAVE

For J.H.

Dull-headed, with dull fingers
I patch once more
the pale brown envelope
still showing under ink scratches
the letterhead of *Mind*.
A chorus of old postmarks
echoes across its face.
It looks so frail
to send so far
and I should tear it across
mindlessly
and find another.
But I'm tired, can't endure
a single new motion
or room or object,
so I cling to this too
as if your tallness moving
against the rainlight
in an Amsterdam flat
might be held awhile
by a handwritten label
or a battered envelope
from your desk.

Once somewhere else
I shan't talk of you
as a singular event
or a beautiful thing I saw
though both are true.
I shan't falsify you
through praising and describing
as I shall other
things I have loved

almost as much.
There in Amsterdam
you'll be living as I
have seen you live
and as I've never seen you.
And I can trust
no plane to bring you
my life out there
in turbid America—
my own life, lived against
facts I keep there.

It wasn't literacy—
the right to read *Mind*—
or suffrage—to vote
for the lesser of two
evils—that were
the great gains, I see now,
when I think of all those women
who suffered ridicule
for us.
But this little piece of ground,
Judith! that two women
in love to the nerves' limit
with two men—
shared out in pieces
to men, children, memories
so different and so draining—
should think it possible
now for the first time
perhaps, to love each other
neither as fellow-victims
nor as a temporary
shadow of something better.
Still shared-out as we are,

lovers, poets, warmers
of men and children
against our flesh, not knowing
from day to day
what we'll fling out on the water
or what pick up
there at the tide's lip,
often tired, as I'm tired now
from sheer distances of soul
we have in one day to cover—
still to get here
to this little spur or headland
and feel now free enough
to leave our weapons somewhere
else—such are the secret
outcomes of revolution!
that two women can meet
no longer as cramped sharers
of a bitter mutual secret
but as two eyes in one brow
receiving at one moment
the rainbow of the world.

1962

ROOTS

For M.L.

Evenings seem endless, now
dark tugs at our sky
harder and earlier
and milkweeds swell to bursting . . .
now in my transatlantic eye

you stand on your terrace
a scarf on your head and in your hands
dead stalks of golden-glow

and now it's for you,
not myself, I shiver
hearing glass doors rattle
at your back, the rustling cough
of a dry clematis vine
your love and toil trained up the walls
of a rented house.

All those roots, Margo!
Didn't you start each slip between your breasts,
each dry seed, carrying some
across frontiers, knotted
into your handkerchief,
haven't you seen your tears
glisten in narrow trenches
where rooted cuttings grope for life?

You, frailer than you look,
long back, long stride, blond hair
coiled up over straight shoulders—
I hear in your ear the wind
lashing in wet from the North Sea
slamming the dahlias flat.

All your work violated
every autumn, every turn of the wrist
guiding the trowel: mocked.
Sleet on brown fibers,
black wilt eating your harvest,
a clean sweep, and you the loser . . .

or is this after all
the liberation your hands fend off
and your eyes implore
when you dream of sudden death
or of beginning anew,
a girl of seventeen, the war just over,
and all the gardens
to dig again?

1963

THE PARTING: II

White morning flows into the mirror.
Her eye, still old with sleep,
meets itself like a sister.

How they slept last night,
the dream that caged them back to back,
was nothing new.

Last words, tears, most often
come wrapped as the everyday
familiar failure.

Now, pulling the comb slowly
through her loosened hair
she tries to find the parting;

it must come out after all:
hidden in all that tangle
there is a way.

1963

WINTER

Dead, dead, dead, dead.
A beast of the Middle Ages
stupefied in its den.
The hairs on its body—a woman's—
cold as hairs on a bulb or tuber.

Nothing so bleakly leaden, you tell me,
as the hyacinth's dull cone
before it bulks into blueness.
Ah, but I'd chosen to be
a woman, not a beast or a tuber!

No one knows where the storks went,
everyone knows they have disappeared.
Something—that woman—seems to have
migrated also; if she lives, she lives
sea-zones away, and the meaning grows colder.

1965

LEAFLETS

(1969)

For Rose Marie and Hayden Carruth

I

Night Watch

ORION

Far back when I went zig-zagging
through tamarack pastures
you were my genius, you
my cast-iron Viking, my helmed
lion-heart king in prison.
Years later now you're young

my fierce half-brother, staring
down from that simplified west
your breast open, your belt dragged down
by an oldfashioned thing, a sword
the last bravado you won't give over
though it weighs you down as you stride

and the stars in it are dim
and maybe have stopped burning.
But you burn, and I know it;
as I throw back my head to take you in
an old transfusion happens again:
divine astronomy is nothing to it.

Indoors I bruise and blunder,
break faith, leave ill enough
alone, a dead child born in the dark.
Night cracks up over the chimney,
pieces of time, frozen geodes
come showering down in the grate.

A man reaches behind my eyes
and finds them empty
a woman's head turns away
from my head in the mirror
children are dying my death
and eating crumbs of my life.

Pity is not your forte.
Calmly you ache up there
pinned aloft in your crow's nest,
my speechless pirate!
You take it all for granted
and when I look you back

it's with a starlike eye
shooting its cold and egotistical spear
where it can do least damage.
Breathe deep! No hurt, no pardon
out here in the cold with you
you with your back to the wall.

1965

HOLDING OUT

The hunters' shack will do,
abandoned, untended, unmended
in its cul-de-sac of alders.
Inside, who knows what
hovel-keeping essentials—
a grey saucepan, a broom, a clock
stopped at last autumn's last hour—
all or any, what matter.

The point is, it's a shelter,
a place more in- than outside.
From that we could begin.
And the wind is surely rising,
snow is in the alders.
Maybe the stovepipe is sound,
maybe the smoke will do us in
at first—no matter.

Late afternoons the ice
squeaks underfoot like mica,
and when the sun drops red and moon-
faced back of the gun-colored firs,
the best intentions are none too good.
Then we have to make a go of it
in the smoke with the dark outside
and our love in our boots at first—
no matter.

1965

FLESH AND BLOOD

For C.

A cracked walk in the garden,
white violets choking in the ivy,
then O then . . .
Everyone else I've had to tell how it was,
only not you.

Nerve-white, the cloud came walking
over the crests of tallest trees.
Doors slammed. We

fell asleep, hot Sundays, in our slips,
two mad little goldfish

fluttering in a drying pond.
Nobody's seen the trouble I've seen
but you.
Our jokes are funnier for that
you'd say
and, Lord, it's true.

1965

IN THE EVENING

Three hours chain-smoking words
and you move on. We stand in the porch,
two archaic figures: a woman and a man.

The old masters, the old sources,
haven't a clue what we're about,
shivering here in the half-dark 'sixties.

Our minds hover in a famous impasse
and cling together. Your hand
grips mine like a railing on an icy night.

The wall of the house is bleeding. Firethorn!
The moon, cracked every which-way,
pushes steadily on.

1966

MISSING THE POINT

There it was, all along,
twisted up in that green vine-thread,
in the skeins of marble,
on the table behind them—those two!
white-faced and undeterred—
everything doubled: forks,
brown glass tumblers, echoing plates,
two crumbled portions of bread.

That was the point that was missed
when they left the room with its wavy light
and pale curtains blowing
and guessed the banquet was over, the picnic
under the leaves was over,
when haggling faces pushed in for a look
and the gingerbread village shrieked outside:
Who's in the wrong? Who's in the wrong?

1966

CITY

From the Dutch of Gerrit Achterberg.

Maybe you spoke to someone
and on that hour your face
printed itself for good.
Where is that man? I need
to find him before he dies
and see you drift across his retina.

You have played with children.
They will run up to me
whenever you
come home free in their dreams.

Houses, realized by you,
slumber in that web.

Streets suppose you
in other streets, and call:
Evening papers . . .
Strawberries . . .

The city has changed hands;
the plan you gave it, fallen through.

1962

DWINGELO

From the Dutch of Gerrit Achterberg.

In the never, still arriving, I find you
again: blue absence keeps knowledge alive,
makes of October an adjusted lens.
The days have almost no clouds left.

Cassiopeia, the Great Bear
let their signals burst by night
to rip into impossibility.
The Pleiades rage silently about.

To wait is the password; and to listen.
In Dwingelo you can hear it whisper,
the void in the radiotelescope.

There too the singing of your nerves is gathered,
becoming graphic on a sheet of paper
not unlike this one here.

1962

THE DEMON LOVER

Fatigue, regrets. The lights
go out in the parking lot
two by two. Snow blindness
settles over the suburb.
Desire. Desire. The nebula
opens in space, unseen,
your heart utters its great beats
in solitude. A new
era is coming in.
Gauche as we are, it seems
we have to play our part.

A plaid dress, silk scarf,
and eyes that go on stinging.
Woman, stand off. The air
glistens like silk.
She's gone. In her place stands
a schoolgirl, morning light,
the half-grown bones
of innocence. Is she

your daughter or your muse,
this tree of blondness
grown up in a field of thorns?

Something piercing and marred.
Take note. Look back. When quick
the whole northeast went black
and prisoners howled and children
ran through the night with candles,
who stood off motionless
side by side while the moon swam up
over the drowned houses?
Who neither touched nor spoke?
whose nape, whose finger-ends
nervelessly lied the hours away?

A voice presses at me.
If I give in it won't
be like the girl the bull rode,
all Rubens flesh and happy moans.
But to be wrestled like a boy
with tongue, hips, knees, nerves, brain . . .
with language?
He doesn't know. He's watching
breasts under a striped blouse,
his bull's head down.
The old wine pours again through my veins.

Goodnight, then. 'Night. Again
we turn our backs and weary
weary we let down.
Things take us hard, no question.
How do you make it, all the way
from here to morning? I touch
you, made of such nerve
and flare and pride and swallowed tears.

Go home. Come to bed. The skies
look in at us, stern.
And this is an old story.

I dreamed about the war.
We were all sitting at table
in a kitchen in Chicago.
The radio had just screamed
that Illinois was the target.
No one felt like leaving,
we sat by the open window
and talked in the sunset.
I'll tell you that joke tomorrow,
you said with your saddest smile,
if I can remember.

The end is just a straw,
a feather furling slowly down,
floating to light by chance, a breath
on the long-loaded scales.
Posterity trembles like a leaf
and we go on making heirs and heirlooms.
The world, we have to make it,
my coexistent friend said, leaning
back in his cell.
Siberia vastly hulks
behind him, which he did not make.

Oh futile tenderness
of touch in a world like this!
how much longer, dear child,
do you think sex will matter?
There might have been a wedding
that never was:
two creatures sprung free
from castiron covenants.

Instead our hands and minds
erotically waver . . .
Lightness is unavailing.

Catalpas wave and spill
their dull strings across this murk of spring.
I ache, brilliantly.
Only where there is language is there world.
In the harp of my hair, compose me
a song. Death's in the air,
we all know that. Still, for an hour,
I'd like to be gay. How could a gay song go?
Why that's your secret, and it shall be mine.
We are our words, and black and bruised and blue.
Under our skins, we're laughing.

In triste veritas?
Take hold, sweet hands, come on . . .
Broken!
When you falter, all eludes.
This is a seasick way,
this almost/never touching, this
drawing-off, this to-and-fro.
Subtlety stalks in your eyes,
your tongue knows what it knows.
I want your secrets—I *will* have them out.
Seasick, I drop into the sea.

1966

JERUSALEM

In my dream, children
are stoning other children
with blackened carob-pods
I dream my son is riding
on an old grey mare
to a half-dead war
on a dead-grey road
through the cactus and thistles
and dried brook-beds.

In my dream, children
are swaddled in smoke
and their uncut hair smolders
even here, here
where trees have no shade
and rocks have no shadow
trees have no memories
only the stones and
the hairs of the head.

I dream his hair is growing
and has never been shorn
from slender temples hanging
like curls of barbed wire
and his first beard is growing
smoldering like fire
his beard is smoke and fire
and I dream him riding
patiently to the war.

What I dream of the city
is how hard it is to leave
and how useless to walk
outside the blasted walls

picking up the shells
from a half-dead war
and I wake up in tears
and hear the sirens screaming
and the carob-tree is bare.

Balfour Street, July 1966

CHARLESTON IN THE 1860's

Derived from the diaries of Mary Boykin Chesnut.

He seized me by the waist and kissed my throat . . .
Your eyes, dear, are they grey or blue,
eyes of an angel?
The carts have passed already with their heaped
night-soil, we breathe again . . .
Is this what war is? Nitrate . . .
But smell the pear,
the jasmine, the violets.
Why does this landscape always sadden you?
Now the freshet is up on every side,
the river comes to our doors,
limbs of primeval trees dip in the swamp.

So we fool on into the black
cloud ahead of us.
Everything human glitters fever-bright—
the thrill of waking up
out of a stagnant life?
There seems a spell upon
your lovers, —all dead of wounds
or blown to pieces . . . Nitrate!
I'm writing, blind with tears of rage.

In vain. Years, death, depopulation, fears,
bondage—these shall all be borne.
No imagination to forestall woe.

1966

NIGHT WATCH

And now, outside, the walls
of black flint, eyeless.
How pale in sleep you lie.
Love: my love is just a breath
blown on the pane and dissolved.
Everything, even you,
cries silently for help, the web
of the spider is ripped with rain,
the geese fly on into the black cloud.
What can I do for you?
what can I do for you?
Can the touch of a finger mend
what a finger's touch has broken?
Blue-eyed now, yellow-haired,
I stand in my old nightmare
beside the track, while you,
and over and over and always you
plod into the deathcars.
Sometimes you smile at me
and I—I smile back at you.
How sweet the odor of the station-master's roses!
How pure, how poster-like the colors of this dream.

1967

THERE ARE SUCH SPRINGLIKE NIGHTS

From the Yiddish of Kadia Molodowsky.

There are such springlike nights here,
when a blade of grass pushes up through the soil
and the fresh dawn is a green pillow
under the skeleton of a dead horse.
And all the limbs of a woman plead for the ache of birth.
And women come to lie down like sick sheep
by the wells—to heal their bodies,
their faces blackened with yearlong thirst for a child's cry.

There are such springlike nights here
when lightning pierces the black soil with silver knives
and pregnant women approach the white tables of the hospital
with quiet steps
and smile at the unborn child
and perhaps at death.

There are such springlike nights here
when a blade of grass pushes up through the soil.

1968

FOR A RUSSIAN POET

1. *The Winter Dream*

Everywhere, snow is falling. Your bandaged foot
drags across huge cobblestones, bells
hammer in distant squares.
Everything we stood against has conquered
and now we're part
of it all. *Life's the main thing,* I hear you say,
but a fog is spreading between this landmass
and the one your voice
mapped so long for me. All that's visible
is walls, endlessly yellow-grey, where
so many risks were taken, the shredded skies
slowly littering both our continents with
the only justice left, burying
footprints, bells and voices with all deliberate speed.

1967

2. *Summer in the Country*

Now, again, every year for years: the life-and-death talk,
late August, forebodings
under the birches, along the water's edge
and between the typed lines

and evenings, tracing a pattern of absurd hopes
in broken nutshells
                    but this year we both
sit after dark with the radio
unable to read, unable to write

trying the blurred edges of broadcasts
for a little truth, taking a walk before bed
wondering what a man can do, asking that
at the verge of tears in a lightning-flash of loneliness.

3. *The Demonstration*

Natalya Gorbanevskaya
13/3 Novopeschanaya Street
Apartment 34

At noon we sit down quietly on the parapet
and unfurl our banners
                              almost immediately
the sound of police whistles
from all corners of Red Square
                              we sit
quietly and offer no resistance
Is this your little boy

we will relive this over and over

the banners torn from our hands
                              blood flowing
a great jagged torn place
in the silence of complicity

that much at least
we did here

In your flat, drinking tea
waiting for the police
your children asleep while you write
quickly, the letters you want to get off
before tomorrow

I'm a ghost at your table
touching poems in a script I can't read

we'll meet each other later

August 1968

NIGHT IN THE KITCHEN

The refrigerator falls silent.
Then other things are audible:
this dull, sheet-metal mind rattling like stage thunder.
The thickness budging forward in these veins
is surely something other
than blood:
say, molten lava.

You will become a black lace cliff fronting a deadpan sea;
nerves, friable as lightning
ending in burnt pine forests.
You are begun, beginning, your black heart drumming
slowly, triumphantly
inside its pacific cave.

1967

5:30 A.M.

Birds and periodic blood.
Old recapitulations.
The fox, panting, fire-eyed,
gone to earth in my chest.
How beautiful we are,
he and I, with our auburn
pelts, our trails of blood,
our miracle escapes,
our whiplash panic flogging us on
to new miracles!
They've supplied us with pills
for bleeding, pills for panic.
Wash them down the sink.
This is truth, then:
dull needle groping in the spinal fluid,
weak acid in the bottom of the cup,
foreboding, foreboding.
No one tells the truth about truth,
that it's what the fox
sees from his scuffled burrow:
dull-jawed, onrushing
killer, being that
inanely single-minded
will have our skins at last.

1967

THE BREAK

All month eating the heart out,
smothering in a fierce insomnia . . .
First the long, spongy summer, drying
out by fits and starts, till a morning
torn off another calendar
when the wind stiffens, chairs
and tables rouse themselves
in a new, unplanned light
and a word flies like a dry leaf down the hall
at the bang of a door.

Then break, October, speak,
non-existent and damning clarity.
Stare me down, thrust
your tongue against mine, break
day, let me stand up
like a table or a chair
in a cold room with the sun beating in
full on the dusty panes.

1967

TWO POEMS

Adapted from Anna Akhmatova.

1.

There's a secret boundary hidden in the waving grasses:
neither the lover nor the expert sensualist
passes it, though mouths press silently together
and the heart is bursting.

And friends—they too are helpless there,
and so with years of fire and joy,
whole histories of freedom
unburdened by sensual languor.

The crazy ones push on to that frontier
while those who have found it are sick with grief . . .
And now you know
why my heart doesn't beat beneath your hand.

2.

On the terrace, violins played
the most heartbreaking songs.
A sharp, fresh smell of the sea
came from oysters on a dish of ice

He said, *I'm a faithful friend,*
touching my dress.
How far from a caress,
the touch of that hand!

The way you stroke a cat, a bird,
the look you give a shapely bareback rider.
In his calm eyes, only laughter
under the light-gold lashes.

And the violins mourn on
behind drifting smoke:
Thank your stars, you're at last alone
with the man you love.

1966

THE KEY

Through a drain grating, something
    glitters and falters,
        glitters again. A scrap of foil,

a coin, a signal, a message
    from the indistinct
        piercing my indistinctness?

How long I have gone round
    and round, spiritless with foreknown defeat,
        in search of that glitter?

Hours, years maybe. The cry of metal
    on asphalt, on iron, the sudden
        ching of a precious loss,

the clear statement
    of something missing. Over and over
        it stops me in my tracks

like a falling star, only
     this is not the universe's loss
          it is mine. If I were only colder,

nearer death, nearer birth, I might let go
     whatever's so bent on staying lost.
         Why not leave the house

locked, to collapse inward among its weeds,
     the letters to darken and flake
        in the drawer, the car

to grow skeletal, aflame with rust
     in the moonlit lot, and walk
        ever after?

O God I am not spiritless,
     but a spirit can be stunned,
        a battery felt going dead

before the light flickers,
     and I've covered this ground too often
        with this yellow disc

within whose beam all's commonplace
     and whose limits are described
        by the whole night.

1967

PICNIC

Sunday in Inwood Park
                 the picnic eaten
the chicken bones scattered
                    for the fox we'll never see
the children playing in the caves
My death is folded in my pocket
                    like a nylon raincoat
What kind of sunlight is it
                 that leaves the rocks so cold?

1967

THE BOOK

For Richard Howard

You, hiding there in your words
like a disgrace
the cast-off son of a family
whose face is written in theirs
who must not be mentioned
who calls collect three times a year
from obscure towns out-of-state
and whose calls are never accepted
You who had to leave alone
and forgot your shadow hanging under the stairs
let me tell you: I have been in the house
I have spoken to all of them
they will not pronounce your name
they only allude to you
rising and sitting, going or coming,
falling asleep and waking,

giving away in marriage or calling for water
on their deathbeds
their faces look into each other and see
you
when they write at night in their diaries they are writing
to you

1968

ABNEGATION

The red fox, the vixen
dancing in the half-light among the junipers,
wise-looking in a sexy way,
Egyptian-supple in her sharpness—
what does she want
with the dreams of dead vixens,
the apotheosis of Reynard,
the literature of fox-hunting?
Only in her nerves the past
sings, a thrill of self-preservation.
I go along down the road
to a house nailed together by Scottish
Covenanters, instinct mortified
in a virgin forest,
and she springs toward her den
every hair on her pelt alive
with tidings of the immaculate present.
They left me a westernness,

a birthright, a redstained, ravelled
afghan of sky.
She has no archives,
no heirlooms, no future
except death
and I could be more
her sister than theirs
who chopped their way across these hills
—a chosen people.

1968

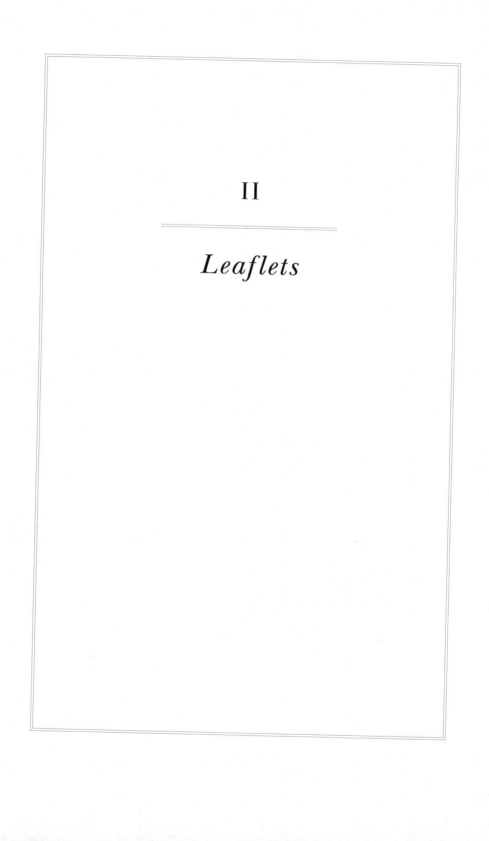

II

Leaflets

WOMEN

For C.R.G.

My three sisters are sitting
on rocks of black obsidian.
For the first time, in this light, I can see who they are.

My first sister is sewing her costume for the procession.
She is going as the Transparent Lady
and all her nerves will be visible.

My second sister is also sewing,
at the seam over her heart which has never healed entirely.
At last, she hopes, this tightness in her chest will ease.

My third sister is gazing
at a dark-red crust spreading westward far out on the sea.
Her stockings are torn but she is beautiful.

1968

IMPLOSIONS

The world's
not wanton
only wild and wavering

I wanted to choose words that even you
would have to be changed by

Take the word
of my pulse, loving and ordinary
Send out your signals, hoist

your dark scribbled flags
but take
my hand

All wars are useless to the dead

My hands are knotted in the rope
and I cannot sound the bell

My hands are frozen to the switch
and I cannot throw it

The foot is in the wheel

When it's finished and we're lying
in a stubble of blistered flowers
eyes gaping, mouths staring
dusted with crushed arterial blues

I'll have done nothing
even for you?

1968

TO FRANTZ FANON

Born Martinique, 1925; dead Washington D.C., 1961.

I don't see your head
sunk, listening   to the throats
of the torturers and the tortured

I don't see your eyes
deep in the blackness   of your skull
they look off from me   into the eyes

of rats and haunted policemen.
What I see best is the length
of your fingers
pressing the pencil
into the barred page

of the French child's copybook
with its Cartesian squares   its grilled
trap of holy geometry
where your night-sweats streamed out
in language

and your death
a black streak on a white bed
in L'Enfant's city where
the fever-bush sweats off

its thick
petals   year after year
on the mass grave
of revolt

1968

CONTINUUM

Waking thickheaded by crow's light
I see the suitcase packed
for your early plane; nothing to do
but follow the wristwatch hands
round to the hour. Life is like money
—you said, finishing the brandy from the cracked
plastic bathroom cup last night—
no use except for what you can get with it.

Yet something wants us delivered up
alive, whatever it is,
that causes me to edge the slatted blind
soundlessly up, leaving you
ten minutes' more sleep, while I look
shivering, lucidifying, down
at that street where the poor are already getting started
and that poster streaking the opposite wall
with the blurred face of a singer whose songs
money can't buy nor air contain
someone yet unloved, whose voice
I may never hear, but go on hoping
to hear, tonight, tomorrow, someday,
as I go on hoping to feel
tears of mercy in the of course impersonal rain.

1968

ON EDGES

When the ice starts to shiver
all across the reflecting basin
or water-lily leaves
dissect a simple surface
the word 'drowning' flows through me.
You built a glassy floor
that held me
as I leaned to fish for old
hooks and toothed tin cans,
stems lashing out like ties of
silk dressing-gowns
archangels of lake-light
gripped in mud.

Now you hand me a torn letter.
On my knees, in the ashes, I could never
fit these ripped-up flakes together.
In the taxi I am still piecing
what syllables I can
translating at top speed like a thinking machine
that types out 'useless' as 'monster'
and 'history' as 'lampshade'.
Crossing the bridge I need all my nerve
to trust to the man-made cables.

The blades on that machine
could cut you to ribbons
but its function is humane.
Is this all I can say of these
delicate hooks, scythe-curved intentions
you and I handle? I'd rather
taste blood, yours or mine, flowing
from a sudden slash, than cut all day
with blunt scissors on dotted lines
like the teacher told.

1968

VIOLENCE

No one knows yet
what he is capable of. Thus: if you
(still drawing me, mouth to mouth
toward the door) had pushed
a gun into my hand
would my fingers have burned, or not,
to dry ice on that metal?

if you'd said, leaving
in a pre-dawn thunderstorm
use this when the time comes
would I have blurted my first *no* that night
or, back without you, bundled
the cold bulk into a drawer
in a cocoon of nightgowns
printed with knots of honeysuckle . . .
Still following you as if your body
were a lantern, an angel of radar,
along the untrustworthy park
or down that block where the cops shoot to kill—
could I have dreamed a violence
like that of finding
your burnt-out cigarettes
planted at random, charred
fuses in a blown-up field?

1968

THE OBSERVER

Completely protected on all sides
by volcanoes
a woman, darkhaired, in stained jeans
sleeps in central Africa.
In her dreams, her notebooks, still
private as maiden diaries,
the mountain gorillas move through their life term;
their gentleness survives
observation. Six bands of them
inhabit, with her, the wooded highland.

When I lay me down to sleep
unsheltered by any natural guardians
from the panicky life-cycle of my tribe
I wake in the old cellblock
observing the daily executions,
rehearsing the laws
I cannot subscribe to,
envying the pale gorilla-scented dawn
she wakes into, the stream where she washes her hair,
the camera-flash of her quiet
eye.

1968

NIGHTBREAK

Something broken   Something
I need   By someone
I love   Next year
will I remember what
This anger   unreal

                              yet
has to be gone through
The sun to set
on this anger
            I go on
head down   into it
The mountain pulsing
Into the oildrum   drops
the ball of fire.

Time is quiet   doesn't break things
or even wound   Things are in danger
from people   The frail clay lamps
of Mesopotamia
row on row under glass
in the ethnological section
little hollows for dried-
up oil   The refugees
with their identical
tales of escape   I don't
collect what I can't use   I need
what can be broken.

In the bed the pieces fly together
and the rifts fill   or else
my body is a list   of wounds
symmetrically placed
a village

blown open   by planes
that did not   finish the job

The enemy has   withdrawn
between raids   become invisible
there are
          no agencies
                    of relief
the darkness becomes utter
Sleep   cracked and flaking
sifts over the shaken   target.

What breaks   is night
not day   The white
scar   splitting
over the east
The crack weeping

Time for the pieces

               to move

dumbly back

            toward each other.

1968

GABRIEL

There are no angels   yet
here comes an angel   one
with a man's face   young
shut-off   the dark
side of the moon   turning to me
and saying: I am the plumed
               serpent   the beast
               with fangs of fire   and a gentle
               heart

But he doesn't say that   His message
drenches his body
he'd want to kill me
for using words to name him

I sit in the bare apartment
reading
words stream past me   poetry
twentieth-century rivers
disturbed surfaces   reflecting clouds
reflecting wrinkled neon
but clogged   and mostly
nothing alive left
in their depths

The angel is barely
Speaking   to me
Once in a horn of light
he stood   or someone like him
salutations in gold-leaf
ribboning from his lips

Today again   the hair streams
to his shoulders
the eyes reflect   something
like a lost country   or so I think
but the ribbon has reeled itself
up
    he isn't giving
or taking any shit
We glance miserably
across the room   at each other

It's true   there are moments
closer and closer together
when words stick   in my throat
                          'the art of love'
                          'the art of words'
I get your message Gabriel
just   will you stay looking
straight at me
awhile longer

1968

LEAFLETS

1.

The big star, and that other
lonely on black glass
overgrown with frozen
lesions, endless night
the Coal Sack gaping
black veins of ice on the pane
spelling a word:
                    Insomnia
not manic but ordinary
to start out of sleep
turning off and on
this seasick neon
vision, this
division

the head clears of sweet smoke
and poison gas

life without caution
the only worth living
love for a man
love for a woman
love for the facts
protectless

that self-defense be not
the arm's first motion

memory not only
cards of identity

that I can live half a year
as I have never lived up to this time—

Chekhov coughing up blood almost daily
the steamer edging in toward the penal colony
chained men dozing on deck
five forest fires lighting the island

lifelong that glare, waiting.

2.

Your face
        stretched like a mask
                begins to tear
as you speak of Che Guevara
Bolivia, Nanterre
I'm too young to be your mother
you're too young to be my brother

your tears are not political
they are real water, burning
as the tears of Telemachus
burned

Over Spanish Harlem the moon
swells up, a fire balloon
fire gnawing the edge
of this crushed-up newspaper

                     now
the bodies come whirling
coal-black, ash-white
out of torn windows
and the death columns blacken

whispering
Who'd choose this life?

We're fighting for a slash of recognition,
a piercing to the pierced heart.
Tell me what you are going through—

but the attention flickers
                    and will flicker
a matchflame in poison air
a thread, a hair of light
                    sum of all answer
to the *Know that I exist!* of all existing things.

3.

If, says the Dahomeyan devil,
someone has courage to enter the fire
the young man will be restored to life.

If, the girl whispers,
I do not go into the fire
I will not be able to live with my soul.

(Her face calm and dark as amber
under the dyed butterfly turban
her back scarified in ostrich-skin patterns.)

4.

Crusaders' wind glinting
off linked scales of sea
ripping the ghostflags
galloping at the fortress

Acre, bloodcaked, lionhearted
raw vomit curdling in the sun
gray walkers walking
straying with a curbed intentness
in and out the inclosures
the gallows, the photographs
of dead Jewish terrorists, aged 15
their fading faces wide-eyed
and out in the crusading sunlight
gray strayers still straying
dusty paths
the mad who live in the dried-up moat
of the War Museum

what are we coming to
what wants these things of us
who wants them

5.

The strain of being born
        over and over has torn your smile into pieces
often I have seen it broken
        and then re-membered
and wondered how a beauty
        so anarch, so ungelded
will be cared for in this world.
        I want to hand you this
leaflet streaming with rain or tears
        but the words coming clear
something you might find crushed into your hand
        after passing a barricade
and stuff in your raincoat pocket.
        I want this to reach you

who told me once that poetry is nothing sacred
    no more sacred that is
than other things in your life—
    to answer yes, if life is uncorrupted
no better poetry is wanted.
    I want this to be yours
in the sense that if you find and read it
    it will be there in you already
and the leaflet then merely something
    to leave behind, a little leaf
in the drawer of a sublet room.
    What else does it come down to
but handing on scraps of paper
    little figurines or phials
no stronger than the dry clay they are baked in
    yet more than dry clay or paper
because the imagination crouches in them.
    If we needed fire to remind us
that all true images
    were scooped out of the mud
where our bodies curse and flounder
    then perhaps that fire is coming
to sponge away the scribes and time-servers
    and much that you would have loved will be lost as well
before you could handle it and know it
    just as we almost miss each other
in the ill cloud of mistrust, who might have touched
    hands quickly, shared food or given blood
for each other. I am thinking how we can use what we have
    to invent what we need.

Winter–Spring 1968

THE RAFTS

For David, Michael and David

Down the river, on rafts you came
floating. The three of you
and others I can't remember.
Stuck to your sleeves, twists of
blurred red rag, old bandages, ribbons
of honor.   Your hands dragged me
aboard.

      Then I sprawled
full length on the lashed poles
laughing, drenched, in rags.

The river's rising!
          they yelled on shore
thru megaphones.
Can't you see
that water's mad, those rafts
are children's toys, that crowd
is heading nowhere?
      My lips
tasted your lips and foreheads
salty with sweat,
then we were laughing, holding off
the scourge of dead branches
overhanging from shore as your
homemade inventions
            danced
              along

1968

III

Ghazals (Homage To Ghalib)

7/12/68
For Sheila Rotner

The clouds are electric in this university.
The lovers astride the tractor burn fissures through the hay.

When I look at that wall I shall think of you
and of what you did not paint there.

Only the truth makes the pain of lifting a hand worthwhile:
the prism staggering under the blows of the raga.

The vanishing-point is the point where he appears.
Two parallel tracks converge, yet there has been no wreck.

To mutilate privacy with a single foolish syllable
is to throw away the search for the one necessary word.

When you read these lines, think of me
and of what I have not written here.

7/13/68

The ones who camped on the slopes, below the bare summit,
saw differently from us, who breathed thin air and kept walking.

Sleeping back-to-back, man and woman, we were more conscious
than either of us awake and alone in the world.

These words are vapor-trails of a plane that has vanished;
by the time I write them out, they are whispering something else.

Do we still have to feel jealous of our creations?
Once they might have outlived us; in this world, we'll die together.

Don't look for me in the room I have left;
the photograph shows just a white rocking-chair, still rocking.

7/14/68: I

In Central Park we talked of our own cowardice.
How many times a day, in this city, are those words spoken?

The tears of the universe aren't all stars, Danton;
some are satellites of brushed aluminum and stainless steel.

He, who was temporary, has joined eternity;
he has deserted us, gone over to the other side.

In the Theatre of the Dust no actor becomes famous.
In the last scene they all are blown away like dust.

"It may be if I had known them I would have loved them."
You were American, Whitman, and those words are yours.

7/14/68: II

Did you think I was talking about my life?
I was trying to drive a tradition up against the wall.

The field they burned over is greener than all the rest.
You have to watch it, he said, the sparks can travel the roots.

Shot back into this earth's atmosphere
our children's children may photograph these stones.

In the red wash of the darkroom, I see myself clearly;
when the print is developed and handed about, the face is
     nothing to me.

For us the work undoes itself over and over:
the grass grows back, the dust collects, the scar breaks open.

7/16/68: I

Blacked-out on a wagon, part of my life cut out forever—
five green hours and forty violet minutes.

A cold spring slowed our lilacs, till a surf broke
violet/white, tender and sensual, misread it if you dare.

I tell you, truth is, at the moment, here
burning outward through our skins.

Eternity streams through my body:
touch it with your hand and see.

Till the walls of the tunnel cave in
and the black river walks on our faces.

7/16/68: II

When they mow the fields, I see the world reformed
as if by snow, or fire, or physical desire.

First snow. Death of the city. Ghosts in the air.
Your shade among the shadows, interviewing the mist.

The mail came every day, but letters were missing;
by this I knew things were not what they ought to be.

The trees in the long park blurring back
into Olmsted's original dream-work.

The impartial scholar writes me from under house arrest.
I hope you are rotting in hell, Montaigne you bastard.

7/17/68

Armitage of scrapiron for the radiations of a moon.
Flower cast in metal, Picasso-woman, sister.

Two hesitant Luna moths regard each other
with the spots on their wings: fascinated.

To resign *yourself*—what an act of betrayal!
—to throw a runaway spirit back to the dogs.

When the ebb-tide pulls hard enough, we are all starfish.
The moon has her way with us, my companion in crime.

At the Aquarium that day, between the white whale's loneliness
and the groupers' mass promiscuities, only ourselves.

7/23/68

When your sperm enters me, it is altered;
when my thought absorbs yours, a world begins.

If the mind of the teacher is not in love with the mind of the student,
he is simply practicing rape, and deserves at best our pity.

To live outside the law! Or, barely within it,
a twig on boiling waters, enclosed inside a bubble

Our words are jammed in an electronic jungle;
sometimes, though, they rise and wheel croaking above the treetops.

An open window; thick summer night; electric fences trilling.
What are you doing here at the edge of the death-camps, Vivaldi?

7/24/68: I

The sapling springs, the milkweed blooms: obsolete Nature.
In the woods I have a vision of asphalt, blindly lingering.

I hardly know the names of the weeds I love.
I have forgotten the names of so many flowers.

I can't live at the hems of that tradition—
will I last to try the beginning of the next?

Killing is different now: no fingers round the throat.
No one feels the wetness of the blood on his hands.

When we fuck, there too are we remoter
than the fucking bodies of lovers used to be?

How many men have touched me with their eyes
more hotly than they later touched me with their lips.

7/24/68: II

The friend I can trust is the one who will let me have my death.
The rest are actors who want me to stay and further the plot.

At the drive-in movie, above the PanaVision,
beyond the projector beams, you project yourself, great Star.

The eye that used to watch us is dead, but open.
Sometimes I still have a sense of being followed.

How long will we be waiting for the police?
How long must I wonder which of my friends would hide me?

Driving at night I feel the Milky Way
streaming above me like the graph of a cry.

7/26/68: I

Last night you wrote on the wall: Revolution is poetry.
Today you needn't write; the wall has tumbled down.

We were taught to respect the appearance behind the reality.
Our senses were out on parole, under surveillance.

A pair of eyes imprisoned for years inside my skull
is burning its way outward, the headaches are terrible.

I'm walking through a rubble of broken sculpture, stumbling
here on the spine of a friend, there on the hand of a brother.

All those joinings! and yet we fought so hard to be unique.
Neither alone, nor in anyone's arms, will we end up sleeping.

7/26/68: II

A dead mosquito, flattened against a door;
his image could survive our comings and our goings.

LeRoi! Eldridge! listen to us, we are ghosts
condemned to haunt the cities where you want to be at home.

The white children turn black on the negative.
The summer clouds blacken inside the camera-skull.

Every mistake that can be made, we are prepared to make;
anything less would fall short of the reality we're dreaming.

Someone has always been desperate, now it's our turn—
we who were free to weep for Othello and laugh at Caliban.

I have learned to smell a *conservateur* a mile away:
they carry illustrated catalogues of all that there is to lose.

7/26/68: III

So many minds in search of bodies
groping their way among artificial limbs.

Of late they write me how they are getting on:
desertion, desertion, is the story of those pages.

A chewed-up nail, the past, splitting yet growing,
the same and not the same; a nervous habit never shaken.

Those stays of tooled whalebone in the Salem museum—
erotic scrimshaw, practical even in lust.

Whoever thought of inserting a ship in a bottle?
Long weeks without women do this to a man.

8/1/68

The order of the small town on the riverbank,
forever at war with the order of the dark and starlit soul.

Were you free then all along, Jim, free at last,
of everything but the white boy's fantasies?

We pleaded guilty till we saw what rectitude was like:
its washed hands, and dead nerve, and sclerotic eye.

I long ago stopped dreaming of pure justice, your honor—
my crime was to believe we could make cruelty obsolete.

The body has been exhumed from the burnt-out bunker;
the teeth counted, the contents of the stomach told over.

And you, Custer the Squaw-killer, hero of primitive schoolrooms—
where are you buried, what is the condition of your bones?

8/4/68

For Aijaz Ahmad

If these are letters, they will have to be misread.
If scribblings on a wall, they must tangle with all the others.

Fuck reds   Black Power   Angel loves Rosita
—and a transistor radio answers in Spanish: *Night must fall.*

Prisoners, soldiers, crouching as always, writing,
explaining the unforgivable to a wife, a mother, a lover.

Those faces are blurred and some have turned away
to which I used to address myself so hotly.

How is it, Ghalib, that your grief, resurrected in pieces,
has found its way to this room from your dark house in Delhi?

When they read this poem of mine, they are translators.
Every existence speaks a language of its own.

8/8/68: I

From here on, all of us will be living
like Galileo turning his first tube at the stars.

Obey the little laws and break the great ones
is the preamble to their constitution.

Even to hope is to leap into the unknown,
under the mocking eyes of the way things are.

There's a war on earth, and in the skull, and in the glassy spaces,
between the existing and the non-existing.

I need to live each day through, have them and know them all,
though I can see from here where I'll be standing at the end.

8/8/68: II
For A.H.C.

A piece of thread ripped-out from a fierce design,
some weaving figured as magic against oppression.

I'm speaking to you as a woman to a man:
when your blood flows I want to hold you in my arms.

How did we get caught up fighting this forest fire,
we, who were only looking for a still place in the woods?

How frail we are, and yet, dispersed, always returning,
the barnacles they keep scraping from the warship's hull.

The hairs on your breast curl so lightly as you lie there,
while the strong heart goes on pounding in its sleep.

POEMS
(1967–1969)

POSTCARD

Rodin's Orpheus, floodlit, hacked,
clawing I don't know what
with the huge toes of an animal,
gripping the air
above the mitered floors
of the Musée . . .

This comes in the mail and I wonder
what it is to be cast in bronze
like the sender;
who wouldn't live, thirsty, drifting,
obscure, freaked-out
but with a future
still lapping at the door
and a dream of language
unlived behind the clouds?

Orpheus hurts all over
but his throat hurts worst of all.
You can see it: the two knobs
of bronze pain in his neck,
the paralysis of his floodlit lips.

1967

WHITE NIGHT

From the Yiddish of Kadia Molodowsky.

White night, my painful joy,
your light is brighter than the dawn.
A white ship is sailing from East Broadway
where I see no sail by day.

A quiet star hands me a ticket
open for all the seas.
I put on my time-worn jacket
and entrust myself to the night.

Where are you taking me, ship?
Who charted us on this course?
The hieroglyphs of the map escape me,
and the arrows of your compass.

I am the one who sees and does not see.
I go along on your deck of secrets,
squeeze shut my baggage on the wreath of sorrows
from all my plucked-out homes.

—Pack in all my blackened pots,
their split lids, the chipped crockeries,
pack in my chaos with its gold-encrusted buttons
since chaos will always be in fashion.

—Pack the letters stamped *Unknown at This Address*—
vanished addresses that sear my eyes,
postmarked with more than years and days;
sucked into my bones and marrow.

—Pack up my shadow that weighs more than my body,
that comes along with its endless exhortations.
Weekdays or holidays, time of flowers or withering,
my shadow is with me, muttering its troubles.

Find me a place of honey cakes and sweetness
where angels and children picnic together
(this is the dream I love best of all),
where the sacred wine fizzes in bottles.

Let me have one sip, here on East Broadway,
for the sake of those old Jews crying in the dark.
I cry my heretic's tears with them,
their sobbing is my sobbing.

I'm a difficult passenger, my ship
is packed with the heavy horns, the *shofars* of grief.
Tighten the sails of night as far as you can,
for the daylight cannot carry me.

Take me somewhere to a place of rest,
of goats in belled hats playing on trombones—
to the Almighty's fresh white sheets
where the hunter's shadow cannot fall.

Take me . . . Yes, take me . . . But you know best
where the sea calmly opens its blue road.
I'm wearier than your oldest tower;
somewhere I've left my heart aside.

1968

THE DAYS: SPRING

He writes: *Let us bear*
our illusions together . . .
I persist in thinking:
every fantasy I have
comes true; who am I
to bear illusions?

He writes: *But who can be*
a saint?—The woman in #9

is locked in the bathroom.
She screams for five hours,
pounds the walls, hears voices
retreating in the hall.
The lock is broken.
The lovers pass and go out to lunch,
boredom sets in by 2 o'clock.

Emptiness of the mirror, and
the failure of the classics.
A look at the ceiling
in pauses of lovemaking:
that immense, scarred domain.

He writes: *The depth of pain
grows all the time.*
We marched and sat down in the street,
she offered her torn newspaper.
Who will survive Amerika?
they sang on Lenox Avenue.

This early summer weekend.
The chance of beginning again.
From always fewer chances
the future plots itself.
I walk Third Avenue,
bare-armed with flowing hair.
Later the stars come out like facts,
my constellation streams at my head,
a woman's body nailed with stars.

1969

TEAR GAS

October 12, 1969: reports of the tear-gassing of demonstrators protesting the treatment of G.I. prisoners in the stockade at Fort Dix, New Jersey.

This is how it feels to do something you are afraid of.
That they are afraid of.

>   (Would it have been different at Fort Dix, beginning
>   to feel the full volume of tears in you, the measure
>   of all you have in you to shed, all you have held
>   back from false pride, false indifference, false
>   courage
>
>   beginning to weep as you weep peeling onions, but
>   endlessly, for the rest of time, tears of chemistry,
>   tears of catalyst, tears of rage, tears for yourself,
>   tears for the tortured men in the stockade and for
>   their torturers
>
>   tears of fear, of the child stepping into the adult
>   field of force, the woman stepping into the male field
>   of violence, tears of relief, that your body was here,
>   you had done it, every last refusal was over)

Here in this house my tears are running wild
in this Vermont of India-madras-colored leaves, of cesspool-
   stricken brooks, of violence licking at old people and
   children
and I am afraid
of the language in my head
I am alone, alone with language
and without meaning
coming back to something written years ago:
our words misunderstand us
wanting a word that will shed itself like a tear

onto the page
leaving its stain

Trying every key in the bunch to get the door even ajar
not knowing whether it's locked or simply jammed from long disuse
trying the keys over and over then throwing the bunch away
staring around for an axe
wondering if the world can be changed like this
if a life can be changed like this

It wasn't completeness I wanted
(the old ideas of a revolution that could be foretold, and once
       arrived at would give us ourselves and each other)
I stopped listening long ago to their descriptions
of the good society

The will to change begins in the body not in the mind
My politics is in my body, accruing and expanding with every
       act of resistance and each of my failures
Locked in the closet at 4 years old I beat the wall with my body
that act is in me still

No, not completeness:
but I needed a way of saying
(this is what they are afraid of)
that could deal with these fragments
I needed to touch you
with a hand, a body
but also with words
I need a language to hear myself with
to see myself in
a language like pigment released on the board
blood-black, sexual green, reds
veined with contradictions
bursting under pressure from the tube
staining the old grain of the wood

like sperm or tears
but this is not what I mean
these images are not what I mean
(I am afraid.)
I mean that I want you to answer me
when I speak badly
that I love you, that we are in danger
that she wants to have your child, that I want us to have mercy
    on each other
that I want to take her hand
that I see you changing
that it was change I loved in you
when I thought I loved completeness
that things I have said which in a few years will be forgotten
matter more to me than this or any poem
and I want you to listen
when I speak badly
not in poems but in tears
not my best but my worst
that these repetitions are beating their way
toward a place where we can no longer be together
where my body no longer will demonstrate outside your stockade
and wheeling through its blind tears will make for the open air
of another kind of action

(I am afraid.)
It's not the worst way to live.

1969

The Will
To Change
(1971)

For David, Pablo and Jacob

What does not change / is the will to change

—Charles Olson, "The Kingfishers"

NOVEMBER 1968

Stripped
you're beginning to float free
up through the smoke of brushfires
and incinerators
the unleafed branches won't hold you
nor the radar aerials

You're what the autumn knew would happen
after the last collapse
of primary color
once the last absolutes were torn to pieces
you could begin

How you broke open, what sheathed you
until this moment
I know nothing about it
my ignorance of you amazes me
now that I watch you
starting to give yourself away
to the wind

1968

STUDY OF HISTORY

Out there.   The mind of the river
as it might be you.

Lights   blotted by unseen hulls
repetitive shapes passing
dull foam crusting the margin
barges sunk below the water-line with silence.
The scow, drudging on.

Lying in the dark, to think of you
and your harsh traffic
gulls pecking your rubbish   natural historians
mourning your lost purity
pleasure cruisers
witlessly careening you

but this
after all
is the narrows and after
all we have never entirely
known what was done to you upstream
what powers trepanned
which of your channels diverted
what rockface leaned to stare
in your upturned
defenseless
face.

1968

PLANETARIUM

Thinking of Caroline Herschel, 1750–1848, astronomer,
sister of William; and others.

A woman in the shape of a monster
a monster in the shape of a woman
the skies are full of them

a woman   'in the snow
among the Clocks and instruments
or measuring the ground with poles'

in her 98 years to discover
8 comets

she whom the moon ruled
like us
levitating into the night sky
riding the polished lenses

Galaxies of women, there
doing penance for impetuousness
ribs chilled
in those spaces   of the mind

An eye,
        'virile, precise and absolutely certain'
        from the mad webs of Uranusborg
                    encountering the NOVA

every impulse of light exploding
from the core
as life flies out of us

Tycho whispering at last
'Let me not seem to have lived in vain'

What we see, we see
and seeing is changing

the light that shrivels a mountain
and leaves a man alive

Heartbeat of the pulsar
heart sweating through my body

The radio impulse
pouring in from Taurus

      I am bombarded yet   I stand

I have been standing all my life in the
direct path of a battery of signals
the most accurately transmitted most
untranslateable language in the universe
I am a galactic cloud so deep   so invo-
luted that a light wave could take 15
years to travel through me   And has
taken   I am an instrument in the shape
of a woman trying to translate pulsations
into images   for the relief of the body
and the reconstruction of the mind.

1968

THE BURNING OF PAPER INSTEAD OF
CHILDREN

> I was in danger of verbalizing my moral impulses out of existence.
>
> —Fr. Daniel Berrigan, on trial in Baltimore

1.

My neighbor, a scientist and art-collector, telephones me in a state
of violent emotion. He tells me that my son and his, aged eleven
and twelve, have on the last day of school burned a mathematics
text-book in the backyard. He has forbidden my son to come to his
house for a week, and has forbidden his own son to leave the house
during that time. "The burning of a book," he says, "arouses terrible
sensations in me, memories of Hitler; there are few things that upset
me so much as the idea of burning a book."

Back there: the library, walled
with green Britannicas
Looking again
in Dürer's *Complete Works*
for MELENCOLIA, the baffled woman

the crocodiles in Herodotus
the Book of the Dead
the *Trial of Jeanne d'Arc,* so blue
I think, It is her color

and they take the book away
because I dream of her too often

love and fear in a house
knowledge of the oppressor

I know it hurts to burn

2.

To imagine a time of silence
or few words
a time of chemistry and music

the hollows above your buttocks
traced by my hand
or, *hair is like flesh,* you said

an age of long silence

relief

from this tongue   the slab of limestone
or reinforced concrete
fanatics and traders
dumped on this coast   wildgreen   clayred
that breathed once
in signals of smoke
sweep of the wind

knowledge of the oppressor
this is the oppressor's language

yet I need it to talk to you

3.

"People suffer highly in poverty and it takes dignity and intelligence
to overcome this suffering. Some of the suffering are: a child did not
had dinner last night: a child steal because he did not have money
to buy it: to hear a mother say she do not have money to buy food
for her children and to see a child without cloth it will make tears
in your eyes."

(the fracture of order
the repair of speech
to overcome this suffering)

4.

We lie under the sheet
after making love, speaking
of loneliness
relieved in a book
relived in a book
so on that page
the clot and fissure
of it appears
words of a man
in pain
a naked word
entering the clot
a hand grasping
through bars:

deliverance

What happens between us
has happened for centuries
we know it from literature

still it happens

sexual jealousy
outflung hand
beating bed

dryness of mouth
after panting

there are books that describe all this
and they are useless

You walk into the woods behind a house
there in that country
you find a temple
built eighteen hundred years ago
you enter without knowing
what it is you enter

so it is with us

no one knows what may happen
though the books tell everything

burn the texts   said Artaud

5.

I am composing on the typewriter late at night, thinking of today.
How well we all spoke. A language is a map of our failures. Fred-
erick Douglass wrote an English purer than Milton's. People suffer
highly in poverty. There are methods but we do not use them. Joan,
who could not read, spoke some peasant form of French. Some of
the suffering are: it is hard to tell the truth; this is America; I cannot
touch you now. In America we have only the present tense. I am in dan-
ger. You are in danger. The burning of a book arouses no sensation in
me. I know it hurts to burn. There are flames of napalm
in Catonsville, Maryland. I know it hurts to burn. The typewriter
is overheated, my mouth is burning, I cannot touch you and this is
the oppressor's language.

1968

I DREAM I'M THE
DEATH OF ORPHEUS

I am walking rapidly through striations of light and dark thrown
      under an arcade.

I am a woman in the prime of life, with certain powers
and those powers severely limited
by authorities whose faces I rarely see.
I am a woman in the prime of life
driving her dead poet in a black Rolls-Royce
through a landscape of twilight and thorns.
A woman with a certain mission
which if obeyed to the letter will leave her intact.
A woman with the nerves of a panther
a woman with contacts among Hell's Angels
a woman feeling the fullness of her powers
at the precise moment when she must not use them
a woman sworn to lucidity
who sees through the mayhem, the smoky fires
of these underground streets
her dead poet learning to walk backward against the wind
on the wrong side of the mirror

1968

THE BLUE GHAZALS

9/21/68

Violently asleep in the old house.
A clock stays awake all night ticking.

Turning, turning their bruised leaves
the trees stay awake all night in the wood.

Talk to me with your body through my dreams.
Tell me what we are going through.

The walls of the room are muttering,
old trees, old utopians, arguing with the wind.

To float like a dead man in a sea of dreams
and half those dreams being dreamed by someone else.

Fifteen years of sleepwalking with you,
wading against the tide, and with the tide.

9/23/68

One day of equinoctial light after another,
moving ourselves through gauzes and fissures of that light.

Early and late I come and set myself against you,
your phallic fist knocking blindly at my door.

The dew is beaded like mercury on the coarsened grass,
the web of the spider is heavy as if with sweat.

Everything is yielding toward a foregone conclusion,
only we are rash enough to go on changing our lives.

An Ashanti woman tilts the flattened basin on her head
to let the water slide downward: I am that woman and that water.

9/26/68: I

A man, a woman, a city.
The city as object of love.

Anger and filth in the basement.
The furnace stoked and blazing.

A sexual heat on the pavements.
Trees erected like statues.

Eyes at the ends of avenues.
Yellow for hesitation.

I'm tired of walking your streets
he says, unable to leave her.

Air of dust and rising sparks,
the city burning her letters.

9/28/68: II
For Wallace Stevens

Ideas of order . . . Sinner of the Florida keys,
you were our poet of revolution all along.

A man isn't what he seems but what he desires:
gaieties of anarchy drumming at the base of the skull.

Would this have left you cold, our scene, its wild parades,
the costumes, banners, incense, flowers, the immense marches?

Disorder is natural, these leaves absently blowing
in the drinking-fountain, filling the statue's crevice.

The use of force in public architecture:
nothing, not even the honeycomb, manifests such control.

9/29/68
For Leroi Jones

Late at night I went walking through your difficult wood,
half-sleepy, half-alert in that thicket of bitter roots.

Who doesn't speak to me, who speaks to me more and more,
but from a face turned off, turned away, a light shut out.

Most of the old lecturers are inaudible or dead.
Prince of the night there are explosions in the hall.

The blackboard scribbled over with dead languages
is falling and killing our children.

Terribly far away I saw your mouth in the wild light:
it seemed to me you were shouting instructions to us all.

12/13/68

They say, if you can tell, clasped tight under the blanket,
the edge of dark from the edge of dawn, your love is a lie.

If I thought of my words as changing minds,
hadn't my mind also to suffer changes?

They measure fever, swab the blisters of the throat,
but the cells of thought go rioting on ignored.

It's the inner ghost that suffers, little spirit
looking out wildly from the clouded pupils.

When will we lie clearheaded in our flesh again
with the cold edge of the night driving us close together?

12/20/68: I

There are days when I seem to have nothing
but these frayed packets, done up with rotting thread.

The shortest day of the year, let it be ours.
Let me give you something: a token for the subway.

(Refuse even
the most beloved old solutions.

That dead man wrote, grief ought to reach the lips.
You must believe I know before you can tell me.

A black run through the tunnelled winter, he and she,
together, touching, yet not side by side.

12/20/68: II

Frost, burning. The city's ill.
We gather like viruses.

The doctors are all on their yachts
watching the beautiful skin-divers.

The peasant mind of the Christian
transfixed on food at the year's turning.

Thinking of marzipan
forget that revolutionary child.

Thought grown senile with sweetness.
You too may visit the Virgins.

In the clear air, hijacked planes
touch down at the forbidden island.

5/4/69

Pain made her conservative.
Where the matches touched her flesh, she wears a scar.

The police arrive at dawn
like death and childbirth.

City of accidents, your true map
is the tangling of all our lifelines.

The moment when a feeling enters the body
is political. This touch is political.

Sometimes I dream we are floating on water
hand-in-hand; and sinking without terror.

PIERROT LE FOU

1.

Suppose you stood facing
a wall
  of photographs
from your unlived life

as you stand looking at these
stills from the unseen film?

Yourself against a wall
curiously stuccoed

Yourself in the doorway
of a kind of watchman's hut

Yourself at a window
signaling to people
you haven't met yet

Yourself in unfamiliar clothes
with the same eyes

2.

On a screen as wide as this, I grope for the titles.
I speak the French language like a schoolgirl of the 'forties.
Those roads remind me of Beauce and the motorcycle.
We rode from Paris to Chartres in the March wind.
He said we should go to Spain but the wind defeated me.
France of the superhighways, I never knew you.
How much the body took in those days, and could take!
A naked lightbulb still simmers in my eyeballs.
In every hotel, I lived on the top floor.

3.

Suppose we had time
and no money
living by our wits
                    telling stories

which stories would you tell?

I would tell the story
of Pierrot Le Fou
who trusted

        not a woman

            but love itself

till his head blew off
not quite intentionally

I would tell all the stories I knew
in which people went wrong
but the nervous system

was right all along

4.

The island blistered our feet.
At first we mispronounced each others' names.
All the leaves of the tree were scribbled with words.
There was a language there but no-one to speak it.
Sometimes each of us was alone.
At noon on the beach our shadows left us.
The net we twisted from memory kept on breaking.
The damaged canoe lay on the beach like a dead animal.
You started keeping a journal on a coconut shell.

5.

When I close my eyes
other films

        have been there all along

a market shot:
bins of turnips, feet
of dead chickens
close-up: a black old woman
buying voodoo medicines

a figure of terrible faith
and I know her needs

Another film:
                  an empty room stacked with old films
I am kneeling on the floor
it is getting dark
                  they want to close the building
and I still haven't found you

Scanning reel after reel
tundras in negative,
the Bowery
            all those scenes
but the light is failing
                and you are missing
from the footage of the march
the railway disaster
the snowbound village

even the shots of the island
miss you
        yet you were there

6.

To record
in order to see

        if you know how the story ends
        why tell it

To record
in order to forget

        the surface is always lucid
        my shadows are under the skin

To record
in order to control

        the eye of the camera
        doesn't weep tears of blood

To record
for that is what one does

        climbing your stairs, over and over
        I memorized the bare walls

        This is my way of coming back

1969

LETTERS: MARCH 1969

1.

Foreknown. The victor
sees the disaster through and through.
His soles grind rocksalt
from roads of the resistance.
He shoulders through rows
of armored faces
he might have loved and lived among.
The victory carried like a corpse
from town to town
begins to crawl in the casket.
The summer swindled on
from town to town, our train
stopping and broiling on the rails
long enough to let on who we were.
The disaster sat up with us all night
drinking bottled water, eating fruit,
talking of the conditions that prevailed.
Outside along the railroad cut
they were singing for our death.

2.

Hopes sparkle like water in the clean carafe.
How little it takes
to restore composure.
White napkins, a tray
of napoleons and cherry tarts
compliments of the airline
which has flown us out of danger.
They are torturing the journalist we drank with
last night in the lounge

but we can't be sure of that
here overlooking the runway
three hours and twenty minutes into another life.
If this is done for us
(and this is done for us)
if we are well men wearing bandages
for disguise
if we can choose our scene
stay out of earshot
break the roll and pour
from the clean carafe
if we can desert like soldiers
abjure like thieves
we may well purchase new virtues at the gate
of the other world.

3.

"I am up at sunrise
collecting data.
The reservoir burns green.
Darling, the knives they have on this block alone
would amaze you.
When they ask my profession I say
I'm a student of weapons systems.
The notes I'm putting together are purely
of sentimental value
my briefcase is I swear useless
to foreign powers, to the police
I am not given I say
to revealing my sources
to handling round copies
of my dossier for perusal.
The vulnerable go unarmed.
I myself walk the floor

a ruinously expensive Swiss hunter's knife
exposed in my brain
eight blades, each one for a distinct purpose,
laid open as on the desk
of an importer or a fence."

4.

Six months back
send carbons you said
but this winter's dashed off in pencil
torn off the pad too fast
for those skills. In the dawn taxi
in the kitchen
burning the succotash
the more I love my life the more
I love you. In a time
of fear. In a city
of fear. in a life
without vacations the paisley fades
winter and summer in the sun
but the best time is now.

My sick friend writes: *what's love?*
This life is nothing, Adrienne!

Her hands bled onto the sill.
She had that trick of reaching outward,
the pane was smashed but only
the Calvinist northwind
spat in from the sea.
She's a shot hero. A dying poet.
Even now, if we went for her—
but they've gone with rags and putty to fix the pane.
She stays in with her mirrors and anger.

I tear up answers
I once gave, postcards
from riot and famine go up on the walls
valentines stuck in the mirror
flame and curl, loyalties dwindle
the bleak light dries our tears
without relief. I keep coming back to you

in my head, but you couldn't know that, and
I have no carbons. Prince of pity,
what eats out of your hand?
the rodent pain, electric
with exhaustion, mazed and shaken?
I'd have sucked the wound in your hand to sleep
but my lips were trembling.
Tell me how to bear myself,
how it's done, the light kiss falling
accurately
on the cracked palm.

1969

PIECES

1. *Breakpoint*

The music of words
received as fact

The steps that wouldn't hold us both
splintering in air

The self withheld in an urn
like ashes

To have loved you better than you loved yourself
—whoever you were, to have loved you—

And still to love but simply
as one of those faces on the street

2. *Relevance*

That erudition
how to confront it

The critics wrote answers
the questions were ours

A breast, a shoulder
chilled at waking

The cup of yoghurt
eaten at noon
and no explanations

The books we borrowed
trying to read each other's minds

Paperbacks piling
on both sides of the fireplace
and piled beside the bed

What difference could it make
that those books came
out of unintelligible pain

as daylight out of the hours

when that light burned
atop the insurance tower
all night like the moon

3. *Memory*

Plugged-in to her body
he came the whole way
but it makes no difference

If not this then what
would fuse a connection

(All that burning intelligence about love
what can it matter

Falling in love on words
and ending in silence
with its double-meanings

Always falling and ending
because this world gives no room
to be what we dreamt of being

Are we, as he said
of the generation that forgets
the lightning-flash, the air-raid

and each other

4. *Time and Place*

Liquid mist burning off
along the highway

Slap of water
Light on shack boards

Hauling of garbage
early in the wet street

Always the same, wherever waking,
the old positions
assumed by the mind

and the new day forms
like a china cup

hard, cream-colored, unbreakable
even in our travels

5. *Revelation*

This morning: read Simone Weil
on the loss of grace

drank a glass of water

remembered the dream that woke me:

some one, some more than one
battering into my room
intent to kill me

I crying your name
its two syllables
ringing through sleep

knowing it vain
knowing
you slept unhearing

crying your name
like a spell

like signs executed

by the superstitious

who are the faithful of this world

1969

OUR WHOLE LIFE

Our whole life a translation
the permissible fibs

and now a knot of lies
eating at itself to get undone

Words bitten thru words

meanings burnt-off like paint
under the blowtorch

All those dead letters
rendered into the oppressor's language

Trying to tell the doctor where it hurts
like the Algerian
who has walked from his village, burning

his whole body a cloud of pain
and there are no words for this

except himself

1969

YOUR LETTER

                    blinds me
like the light of that surf
you thrust your body in
for punishment

or the river of fiery fenders
and windshields
you pour yourself into
driving north to S.F.
on that coast of chrome and oil

I watch for any signal
the tremor of courage
in the seismograph

a flash
where I thought the glare
was steady, smogged & tame

1969

STAND UP

Stand up in my nightgown at the window
almost naked behind black glass

Off from the line of trees the road
beaten, bare, we walked

in the light of the bare, beaten moon.
Almost, you spoke to me. The road

swings past swampground
the soft spots of the earth

you might sink through into location
where their cameras are set up

the underground film-makers waiting to make their film
waiting for you

their cameras pivot toward your head and the film burns
but you're not talking

If I am there you have forgotten my name
you think perhaps 'a woman'

and you drift on, drifter, through the frames
of the movie they are making of this time.

A whole soundtrack of your silence
a whole film

of dark nights and darker rooms
and blank sheets of paper, bare . . .

1969

THE STELAE

For Arnold Rich

Last night I met you in my sister's house
risen from the dead
showing me your collection

You are almost at the point of giving things away

It's the stelae on the walls I want
that I never saw before

You offer other objects
I have seen time and time again

I think you think you are giving me
something precious

The stelae are so unlike you
swart, indifferent, incised with signs
you have never deciphered

I never knew you had them
I wonder if you are giving them away

1969

SNOW

when it comes down turning
itself in clusters before the flat
light of the shortest day

you see how all turns away
from us how we turn
into our shadows you can see
how we are tested

the individual crystal on the
black skirt of the maxi-coat
under the lens

was it a whole day or just a lifetime
spent studying crystals

on the fire escape while the 'Sixties
were running out
could you see

how the black ladder spun away from us
into whiteness
how over and over
a star became a tear

if no two are alike
then what are we doing
with these diagrams of loss

1969

THE WILL TO CHANGE

1.

For L D., Dead 11/69

That Chinese restaurant was a joke
with its repeating fountains

& chopsticks in tissue paper
The vodka was too sweet

the beancurd too hot
You came with your Egyptian hieroglyph

your angel's smile
Almost the next day

as surely as if shot
you were thin air

At the risk of appearing ridiculous—
we take back this halfworld for you

and all whose murders accrue
past your death

2.

For Sandra Levinson

Knocked down in the canefield
by a clumsily swung machete

she is helped to her feet
by Fidel

and snapped by photographers
the blonde Yanqui in jeans

We're living through a time
that needs to be lived through us

(and in the morning papers
Bobby Seale, chalked

by the courtroom artist
defaced by the gag)

3.
For D.J.L.

Beardless again, phoning
from a storefront in Yorkville

. . . we need a typewriter, a crib
& Michael's number . . .

I swim to you thru dead
latitudes of fever

. . . accepting the discipline . . .
You mean your old freedom

to disappear—you miss that?
. . . but I can dig having lost it . . .

David, I could dig losing everything.
Knowing what you mean, to make that leap

bite into the fear, over & over
& survive. Hoarding my 'liberty'

like a compulsive—more
than I can use up in a lifetime—

two dozen oranges in the refrigerator
for one American weekend

4.
For A.H.C.

At the wings of the mirror, peacock plumes
from the Feast of San Gennaro

gaze thru the dark
All night the A-train forages

under our bedroom
All night I dream of a man

black, gagged, shackled, coffined
in a courtroom where I am

passive, white & silent
though my mouth is free

All night I see his eyes
iridescent under torture

and hear the shuddering of the earth
as the trains tear us apart

5.

The cabdriver from the Bronx
screaming: 'This city's GOTTA die!'

dynamiting it hourly from his soul
as surely as any terrorist

Burning the bodies of the scum on welfare
ejaculating into the flames

(*and,* said Freud,
who welcomed it when it was done?)

the professors of the fact
that someone has suffered

seeking truth in a mist of librium
the artists talking of freedom

in their chains

1969–1970

THE PHOTOGRAPH OF THE UNMADE BED

Cruelty is rarely conscious
One slip of the tongue

one exposure
among so many

a thrust in the dark
to see if there's pain there

I never asked you to explain
that act of violence

what dazed me was our ignorance
of our will to hurt each other

•

In a flash I understand
how poems are unlike photographs

(the one saying   This could be
the other   This was

The image
isn't responsible

for our uses of it
It is intentionless

A long strand of dark hair
in the washbasin

is innocent and yet
such things have done harm

•

These snapshots taken by ghetto children
given for Christmas

Objects blurring into perceptions
No 'art,' only the faults

of the film, the faults of the time
Did mere indifference blister

these panes, eat these walls,
shrivel and scrub these trees—

mere indifference? I tell you
cruelty is rarely conscious

the done and the undone blur
into one photograph of failure

•

This crust of bread we try to share
this name traced on a window

this word I paste together
like a child fumbling

with paste and scissors
this writing in the sky with smoke

this silence

this lettering chalked on the ruins
this alphabet of the dumb

this feather held to lips
that still breathe and are warm

1969

IMAGES FOR GODARD

1.

Language as city:: Wittgenstein
Driving to the limits
of the city of words

the superhighway streams
like a comic strip

to newer suburbs
casements of shockproof glass

where no one yet looks out
or toward the coast where even now

the squatters in their shacks
await eviction

When all conversation
becomes an interview
under duress

when we come to the limits
of the city

my face must have a meaning

2.

To know the extremes of light
I sit in this darkness

To see the present flashing
in a rearview mirror

blued in a plateglass pane
reddened in the reflection

of the red Triomphe
parked at the edge of the sea

the sea glittering in the sun
the swirls of nebula

in the espresso cup
raindrops, neon spectra

on a vinyl raincoat

3.

To love, to move perpetually
as the body changes

a dozen times a day
the temperature of the skin

the feeling of rise & fall
deadweight & buoyancy

the eye sunk inward
the eye bleeding with speech

('for that moment at least
I wás you—')

To be stopped, to shoot the same scene
over & over

4.

At the end of *Alphaville*
she says *I love you*

and the film begins
that you've said you'd never make

because it's impossible
'things as difficult to show

as horror & war & sickness are'

meaning: love,
to speak in the mouth

to touch the breast
for a woman

to know the sex of a man
That film begins here

yet you don't show it
we leave the theatre

suffering from that

5.

Interior monologue of the poet:
the notes for the poem are the only poem

the mind collecting, devouring
all these destructibles

the unmade studio couch the air
shifting the abalone shells

the mind of the poet is the only poem
the poet is at the movies

dreaming the film-maker's dream but differently
free in the dark as if asleep

free in the dusty beam of the projector
the mind of the poet is changing

the moment of change is the only poem

1970

A VALEDICTION
FORBIDDING MOURNING

My swirling wants. Your frozen lips.
The grammar turned and attacked me.
Themes, written under duress.
Emptiness of the notations.

They gave me a drug that slowed the healing of wounds.

I want you to see this before I leave:
the experience of repetition as death
the failure of criticism to locate the pain
the poster in the bus that said:
my bleeding is under control.

A red plant in a cemetery of plastic wreaths.

A last attempt: the language is a dialect called metaphor.
These images go unglossed: hair, glacier, flashlight.
When I think of a landscape I am thinking of a time.
When I talk of taking a trip I mean forever.
I could say: those mountains have a meaning
but further than that I could not say.

To do something very common, in my own way.

1970

SHOOTING SCRIPT
PART I: 11/69–2/70

1.

We were bound on the wheel of an endless conversation.

Inside this shell, a tide waiting for someone to enter.

A monologue waiting for you to interrupt it.

A man wading into the surf. The dialogue of the rock with the breaker.

The wave changed instantly by the rock; the rock changed by the wave returning over and over.

The dialogue that lasts all night or a whole lifetime.

A conversation of sounds melting constantly into rhythms.

A shell waiting for you to listen.

A tide that ebbs and flows against a deserted continent.

A cycle whose rhythm begins to change the meanings of words.

A wheel of blinding waves of light, the spokes pulsing out from where we hang together in the turning of an endless conversation.

The meaning that searches for its word like a hermit crab.

A monologue that waits for one listener.

An ear filled with one sound only.

A shell penetrated by meaning.

2. *Ghazal V*
Adapted from Mirza Ghalib.

Even when I thought I prayed, I was talking to myself; when I
found the door shut, I simply walked away.

We all accept Your claim to be unique; the stone lips, the
carved limbs, were never your true portrait.

Grief held back from the lips wears at the heart; the drop that
refused to join the river dried up in the dust.

Now tell me your story till the blood drips from your lashes. Any
other version belongs to your folklore, or ours.

To see the Tigris in a water-drop . . . Either you were playing
games with me, or you never cared to learn the structure of my
language.

3.

The old blanket. The crumbs of rubbed wool turning up.

Where we lay and breakfasted. The stains of tea. The squares
of winter light projected on the wool.

You, sleeping with closed windows. I, sleeping in the silver
nitrate burn of zero air.

Where it can snow, I'm at home; the crystals accumulating spell
out my story.

The cold encrustation thickening on the ledge.

The arrow-headed facts, accumulating, till a whole city is
taken over.

Midwinter and the loss of love, going comes before gone, over and over the point is missed and still the blind will turns for its target.

4.

In my imagination I was the pivot of a fresh beginning.

In rafts they came over the sea; on the island they put up those stones by methods we can only guess at.

If the vegetation grows as thick as this, how can we see what they were seeing?

It is all being made clear, with bulldozers, at Angkor Wat.

The verdure was a false mystery; the baring of the stones is no solution for us now.

Defoliation progresses; concrete is poured, sheets of glass hauled overland in huge trucks and at great cost.

Here we never travailed, never took off our shoes to walk the final mile.

Come and look into this cellar-hole; this is the foundling of the woods.

Humans lived here once; it became sacred only when they went away.

5.

Of simple choice they are the villagers; their clothes come with them like red clay roads they have been walking.

The sole of the foot is a map, the palm of the hand a letter,
learned by heart and worn close to the body.

They seemed strange to me, till I began to recall their dialect.

Poking the spade into the dry loam, listening for the tick of
broken pottery, hoarding the brown and black bits in a dented can.

Evenings, at the table, turning the findings out, pushing them
around with a finger, beginning to dream of fitting them together.

Hiding all this work from them, although they might have helped
me.

Going up at night, hiding the tin can in a closet, where the
linoleum lies in shatters on a back shelf.

Sleeping to dream of the unformed, the veil of water pouring over
the wet clay, the rhythms of choice, the lost methods.

6.

You are beside me like a wall; I touch you with my fingers and
keep moving through the bad light.

At this time of year when faces turn aside, it is amazing that your
eyes are to be met.

A bad light is one like this, that flickers and diffuses itself along
the edge of a frontier.

No, I don't invest you with anything; I am counting on your
weakness as much as on your strength.

This light eats away at the clarities I had fixed on; it moves up like a rodent at the edge of the raked paths.

Your clarities may not reach me; but your attention will.

It is to know that I too have no mythic powers; it is to see the liability of all my treasures.

You will have to see all this for a long time alone.

You are beside me like a wall; I touch you with my fingers and keep trying to move through the bad light.

7.

Picking the wax to crumbs in the iron lip of the candelabrum.

Fingering down the thread of the maze where the green strand cuts across the violent strand.

Picking apart the strands of pain; a warp of wool dipped in burning wax.

When the flame shrinks to a blue bead, there is danger; the change of light in a flickering situation.

Stretched on the loom the light expands; the smell of a smell of burning.

When the change leaves you dark, when the wax cools in the socket, when I thought I prayed, when I was talking to myself under the cover of my darkness.

Someone who never said, "What do you feel?" someone who sat across from me, taking the crumbs of wax as I picked them apart and handed them over.

PART II: 3–7/70

8.

For Hugh Seidman

A woman waking behind grimed blinds slatted across a courtyard
she never looks into.

Thinking of the force of a waterfall, the slash of cold air from the
thickest water of the falls, slicing the green and ochre afternoon in
which he turns his head and walks away.

Thinking of that place as an existence.

A woman reaching for the glass of water left all night on the bureau,
the half-done poem, the immediate relief.

Entering the poem as a method of leaving the room.

Entering the paper airplane of the poem, which somewhere before
its destination starts curling into ash and comes apart.

The woman is too heavy for the poem, she is a swollenness, a foot,
an arm, gone asleep, grown absurd and out of bounds.

Rooted to memory like a wedge in a block of wood; she takes the
pressure of her thought but cannot resist it.

You call this a poetry of false problems, the shotgun wedding of the
mind, the subversion of choice by language.

Instead of the alternative: to pull the sooty strings to set the
window bare to purge the room with light to feel the sun breaking
in on the courtyard and the steamheat smothering in the shut-off
pipes.

To feel existence as this time, this place, the pathos and force
of the lumps of snow gritted and melting in the unloved corners of
the courtyard.

9. (Newsreel)

This would not be the war we fought in. See, the foliage is
heavier, there were no hills of that size there.

But I find it impossible not to look for actual persons known
to me and not seen since; impossible not to look for myself.

The scenery angers me, I know there is something wrong, the sun
is too high, the grass too trampled, the peasants' faces too broad,
and the main square of the capital had no arcades like those.

Yet the dead look right, and the roofs of the huts, and the crashed
fuselage burning among the ferns.

But this is not the war I came to see, buying my ticket, stumbling
through the darkness, finding my place among the sleepers and
masturbators in the dark.

I thought of seeing the General who cursed us, whose name they
gave to an expressway; I wanted to see the faces of the dead when
they were living.

Once I know they filmed us, back at the camp behind the lines,
taking showers under the trees and showing pictures of our girls.

Somewhere there is a film of the war we fought in, and it must
contain the flares, the souvenirs, the shadows of the netted brush,
the standing in line of the innocent, the hills that were not of
this size.

Somewhere my body goes taut under the deluge, somewhere I am naked behind the lines, washing my body in the water of that war.

Someone has that war stored up in metal canisters, a memory he cannot use, somewhere my innocence is proven with my guilt, but this would not be the war I fought in.

10.

For Valerie Glauber

They come to you with their descriptions of your soul.

They come and drop their mementoes at the foot of your bed; their feathers, ferns, fans, grasses from the western mountains.

They wait for you to unfold for them like a paper flower, a secret springing open in a glass of water.

They believe your future has a history and that it is themselves.

They have family trees to plant for you, photographs of dead children, old bracelets and rings they want to fasten onto you.

And, in spite of this, you live alone.

Your secret hangs in the open like Poe's purloined letter; their longing and their methods will never let them find it.

Your secret cries out in the dark and hushes; when they start out of sleep they think you are innocent.

You hang among them like the icon in a Russian play; living your own intenser life behind the lamp they light in front of you.

You are spilt here like mercury on a marble counter, liquefying into many globes, each silvered like a planet caught in a lens.

You are a mirror lost in a brook, an eye reflecting a torrent of reflections.

You are a letter written, folded, burnt to ash, and mailed in an envelope to another continent.

11.

The mare's skeleton in the clearing: another sign of life.

When you pull the embedded bones up from the soil, the flies collect again.

The pelvis, the open archway, staring at me like an eye.

In the desert these bones would be burnt white; a green bloom grows on them in the woods.

Did she break her leg or die of poison?

What was it like when the scavengers came?

So many questions unanswered, yet the statement is here and clear.

With what joy you handled the skull, set back the teeth spilt in the grass, hinged back the jaw on the jaw.

With what joy we left the woods, swinging our sticks, miming the speech of noble savages, of the fathers of our country, bursting into the full sun of the uncut field.

12.

I was looking for a way out of a lifetime's consolations.

We walked in the wholesale district: closed warehouses, windows, steeped in sun.

I said: those cloths are very old. You said: they have lain in that window a long time.

When the skeletons of the projects shut off the sunset, when the sense of the Hudson leaves us, when only by loss of light in the east do I know that I am living in the west.

When I give up being paraphrased, when I let go, when the beautiful solutions in their crystal flasks have dried up in the sun, when the lightbulb bursts on lighting, when the dead bulb rattles like a seed-pod.

Those cloths are very old, they are mummies' cloths, they have lain in graves, they were not intended to be sold, the tragedy of this mistake will soon be clear.

Vacillant needles of Manhattan, describing hour & weather; buying these descriptions at the cost of missing every other point.

13.

We are driven to odd attempts; once it would not have occurred to me to put out in a boat, not on a night like this.

Still, it was an instrument, and I had pledged myself to try any instrument that came my way. Never to refuse one from conviction of incompetence.

A long time I was simply learning to handle the skiff; I had no special training and my own training was against me.

I had always heard that darkness and water were a threat.

In spite of this, darkness and water helped me to arrive here.

I watched the lights on the shore I had left for a long time; each one, it seemed to me, was a light I might have lit, in the old days.

14.

Whatever it was: the grains of the glacier caked in the boot-cleats; ashes spilled on white formica.

The death-col viewed through power-glasses; the cube of ice melting on stainless steel.

Whatever it was, the image that stopped you, the one on which you came to grief, projecting it over & over on empty walls.

Now to give up the temptations of the projector; to see instead the web of cracks filtering across the plaster.

To read there the map of the future, the roads radiating from the initial split, the filaments thrown out from that impasse.

To reread the instructions on your palm; to find there how the lifeline, broken, keeps its direction.

To read the etched rays of the bullet-hole left years ago in the glass; to know in every distortion of the light what fracture is.

To put the prism in your pocket, the thin glass lens, the map
of the inner city, the little book with gridded pages.

To pull yourself up by your own roots; to eat the last meal in your old
neighborhood.

DIVING INTO THE WRECK

WRECK

(1971–1972)

I

Perhaps my life is nothing but an image of this kind; perhaps I am doomed to retrace my steps under the illusion that I am exploring, doomed to try and learn what I should simply recognize, learning a mere fraction of what I have forgotten.

—André Breton, *Nadja*

There is no private life which is not determined by a wider public life.

—George Eliot

TRYING TO TALK WITH A MAN

Out in this desert we are testing bombs,

that's why we came here.

Sometimes I feel an underground river
forcing its way between deformed cliffs
an acute angle of understanding
moving itself like a locus of the sun
into this condemned scenery.

What we've had to give up to get here—
whole LP collections, films we starred in
playing in the neighborhoods, bakery windows
full of dry, chocolate-filled Jewish cookies,
the language of love-letters, of suicide notes,
afternoons on the riverbank
pretending to be children

Coming out to this desert
we meant to change the face of
driving among dull green succulents
walking at noon in the ghost town
surrounded by a silence

that sounds like the silence of the place
except that it came with us
and is familiar
and everything we were saying until now
was an effort to blot it out—
Coming out here we are up against it

Out here I feel more helpless
with you than without you
You mention the danger
and list the equipment

we talk of people caring for each other
in emergencies—laceration, thirst—
but you look at me like an emergency

Your dry heat feels like power
your eyes are stars of a different magnitude
they reflect lights that spell out: EXIT
when you get up and pace the floor

talking of the danger
as if it were not ourselves
as if we were testing anything else.

1971

WHEN WE DEAD AWAKEN

For E.Y.

1.   Trying to tell you how
       the anatomy of the park
       through stained panes, the way
       guerrillas are advancing
       through minefields, the trash
       burning endlessly in the dump
       to return to heaven like a stain—
       everything outside our skins is an image
       of this affliction:
       stones on my table, carried by hand
       from scenes I trusted
       souvenirs of what I once described
       as happiness
       everything outside my skin
       speaks of the fault that sends me limping

even the scars of my decisions
even the sunblaze in the mica-vein
even you, fellow-creature, sister,
sitting across from me, dark with love,
working like me to pick apart
working with me to remake
this trailing knitted thing, this cloth of darkness,
this woman's garment, trying to save the skein.

2.   The fact of being separate
enters your livelihood like a piece of furniture
—a chest of seventeenth-century wood
from somewhere in the North.
It has a huge lock shaped like a woman's head
but the key has not been found.
In the compartments are other keys
to lost doors, an eye of glass.
Slowly you begin to add
things of your own.
You come and go reflected in its panels.
You give up keeping track of anniversaries,
you begin to write in your diaries
more honestly than ever.

3.   The lovely landscape of southern Ohio
betrayed by strip mining, the
thick gold band on the adulterer's finger
the blurred programs of the offshore pirate station
are causes for hesitation.
Here in the matrix of need and anger, the
disproof of what we thought possible
failures of medication
doubts of another's existence
—tell it over and over, the words
get thick with unmeaning—
yet never have we been closer to the truth

of the lies we were living, listen to me:
the faithfulness I can imagine would be a weed
flowering in tar, a blue energy piercing
the massed atoms of a bedrock disbelief.

1971

WAKING IN THE DARK

1.

The thing that arrests me is
    how we are composed of molecules

    (he showed me the figure in the paving stones)

    arranged without our knowledge and consent

        like the wirephoto composed
        of millions of dots

        in which the man from Bangladesh
        walks starving
            on the front page
            knowing nothing about it

        which is his presence for the world

2.

We were standing in line outside of something
two by two, or alone in pairs, or simply alone,

looking into windows full of scissors,
windows full of shoes. The street was closing,
the city was closing, would we be the lucky ones
to make it? They were showing
in a glass case, the Man Without A Country.
We held up our passports in his face, we wept for him.

They are dumping animal blood into the sea
to bring up the sharks. Sometimes every
aperture of my body
leaks blood. I don't know whether
to pretend that this is natural.
Is there a law about this, a law of nature?
You worship the blood
you call it hysterical bleeding
you want to drink it like milk
you dip your finger into it and write
you faint at the smell of it
you dream of dumping me into the sea.

3.

The tragedy of sex
lies around us, a woodlot
the axes are sharpened for.
The old shelters and huts
stare through the clearing with a certain resolution
—the hermit's cabin, the hunters' shack—
scenes of masturbation
and dirty jokes.
A man's world. But finished.
They themselves have sold it to the machines.
I walk the unconscious forest,
a woman dressed in old army fatigues
that have shrunk to fit her, I am lost
at moments, I feel dazed

by the sun pawing between the trees,
cold in the bog and lichen of the thicket.
Nothing will save this. I am alone,
kicking the last rotting logs
with their strange smell of life, not death,
wondering what on earth it all might have become.

4.

Clarity,
            spray

blinding and purging

spears of sun striking the water

the bodies riding the air
like gliders

the bodies in slow motion

falling
into the pool
at the Berlin Olympics

control; loss of control

the bodies rising
arching back to the tower
time reeling backward

clarity of open air
before the dark chambers
with the shower-heads

the bodies falling again
freely

          faster than light
the water opening
like air
like realization

A woman made this film
against

the law
of gravity

5.

All night dreaming of a body
space weighs on differently from mine
We are making love in the street
the traffic flows off from us
pouring back like a sheet
the asphalt stirs with tenderness
there is no dismay
we move together like underwater plants

Over and over, starting to wake
I dive back to discover you
still whispering, *touch me,* we go on
streaming through the slow
citylight forest ocean
stirring our body hair

But this is the saying of a dream
on waking
I wish there were somewhere

actual we could stand
handing the power-glasses back and forth
looking at the earth, the wildwood
where the split began

1971

INCIPIENCE

1.   To live, to lie awake
under scarred plaster
while ice is forming over the earth
at an hour when nothing can be done
to further any decision

to know the composing of the thread
inside the spider's body
first atoms of the web
visible tomorrow

to feel the fiery future
of every matchstick in the kitchen

Nothing can be done
but by inches. I write out my life
hour by hour, word by word
gazing into the anger of old women on the bus
numbering the striations
of air inside the ice cube
imagining the existence
of something uncreated
this poem
our lives

2.   A man is asleep in the next room
           We are his dreams
           We have the heads and breasts of women
           the bodies of birds of prey
           Sometimes we turn into silver serpents
    While we sit up smoking and talking of how to live
    he turns on the bed and murmurs

    A man is asleep in the next room
           A neurosurgeon enters his dream
           and begins to dissect his brain
           She does not look like a nurse
           she is absorbed in her work
           she has a stern, delicate face like Marie Curie
    She is not/might be either of us

    A man is asleep in the next room
           He has spent a whole day
           standing, throwing stones into the black pool
           which keeps its blackness
Outside the frame of his dream we are stumbling up the hill
    hand in hand, stumbling and guiding each other
    over the scarred volcanic rock

1971

AFTER TWENTY YEARS
For A.P.C.

Two women sit at a table by a window. Light breaks
unevenly on both of them.
Their talk is a striking of sparks
which passers-by in the street observe
as a glitter in the glass of that window.

Two women in the prime of life.
Their babies are old enough to have babies.
Loneliness has been part of their story for twenty years,
the dark edge of the clever tongue,
the obscure underside of the imagination.
It is snow and thunder in the street.
While they speak the lightning flashes purple.
it is strange to be so many women,
eating and drinking at the same table,
those who bathed their children in the same basin
who kept their secrets from each other
walked the floors of their lives in separate rooms
and flow into history now as the woman of their time
living in the prime of life
as in a city where nothing is forbidden
and nothing permanent.

1971

THE MIRROR IN WHICH TWO ARE SEEN AS ONE

1.

She is the one you call sister.
Her simplest act has glamour,
as when she scales a fish the knife
flashes in her long fingers
no motion wasted or when
rapidly talking of love
she steel-wool burnishes
the battered kettle

Love-apples cramp you sideways
with sudden emptiness
the cereals glutting you, the grains
ripe clusters picked by hand
Love: the refrigerator
with open door
the ripe steaks bleeding
their hearts out in plastic film
the whipped butter, the apricots
the sour leftovers

A crate is waiting in the orchard
for you to fill it
your hands are raw with scraping
the sharp bark, the thorns
of this succulent tree
Pick, pick, pick
this harvest is a failure
the juice runs down your cheekbones
like sweat or tears

2.

She is the one you call sister
you blaze like lightning about the room
flicker around her like fire
dazzle yourself in her wide eyes
listing her unfelt needs
thrusting the tenets of your life
into her hands

She moves through a world of India print
her body dappled
with softness, the paisley swells at her hip
walking the street in her cotton shift

buying fresh figs because you love them
photographing the ghetto because you took her there

Why are you crying dry up your tears
we are sisters
words fail you in the stare of her hunger
you hand her another book
scored by your pencil
you hand her a record
of two flutes in India reciting

3.

Late summer night the insects
fry in the yellowed lightglobe
your skin burns gold in its light
In this mirror, who are you? Dreams of the nunnery
with its discipline, the nursery
with its nurse, the hospital
where all the powerful ones are masked
the graveyard where you sit on the graves
of women who died in childbirth
and women who died at birth

Dreams of your sister's birth
your mother dying in childbirth over and over
not knowing how to stop
bearing you over and over

your mother dead and you unborn
your two hands grasping your head
drawing it down against the blade of life
your nerves the nerves of a midwife
learning her trade

1971

FROM THE PRISON HOUSE

Underneath my lids another eye has opened
it looks nakedly
at the light

that soaks in from the world of pain
even when I sleep

Steadily it regards
everything I am going through

and more

it sees the clubs and rifle-butts
rising and falling
it sees

detail not on TV

the fingers of the policewoman
searching the cunt of the young prostitute
it sees

the roaches dropping into the pan
where they cook the pork
in the House of D

it sees
the violence
embedded in silence

This eye
is not for weeping
its vision
must be unblurred

though tears are on my face

its intent is clarity
it must forget
nothing

September 1971

THE STRANGER

Looking as I've looked before, straight down the heart
of the street to the river
walking the rivers of the avenues
feeling the shudder of the caves beneath the asphalt
watching the lights turn on in the towers
walking as I've walked before
like a man, like a woman, in the city
my visionary anger cleansing my sight
and the detailed perceptions of mercy
flowering from that anger

if I come into a room out of the sharp misty light
and hear them talking a dead language
if they ask me my identity
what can I say but
I am the androgyne
I am the living mind you fail to describe
in your dead language
the lost noun, the verb surviving
only in the infinitive
the letters of my name are written under the lids
of the newborn child

1972

SONG

You're wondering if I'm lonely:
OK then, yes, I'm lonely
as a plane rides lonely and level
on its radio beam, aiming
across the Rockies
for the blue-strung aisles
of an airfield on the ocean

You want to ask, am I lonely?
Well, of course, lonely
as a woman driving across country
day after day, leaving behind
mile after mile
little towns she might have stopped
and lived and died in, lonely

If I'm lonely
it must be the loneliness
of waking first, of breathing
dawn's first cold breath on the city
of being the one awake
in a house wrapped in sleep

If I'm lonely
it's with the rowboat ice-fast on the shore
in the last red light of the year
that knows what it is, that knows it's neither
ice nor mud nor winter light
but wood, with a gift for burning

1971

DIALOGUE

She sits with one hand poised against her head, the
other turning an old ring to the light
for hours our talk has beaten
like rain against the screens
a sense of August and heat-lightning
I get up, go to make tea, come back
we look at each other
then she says (and this is what I live through
over and over)—she says: *I do not know*
if sex is an illusion

I do not know
who I was when I did those things
or who I said I was
or whether I willed to feel
what I had read about
or who in fact was there with me
or whether I knew, even then
that there was doubt about these things

1972

DIVING INTO THE WRECK

First having read the book of myths,
and loaded the camera,
and checked the edge of the knife-blade,
I put on
the body-armor of black rubber
the absurd flippers
the grave and awkward mask.

I am having to do this
not like Cousteau with his
assiduous team
aboard the sun-flooded schooner
but here alone.

There is a ladder.
The ladder is always there
hanging innocently
close to the side of the schooner.
We know what it is for,
we who have used it.
Otherwise
it's a piece of maritime floss
some sundry equipment.

I go down.
Rung after rung and still
the oxygen immerses me
the blue light
the clear atoms
of our human air.
I go down.
My flippers cripple me,
I crawl like an insect down the ladder
and there is no one
to tell me when the ocean
will begin.

First the air is blue and then
it is bluer and then green and then
black I am blacking out and yet
my mask is powerful
it pumps my blood with power
the sea is another story
the sea is not a question of power

I have to learn alone
to turn my body without force
in the deep element.

And now: it is easy to forget
what I came for
among so many who have always
lived here
swaying their crenellated fans
between the reefs
and besides
you breathe differently down here.

I came to explore the wreck.
The words are purposes.
The words are maps.
I came to see the damage that was done
and the treasures that prevail.
I stroke the beam of my lamp
slowly along the flank
of something more permanent
than fish or weed

the thing I came for:
the wreck and not the story of the wreck
the thing itself and not the myth
the drowned face always staring
toward the sun
the evidence of damage
worn by salt and sway into this threadbare beauty
the ribs of the disaster
curving their assertion
among the tentative haunters.

This is the place.
And I am here, the mermaid whose dark hair
streams black, the merman in his armored body
We circle silently
about the wreck
we dive into the hold.
I am she: I am he

whose drowned face sleeps with open eyes
whose breasts still bear the stress
whose silver, copper, vermeil cargo lies
obscurely inside barrels
half-wedged and left to rot
we are the half-destroyed instruments
that once held to a course
the water-eaten log
the fouled compass

We are, I am, you are
by cowardice or courage
the one who find our way
back to this scene
carrying a knife, a camera
a book of myths
in which
our names do not appear.

1972

II

The Phenomenology
of Anger

THE PHENOMENOLOGY OF ANGER

1. The freedom of the wholly mad
to smear & play with her madness
write with her fingers dipped in it
the length of a room

which is not, of course, the freedom
you have, walking on Broadway
to stop & turn back or go on
10 blocks; 20 blocks

but feels enviable maybe
to the compromised

curled in the placenta of the real
which was to feed & which is strangling her.

2. Trying to light a log that's lain in the damp
as long as this house has stood:
even with dry sticks I can't get started
even with thorns.
I twist last year into a knot of old headlines
—this rose won't bloom.

How does a pile of rags the machinist wiped his hands on
feel in its cupboard, hour upon hour?
Each day during the heat-wave
they took the temperature of the haymow.
I huddled fugitive
in the warm sweet simmer of the hay

muttering: *Come.*

3. Flat heartland of winter.
The moonmen come back from the moon
the firemen come out of the fire.
Time without a taste: time without decisions.

Self-hatred, a monotone in the mind.
The shallowness of a life lived in exile
even in the hot countries.
Cleaver, staring into a window full of knives.

4. White light splits the room.
Table.   Window.   Lampshade.   You.

My hands, sticky in a new way.
Menstrual blood
seeming to leak from your side.

Will the judges try to tell me
which was the blood of whom?

5. Madness.   Suicide.   Murder.
Is there no way out but these?
The enemy, always just out of sight
snowshoeing the next forest, shrouded
in a snowy blur, abominable snowman
—at once the most destructive
and the most elusive being
gunning down the babies at My Lai
vanishing in the face of confrontation.

The prince of air and darkness
computing body counts, masturbating
in the factory
of facts.

6. Fantasies of murder: not enough:
to kill is to cut off from pain
but the killer goes on hurting

Not enough. When I dream of meeting
the enemy, this is my dream:

white acetylene
ripples from my body
effortlessly released
perfectly trained
on the true enemy

raking his body down to the thread
of existence
burning away his lie
leaving him in a new
world; a changed
man

7. I suddenly see the world
as no longer viable:
you are out there burning the crops
with some new sublimate
This morning you left the bed
we still share
and went out to spread impotence
upon the world

I hate you.
I hate the mask you wear, your eyes
assuming a depth
they do not possess, drawing me
into the grotto of your skull
the landscape of bone
I hate your words
they make me think of fake

revolutionary bills
crisp imitation parchment
they sell at battlefields.

Last night, in this room, weeping
I asked you: *what are you feeling?*
do you feel anything?

Now in the torsion of your body
as you defoliate the fields we lived from
I have your answer.

8. Dogeared earth. Wormeaten moon.
A pale cross-hatching of silver
lies like a wire screen on the black
water. All these phenomena
are temporary.

I would have loved to live in a world
of women and men gaily
in collusion with green leaves, stalks,
building mineral cities, transparent domes,
little huts of woven grass
each with its own pattern—
a conspiracy to coexist
with the Crab Nebula, the exploding
universe, the Mind—

9. *The only real love I have ever felt*
was for children and other women.
Everything else was lust, pity,
self-hatred, pity, lust.
This is a woman's confession.
Now, look again at the face
of Botticelli's Venus, Kali,
the Judith of Chartres
with her so-called smile.

10. how we are burning up our lives
testimony:

> the subway
> hurtling to Brooklyn
> her head on her knees
> asleep or drugged

la vía del tren subterráneo
es peligrosa

> many sleep
> the whole way
> others sit
> staring holes of fire into the air
> others plan rebellion:
> night after night
> awake in prison, my mind
> licked at the mattress like a flame
> till the cellblock went up roaring

> Thoreau setting fire to the woods

Every act of becoming conscious
(it says here in this book)
is an unnatural act

1972

III

I saw a beggar leaning on his crutch,
He said to me: Why do you ask for so much?
I saw a woman leaning on a door,
She said, Why not, why not, why not ask for more?

—Leonard Cohen's "Bird on the Wire"
(as sung by Judy Collins)

MERCED

Fantasies of old age:
they have rounded us up
in a rest-camp for the outworn.
Somewhere in some dustbowl
a barbed-wire cantonment
of low-cost dustcolored prefab
buildings, smelling of shame
and hopeless incontinence
identical clothes of disposable
paper, identical rations
of chemically flavored food
Death in order, by gas,
hypodermics daily
to neutralize despair
So I imagine my world
in my seventieth year alive
and outside the barbed wire
a purposeless exchange
of consciousness for the absence
of pain. We will call this life.

Yet only last summer I
burned my feet in the sand
of that valley traced by the thread
of the cold quick river Merced
watered by plummets of white
When I swam, my body ached
from the righteous cold
when I lay back floating the jays
flittered from pine to pine
and the shade moved hour by hour
across El Capitan
Our wine cooled in the water

and I watched my sons, half-men
half-children, testing their part
in a world almost archaic
so precious by this time
that merely to step in pure water
or stare into clear air
is to feel a spasm of pain.

For weeks now a rage
has possessed my body, driving
now out upon men and women
now inward upon myself
Walking Amsterdam Avenue
I find myself in tears
without knowing which thought
forced water to my eyes
To speak to another human
becomes a risk
I think of Norman Morrison
the Buddhists of Saigon
the black teacher last week
who put himself to death
to waken guilt in hearts
too numb to get the message
in a world masculinity made
unfit for women or men
Taking off in a plane
I look down at the city
which meant life to me, not death
and think that somewhere there
a cold center, composed
of pieces of human beings
metabolized, restructured
by a process they do not feel
is spreading in our midst
and taking over our minds

a thing that feels neither guilt
nor rage: that is unable
to hate, therefore to love.

1972

A PRIMARY GROUND

> But he must have more than that. It was sympathy he wanted, to be
> assured of his genius, first of all, and then to be taken within the circle
> of life, warmed and soothed, to have his sense restored to him, his bar-
> renness made fertile, and all the rooms of the house made full of life . . .
>
> —Virginia Woolf, *To the Lighthouse*

And this is how you live: a woman, children
protect you from the abyss
you move near, turning on the news
eating Thanksgiving with its pumpkin teeth
drinking the last wine
from the cellar of your wedding

It all seems innocent enough, this sin
of wedlock: you, your wife, your children
leaning across the unfilled plates
passing the salt
down a cloth ironed by a woman
with aching legs
Now they go out to play
in the coarse, rough November air
that smells of soft-coal smoke, the river,
burnt sweet-potato pie.

Sensuality dessicates in words—
risks of the portage, risks of the glacier
never taken
Protection is the genius of your house
the pressure of the steam iron
flattens the linen cloth again
chestnuts puréed with care are dutifully eaten
in every room the furniture reflects you
larger than life, or dwindling

Emptiness
thrust like a batch of letters to the furthest
dark of a drawer
But there is something else:
your wife's twin sister, speechless
is dying in the house
You and your wife take turns
carrying up the trays,
understanding her case, trying to make her understand.

1972

TRANSLATIONS

You show me the poems of some woman
my age, or younger
translated from your language

Certain words occur: *enemy, oven, sorrow*
enough to let me know
she's a woman of my time

obsessed

with Love, our subject:
we've trained it like ivy to our walls
baked it like bread in our ovens
worn it like lead on our ankles
watched it through binoculars as if
it were a helicopter
bringing food to our famine
or the satellite
of a hostile power

I begin to see that woman
doing things: stirring rice
ironing a skirt
typing a manuscript till dawn

trying to make a call
from a phonebooth

The phone rings unanswered
in a man's bedroom
she hears him telling someone else
Never mind. She'll get tired.
hears him telling her story to her sister

who becomes her enemy
and will in her own time
light her own way to sorrow

ignorant of the fact this way of grief
is shared, unnecessary
and political

1972

LIVING IN THE CAVE

Reading the Parable of the Cave
While living in the cave,

                         black moss
deadening my footsteps
candles stuck on rock-ledges
weakening my eyes

These things around me, with their
daily requirements:

                    fill me, empty me
talk to me, warm me, let me
suck on you

Every one of them has a plan that depends on me

stalactites want to become
stalagmites
veins of ore
imagine their preciousness

candles see themselves disembodied
into gas
and taking flight

the bat hangs dreaming
of an airy world

None of them, not one
sees me
as I see them

1972

THE NINTH SYMPHONY
OF BEETHOVEN UNDERSTOOD AT LAST
AS A SEXUAL MESSAGE

A man in terror of impotence
or infertility, not knowing the difference
a man trying to tell something
howling from the climacteric
music of the entirely
isolated soul
yelling at Joy from the tunnel of the ego
music without the ghost
of another person in it, music
trying to tell something the man
does not want out, would keep if he could
gagged and bound and flogged with chords of Joy
where everything is silence and the
beating of a bloody fist upon
a splintered table

1972

RAPE

There is a cop who is both prowler and father:
he comes from your block, grew up with your brothers,
had certain ideals.
You hardly know him in his boots and silver badge,
on horseback, one hand touching his gun.

You hardly know him but you have to get to know him:
he has access to machinery that could kill you.
He and his stallion clop like warlords among the trash,
his ideals stand in the air, a frozen cloud
from between his unsmiling lips.

And so, when the time comes, you have to turn to him,
the maniac's sperm still greasing your thighs,
your mind whirling like crazy. You have to confess
to him, you are guilty of the crime
of having been forced.

And you see his blue eyes, the blue eyes of all the family
whom you used to know, grow narrow and glisten,
his hand types out the details
and he wants them all
but the hysteria in your voice pleases him best.

You hardly know him but now he thinks he knows you:
he has taken down your worst moment
on a machine and filed it in a file.
He knows, or thinks he knows, how much you imagined;
he knows, or thinks he knows, what you secretly wanted.

He has access to machinery that could get you put away:
and if, in the sickening light of the precinct,
and if, in the sickening light of the precinct,
your details sound like a portrait of your confessor,
will you swallow, will you deny them, will you lie your way home?

1972

BURNING ONESELF IN

In a bookstore on the East Side
I read a veteran's testimony:

the running down, for no reason
of an old woman in South Vietnam
by a U.S. Army truck

The heat-wave is over
Lifeless, sunny, the East Side
rests under its awnings

Another summer
The flames go on feeding

and a dull heat permeates the ground
of the mind, the burn has settled in
as if it had no more question

of its right to go on devouring
the rest of a lifetime,
the rest of history

Pieces of information, like this one
blow onto the heap

they keep it fed, whether we will it or not,
another summer, and another
of suffering quietly

in bookstores, in the parks
however we may scream we are
suffering quietly

1972

BURNING ONESELF OUT

For E.K.

We can look into the stove tonight
as into a mirror, yes,

the serrated log, the yellow-blue
gaseous core

the crimson-flittered grey ash, yes,
I know inside my eyelids
and underneath my skin

Time takes hold of us like a draft
upward, drawing at the heats
in the belly, in the brain

You told me of setting your hand
into the print of a long-dead Indian
and for a moment, I knew that hand,

that print, that rock,
that sun producing powerful dreams
A word can do this

or, as tonight, the mirror of the fire
of my mind, burning as if it could go on
burning itself, burning down

feeding on everything
till there is nothing in life
that has not fed that fire

1972

FOR A SISTER

Natalya Gorbanevskaya, two years incarcerated in a Soviet penal mental asylum for
her political activism; and others

I trust none of them. Only my existence
thrown out in the world like a towchain
battered and twisted in many chance connections,
being pulled this way, pulling in that.

I have to steal the sense of dust on your floor,
milk souring in your pantry
after they came and took you.
I'm forced to guess at the look you threw backward.

A few paragraphs in the papers,
allowing for printers' errors, wilful omissions,
the trained violence of doctors.
I don't trust them, but I'm learning how to use them.

Little by little out of the blurred conjectures
your face clears, a sunken marble
slowly cranked up from underwater.
I feel the ropes straining under their load of despair.

They searched you for contraband, they made their notations.
A look of intelligence could get you twenty years.
Better to trace nonexistent circles with your finger,
try to imitate the smile of the permanently dulled.

My images. This metaphor for what happens.
A geranium in flames on a green cloth
becomes yours. You, coming home after years
to light the stove, get out the typewriter and begin again. Your story.

1972

FOR THE DEAD

I dreamed I called you on the telephone
to say: *Be kinder to yourself*
but you were sick and would not answer

The waste of my love goes on this way
trying to save you from yourself

I have always wondered about the leftover
energy, water rushing down a hill
long after the rains have stopped

or the fire you want to go to bed from
but cannot leave, burning-down but not burnt-down
the red coals more extreme, more curious
in their flashing and dying
than you wish they were
sitting there long after midnight

1972

FROM A SURVIVOR

The pact that we made was the ordinary pact
of men & women in those days

I don't know who we thought we were
that our personalities
could resist the failures of the race

Lucky or unlucky, we didn't know
the race had failures of that order
and that we were going to share them

Like everybody else, we thought of ourselves as special

Your body is as vivid to me
as it ever was: even more

since my feeling for it is clearer:
I know what it could do and could not do

it is no longer
the body of a god
or anything with power over my life

Next year it would have been 20 years
and you are wastefully dead
who might have made the leap
we talked, too late, of making

which I live now
not as a leap
but a succession of brief, amazing movements

each one making possible the next

1972

AUGUST

Two horses in yellow light
eating windfall apples under a tree

as summer tears apart   milkweeds stagger
and grasses grow more ragged

They say there are ions in the sun
neutralizing magnetic fields on earth

Some way to explain
what this week has been, and the one before it!

If I am flesh sunning on rock
if I am brain burning in fluorescent light

if I am dream like a wire with fire
throbbing along it

if I am death to man
I have to know it

His mind is too simple, I cannot go on
sharing his nightmares

My own are becoming clearer, they open
into prehistory

which looks like a village lit with blood
where all the fathers are crying: *My son is mine!*

1972

IV

Meditations for a Savage Child

MEDITATIONS FOR A SAVAGE CHILD

The prose passages are from J.-M. Itard's account of *The Wild Boy of Aveyron*,
as translated by G. and M. Humphrey.

I

*There was a profound indifference to the objects of our pleasures and of our ficti-
tious needs; there was still . . . so intense a passion for the freedom of the fields
. . . that he would certainly have escaped into the forest had not the most rigid
precautions been taken . . .*

In their own way, by their own lights
they tried to care for you
tried to teach you to care
for objects of their caring:

        glossed oak planks, glass
        whirled in a fire
        to impossible thinness

to teach you names
for things
you did not need

        muslin shirred against the sun
        linen on a sack of feathers
        locks, keys
        boxes with coins inside

they tried to make you feel
the importance of

        a piece of cowhide
        sewn around a bundle
        of leaves impressed with signs

to teach you language:
the thread their lives
were strung on

II

When considered from a more general and philosophic point of view, these scars
bear witness . . . against the feebleness and insufficiency of man when left
entirely to himself, and in favor of the resources of nature which . . . work openly
to repair and conserve that which she tends secretly to impair and destroy.

I keep thinking about the lesson of the human ear
which stands for music, which stands for balance—
or the cat's ear which I can study better
the whorls and ridges exposed
It seems a hint dropped about the inside of the skull
which I cannot see
lobe, zone, that part of the brain
which is pure survival

The most primitive part
I go back into at night
pushing the leathern curtain
with naked fingers
then
with naked body

There where every wound is registered
as scar tissue

A cave of scars!
ancient, archaic wallpaper
built up, layer on layer
from the earliest, dream-white
to yesterday's, a red-black scrawl
a red mouth slowly closing

Go back so far there is another language
go back far enough the language
is no longer personal

these scars bear witness
but whether to repair
or to destruction
I no longer know

III

*It is true that there is visible on the throat a very extended scar which might
throw some doubt upon the soundness of the underlying parts if one were not
reassured by the appearance of the scar . . .*

When I try to speak
my throat is cut
and, it seems, by his hand

The sounds I make are prehuman, radical
the telephone is always
ripped-out

and he sleeps on
Yet always the tissue
grows over, white as silk

hardly a blemish
maybe a hieroglyph for scream

Child, no wonder you never wholly
trusted your keepers

IV

*A hand with the will rather than the habit of crime had wished to make an
attempt on the life of this child . . . left for dead in the woods, he will have owed
the prompt recovery of his wound to the help of nature alone.*

In the 18th century infanticide
reaches epidemic proportions:
old prints attest to it: starving mothers
smothering babies in sleep
abandoning newborns in sleet
on the poorhouse steps
gin-blurred, setting fire to the room

I keep thinking of the flights we used to take
on the grapevine across the gully
littered with beer-bottles where dragonflies flashed
we were 10, 11 years old
wild little girls with boyish bodies
flying over the moist
shadow-mottled earth
till they warned us to stay away from there

Later they pointed out
the venetian blinds
of the abortionist's house
we shivered

Men can do things to you
was all they said

V

And finally, my Lord, looking at this long experiment . . . whether it be consid-
ered as the methodical education of a savage or as no more than the physical
and moral treatment of one of those creatures ill-favored by nature, rejected by
society and abandoned by medicine, the care that has been taken and ought
still to be taken of him, the changes that have taken place, and those that can
be hoped for, the voice of humanity, the interest inspired by such a desertion
and a destiny so strange—all these things recommend this extraordinary young

man to the attention of scientists, to the solicitude of administrators, and to the
protection of the government.

1.   The doctor in "Uncle Vanya":
        They will call us fools,
        blind, ignorant, they will
        despise us

        devourers of the forest
        leaving teeth of metal in every tree
        so the tree can neither grow
        nor be cut for lumber

        Does the primeval forest
        weep
        for its devourers

        does nature mourn
        our existence

        is the child with arms
        burnt to the flesh of its sides
        weeping eyelessly for man

2.   At the end of the distinguished doctor's
    lecture
    a young woman raises her hand:

        You have the power
        in your hands, you control our lives—
        why do you want our pity too?

        Why are men afraid
        why do you pity yourselves
        why do the administrators

lack solicitude, the government
refuse protection,

why should the wild child
weep for the scientists
why

1972

POEMS
(1973–1974)

DIEN BIEN PHU

A nurse on the battlefield
wounded herself, but working

    dreams
        that each man she touches
        is a human grenade
                an anti-personnel weapon
                that can explode in her arms

    How long
        can she go on like this
        putting mercy
        ahead of survival

She is walking
in a white dress stained
with earth and blood

            down a road lined
            with fields long
            given up   blasted

    cemeteries of one name
    or two

    A hand
juts out like barbed wire
it is terribly alone

if she takes it
        will it slash her wrists again

if she passes it by

       will she turn into a case
       of shell-shock, eyes
       glazed forever on the

              blank chart of
              amnesia

1973

ESSENTIAL RESOURCES

I don't know
how late it is. I'm writing
with a chewed blunted lead
under a bridge while snow blankets the city
or with a greasy ballpoint
the nurse left
in a ward of amnesiacs who can be trusted
not to take notes

You talk of a film we could make
with women's faces naked
of make-up, the mist of sweat
on a forehead, lips dry
the little bloodspot from a coldsore

I know the inmates are encouraged
to express themselves
I'm wondering how

I long to create something
that can't be used to keep us passive:
I want to write
a script about plumbing, how every pipe
is joined
to every other

the wash of pure water and sewage
side by side

or about the electrical system
a study of the sources of energy
till in the final shot
the whole screen goes dark
and the keepers of order are screaming

I forget
what year it is. I am thinking
of films we have made but cannot show
yet, films of the mind unfolding
and our faces, still young
sweated with desire and
premature clarity

1973

BLOOD-SISTER

For Cynthia

Shoring up the ocean. A railroad track
ran close to the coast for miles
through the potato-fields, bringing us
to summer. Weeds blur the ties,
sludge clots the beaches.

During the war, the shells we found—
salmon-and-silver coins
sand dollars dripping sand
like dust. We were dressed
in navy dotted-swiss dresses in the train
not to show the soot. Like dolls
we sat with our dolls in the station.

When did we begin to dress ourselves?

Now I'm wearing jeans spider-webbed
with creases, a black sweater bought years ago
worn almost daily since
the ocean has undergone a tracheotomy
and lost its resonance
you wear a jersey the color of
Navaho turquoise and sand
you are holding a naked baby girl
she laughs into your eyes
we sit at your table drinking coffee
light flashes off unwashed sheetglass
you are more beautiful than you have ever been

we talk of destruction and creation
ice fits itself around each twig of the lilac

like a fist of law and order
your imagination burns like a bulb in the frozen soil
the fierce shoots knock
at the roof of waiting

when summer comes the ocean may be closed for good
we will turn
to the desert
where survival
takes naked and fiery forms

1973

THE WAVE

For J.B.

To give you back this wave
I would have to give back
the black
spaces

fretted with film of spray,
darker and deeper than the mind
they are emblems of

Not only the creator fury
of the whitest churn

the caldron of all life
but the blankness underlying

Thinking of the sea I think of light
lacing, lancing the water
the blue knife of a radiant consciousness
bent by the waves of vision as it pierces
to the deepest grotto

And I think of those lives we tried to live
in our globed helmets, self-enclosed
bodies self-illumined gliding
safe from the turbulence

and how, miraculously, we failed

1973

RE-FORMING THE CRYSTAL

I am trying to imagine
how it feels to you
to want a woman

trying to hallucinate
desire
centered in a cock
focused like a burning-glass

desire without discrimination:
to want a woman like a fix

Desire: yes: the sudden knowledge, like coming out of 'flu, that the
body is sexual. Walking in the streets with that knowledge. That eve-
ning in the plane from Pittsburgh, fantasizing going to meet you.
Walking through the airport blazing with energy and joy. But know-

ing all along that you were not the source of that energy and joy; you were a man, a stranger, a name, a voice on the telephone, a friend; this desire was mine, this energy my energy; it could be used a hundred ways, and going to meet you could be one of them.

Tonight is a different kind of night.
I sit in the car, racing the engine,
calculating the thinness of the ice.
In my head I am already threading the beltways
that rim this city,
all the old roads that used to wander the country
having been lost.
Tonight I understand
my photo on the license is not me,
my
name on the marriage-contract was not mine.
If I remind you of my father's favorite daughter,
look again. The woman
I needed to call my mother
was silenced before I was born.

Tonight if the battery charges I want to take the car out on sheet-ice; I want to understand my fear both of the machine and of the accidents of nature. My desire for you is not trivial; I can compare it with the greatest of those accidents. But the energy it draws on might lead to racing a cold engine, cracking the frozen spiderweb, parachuting into the field of a poem wired with danger, or to a trip through gorges and canyons, into the cratered night of female memory, where delicately and with intense care the chieftainess inscribes upon the ribs of the volcano the name of the one she has chosen.

1973

THE FOURTH MONTH OF THE
LANDSCAPE ARCHITECT

It is asleep in my body.
For now, I am myself,
like anyone, like a man
whose body contains simply: itself.
I draw a too-big sweater
over my breasts, walk into the drafting-room
and stand there, balancing.
The sun sprays acid points of light
on the tools of my trade, the metal,
the edged instruments. My work has always been
with edges. For a while I listen:
will there be a knock, is the neighbor
so near me stirring behind his walls?
The neighbor is quiet. I am not
a body, I am no body, I am I,
a pair of hands ending in fingers
that think like a brain.
I draw a sheet of paper toward me
on the slanted drafting-table.
I start to imagine
plans for a house, a park
stretching in every direction to the horizon
which is no horizon
which is merely a circle of volcanoes.
I touch stylus, T-square, pens
of immeasurable fineness,
the hard-edge. I am I,
this India ink my rain
which can irrigate gardens, terraces
dissolve or project horizons
flowing like lava from the volcano of the inkpot
at the stirring of my mind.
A city waits at the back of my skull

eating its heart out to be born:
how design the first
city of the moon? how shall I see it
for all of us who are done
with enclosed spaces, purdah, the salon, the sweatshop loft,
the ingenuity of the cloister?
My mind flies at the moon
beating, a pale-green kite.
Something else is beating.
In my body.
Spaces fold in. I'm caught
in the enclosure of the crib my body
where every thought I think
simply loosens to life another life.

1973

THE ALLEGED MURDERESS
WALKING IN HER CELL

Nine months we conspired:
first in panic, then in a quieter dread,
finally an unfamiliar kind of peace.
In the new year voices began,
they said I'd helped beat a man to death,
even my lover said so.
You were no bigger than a cyst
then, a bead of life
lit from within.
I took that life in my hands
with mine; a key turned
and the voices shrank away.
Then began that whispered conversation

telling each other we were alive,
twins in the prison womb,
exchanging vows against the future.
Justice, they say, and clemency
installed our nursery in the house
of detention. I don't know what
it means, that we have each other.
Do they mean to—can they use you
against me? I walk up and down
more at peace than in any prison night
here or outside—
your warmth washing into my ribcage
your frail silken skull asleep against my throat
your anxious pleading stilled—
unable to remember
whether or not I ever killed
whether I ever lived
without this—the blue pulse of your life
with its blind stroke: *Not-Guilty*
fledging my twenty-one-year life
of unmeaning, my worthless life
they framed in their contempt.

1973

WHITE NIGHT

Light at a window. Someone up
at this snail-still hour.
We who work this way have often worked
in solitude. I've had to guess at her
sewing her skin together as I sew mine
though
with a different
stitch.

Dawn after dawn, this neighbor
burns like a candle
dragging her bedspread through the dark house
to her dark bed
her head
full of runes, syllables, refrains,
this accurate dreamer

sleepwalks the kitchen
like a white moth,
an elephant, a guilt.
Somebody tried to put her
to rest under an afghan
knitted with wools the color of grass and blood

but she has risen. Her lamplight
licks at the icy panes
and melts into the dawn.
They will never prevent her
who sleep the stone sleep of the past,
the sleep of the drugged.
One crystal second, I flash

an eye across the cold
unwrapping of light between us
into her darkness-lancing eye
—that's all. Dawn is the test, the agony
but we were meant to see it:
After this, we may sleep, my sister,
while the flames rise higher and higher, we can sleep.

1974

AMNESIA

I almost trust myself to know
when we're getting to that scene—
call it the snow-scene in *Citizen Kane:*

the mother handing over her son
the earliest American dream
shot in a black-and-white

where every flake of snow
is incandescent
with its own burden, adding-

up, always adding-up to the
cold blur of the past
But first there is the picture of the past

simple and pitiless as the deed
truly was
the putting-away of a childish thing

Becoming a man means leaving
someone, or something—
still, why

must the snow-scene blot itself out
the flakes come down so fast
so heavy, so unrevealing

over the something that gets left behind?

1974

FOR L.G.: UNSEEN FOR TWENTY YEARS

A blue-grained line circles a fragment of the mind
drawn in ancient crayon:
out of the blue, your tightstrung smile—

often in the first snow
that even here smells only of itself
even on this Broadway limped by cripples
and the self-despising
Still, in that smell, another snow,
another world: we're walking
grey boulevards traced with white
in Paris, the early 'fifties
of invincible ignorance:

or, a cold spring:
I clasp your hips on the bike
shearing the empty plain in March
teeth gritted in the wind
searching for Chartres:
we doze
in the boat-train

we who were friends and thought
women and men should be lovers

Your face: taut as a mask of wires, a fencer's mask
half-turned away, the one night, walking
the City of Love, so cold
we warmed our nerves with wine
at every all-night café
to keep on walking, talking
Your words have drifted back for twenty years:

I have to tell you—maybe I'm not a man—
I can't do it with women—but I'd like
to hold you, to know what it's like
to sleep and wake together—

the one night in all our weeks of talk
you talked of fear
     I wonder

what words of mine drift back to you?
Something like:
    But you're a man, I know it—
the swiftness of your mind is masculine—?

—some set-piece I'd learned to embroider
in my woman's education
while the needle scarred my hand?

Of course, you're a man. I like you. What else could you be?
what else, what else,
what bloody else . . .

Given the cruelty of our times and customs,
maybe you hate these memories,
the ignorance, the innocence we shared:
maybe you cruise the SoHo cocktail parties
the Vancouver bar-scene
stalking yourself as I can see you still:
young, tense, amorphous, longing—

maybe you live out your double life
in the Berkeley hills, with a wife
who stuns her mind into indifference
with Scotch and saunas
while you arrange your own humiliations
downtown

(and, yes, I've played my scenes
of favorite daughter, child-bride, token woman, muse
listening now and then
as a drunken poet muttered into my hair:
I can't make it with women I admire—)

maybe you've found or fought
through to a kind of faithfulness
in the strange coexistence
of two of any gender

But we were talking in 1952
of the fear of being cripples in a world
of perfect women and men:
we were the givens and the stake
and we did badly

and, dear heart, I know, had a lover gestured
you'd have left me
for a man, as I left you,
as we left each other, seeking the love of men.

1974

FAMILY ROMANCE

(the brothers speak)

Our mother went away and our father was the king
always absent at the wars

We had to make it together or not at all
in the black forest

cutting paths, stumbling on the witch's house
long empty

gathering wood and mushrooms, gathering everything
we needed in a wordless collusion

Sometimes we pretended the witch had been our mother
and would come back

we loved each other with a passion understood
like the great roots of the wood

In another country we might have fought each other
and died of fraternal wounds

conspiring each alone for the father's blessing,
the birthright, the mother

Since we had no father to bless us, we were free
and our birthright was each other

our life was harsh and simple; we slept deeply
and we thought our mother came and watched us sleeping

1974

FROM AN OLD HOUSE IN AMERICA

1.

Deliberately, long ago
the carcasses

of old bugs crumbled
into the rut of the window

and we started sleeping here
Fresh June bugs batter this June's

screens, June-lightning batters
the spiderweb

I sweep the wood-dust
from the wood-box

the snout of the vacuum cleaner
sucks the past away

2.

Other lives were lived here:
mostly un-articulate

yet someone left her creamy signature
in the trail of rusticated

narcissus straggling up
through meadowgrass and vetch

Families breathed close
boxed-in from the cold

hard times, short growing season
the old rainwater cistern
hulks in the cellar

3.

Like turning through the contents of a drawer:
these rusted screws, this empty vial

useless, this box of watercolor paints
dried to insolubility—

but this—
this pack of cards with no card missing

still playable
and three good fuses

and this toy: a little truck
scarred red, yet all its wheels still turn

The humble tenacity of things
waiting for people, waiting for months, for years

4.

Often rebuked, yet always back returning
I place my hand on the hand

of the dead, invisible palm-print
on the doorframe

spiked with daylilies, green leaves
catching in the screen door

or I read the backs of old postcards
curling from thumbtacks, winter and summer

fading through cobweb-tinted panes—
white church in Norway

Dutch hyacinths bleeding azure
red beach on Corsica

set-pieces of the world
stuck to this house of plank

I flash on wife and husband
embattled, in the years

that dried, dim ink was wet
those signatures

5.

If they call me man-hater, you
would have known it for a lie

but the *you* I want to speak to
has become your death

If I dream of you these days
I know my dreams are mine and not of you

yet something hangs between us
older and stranger than ourselves

like a translucent curtain, a sheet of water
a dusty window

the irreducible, incomplete connection
between the dead and living

or between man and woman in this
savagely fathered and unmothered world

6.

The other side of a translucent
curtain, a sheet of water

a dusty window, Non-being
utters its flat tones

the speech of an actor learning his lines
phonetically

the final autistic statement
of the self-destroyer

All my energy reaches out tonight
to comprehend a miracle beyond

raising the dead: the undead to watch
back on the road of birth

7.

I am an American woman:
I turn that over

like a leaf pressed in a book
I stop and look up from

into the coals of the stove
or the black square of the window

Foot-slogging through the Bering Strait
jumping from the *Arbella* to my death

chained to the corpse beside me
I feel my pains begin

I am washed up on this continent
shipped here to be fruitful

my body a hollow ship
bearing sons to the wilderness

sons who ride away
on horseback, daughters

whose juices drain like mine
into the *arroyo* of stillbirths, massacres

Hanged as witches, sold as breeding-wenches
my sisters leave me

I am not the wheatfield
nor the virgin forest

I never chose this place
yet I am of it now

In my decent collar, in the daguerreotype
I pierce its legend with my look

my hands wring the necks of prairie chickens
I am used to blood

When the men hit the hobo track
I stay on with the children

my power is brief and local
but I know my power

I have lived in isolation
from other women, so much

in the mining camps, the first cities
the Great Plains winters

Most of the time, in my sex, I was alone

8.

Tonight in this northeast kingdom
striated iris stand in a jar with daisies

the porcupine gnaws in the shed
fireflies beat and simmer

caterpillars begin again
their long, innocent climb

the length of leaves of burdock
or webbing of a garden chair

plain and ordinary things
speak softly

the light square on old wallpaper
where a poster has fallen down

Robert Indiana's LOVE
leftover of a decade

9.

I do not want to simplify
Or: I would simplify

by naming the complexity
It was made over-simple all along

the separation of powers
the allotment of sufferings

her spine cracking in labor
his plow driving across the Indian graves

her hand unconscious on the cradle, her mind
with the wild geese

his mother-hatred driving him
into exile from the earth

the refugee couple with their cardboard luggage
standing on the ramshackle landing-stage

he with fingers frozen around his Law
she with her down quilt sewn through iron nights

—the weight of the old world, plucked
drags after them, a random feather-bed

10.

Her children dead of diphtheria, she
set herself on fire with kerosene

(O Lord I was unworthy
Thou didst find me out)

she left the kitchen scrubbed
down to the marrow of its boards

"The penalty for barrenness
is emptiness

my punishment is my crime
what I have failed to do, is me . . ."

—Another month without a show
and this the seventh year

O Father let this thing pass out of me
I swear to You

I will live for the others, asking nothing
I will ask nothing, ever, for myself

11.

Out back of this old house
datura tangles with a gentler weed

its spiked pods smelling
of bad dreams and death

I reach through the dark, groping
past spines of nightmare

to brush the leaves of sensuality
A dream of tenderness

wrestles with all I know of history
I cannot now lie down

with a man who fears my power
or reaches for me as for death

or with a lover who imagines
we are not in danger

12.

If it was lust that had defined us—
their lust and fear of our deep places

we have done our time
as faceless torsos licked by fire

we are in the open, on our way—
our counterparts

the pinyon jay, the small
gilt-winged insect

the Cessna throbbing level
the raven floating in the gorge

the rose and violet vulva of the earth
filling with darkness

yet deep within a single sparkle
of red, a human fire

and near and yet above the western planet
calmly biding her time

13.

They were the distractions, lust and fear
but are

themselves a key
Everything that can be used, will be:

the fathers in their ceremonies
the genital contests

the cleansing of blood from pubic hair
the placenta buried and guarded

their terror of blinding
by the look of her who bore them

If you do not believe
that fear and hatred

read the lesson again
in the old dialect

14.

But can't you see me as a human being
he said

What is a human being
she said

I try to understand
he said

what will you undertake
she said

will you punish me for history
he said

what will you undertake
she said

do you believe in collective guilt
he said

let me look in your eyes
she said

15.

Who is here. The Erinyes.
One to sit in judgment.

One to speak tenderness.
One to inscribe the verdict on the canyon wall.

If you have not confessed
the damage

if you have not recognized
the Mother of reparations

if you have not come to terms
with the women in the mirror

if you have not come to terms
with the inscription

the terms of the ordeal
the discipline   the verdict

if still you are on your way
still She awaits your coming

16.

"Such women are dangerous
to the order of things"

and yes, we will be dangerous
to ourselves

groping through spines of nightmare
(*datura* tangling with a simpler herb)

because the line dividing
lucidity from darkness

is yet to be marked out

Isolation, the dream
of the frontier woman

leveling her rifle along
the homestead fence

still snares our pride
—a suicidal leaf

laid under the burning-glass
in the sun's eye

Any woman's death diminishes me

1974

THE FACT OF A DOORFRAME

means there is something to hold
onto with both hands
while slowly thrusting my forehead against the wood
and taking it away
one of the oldest motions of suffering
as Makeba sings
a courage-song for warriors
music is suffering made powerful

I think of the story
of the goose-girl who passed through the high gate
where the head of her favorite mare
was nailed to the arch
and in a human voice
If she could see thee now, thy mother's heart would break
said the head
of Falada

Now, again, poetry,
violent, arcane, common,
hewn of the commonest living substance
into archway, portal, frame
I grasp for you, your bloodstained splinters, your
ancient and stubborn poise
—as the earth trembles—
burning out from the grain

1974

THE DREAM OF A
COMMON LANGUAGE

(1974–1977)

I go where I love and where I am loved,
into the snow;

I go to the things I love
with no thought of duty or pity

—H. D., *The Flowering of the Rod*

I

Power

POWER

Living   in the earth-deposits   of our history

Today a backhoe divulged   out of a crumbling flank of earth
one bottle   amber   perfect   a hundred-year-old
cure for fever   or melancholy   a tonic
for living on this earth   in the winters of this climate

Today I was reading about Marie Curie:
she must have known she suffered   from radiation sickness
her body bombarded for years   by the element
she had purified
It seems she denied to the end
the source of the cataracts on her eyes
the cracked and suppurating skin   of her finger-ends
till she could no longer hold   a test-tube or a pencil

She died   a famous woman   denying
her wounds
denying
her wounds   came   from the same source as her power

1974

PHANTASIA FOR ELVIRA SHATAYEV

(Leader of a women's climbing team, all of whom died in a
storm on Lenin Peak, August 1974. Later, Shatayev's
husband found and buried the bodies.)

The cold felt cold until our blood
grew colder   then the wind
died down and we slept

If in this sleep I speak
It's with a voice no longer personal
(I want to say   *with voices*)
When the wind tore   our breath from us at last
we had no need of words
For months   for years   each one of us
had felt her own *yes*   growing in her
slowly forming   as she stood at windows   waited
for trains   mended her rucksack   combed her hair
What we were to learn   was simply   what we had
up here   as out of all words   that *yes*   gathered
its forces   fused itself   and only just in time
to meet a *No* of no degrees
the black hole   sucking the world in

I feel you climbing toward me
your cleated bootsoles leaving   their geometric bite
colossally embossed   on microscopic crystals
as when I trailed you in the Caucasus
Now I am further
ahead   than either of us dreamed   anyone would be
I have become

the white snow packed like asphalt by the wind
the women I love   lightly flung   against the mountain
that blue sky
our frozen eyes unribboned   through the storm
we could have stitched that blueness   together   like a quilt

You come (I know this)   with your love   your loss
strapped to your body   with your tape-recorder   camera
ice-pick   against advisement
to give us burial in the snow   and in your mind
While my body lies out here
flashing like a prism   into your eyes
how could you sleep   You climbed here for yourself
we climbed for ourselves

When you have buried us   told your story
ours does not end   we stream
into the unfinished   the unbegun
the possible
Every cell's core of heat   pulsed out of us
into the thin air   of the universe
the armature of rock beneath these snows
this mountain   which has taken   the imprint of our minds
through changes elemental and minute
as those we underwent
to bring each other here
choosing ourselves   each other   and this life
whose every breath   and grasp   and further foothold
is somewhere   still enacted   and continuing

In the diary I wrote: *Now we are ready*
and each of us knows it   I have never loved
like this   I have never seen
my own forces so taken up and shared
and given back
After the long training   the early sieges
we are moving almost effortlessly in our love

In the diary as the wind   began to tear
at the tents over us   I wrote:
We know now we have always been in danger
down in our separateness
and now up here together   but till now
we had not touched our strength

In the diary torn from my fingers I had written:
What does love mean
What does it mean   "to survive"
A cable of blue fire ropes our bodies
burning together in the snow   We will not live
to settle for less   We have dreamed of this
all of our lives

1974

ORIGINS AND HISTORY
OF CONSCIOUSNESS

I

Night-life. Letters, journals, bourbon
sloshed in the glass. Poems crucified on the wall,
dissected, their bird-wings severed
like trophies. No one lives in this room
without living through some kind of crisis.

No one lives in this room
without confronting the whiteness of the wall
behind the poems, planks of books,
photographs of dead heroines.
Without contemplating last and late
the true nature of poetry. The drive
to connect. The dream of a common language.

Thinking of lovers, their blind faith, their
experienced crucifixions,
my envy is not simple. I have dreamed of going to bed
as walking into clear water ringed by a snowy wood
white as cold sheets, thinking, *I'll freeze in there.*
My bare feet are numbed already by the snow
but the water
is mild, I sink and float
like a warm amphibious animal
that has broken the net, has run
through fields of snow leaving no print;
this water washes off the scent—
You are clear now
of the hunter, the trapper
the wardens of the mind—

yet the warm animal dreams on
of another animal
swimming under the snow-flecked surface of the pool,
and wakes, and sleeps again.

No one sleeps in this room without
the dream of a common language.

II

It was simple to meet you, simple to take your eyes
into mine, saying: these are eyes I have known
from the first. . . . It was simple to touch you
against the hacked background, the grain of what we
had been, the choices, years. . . . It was even simple
to take each other's lives in our hands, as bodies.

What is not simple: to wake from drowning
from where the ocean beat inside us like an afterbirth
into this common, acute particularity
these two selves who walked half a lifetime untouching—
to wake to something deceptively simple: a glass
sweated with dew, a ring of the telephone, a scream
of someone beaten up far down in the street
causing each of us to listen to her own inward scream

knowing the mind of the mugger and the mugged
as any woman must who stands to survive this city,
this century, this life . . .
each of us having loved the flesh in its clenched or loosened beauty
better than trees or music (yet loving those too
as if they were flesh—and they are—but the flesh
of beings unfathomed as yet in our roughly literal life).

III

It's simple to wake from sleep with a stranger,
dress, go out, drink coffee,
enter a life again. It isn't simple
to wake from sleep into the neighborhood
of one neither strange nor familiar
whom we have chosen to trust. Trusting, untrusting,
we lowered ourselves into this, let ourselves
downward hand over hand as on a rope that quivered
over the unsearched. . . . We did this. Conceived
of each other, conceived each other in a darkness
which I remember as drenched in light.
                                  I want to call this, life.

But I can't call it life until we start to move
beyond this secret circle of fire
where our bodies are giant shadows flung on a wall
where the night becomes our inner darkness, and sleeps
like a dumb beast, head on her paws, in the corner.

1972–1974

SPLITTINGS

1.

My body opens over San Francisco like the day-
light raining down   each pore crying the change of light
I am not with her   I have been waking off and on
all night to that pain   not simply absence but
the presence of the past   destructive
to living here and now   Yet if I could instruct
myself, if we could learn to learn from pain
even as it grasps us   if the mind, the mind that lives
in this body could refuse   to let itself be crushed
in that grasp   it would loosen   Pain would have to stand
off from me and listen   its dark breath still on me
but the mind could begin to speak to pain
and pain would have to answer:

We are older now

we have met before   these are my hands before your eyes
my figure blotting out   all that is not mine
I am the pain of division   creator of divisions
it is I who blot your lover from you
and not the time-zones nor the miles
It is not separation calls me forth   but I
who am separation   And remember
I have no existence   apart from you

2.

I believe I am choosing something new
not to suffer uselessly   yet still to feel
Does the infant memorize the body of the mother
and create her in absence?   or simply cry
primordial loneliness?   does the bed of the stream
once diverted   mourning   remember wetness?
But we, we live so much in these
configurations of the past   I choose
to separate her   from my past we have not shared
I choose not to suffer uselessly
to detect primordial pain as it stalks toward me
flashing its bleak torch in my eyes   blotting out
her particular being   the details of her love
I will not be divided   from her or from myself
by myths of separation
while her mind and body in Manhattan are more with me
than the smell of eucalyptus coolly burning   on these hills

3.

The world tells me I am its creature
I am raked by eyes   brushed by hands
I want to crawl into her for refuge   lay my head
in the space   between her breast and shoulder
abnegating power for love
as women have done   or hiding
from power in her love like a man
I refuse these givens   the splitting
between love and action   I am choosing
not to suffer uselessly   and not to use her
I choose to love   this time   for once
with all my intelligence

1974

HUNGER

For Audre Lorde

1.

A fogged hill-scene on an enormous continent,
intimacy rigged with terrors,
a sequence of blurs the Chinese painter's ink-stick planned,
a scene of desolation comforted
by two human figures recklessly exposed,
leaning together in a sticklike boat
in the foreground. Maybe we look like this,
I don't know. I'm wondering
whether we even have what we think we have—
lighted windows signifying shelter,

a film of domesticity
over fragile roofs. I know I'm partly somewhere else—
huts strung across a drought-stretched land
not mine, dried breasts, mine and not mine, a mother
watching my children shrink with hunger.
I live in my Western skin,
my Western vision, torn
and flung to what I can't control or even fathom.
Quantify suffering, you could rule the world.

2.

They cán rule the world while they can persuade us
our pain belongs in some order.
Is death by famine worse than death by suicide,
than a life of famine and suicide, if a black lesbian dies,
if a white prostitute dies, if a woman genius
starves herself to feed others,
self-hatred battening on her body?
Something that kills us or leaves us half-alive
is raging under the name of an "act of god"
in Chad, in Niger, in the Upper Volta—
yes, that male god that acts on us and on our children,
that male State that acts on us and on our children
till our brains are blunted by malnutrition,
yet sharpened by the passion for survival,
our powers expended daily on the struggle
to hand a kind of life on to our children,
to change reality for our lovers
even in a single trembling drop of water.

3.

We can look at each other through both our lifetimes
like those two figures in the sticklike boat
flung together in the Chinese ink-scene;
even our intimacies are rigged with terror.
Quantify suffering? My guilt at least is open,
I stand convicted by all my convictions—
you, too. We shrink from touching
our power, we shrink away, we starve ourselves
and each other, we're scared shitless
of what it could be to take and use our love,
hose it on a city, on a world,
to wield and guide its spray, destroying
poisons, parasites, rats, viruses—
like the terrible mothers we long and dread to be.

4.

The decision to feed the world
is the real decision. No revolution
has chosen it. For that choice requires
that women shall be free.
I choke on the taste of bread in North America
but the taste of hunger in North America
is poisoning me. Yes, I'm alive to write these words,
to leaf through Kollwitz's women
huddling the stricken children into their stricken arms
the "mothers" drained of milk, the "survivors" driven
to self-abortion, self-starvation, to a vision
bitter, concrete, and wordless.
I'm alive to want more than life,
want it for others starving and unborn,
to name the deprivations boring
into my will, my affections, into the brains

of daughters, sisters, lovers caught in the crossfire
of terrorists of the mind.
In the black mirror of the subway window
hangs my own face, hollow with anger and desire.
Swathed in exhaustion, on the trampled newsprint,
a woman shields a dead child from the camera.
The passion to be inscribes her body.
Until we find each other, we are alone.

1974–1975

TO A POET

Ice splits   under the metal
shovel   another day
hazed light off fogged panes
cruelty of winter   landlocked   your life
wrapped round you   in your twenties
an old bathrobe   dragged down
with milkstains   tearstains   dust

Scraping eggcrust from the child's
dried dish   skimming the skin
from cooled milk   wringing diapers
Language floats at the vanishing-point
incarnate   breathes the fluorescent bulb
primary   states the scarred grain of the floor
and on the ceiling in torn plaster laughs   *imago*

> *and I have fears that you will cease to be*
> *before your pen has glean'd your teeming brain*

for you are not a suicide
but no-one calls this murder
Small mouths, needy, suck you: *This is love*

I write this   not for you
who fight to write your own
words   fighting up the falls
but for another woman   dumb
with loneliness   dust   seeping plastic bags
with children in a house
where language floats and spins
abortion   in
the bowl

1974

CARTOGRAPHIES OF SILENCE

1.

A conversation begins
with a lie. And each

speaker of the so-called common language feels
the ice-floe split, the drift apart

as if powerless, as if up against
a force of nature

A poem can begin
with a lie. And be torn up.

A conversation has other laws
recharges itself with its own

false energy. Cannot be torn
up. Infiltrates our blood. Repeats itself.

Inscribes with its unreturning stylus
the isolation it denies.

2.

The classical music station
playing hour upon hour in the apartment

the picking up and picking up
and again picking up the telephone

The syllables uttering
the old script over and over

The loneliness of the liar
living in the formal network of the lie

twisting the dials to drown the terror
beneath the unsaid word

3.

The technology of silence
The rituals, etiquette

the blurring of terms
silence not absence

of words or music or even
raw sounds

Silence can be a plan
rigorously executed

the blueprint to a life

It is a presence
it has a history a   form

Do not confuse it
with any kind of absence

4.

How calm, how inoffensive these words
begin to seem to me

though begun in grief and anger
Can I break through this film of the abstract

without wounding myself or you
there is enough pain here

This is why the classical or the jazz music station plays?
to give a ground of meaning to our pain?

5.

The silence that strips bare:
In Dreyer's *Passion of Joan*

Falconetti's face, hair shorn, a great geography
mutely surveyed by the camera

If there were a poetry where this could happen
not as blank spaces or as words

stretched like a skin over meanings
but as silence falls at the end

of a night through which two people
have talked till dawn

6.

The scream
of an illegitimate voice

It has ceased to hear itself, therefore
it asks itself

How dó I exist?

This was the silence I wanted to break in you
I had questions but you would not answer

I had answers but you could not use them
This is useless to you and perhaps to others

7.

It was an old theme even for me:
Language cannot do everything—

chalk it on the walls where the dead poets
lie in their mausoleums

If at the will of the poet the poem
could turn into a thing

a granite flank laid bare, a lifted head
alight with dew

If it could simply look you in the face
with naked eyeballs, not letting you turn

till you, and I who long to make this thing,
were finally clarified together in its stare

8.

No. Let me have this dust,
these pale clouds dourly lingering, these words

moving with ferocious accuracy
like the blind child's fingers

or the newborn infant's mouth
violent with hunger

No one can give me, I have long ago
taken this method

whether of bran pouring from the loose-woven sack
or of the bunsen-flame turned low and blue

If from time to time I envy
the pure annunciations to the eye

the *visio beatifica*
if from time to time I long to turn

like the Eleusinian hierophant
holding up a simple ear of grain

for return to the concrete and everlasting world
what in fact I keep choosing

are these words, these whispers, conversations
from which time after time the truth breaks moist and green.

1975

THE LIONESS

The scent of her beauty draws me to her place.
The desert stretches, edge from edge.
Rock. Silver grasses. Drinking-hole.
The starry sky.
The lioness pauses
in her back-and-forth pacing of three yards square
and looks at me. Her eyes
are truthful. They mirror rivers,
seacoasts, volcanoes, the warmth
of moon-bathed promontories.
Under her haunches' golden hide
flows an innate, half-abnegated power.
Her walk
is bounded. Three square yards
encompass where she goes.

In country like this. I say, *the problem is always*
one of straying too far, not of staying
within bounds. There are caves,
high rocks, you don't explore. Yet you know
they exist. Her proud, vulnerable head
sniffs toward them. It is her country, she
knows they exist.

I come towards her in the starlight.
I look into her eyes
as one who loves can look.
entering the space behind her eyeballs,
leaving myself outside.
So, at last, through her pupils,

I see what she is seeing:
between her and the river's flood,
the volcano veiled in rainbow,
a pen that measures three yards square.
Lashed bars.
The cage.
The penance.

1975

II

Twenty-One Love Poems

I

Wherever in this city, screens flicker
with pornography, with science-fiction vampires,
victimized hirelings bending to the lash,
we also have to walk . . . if simply as we walk
through the rainsoaked garbage, the tabloid cruelties
of our own neighborhoods.
We need to grasp our lives inseparable
from those rancid dreams, that blurt of metal, those disgraces,
and the red begonia perilously flashing
from a tenement sill six stories high,
or the long-legged young girls playing ball
in the junior highschool playground.
No one has imagined us. We want to live like trees,
sycamores blazing through the sulfuric air,
dappled with scars, still exuberantly budding,
our animal passion rooted in the city.

II

I wake up in your bed. I know I have been dreaming.
Much earlier, the alarm broke us from each other,
you've been at your desk for hours. I know what I dreamed:
our friend the poet comes into my room
where I've been writing for days,
drafts, carbons, poems are scattered everywhere,
and I want to show her one poem
which is the poem of my life. But I hesitate,
and wake. You've kissed my hair
to wake me. *I dreamed you were a poem,*
I say, *a poem I wanted to show someone . . .*
and I laugh and fall dreaming again

of the desire to show you to everyone I love,
to move openly together
in the pull of gravity, which is not simple,
which carries the feathered grass a long way down the upbreathing air.

III

Since we're not young, weeks have to do time
for years of missing each other. Yet only this odd warp
in time tells me we're not young.
Did I ever walk the morning streets at twenty,
my limbs streaming with a purer joy?
did I lean from any window over the city
listening for the future
as I listen here with nerves tuned for your ring?
And you, you move toward me with the same tempo.
Your eyes are everlasting, the green spark
of the blue-eyed grass of early summer,
the green-blue wild cress washed by the spring.
At twenty, yes: we thought we'd live forever.
At forty-five, I want to know even our limits.
I touch you knowing we weren't born tomorrow,
and somehow, each of us will help the other live,
and somewhere, each of us must help the other die.

IV

I come home from you through the early light of spring
flashing off ordinary walls, the Pez Dorado,
the Discount Wares, the shoe-store. . . . I'm lugging my sack
of groceries, I dash for the elevator
where a man, taut, elderly, carefully composed
lets the door almost close on me.—*For god's sake hold it!*
I croak at him.—*Hysterical,*—he breathes my way.

I let myself into the kitchen, unload my bundles,
make coffee, open the window, put on Nina Simone
singing *Here comes the sun*. . . . I open the mail,
drinking delicious coffee, delicious music,
my body still both light and heavy with you. The mail
lets fall a Xerox of something written by a man
aged 27, a hostage, tortured in prison:
My genitals have been the object of such a sadistic display
they keep me constantly awake with the pain . . .
Do whatever you can to survive.
You know, I think that men love wars . . .
And my incurable anger, my unmendable wounds
break open further with tears, I am crying helplessly,
and they still control the world, and you are not in my arms.

V

This apartment full of books could crack open
to the thick jaws, the bulging eyes
of monsters, easily: Once open the books, you have to face
the underside of everything you've loved—
the rack and pincers held in readiness, the gag
even the best voices have had to mumble through,
the silence burying unwanted children—
women, deviants, witnesses—in desert sand.
Kenneth tells me he's been arranging his books
so he can look at Blake and Kafka while he types;
yes; and we still have to reckon with Swift
loathing the woman's flesh while praising her mind,
Goethe's dread of the Mothers, Claudel vilifying Gide,
and the ghosts—their hands clasped for centuries—
of artists dying in childbirth, wise-women charred at the stake,
centuries of books unwritten piled behind these shelves;

and we still have to stare into the absence
of men who would not, women who could not, speak
to our life—this still unexcavated hole
called civilization, this act of translation, this half-world.

VI

Your small hands, precisely equal to my own—
only the thumb is larger, longer—in these hands
I could trust the world, or in many hands like these,
handling power-tools or steering-wheel
or touching a human face. . . . Such hands could turn
the unborn child rightways in the birth canal
or pilot the exploratory rescue-ship
through icebergs, or piece together
the fine, needle-like sherds of a great krater-cup
bearing on its sides
figures of ecstatic women striding
to the sibyl's den or the Eleusinian cave—
such hands might carry out an unavoidable violence
with such restraint, with such a grasp
of the range and limits of violence
that violence ever after would be obsolete.

VII

What kind of beast would turn its life into words?
What atonement is this all about?
—and yet, writing words like these, I'm also living.
Is all this close to the wolverines' howled signals,
that modulated cantata of the wild?
or, when away from you I try to create you in words,
am I simply using you, like a river or a war?
And how have I used rivers, how have I used wars

to escape writing of the worst thing of all—
not the crimes of others, not even our own death,
but the failure to want our freedom passionately enough
so that blighted elms, sick rivers, massacres would seem
mere emblems of that desecration of ourselves?

VIII

I can see myself years back at Sunion,
hurting with an infected foot, Philoctetes
in woman's form, limping the long path,
lying on a headland over the dark sea,
looking down the red rocks to where a soundless curl
of white told me a wave had struck,
imagining the pull of that water from that height,
knowing deliberate suicide wasn't my métier,
yet all the time nursing, measuring that wound.
Well, that's finished. The woman who cherished
her suffering is dead. I am her descendant.
I love the scar-tissue she handed on to me,
but I want to go on from here with you
fighting the temptation to make a career of pain.

IX

Your silence today is a pond where drowned things live
I want to see raised dripping and brought into the sun.
It's not my own face I see there, but other faces,
even your face at another age.
Whatever's lost there is needed by both of us—
a watch of old gold, a water-blurred fever chart,
a key. . . . Even the silt and pebbles of the bottom
deserve their glint of recognition. I fear this silence,
this inarticulate life. I'm waiting

for a wind that will gently open this sheeted water
for once, and show me what I can do
for you, who have often made the unnameable
nameable for others, even for me.

X

Your dog, tranquil and innocent, dozes through
our cries, our murmured dawn conspiracies
our telephone calls. She knows—what can she know?
If in my human arrogance I claim to read
her eyes, I find there only my own animal thoughts:
that creatures must find each other for bodily comfort,
that voices of the psyche drive through the flesh
further than the dense brain could have foretold,
that the planetary nights are growing cold for those
on the same journey who want to touch
one creature-traveler clear to the end;
that without tenderness, we are in hell.

XI

Every peak is a crater. This is the law of volcanoes,
making them eternally and visibly female.
No height without depth, without a burning core,
though our straw soles shred on the hardened lava.
I want to travel with you to every sacred mountain
smoking within like the sibyl stooped over her tripod,
I want to reach for your hand as we scale the path,
to feel your arteries glowing in my clasp,
never failing to note the small, jewel-like flower
unfamiliar to us, nameless till we rename her,
that clings to the slowly altering rock—
that detail outside ourselves that brings us to ourselves,
was here before us, knew we would come, and sees beyond us.

XII

Sleeping, turning in turn like planets
rotating in their midnight meadow:
a touch is enough to let us know
we're not alone in the universe, even in sleep:
the dream-ghosts of two worlds
walking their ghost-towns, almost address each other.
I've wakened to your muttered words
spoken light- or dark-years away
as if my own voice had spoken.
But we have different voices, even in sleep,
and our bodies, so alike, are yet so different
and the past echoing through our bloodstreams
is freighted with different language, different meanings—
though in any chronicle of the world we share
it could be written with new meaning
we were two lovers of one gender,
we were two women of one generation.

XIII

The rules break like a thermometer,
quicksilver spills across the charted systems,
we're out in a country that has no language
no laws, we're chasing the raven and the wren
through gorges unexplored since dawn
whatever we do together is pure invention
the maps they gave us were out of date
by years . . . we're driving through the desert
wondering if the water will hold out
the hallucinations turn to simple villages
the music on the radio comes clear—
neither *Rosenkavalier* nor *Götterdämmerung*
but a woman's voice singing old songs

with new words, with a quiet bass, a flute
plucked and fingered by women outside the law.

XIV

It was your vision of the pilot
confirmed my vision of you: you said, *He keeps*
on steering headlong into the waves, on purpose
while we crouched in the open hatchway
vomiting into plastic bags
for three hours between St. Pierre and Miquelon.
I never felt closer to you.
In the close cabin where the honeymoon couples
huddled in each other's laps and arms
I put my hand on your thigh
to comfort both of us, your hand came over mine,
we stayed that way, suffering together
in our bodies, as if all suffering
were physical, we touched so in the presence
of strangers who knew nothing and cared less
vomiting their private pain
as if all suffering were physical.

(THE FLOATING POEM, UNNUMBERED)

Whatever happens with us, your body
will haunt mine—tender, delicate
your lovemaking, like the half-curled frond
of the fiddlehead fern in forests
just washed by sun. Your traveled, generous thighs
between which my whole face has come and come—
the innocence and wisdom of the place my tongue has found there—
the live, insatiate dance of your nipples in my mouth—
your touch on me, firm, protective, searching

me out, your strong tongue and slender fingers
reaching where I had been waiting years for you
in my rose-wet cave—whatever happens, this is.

XV

If I lay on that beach with you
white, empty, pure green water warmed by the Gulf Stream
and lying on that beach we could not stay
because the wind drove fine sand against us
as if it were against us
if we tried to withstand it and we failed—
if we drove to another place
to sleep in each other's arms
and the beds were narrow like prisoners' cots
and we were tired and did not sleep together
and this was what we found, so this is what we did—
was the failure ours?
If I cling to circumstances I could feel
not responsible. Only she who says
she did not choose, is the loser in the end.

XVI

Across a city from you, I'm with you,
just as an August night
moony, inlet-warm, seabathed, I watched you sleep,
the scrubbed, sheenless wood of the dressing-table
cluttered with our brushes, books, vials in the moonlight—
or a salt-mist orchard, lying at your side
watching red sunset through the screendoor of the cabin,
G minor Mozart on the tape-recorder,
falling asleep to the music of the sea.
This island of Manhattan is wide enough

for both of us, and narrow:
I can hear your breath tonight, I know how your face
lies upturned, the halflight tracing
your generous, delicate mouth
where grief and laughter sleep together.

XVII

No one's fated or doomed to love anyone.
The accidents happen, we're not heroines,
they happen in our lives like car crashes,
books that change us, neighborhoods
we move into and come to love.
Tristan und Isolde is scarcely the story,
women at least should know the difference
between love and death. No poison cup,
no penance. Merely a notion that the tape-recorder
should have caught some ghost of us: that tape-recorder
not merely played but should have listened to us,
and could instruct those after us:
this we were, this is how we tried to love,
and these are the forces they had ranged against us,
and these are the forces we had ranged within us,
within us and against us, against us and within us.

XVIII

Rain on the West Side Highway,
red light at Riverside:
the more I live the more I think
two people together is a miracle.
You're telling the story of your life
for once, a tremor breaks the surface of your words.
The story of our lives becomes our lives.
Now you're in fugue across what some I'm sure
Victorian poet called the *salt estranging sea*.

Those are the words that come to mind.
I feel estrangement, yes. As I've felt dawn
pushing toward daybreak. Something: a cleft of light—?
Close between grief and anger, a space opens
where I am Adrienne alone. And growing colder.

XIX

Can it be growing colder when I begin
to touch myself again, adhesions pull away?
When slowly the naked face turns from staring backward
and looks into the present,
the eye of winter, city, anger, poverty, and death
and the lips part and say: *I mean to go on living?*
Am I speaking coldly when I tell you in a dream
or in this poem, *There are no miracles?*
(I told you from the first I wanted daily life,
this island of Manhattan was island enough for me.)
If I could let you know—
two women together is a work
nothing in civilization has made simple,
two people together is a work
heroic in its ordinariness,
the slow-picked, halting traverse of a pitch
where the fiercest attention becomes routine
—look at the faces of those who have chosen it.

XX

That conversation we were always on the edge
of having, runs on in my head,
at night the Hudson trembles in New Jersey light
polluted water yet reflecting even
sometimes the moon

and I discern a woman
I loved, drowning in secrets, fear wound round her throat
and choking her like hair. And this is she
with whom I tried to speak, whose hurt, expressive head
turning aside from pain, is dragged down deeper
where it cannot hear me,
and soon I shall know I was talking to my own soul.

XXI

The dark lintels, the blue and foreign stones
of the great round rippled by stone implements
the midsummer night light rising from beneath
the horizon—when I said "a cleft of light"
I meant this. And this is not Stonehenge
simply nor any place but the mind
casting back to where her solitude,
shared, could be chosen without loneliness,
not easily nor without pains to stake out
the circle, the heavy shadows, the great light.
I choose to be a figure in that light,
half-blotted by darkness, something moving
across that space, the color of stone
greeting the moon, yet more than stone
a woman. I choose to walk here. And to draw this circle.

1974–1976

III

Not Somewhere Else,
But Here

NOT SOMEWHERE ELSE, BUT HERE

Courage   Her face in the leaves   the polygons
of the paving   Her   out of touch
Courage to breathe   The death of October
Spilt wine   The unbuilt house   The unmade life
Graffiti   without memory   grown conventional
scrawling the least wall   *god loves you   voice of the ghetto*
Death of the city   Her face
sleeping   Her quick stride   Her
running   Search for a private space   The city
caving in from within   The lessons badly
learned   Or not at all   The unbuilt world
This one love flowing   Touching other
lives   Spilt love   The least wall caving

To have enough courage   The life that must be lived
in terrible October
Sudden immersion in yellows   streaked blood   The fast rain
Faces   Inscriptions   Trying to teach
unlearnable lessons   October   This one love
Repetitions   from other lives   The deaths
that must be lived   Denials   Blank walls
Our quick stride side by side   Her fugue

Bad air in the tunnels   *voice of the ghetto   god loves you*
My face   pale in the window   anger is pale
the blood shrinks to the heart
the head severed   it does not pay to feel

Her face   The fast rain tearing   Courage
to feel this   To tell of this   to be alive
Trying to learn   unteachable lessons

The fugue   Blood in my eyes   The careful sutures
ripped open   The hands that touch me   Shall it be said
I am not alone
Spilt love   seeking its level   flooding other
lives   that must be lived   not somewhere else
but here   seeing through blood   nothing is lost

1974

UPPER BROADWAY

The leafbud straggles forth
toward the frigid light of the airshaft   this is faith
this pale extension of a day
when looking up   you know   something is changing
winter has turned   though the wind is colder
Three streets away   a roof collapses   onto people
who thought they still had time   Time out of mind

I have written so many words
wanting to live inside you
to be of use to you

Now I must write for myself   for this blind
woman scratching the pavement   with her wand of thought
this slippered crone   inching on icy streets
reaching into wire trashbaskets   pulling out
what was thrown away   and infinitely precious

I look at my hands and see   they are still unfinished
I look at the vine and see the leafbud
inching towards life

I look at my face in the glass and see
a halfborn woman

1975

PAULA BECKER TO CLARA WESTHOFF

Paula Becker 1876–1907

Clara Westhoff 1878–1954

became friends at Worpswede, an artists' colony near Bremen, Germany, summer 1899. In January 1900, spent a half-year together in Paris, where Paula painted and Clara studied sculpture with Rodin. In August they returned to Worpswede, and spent the next winter together in Berlin. In 1901, Clara married the poet Rainer Maria Rilke; soon after, Paula married the painter Otto Modersohn. She died in a hemorrhage after childbirth, murmuring, *What a pity!*

The autumn feels slowed down,
summer still holds on here, even the light
seems to last longer than it should
or maybe I'm using it to the thin edge.
The moon rolls in the air. I didn't want this child.
You're the only one I've told.
I want a child maybe, someday, but not now.
Otto has a calm, complacent way
of following me with his eyes, as if to say
Soon you'll have your hands full!
And yes, I will; this child will be mine
not his, the failures, if I fail
will be all mine. We're not good, Clara,
at learning to prevent these things,
and once we have a child, it *is* ours.
But lately, I feel beyond Otto or anyone.
I know now the kind of work I have to do.
It takes such energy! I have the feeling I'm

moving somewhere, patiently, impatiently,
in my loneliness. I'm looking everywhere in nature
for new forms, old forms in new places,
the planes of an antique mouth, let's say, among the leaves.
I know and do not know
what I am searching for.
Remember those months in the studio together,
you up to your strong forearms in wet clay,
I trying to make something of the strange impressions
assailing me—the Japanese
flowers and birds on silk, the drunks
sheltering in the Louvre, that river-light,
those faces. . . . Did we know exactly
why we were there? Paris unnerved you,
you found it too much, yet you went on
with your work . . . and later we met there again,
both married then, and I thought you and Rilke
both seemed unnerved. I felt a kind of joylessness
between you. Of course he and I
have had our difficulties. Maybe I was jealous
of him, to begin with, taking you from me,
maybe I married Otto to fill up
my loneliness for you.
Rainer, of course, *knows* more than Otto knows,
he believes in women. But he feeds on us,
like all of them. His whole life, his art
is protected by women. Which of us could say that?
Which of us, Clara, hasn't had to take that leap
out beyond our being women
to save our work? or is it to save ourselves?
Marriage is lonelier than solitude.
Do you know: I was dreaming I had died
giving birth to the child.
I couldn't paint or speak or even move.
My child—I think—survived me. But what was funny
in the dream was, Rainer had written my requiem—

a long, beautiful poem, and calling me his friend.
I was *your* friend
but in the dream you didn't say a word.
In the dream his poem was like a letter
to someone who has no right
to be there but must be treated gently, like a guest
who comes on the wrong day. Clara, why don't I dream of you?
That photo of the two of us—I have it still,
you and I looking hard into each other
and my painting behind us. How we used to work
side by side! And how I've worked since then
trying to create according to our plan
that we'd bring, against all odds, our full power
to every subject. Hold back nothing
because we were women. Clara, our strength still lies
in the things we used to talk about:
how life and death take one another's hands,
the struggle for truth, our old pledge against guilt.
And now I feel dawn and the coming day.
I love waking in my studio, seeing my pictures
come alive in the light. Sometimes I feel
it is myself that kicks inside me,
myself I must give suck to, love . . .
I wish we could have done this for each other
all our lives, but we can't . . .
They say a pregnant woman
dreams of her own death. But life and death
take one another's hands. Clara, I feel so full
of work, the life I see ahead, and love
for you, who of all people
however badly I say this
will hear all I say and cannot say.

1975–1976

NIGHTS AND DAYS

The stars will come out over and over
the hyacinths rise like flames
from the windswept turf down the middle of upper Broadway
where the desolate take the sun
the days will run together and stream into years
as the rivers freeze and burn
and I ask myself and you, which of our visions will claim us
which will we claim
how will we go on living
how will we touch, what will we know
what will we say to each other.

Pictures form and dissolve in my head:
we are walking in a city
you fled, came back to and come back to still
which I saw once through winter frost
years back, before I knew you,
before I knew myself.
We are walking streets you have by heart from childhood
streets you have graven and erased in dreams:
scrolled portals, trees, nineteenth-century statues.
We are holding hands so I can see
everything as you see it
I follow you into your dreams
your past, the places
none of us can explain to anyone.

We are standing in the wind
on an empty beach, the onslaught of the surf
tells me Point Reyes, or maybe some northern
Pacific shoreline neither of us has seen.
In its fine spectral mist our hair
is grey as the sea
someone who saw us far-off would say we were two old women

Norns, perhaps, or sisters of the spray
but our breasts are beginning to sing together
your eyes are on my mouth

I wake early in the morning
in a bed we have shared for years
lie watching your innocent, sacred sleep
as if for the first time.
We have been together so many nights and days
this day is not unusual.
I walk to an eastern window, pull up the blinds:
the city around us is still
on a clear October morning
wrapped in her indestructible light.

The stars will come out over and over
the hyacinths rise like flames
from the windswept turf down the middle of upper Broadway
where the desolate take the sun
the days will run together and stream into years
as the rivers freeze and burn
and I ask myself and you, which of our visions will claim us
which will we claim
how will we go on living
how will we touch, what will we know
what will we say to each other.

1976

SIBLING MYSTERIES

For C.R.

1.

Remind me how we walked
trying the planetary rock
for foothold

testing the rims of canyons
fields of sheer
ice in the midnight sun

smelling the rains before they came
feeling the fullness of the moon
before moonrise

unbalanced by the life
moving in us, then lightened
yet weighted still

by children on our backs
at our hips, as we made fire
scooped clay   lifted water

Remind me how the stream
wetted the clay   between our palms
and how the flame

licked it to mineral colors
how we traced our signs by torchlight
in the deep chambers of the caves

and how we drew the quills
of porcupines between our teeth
to a keen thinness

and brushed the twisted raffia into velvet
and bled our lunar knowledge thirteen times
upon the furrows

I know by heart, and still
I need to have you tell me,
hold me, remind me

2.

Remind me how we loved our mother's body
our mouths drawing the first
thin sweetness from her nipples

our faces dreaming hour on hour
in the salt smell of her lap   Remind me
how her touch melted childgrief

how she floated great and tender in our dark
or stood guard over us
against our willing

and how we thought she loved
the strange male body first
that took, that took, whose taking seemed a law

and how she sent us weeping
into that law
how we remet her in our childbirth visions

erect, enthroned, above
a spiral stair
and crawled and panted toward her

I know, I remember, but
hold me, remind me
of how her woman's flesh was made taboo to us

3.

And how beneath the veil
black gauze or white, the dragging
bangles, the amulets, we dreamed   And how beneath

the strange male bodies
we sank in terror or in resignation
and how we taught them tenderness—

the holding-back, the play,
the floating of a finger
the secrets of the nipple

And how we ate and drank
their leavings, how we served them
in silence, how we told

among ourselves our secrets, wept and laughed
passed bark and root and berry
from hand to hand, whispering each one's power

washing the bodies of the dead
making celebrations of doing laundry
piecing our lore in quilted galaxies

how we dwelt in two worlds
the daughters and the mothers
in the kingdom of the sons

4.

Tell me again because I need to hear
how we bore our mother-secrets
straight to the end

tied in unlawful rags
between our breasts
muttered in blood

in looks exchanged at the feast
where the fathers sucked the bones
and struck their bargains

in the open square when noon
battered our shaven heads
and the flames curled transparent in the sun

in boats of skin on the ice-floe
—the pregnant set to drift,
too many mouths for feeding—

how sister gazed at sister
reaching through mirrored pupils
back to the mother

5.

C. had a son on June 18th . . . I feel acutely that we are strangers, my sister and I; we don't get through to each other, or say what we really feel. This depressed me violently on that occasion, when I wanted to have only generous and simple feelings towards her, of pleasure in her joy, affection for all that was hers. But we are not really friends, and act the part of sisters. I don't know what really gives her pain or joy, nor does she know how I am happy or how I suffer.

(1963)

There were years you and I
hardly spoke to each other

then one whole night
our father dying upstairs

we burned our childhood, reams of paper,
talking till the birds sang

Your face across a table now: dark
with illumination

This face I have watched changing
for forty years

has watched me changing
this mind has wrenched my thought

I feel the separateness
of cells in us, split-second choice

of one ovum for one sperm?
We have seized different weapons

our hair has fallen long
or short at different times

words flash from you I never thought of
we are translations into different dialects

of a text still being written
in the original

yet our eyes drink from each other
our lives were driven down the same dark canal

6.

We have returned so far
that house of childhood seems absurd

its secrets a fallen hair, a grain of dust
on the photographic plate

we are eternally exposing to the universe
I call you from another planet

to tell a dream
Light-years away, you weep with me

The daughters never were
true brides of the father

the daughters were to begin with
brides of the mother

then brides of each other
under a different law

Let me hold and tell you

1976

A WOMAN DEAD IN HER FORTIES

1.

Your breasts/   sliced-off   The scars
dimmed   as they would have to be
years later

All the women I grew up with are sitting
half-naked on rocks   in sun
we look at each other and
are not ashamed

and you too have taken off your blouse
but this was not what you wanted:

to show your scarred, deleted torso

I barely glance at you
as if my look could scald you
though I'm the one who loved you

I want to touch my fingers
to where your breasts had been
but we never did such things

You hadn't thought everyone
would look so perfect
unmutilated

you pull on
your blouse again: stern statement:

There are things I will not share
with everyone

2.

You send me back to share
my own scars   first of all
with myself

What did I hide from her
what have I denied her
what losses suffered

how in this ignorant body
did she hide

waiting for her release
till uncontrollable light began to pour

from every wound and suture
and all the sacred openings

3.

Wartime.   We sit on warm
weathered, softening grey boards

the ladder glimmers where you told me
the leeches swim

I smell the flame
of kerosene   the pine

boards where we sleep side by side
in narrow cots

the night-meadow exhaling
its darkness   calling

child into woman
child into woman
woman

4.

Most of our love from the age of nine
took the form of jokes and mute

loyalty: you fought a girl
who said she'd knock me down

we did each other's homework
wrote letters   kept in touch, untouching

lied about our lives: I wearing
the face of the proper marriage

you the face of the independent woman
We cleaved to each other across that space

fingering webs
of love and estrangement   till the day

the gynecologist touched your breast
and found a palpable hardness

5.

You played heroic, necessary
games with death

since in your neo-protestant tribe the void
was supposed not to exist

except as a fashionable concept
you had no traffic with

I wish you were here tonight   I want
to yell at you

Don't accept
Don't give in

But would I be meaning your brave
irreproachable life, you dean of women, or

your unfair, unfashionable, unforgivable
woman's death?

6.

You are every woman I ever loved
and disavowed

a bloody incandescent chord strung out
across years, tracts of space

How can I reconcile this passion
with our modesty

your Calvinist heritage
my girlhood frozen into forms

how can I go on this mission
without you

you, who might have told me
everything you feel is true?

7.

Time after time in dreams you rise
reproachful

once from a wheelchair pushed by your father
across a lethal expressway

Of all my dead it's you
who come to me unfinished

You left me amber beads
Strung with turquoise from an Egyptian grave

I wear them wondering
How am I true to you?

I'm half-afraid to write poetry
for you   who never read it much

and I'm left laboring
with the secrets and the silence

In plain language: I never told you how I loved you
we never talked at your deathbed of your death

8.

One autumn evening in a train
catching the diamond-flash of sunset

in puddles along the Hudson
I thought: *I understand*

life and death now, the choices
I didn't know your choice

or how by then you had no choice
how the body tells the truth in its rush of cells

Most of our love took the form
of mute loyalty

we never spoke at your deathbed of your death

but from here on
I want more crazy mourning, more howl, more keening

We stayed mute and disloyal
because we were afraid

I would have touched my fingers
to where your breasts had been
but we never did such things

1974–1977

MOTHER-RIGHT

For M.H.

Woman and child   running
in a field   A man planted
on the horizon

Two hands   one long, slim   one
small, starlike   clasped
in the razor wind

Her hair cut short for faster travel
the child's curls grazing his shoulders
the hawk-winged cloud   over their heads

The man is walking boundaries
measuring   He believes in what is his
the grass   the waters underneath   the air

the air   through which child and mother
are running   the boy singing
the woman   eyes sharpened in the light
heart stumbling   making for the open

1977

NATURAL RESOURCES

1.

The core of the strong hill: not understood:
the mulch-heat of the underwood

where unforeseen the forest fire unfurls;
the heat, the privacy of the mines;

the rainbow laboring to extend herself
where neither men nor cattle understand,

arching her lusters over rut and stubble
purely to reach where she must go;

the emerald lying against the silver vein
waiting for light to reach it, breathing in pain;

the miner laboring beneath
the ray of the headlamp: a weight like death.

2.

The miner is no metaphor. She goes
into the cage like the rest, is flung

downward by gravity like them, must change
her body like the rest to fit a crevice

to work a lode
on her the pick hangs heavy, the bad air

lies thick, the mountain presses in on her
with boulder, timber, fog
slowly the mountain's dust descends
into the fibers of her lungs.

3.

The cage drops into the dark,
the routine of life goes on:

a woman turns a doorknob, but so slowly
so quietly, that no one wakes

and it is she alone who gazes
into the dark of bedrooms, ascertains

how they sleep, who needs her touch
what window blows the ice of February

into the room and who must be protected:
It is only she who sees; who was trained to see.

4.

Could you imagine a world of women only,
the interviewer asked. *Can you imagine*

a world where women are absent. (He believed
he was joking.) Yet I have to imagine

at one and the same moment, both. Because
I live in both. *Can you imagine,*

the interviewer asked, *a world of men?*
(He thought he was joking.) *If so, then,*

a world where men are absent?
Absently, wearily, I answered: Yes.

5.

The phantom of the man-who-would-understand,
the lost brother, the twin—

for him did we leave our mothers,
deny our sisters, over and over?

did we invent him, conjure him
over the charring log,

nights, late, in the snowbound cabin
did we dream or scry his face

in the liquid embers,
the man-who-would-dare-to-know-us?

6.

It was never the rapist:
it was the brother, lost,

the comrade/twin whose palm
would bear a lifeline like our own:

decisive, arrowy,
forked-lightning of insatiate desire

It was never the crude pestle, the blind
ramrod we were after:

merely a fellow-creature
with natural resources equal to our own

7.

Meanwhile, another kind of being
was constructing itself, blindly

—a mutant, some have said:
the blood-compelled exemplar

of a "botched civilization"
as one of them called it

children picking up guns
for that is what it means to be a man

We have lived with violence for seven years
It was not worth one single life—

but the patriot's fist is at her throat,
her voice is in mortal danger

and that kind of being has lain in our beds
declaring itself our desire

requiring women's blood for life
a woman's breast to lay its nightmare on

8.

And that kind of being has other forms:
a passivity we mistake

—in the desperation of our search—
for gentleness

But gentleness is active
gentleness swabs the crusted stump

invents more merciful instruments
to touch the wound beyond the wound

does not faint with disgust
will not be driven off

keeps bearing witness calmly
against the predator, the parasite

9.

I am tired of faintheartedness,
their having to be *exceptional*

to do what an ordinary woman
does in the course of things

I am tired of women stooping to half our height
to bring the essential vein to light

tired of the waste of what we bear
with such cost, such elation, into sight

(—for what becomes of what the miner probes
and carves from the mountain's body in her pain?)

10.

This is what I am: watching the spider
rebuild—"patiently", they say,

but I recognize in her
impatience—my own—

the passion to make and make again
where such unmaking reigns

the refusal to be a victim
we have lived with violence so long

Am I to go on saying
for myself, for her

This is my body,
take and destroy it?

11.

The enormity of the simplest things:
in this cold barn tables are spread

with china saucers, shoehorns
of german silver, a gilt-edged book

that opens into a picture-frame—
a biscuit-tin of the thirties.

Outside, the north lies vast
with unshed snow, everything is

at once remote and familiar
each house contains what it must

women simmer carcasses
of clean-picked turkeys, store away

the cleaned cutglass and soak the linen cloths
Dark rushes early at the panes

12.

These things by women saved
are all we have of them

or of those dear to them
these ribboned letters, snapshots

faithfully glued for years
onto the scrapbook page

these scraps, turned into patchwork,
doll-gowns, clean white rags

for stanching blood
the bride's tea-yellow handkerchief

the child's height penciled on the cellar door
In this cold barn we dream

a universe of humble things—
and without these, no memory

no faithfulness, no purpose for the future
no honor to the past

13.

There are words I cannot choose again:
humanism   androgyny

Such words have no shame in them, no diffidence
before the raging stoic grandmothers:

their glint is too shallow, like a dye
that does not permeate

the fibers of actual life
as we live it, now:

this fraying blanket with its ancient stains
we pull across the sick child's shoulder

or wrap around the senseless legs
of the hero trained to kill

this weaving, ragged because incomplete
we turn our hands to, interrupted

over and over, handed down
unfinished, found in the drawer

of an old dresser in the barn,
her vanished pride and care

still urging us, urging on
our works, to close the gap

in the Great Nebula
to help the earth deliver.

14.

The women who first knew themselves
miners, are dead. The rainbow flies

like a flying buttress from the walls
of cloud, the silver-and-green vein

awaits the battering of the pick
the dark lode weeps for light

My heart is moved by all I cannot save:
so much has been destroyed

I have to cast my lot with those
who age after age, perversely,

with no extraordinary power,
reconstitute the world.

1977

TOWARD THE SOLSTICE

The thirtieth of November.
Snow is starting to fall.
A peculiar silence is spreading
over the fields, the maple grove.
It is the thirtieth of May,
rain pours on ancient bushes, runs
down the youngest blade of grass.
I am trying to hold in one steady glance
all the parts of my life.
A spring torrent races
on this old slanting roof,
the slanted field below
thickens with winter's first whiteness.
Thistles dried to sticks in last year's wind
stand nakedly in the green,
stand sullenly in the slowly whitening,
field.

       My brain glows
more violently, more avidly
the quieter, the thicker
the quilt of crystals settles,
the louder, more relentlessly
the torrent beats itself out
on the old boards and shingles.
It is the thirtieth of May,
the thirtieth of November,
a beginning or an end,
we are moving into the solstice
and there is so much here
I still do not understand.

If I could make sense of how
my life is still tangled

with dead weeds, thistles,
enormous burdocks, burdens
slowly shifting under
this first fall of snow,
beaten by this early, racking rain
calling all new life to declare itself strong
or die,
         if I could know
in what language to address
the spirits that claim a place
beneath these low and simple ceilings,
tenants that neither speak nor stir
yet dwell in mute insistence
till I can feel utterly ghosted in this house.

If history is a spider-thread
spun over and over though brushed away
it seems I might some twilight
or dawn in the hushed country light
discern its greyness stretching
from molding or doorframe, out
into the empty dooryard
and following it climb
the path into the pinewoods,
tracing from tree to tree
in the failing light, in the slowly
lucidifying day
its constant, purposive trail,
till I reach whatever cellar hole
filling with snowflakes or lichen,
whatever fallen shack
or unremembered clearing
I am meant to have found
and there, under the first or last
star, trusting to instinct
the words would come to mind

I have failed or forgotten to say
year after year, winter
after summer, the right rune
to ease the hold of the past
upon the rest of my life
and ease my hold on the past.

If some rite of separation
is still unaccomplished
between myself and the long-gone
tenants of this house,
between myself and my childhood,
and the childhood of my children,
it is I who have neglected
to perform the needed acts,
set water in corners, light and eucalyptus
in front of mirrors,
or merely pause and listen
to my own pulse vibrating
lightly as falling snow,
relentlessly as the rainstorm,
and hear what it has been saying.
It seems I am still waiting
for them to make some clear demand
some articulate sound or gesture,
for release to come from anywhere
but from inside myself.

A decade of cutting away
dead flesh, cauterizing
old scars ripped open over and over
and still it is not enough.
A decade of performing
the loving humdrum acts
of attention to this house
transplanting lilac suckers,

washing panes, scrubbing
wood-smoke from splitting paint,
sweeping stairs, brushing the thread
of the spider aside,
and so much yet undone,
a woman's work, the solstice nearing,
and my hand still suspended
as if above a letter
I long and dread to close.

1977

TRANSCENDENTAL ETUDE

For Michelle Cliff

This August evening I've been driving
over backroads fringed with queen anne's lace
my car startling young deer in meadows—one
gave a hoarse intake of her breath and all
four fawns sprang after her
into the dark maples.
Three months from today they'll be fair game
for the hit-and-run hunters, glorying
in a weekend's destructive power.
triggers fingered by drunken gunmen, sometimes
so inept as to leave the shattered animal
stunned in her blood. But this evening deep in summer
the deer are still alive and free,
nibbling apples from early-laden boughs
so weighted, so englobed
with already yellowing fruit
they seem eternal, Hesperidean
in the clear-tuned, cricket-throbbing air.

Later I stood in the dooryard,
my nerves singing the immense
fragility of all this sweetness,
this green world already sentimentalized, photographed,
advertised to death. Yet, it persists
stubbornly beyond the fake Vermont
of antique barnboards glazed into discothèques,
artificial snow, the sick Vermont of children
conceived in apathy, grown to winters
of rotgut violence,
poverty gnashing its teeth like a blind cat at their lives.
Still, it persists. Turning off onto a dirt road
from the raw cuts bulldozed through a quiet village
for the tourist run to Canada,
I've sat on a stone fence above a great, soft, sloping field
of musing heifers, a farmstead
slanting its planes calmly in the calm light,
a dead elm raising bleached arms
above a green so dense with life,
minute, momentary life—slugs, moles, pheasants, gnats,
spiders, moths, hummingbirds, groundhogs, butterflies—
a lifetime is too narrow
to understand it all, beginning with the huge
rockshelves that underlie all that life.

No one ever told us we had to study our lives,
make of our lives a study, as if learning natural history
or music, that we should begin
with the simple exercises first
and slowly go on trying
the hard ones, practicing till strength
and accuracy became one with the daring
to leap into transcendence, take the chance
of breaking down in the wild arpeggio
or faulting the full sentence of the fugue.
—And in fact we can't live like that: we take on

everything at once before we've even begun
to read or mark time, we're forced to begin
in the midst of the hardest movement,
the one already sounding as we are born.
At most we're allowed a few months
of simply listening to the simple line
of a woman's voice singing a child
against her heart. Everything else is too soon,
too sudden, the wrenching-apart, that woman's heartbeat
heard ever after from a distance,
the loss of that ground-note echoing
whenever we are happy, or in despair.

Everything else seems beyond us,
we aren't ready for it, nothing that was said
is true for us, caught naked in the argument,
the counterpoint, trying to sightread
what our fingers can't keep up with, learn by heart
what we can't even read. And yet
it *is* this we were born to. We aren't virtuosi
or child prodigies, there are no prodigies
in this realm, only a half-blind, stubborn
cleaving to the timbre, the tones of what we are
—even when all the texts describe it differently.

And we're not performers, like Liszt, competing
against the world for speed and brilliance
(the 79-year-old pianist said, when I asked her
What makes a virtuoso?—Competitiveness.)
The longer I live the more I mistrust
theatricality, the false glamour cast
by performance, the more I know its poverty beside
the truths we are salvaging from
the splitting-open of our lives.
The woman who sits watching, listening,
eyes moving in the darkness

is rehearsing in her body, hearing-out in her blood
a score touched off in her perhaps
by some words, a few chords, from the stage:
a tale only she can tell.

But there come times—perhaps this is one of them—
when we have to take ourselves more seriously or die;
when we have to pull back from the incantations,
rhythms we've moved to thoughtlessly,
and disenthrall ourselves, bestow
ourselves to silence, or a deeper listening, cleansed
of oratory, formulas, choruses, laments, static
crowding the wires. We cut the wires,
find ourselves in free-fall, as if
our true home were the undimensional
solitudes, the rift
in the Great Nebula.
No one who survives to speak
new language, has avoided this:
the cutting-away of an old force that held her
rooted to an old ground
the pitch of utter loneliness
where she herself and all creation
seem equally dispersed, weightless, her being a cry
to which no echo comes or can ever come.

But in fact we were always like this,
rootless, dismembered: knowing it makes the difference.
Birth stripped our birthright from us,
tore us from a woman, from women, from ourselves
so early on
and the whole chorus throbbing at our ears
like midges, told us nothing, nothing
of origins, nothing we needed
to know, nothing that could re-member us.

Only: that it is unnatural,
the homesickness for a woman, for ourselves,
for that acute joy at the shadow her head and arms
cast on a wall, her heavy or slender
thighs on which we lay, flesh against flesh,
eyes steady on the face of love; smell of her milk, her sweat,
terror of her disappearance, all fused in this hunger
for the element they have called most dangerous, to be
lifted breathtaken on her breast, to rock within her
—even if beaten back, stranded again, to apprehend
in a sudden brine-clear thought
trembling like the tiny, orbed, endangered
egg-sac of a new world:
This is what she was to me, and this
is how I can love myself—
as only a woman can love me.

Homesick for myself, for her—as, after the heatwave
breaks, the clear tones of the world
manifest: cloud, bough, wall, insect, the very soul of light:
homesick as the fluted vault of desire
articulates itself: *I am the lover and the loved,*
home and wanderer, she who splits
firewood and she who knocks, a stranger
in the storm, two women, eye to eye
measuring each other's spirit, each other's
limitless desire,
                    a whole new poetry beginning here.

Vision begins to happen in such a life
as if a woman quietly walked away
from the argument and jargon in a room
and sitting down in the kitchen, began turning in her lap
bits of yarn, calico and velvet scraps,
laying them out absently on the scrubbed boards
in the lamplight, with small rainbow-colored shells

sent in cotton-wool from somewhere far away,
and skeins of milkweed from the nearest meadow—
original domestic silk, the finest findings—
and the darkblue petal of the petunia,
and the dry darkbrown lace of seaweed;
not forgotten either, the shed silver
whisker of the cat,
the spiral of paper-wasp-nest curling
beside the finch's yellow feather.
Such a composition has nothing to do with eternity,
the striving for greatness, brilliance—
only with the musing of a mind
one with her body, experienced fingers quietly pushing
dark against bright, silk against roughness,
pulling the tenets of a life together
with no mere will to mastery,
only care for the many-lived, unending
forms in which she finds herself,
becoming now the sherd of broken glass
slicing light in a corner, dangerous
to flesh, now the plentiful, soft leaf
that wrapped round the throbbing finger, soothes the wound;
and now the stone foundation, rockshelf further
forming underneath everything that grows.

1977

A WILD PATIENCE
HAS TAKEN ME
THIS FAR
(1978–1981)

THE IMAGES

    Close to your body, in the
    pain of the city
I turn. My hand half-sleeping reaches, finds
        some part of you, touch knows you before language
        names in the brain. Out in the dark
a howl, police sirens, emergency
        our 3 a.m. familiar, ripping the sheath of sleep
        registering pure force as if all transpired—
the swell of cruelty and helplessness—
        in one block between West End
        and Riverside. In my dreams the Hudson
rules the night like a right-hand margin
        drawn against the updraft
        of burning life, the tongueless cries
of the city. I turn again, slip my arm
        under the pillow turned for relief,
        your breathing traces my shoulder. Two women sleeping
together have more than their sleep to defend.

    And what can reconcile me
    that you, the woman whose hand
sensual and protective, brushes me in sleep,
        go down each morning into such a city?
        I will not, cannot withhold
your body or my own from its chosen danger
        but when did we ever choose
        to see our bodies strung
in bondage and crucifixion across the exhausted air
        when did we choose
        to be lynched on the queasy electric signs
of midtown when did we choose
        to become the masturbator's fix
        emblem of rape in Riverside Park   the campground
        at Bandol   the beach at Sydney?

We are trying to live
in a clearheaded tenderness—
I speak not merely of us, our lives
are "moral and ordinary"
as the lives of numberless women—
I pretend the Hudson is a right-hand margin
drawn against fear and woman-loathing
(water as purification, river as boundary)
but I know my imagination lies:
in the name of freedom of speech
they are lynching us no law is on our side
there are no boundaries
no-man's-land does not exist.

I can never romanticize language again
never deny its power for disguise for mystification
but the same could be said for music
or any form created
painted ceilings beaten gold worm-worn Pietàs
reorganizing victimization   frescoes translating
violence into patterns so powerful and pure
we continually fail to ask are they true for us.

When I walked among time-battered stones
thinking already of you
when I sat near the sea
among parched yet flowering weeds
when I drew in my notebook
the thorned purple-tongued flower, each petal
protected by its thorn-leaf
I was mute
innocent of grammar as the waves
irrhythmically washing   I felt washed clean
of the guilt of words   there was no word to read
in the book of that earth   no perjury
the tower of Babel fallen once and for all

light drank at my body
thinking of you I felt free
in the cicadas' pulse, their encircling praise.

When I saw hér face, she of the several faces
staring   indrawn   in judgment   laughing for joy
her serpents twisting   her arms raised
her breasts   gazing
when I looked into hér world
I wished to cry loose my soul
into her, to become
free of speech   at last.

And so I came home   a woman starving
for images
to say my hunger is so old
so fundamental, that all the lost
crumbled   burnt   smashed   shattered   defaced
overpainted   concealed and falsely named
faces of every past we have searched together
in all the ages
could rise   reassemble   re-collect   re-member
themselves as I recollected myself in that presence
as every night close to your body
in the pain of the city, turning
I am remembered by you, remember you
even as we are dismembered
on the cinema screens, the white expensive walls
of collectors, the newsrags blowing the streets
—and it would not be enough.
This is the war of the images.
We are the thorn-leaf guarding the purple-tongued flower
each to each.

1976–1978

COAST TO COAST

There are days when housework seems the only
outlet   old funnel I've poured caldrons through
old servitude   In grief and fury bending
to the accustomed tasks   the vacuum cleaner plowing
realms of dust   the mirror scoured   grey webs
behind framed photographs   brushed away
the grey-seamed sky enormous in the west
snow gathering in corners   of the north

Seeing through the prism
you who gave it me
                          You, bearing ceaselessly
yourself   the witness
Rainbow dissolves the Hudson   This chary, stinting
skin of late winter   ice   forming and breaking up
The unprotected seeing it through
with their ordinary valor

Rainbow composed of ordinary light
February-flat
grey-white of a cheap enamelled pan
breaking into veridian, azure, violet
You write: *Three and a half weeks lost from writing.* . . .
I think of the word *protection*
who it is we try to protect   and why

Seeing through the prism   Your face, fog-hollowed   burning
cold of eucalyptus hung with butterflies
lavender of rockbloom
O and your anger uttered in silence word and stammer
shattering the fog   lances of sun
piercing the grey Pacific   unanswerable tide
carving itself in clefts and fissures of the rock
Beauty of your breasts   your hands

turning a stone a shell a weed a prism   in coastal light
traveller and witness
the passion of the speechless
driving your speech
protectless

If you can read and understand this poem
send something back: a burning strand of hair
a still-warm, still-liquid drop of blood
a shell
thickened from being battered year on year
send something back.

1978

INTEGRITY

the quality or state of being complete: unbroken condition: entirety

—Webster's

A wild patience has taken me this far

as if I had to bring to shore
a boat with a spasmodic outboard motor
old sweaters, nets, spray-mottled books
tossed in the prow
some kind of sun burning my shoulder-blades.
Splashing the oarlocks. Burning through.
Your fore-arms can get scalded, licked with pain
in a sun blotted like unspoken anger
behind a casual mist.

The length of daylight
this far north, in this
forty-ninth year of my life
is critical.

The light is critical: of me, of this
long-dreamed, involuntary landing
on the arm of an inland sea.
The glitter of the shoal
depleting into shadow
I recognize: the stand of pines
violet-black really, green in the old postcard
but really I have nothing but myself
to go by; nothing
stands in the realm of pure necessity
except what my hands can hold.

Nothing but myself? . . . My selves.
After so long, this answer.
As if I had always known
I steer the boat in, simply.
The motor dying on the pebbles
cicadas taking up the hum
dropped in the silence.

Anger and tenderness: my selves.
And now I can believe they breathe in me
as angels, not polarities.
Anger and tenderness: the spider's genius
to spin and weave in the same action
from her own body, anywhere—
even from a broken web.

The cabin in the stand of pines
is still for sale. I know this. Know the print
of the last foot, the hand that slammed and locked that door,

then stopped to wreathe the rain-smashed clematis
back on the trellis
for no one's sake except its own.
I know the chart nailed to the wallboards
the icy kettle squatting on the burner.
The hands that hammered in those nails
emptied that kettle one last time
are these two hands
and they have caught the baby leaping
from between trembling legs
and they have worked the vacuum aspirator
and stroked the sweated temples
and steered the boat here through this hot
misblotted sunlight, critical light
imperceptibly scalding
the skin these hands will also salve.

1978

CULTURE AND ANARCHY

Leafshade stirring on lichened bark
       Daylilies
run wild, "escaped" the botanists call it
from dooryard to meadow to roadside

Life-tingle of angled light
       late summer
sharpening toward fall, each year more sharply

This headlong, loved, escaping life

Rainy days at the kitchen table typing,
heaped up letters, a dry moth's
perfectly mosaiced wings, pamphlets on rape,
forced sterilization, snapshots in color
of an Alabama woman still quilting in her nineties,
The Life and Work of Susan B. Anthony. . . .

> *I stained and varnished*
> *the library bookcase today and superintended*
> *the plowing of the orchard.* . . .
> *Fitted out a fugitive slave for Canada*
> *with the help of Harriet Tubman.* . . .
> *The women's committee failed*
> *to report. I am mortified to death for them.* . . .
> *Washed every window in the house today.*
> *Put a quilted petticoat in the frame.*
> *Commenced Mrs. Browning's Portuguese*
> *Sonnets. Have just finished*
> *Casa Guidi Windows, a grand poem*
> *and so fitting to our struggle.* . . .
> *To forever blot out slavery is the only*
> *possible compensation for this*
> *merciless war.* . . .

> *The all-alone feeling will creep over me.* . . .

Upstairs, long silence, then
again, the sudden torrent of your typing

Rough drafts we share, each reading
her own page over the other's shoulder
trying to see afresh

An energy I cannot even yet
take for granted: picking up a book

of the nineteenth century, reading there the name
of the woman whose book you found
in the old town Athenaeum
beginning to stitch together
Elizabeth Ellet
Elizabeth Barrett
Elizabeth Blackwell
Frances Kemble
Ida B. Wells-Barnett
Susan B. Anthony

> *On Saturday Mrs. Ford took us to Haworth,*
> *the home of the Brontë sisters. . . .*
> *A most sad day it was to me*
> *as I looked into the little parlor where*
> *the sisters walked up and down*
> *with their arms around each other*
> *and planned their novels. . . .*
> *How much the world of literature has lost*
> *because of their short and ill-environed lives*

we can only guess. . . .

Anarchy of August: as if already
autumnal gases glowed in darkness underground
the meadows roughen, grow guttural
with goldenrod, milkweed's late-summer lilac,
cat-tails, the wild lily brazening,
dooryards overflowing in late, rough-headed
bloom: bushes of orange daisies, purple mallow,
the thistle blazing in her clump of knives,
and the great SUNFLOWER turns

Haze wiping out the hills. Mornings like milk,
the mind wading, treading water, the line of vision blind
the pages of the book cling to the hand

words hang in a suspension
the prism hanging in the windowframe
is blank
A stillness building all day long to thunder
as the weedpod swells and thickens
No one can call this calm

> Jane Addams, marking time
> in Europe: *During most*
> *of that time I was absolutely at sea*
> *so far as any moral purpose was concerned*
> *clinging only to the desire to live*
> *in a really living world*
> *refusing to be content*
> *with a shadowy intellectual*
> *or aesthetic reflection*

finally the bursting of the sky
power, release

by sheets by ropes of water, wind
driving before or after
the book laid face-down on the table
spirit travelling the lines of storm
leaping the torrent   all that water
already smelling of earth

> Elizabeth Barrett to Anna Jameson:
> *. . . and is it possible you think*
> *a woman has no business with questions*
> *like the question of slavery?*
> *Then she had better use a pen no more.*
> *She had better subside into slavery*
> *and concubinage herself, I think, . . .*
> *and take no rank among thinkers and speakers.*

Early dark; still raining; the electricity
out. On the littered table
a transparent globe half-filled
with liquid light, the soaked wick quietly
drinking, turning to flame
that faintly stains the slim glass chimney:
ancient, fragile contrivance

light welling, searching the shadows

Matilda Joslyn Gage; Harriet Tubman;
Ida B. Wells-Barnett; Maria Mitchell;
Anna Howard Shaw; Sojourner Truth;
Elizabeth Cady Stanton; Harriet Hosmer;
Clara Barton; Harriet Beecher Stowe;
Ida Husted Harper; Ernestine Rose

and all those without names
because of their short and ill-environed lives

False dawn. Gossamer tents in wet grass: leaflets
dissolving within hours,
spun of necessity and
leaving no trace

The heavy volumes, calf, with titles in smooth
leather, red and black, gilt letters spelling:
THE HISTORY OF HUMAN SUFFERING

I brush my hand across my eyes
—this is a dream, I think—and read:
THE HISTORY OF WOMAN SUFFRAGE

> *of a movement*
> *for many years unnoticed*
> *or greatly misrepresented in the public press*

its records usually not considered
of sufficient value to be
officially preserved

and conjure up again
THE HISTORY OF HUMAN SUFFERING
like bound back issues of a periodical
stretching for miles
OF HUMAN SUFFERING: borne,
tended, soothed, cauterized,
stanched, cleansed, absorbed, endured
by women

our records usually not considered
of sufficient value to be
officially preserved

The strongest reason
for giving woman all the opportunities
for higher education, for the full
development of her forces of mind and body . . .
the most enlarged freedom of thought and action
a complete emancipation
from all the crippling influences of fear—
is the solitude and personal
responsibility
of her own individual life.

Late afternoon: long silence.
Your notes on yellow foolscap drift on the table
you go down to the garden to pick chard
while the strength is in the leaves
crimson stems veining upward into green
How you have given back to me
my dream of a common language
my solitude of self.

I slice the beetroots to the core,
each one contains a different landscape
of bloodlight filaments, distinct rose-purple
striations like the oldest
strata of a Southwestern canyon
an undiscovered planet laid open in the lens

> *I should miss you more than any other*
> *living being from this earth. . .*
> *Yes, our work is one,*
> *we are one in aim and sympathy*
> *and we should be together. . . .*

1978

FOR JULIA IN NEBRASKA

Here on the divide between the Republican and the Little Blue lived some of the
most courageous people of the frontier. Their fortunes and their loves live again in
the writings of Willa Cather, daughter of the plains and interpreter of man's growth
in these fields and in the valleys beyond.

On this beautiful, ever-changing land, man fought to establish a home. In her vision
of the plow against the sun, symbol of the beauty and importance of work, Willa
Cather caught the eternal blending of earth and sky. . . .

In the Midwest of Willa Cather
the railroad looks like a braid of hair
a grandmother's strong hands plaited
straight down a grand-daughter's back.
Out there last autumn the streets
dreamed copper-lustre, the fields
of winter wheat whispered long snows yet to fall
we were talking of matrices

and now it's spring again already.
This stormy Sunday lashed with rain
I call you in Nebraska
hear you're planting your garden
sanding and oiling a burl of wood
hear in your voice the intention to
survive the long war between mind and body
and we make a promise to talk
this year, about growing older

and I think: we're making a pledge.
Though not much in books of ritual
is useful between women
we still can make vows together
long distance, in electrical code:
Today you were promising me
to live, and I took your word,
Julia, as if it were my own:
we'll live to grow old and talk about it too.

I've listened to your words
seen you stand by the caldron's glare
rendering grammar by the heat
of your womanly wrath.
Brave linguist, bearing your double axe and shield
painfully honed and polished,
no word lies cool on your tongue
bent on restoring meaning to
our lesbian names, in quiet fury
weaving the chronicle so violently torn.

On this beautiful, ever-changing land
—the historical marker says—
man fought to establish a home
(fought whom? the marker is mute.)
They named this Catherland, for Willa Cather,

lesbian—the marker is mute,
the marker white men set on a soil
of broken treaties, Indian blood,
women wiped out in childbirths, massacres—
for Willa Cather, lesbian,
whose letters were burnt in shame.

Dear Julia, Willa knew at her death
that the very air was changing
that her Archbishop's skies
would hardly survive his life
she knew as well that history
is neither your script nor mine
it is the pictograph
from which the young must learn
like Tom Outland, from people
discredited or dead
that it needs a telling as plain
as the prairie, as the tale
of a young girl or an old woman
told by tongues that loved them

And Willa who could not tell
her own story as it was
left us her stern and delicate
respect for the lives she loved—
How are we going to do better?
for that's the question that lies
beyond our excavations,
the question I ask of you
and myself, when our maps diverge,
when we miss signals, fail—

And if I've written in passion,
Live, Julia! what was I writing
but my own pledge to myself

where the love of women is rooted?
And what was I invoking
but the matrices we weave
web upon web, delicate rafters
flung in audacity to the prairie skies
nets of telepathy contrived
to outlast the iron road
laid out in blood across the land they called virgin—
nets, strands, a braid of hair
a grandmother's strong hands plaited
straight down a grand-daughter's back.

1978, 1981

TRANSIT

When I meet the skier she is always
walking, skis and poles shouldered, toward the mountain
free-swinging in worn boots
over the path new-sifted with fresh snow
her greying dark hair almost hidden by
a cap of many colors
her fifty-year-old, strong, impatient body
dressed for cold and speed
her eyes level with mine

And when we pass each other I look into her face
wondering what we have in common
where our minds converge
for we do not pass each other, she passes me
as I halt beside the fence tangled in snow,
she passes me as I shall never pass her
in this life

Yet I remember us together
climbing Chocorua, summer nineteen-forty-five
details of vegetation beyond the timberline
lichens, wildflowers, birds,
amazement when the trail broke out onto the granite ledge
sloped over blue lakes, green pines, giddy air
like dreams of flying

When sisters separate they haunt each other
as she, who I might once have been, haunts me
or is it I who do the haunting
halting and watching on the path
how she appears again through lightly-blowing
crystals, how her strong knees carry her,
how unaware she is, how simple
this is for her, how without let or hindrance
she travels in her body
until the point of passing, where the skier
and the cripple must decide
to recognize each other?

1979

FOR MEMORY

Old words: *trust fidelity*
Nothing new yet to take their place.

I rake leaves, clear the lawn, October grass
painfully green beneath the gold
and in this silent labor thoughts of you
start up
I hear your voice: *disloyalty   betrayal*
stinging the wires

I stuff the old leaves into sacks
and still they fall and still
I see my work undone

One shivering rainswept afternoon
and the whole job to be done over

I can't know what you know
unless you tell me
there are gashes in our understandings
of this world
We came together in a common
fury of direction
barely mentioning difference
(what drew our finest hairs
to fire
the deep, difficult troughs
unvoiced)
I fell through a basement railing
the first day of school and cut my forehead open—
did I ever tell you? More than forty years

and I still remember smelling my own blood
like the smell of a new schoolbook

And did you ever tell me
how your mother called you in from play
and from whom? To what? These atoms filmed by ordinary dust
that common life we each and all bent out of orbit from
to which we must return simply to say
this is where I came from
this is what I knew

The past is not a husk   yet change goes on

Freedom. It isn't once, to walk out
under the Milky Way, feeling the rivers
of light, the fields of dark—
freedom is daily, prose-bound, routine
remembering. Putting together, inch by inch
the starry worlds. From all the lost collections.

1979

WHAT IS POSSIBLE

A clear night   if the mind were clear

If the mind were simple, if the mind were bare
of all but the most classic necessities:
wooden spoon   knife   mirror
cup   lamp   chisel
a comb passing through hair beside a window
a sheet
          thrown back by the sleeper

A clear night in which two planets
seem to clasp each other   in which the earthly grasses
shift like silk in starlight
                    If the mind were clear
and if the mind were simple   you could take this mind
this particular state   and say
This is how I would live if I could choose:
this is what is possible

A clear night.   But the mind
of the woman imagining all this   the mind
that allows all this to be possible
is not clear as the night

is never simple   cannot clasp
its truths as the transiting planets clasp each other
does not so easily

           work free from remorse

does not so easily

          manage the miracle

for which mind is famous

              or used to be famous

does not at will become abstract and pure

this woman's mind

does not even will that miracle
having a different mission

          in the universe

If the mind were simple   if the mind were bare
it might resemble a room   a swept interior
but how could this now   be possible

given the voices of the ghost-towns
their tiny and vast configurations
needing to be deciphered

           the oracular night

with its densely working sounds

if it could ever come down to anything like
a comb passing through hair beside a window

no more than that

        a sheet
        thrown back by the sleeper

but the mind
of the woman thinking this   is wrapped in battle
is on another mission
a stalk of grass   dried feathery weed   rooted in snow
in frozen air stirring   a fierce wand graphing

Her finger also tracing
pages of a book
knowing better than the poem she reads

knowing through the poem

through ice-feathered panes
the winter

flexing its talons
the hawk-wind

poised to kill

1980

FOR ETHEL ROSENBERG

convicted, with her husband, of "conspiracy to commit espionage": killed in the electric chair June 19, 1953

1.

Europe 1953:
throughout my random sleepwalk
the words

scratched on walls, on pavements
painted over railway arches
Liberez les Rosenberg!

Escaping from home I found
home everywhere:
the Jewish question, Communism

marriage itself
a question of loyalty
or punishment

my Jewish father writing me
letters of seventeen pages
finely inscribed harangues

questions of loyalty
and punishment
One week before my wedding

that couple gets the chair
the volts grapple her, don't
kill her fast enough

Liberez les Rosenberg!
I hadn't realized
our family arguments were so important

my narrow understanding
of crime   of punishment
no language for this torment

mystery of that marriage
always both faces
on every front page in the world

Something so shocking   so
unfathomable
it must be pushed aside

2.

She sank however into my soul   A weight of sadness
I hardly can register how deep
her memory has sunk   that wife and mother

like so many
who seemed to get nothing out of any of it
except her children

that daughter   of a family
like so many
needing its female monster

she, actually wishing to be   *an artist*
wanting out of poverty
possibly also really wanting

                              revolution

that woman   strapped in the chair
no fear and no regrets
charged by posterity

not with selling secrets to the Communists
but with wanting   *to distinguish*
herself   being a bad daughter   a bad mother

And I   walking to my wedding
by the same token a bad daughter   a bad sister
my forces focussed

on that hardly revolutionary effort
Her life and death   the possible
ranges of disloyalty

so painful   so unfathomable
they must be pushed aside
ignored for years

3.

Her mother testifies against her
Her brother testifies against her
After her death

she becomes a natural prey for pornographers
her death itself a scene
her body *sizzling*   *half-strapped*   *whipped like a sail*

She becomes the extremest victim
described nonetheless as *rigid of will*
what are her politics by then   no one knows

Her figure sinks into my soul
a drowned statue
sealed in lead

For years it has lain there   unabsorbed
first as part of that dead couple
on the front pages of the world   the week

I gave myself in marriage
then slowly severing   drifting apart
a separate death   a life unto itself

no longer *the Rosenbergs*
no longer the chosen scapegoat
the family monster

till I hear how she sang
a prostitute to sleep
in the Women's House of Detention

Ethel Greenglass Rosenberg   would you
have marched to take back the night
collected signatures

for battered women who kill
What would you have to tell us
would you have burst the net

4.

Why do I even want to call her up
to console my pain   (she feels no pain at all)
why do I wish to put such questions

to ease myself   (she feels no pain at all
she   finally burned to death   like so many)
why all this exercise of hindsight?

since   if I imagine her at all
I have to imagine first
the pain inflicted on her   by women

her mother testifies against her
her sister-in-law testifies against her
and how she sees it

not the impersonal forces
not the historical reasons
why they might have hated her strength

If I have held her at arm's length till now
if I have still believed it was
my loyalty, my punishment at stake

if I dare imagine her surviving
I must be fair to what she must have lived through
I must allow her to be at last

political in her ways   not in mine
her urgencies perhaps   impervious to mine
defining revolution as she defines it

or, bored to the marrow of her bones
with "politics"
bored with the vast boredom of long pain

small; tiny in fact; in her late sixties
liking her room   her private life
living alone perhaps

no one you could interview
maybe filling a notebook herself
with secrets she has never sold

1980

MOTHER-IN-LAW

Tell me something
                    you say
    Not: What are you working on now, is there anyone special,
    how is the job
    do you mind coming back to an empty house

what do you do on Sundays
Tell me something . . .
                    Some secret
we both know and have never spoken?
Some sentence that could flood with light
your life, mine?
Tell me what daughters tell their mothers
everywhere in the world, and I and only I
even have to ask. . . .
Tell me something.
    Lately, I hear it: Tell me something true,
    daughter-in-law, before we part,
    tell me something true before I die

    And time was when I tried.
You married my son, and so
strange as you are, you're my daughter
Tell me. . . .
    I've been trying to tell you, mother-in-law
    that I think I'm breaking in two
    and half of me doesn't even want to love
    I can polish this table to satin because I don't care
    I am trying to tell you, I envy
    the people in mental hospitals their freedom
    and I can't live on placebos
    or Valium, like you

A cut lemon scours the smell of fish away
You'll feel better when the children are in school
    I would try to tell you, mother-in-law
    but my anger takes fire from yours and in the oven
    the meal bursts into flames
Daughter-in-law, before we part
tell me something true
    I polished the table, mother-in-law
    and scrubbed the knives with half a lemon

the way you showed me to do
I wish I could tell you—
                    Tell me!
They think I'm weak and hold
things back from me. I agreed to this years ago.
Daughter-in-law, strange as you are,
tell me something true

tell me something
                    Your son is dead
ten years, I am a lesbian,
my children are themselves.
Mother-in-law, before we part
shall we try again? Strange as I am,
strange as you are? What do mothers
ask their own daughters, everywhere in the world?
Is there a question?
                    Ask me something.

1980

HEROINES

Exceptional
          even deviant
                    you draw your long skirts
across the nineteenth century
                    Your mind
burns long after death
                    not like the harbor beacon
but like a pyre of driftwood
                    on the beach
                              You are spared

illiteracy
>   death by pneumonia
>   teeth which leave the gums
the seamstress' clouded eyes
>   the mill-girl's shortening breath
by a collection
>   of circumstances
>   soon to be known as
class privilege
>   The law says you can possess nothing
>   in a world
where property is everything
>   You belong first to your father
then to him who
>   chooses you
>   if you fail to marry
you are without recourse
>   unable to earn
>   a workingman's salary
forbidden to vote
>   forbidden to speak
>   in public

if married you are legally dead
>   the law says
you may not bequeath property
>   save to your children
or male kin
>   that your husband
>   has the right
of the slaveholder
>   to hunt down and re-possess you
>   should you escape
You may inherit slaves
>   but have no power to free them

your skin is fair

        you have been taught that light

came

    to the Dark Continent

          with white power

that the Indians

       live in filth

         and occult animal rites

Your mother wore corsets

        to choke her spirit

            which if you refuse

you are jeered for refusing

        you have heard many sermons

and have carried

      your own interpretations

           locked in your heart

You are a woman

      strong in health

         through a collection

of circumstances

      soon to be known

          as class privilege

which if you break

      the social compact

         you lose outright

When you open your mouth in public

        human excrement

           is flung at you

you are exceptional

      in personal circumstance

          in indignation

you give up believing

      in protection

       in Scripture

in man-made laws
                    respectable as you look
                                     you are an outlaw
Your mind burns
                    not like the harbor beacon
                                 but like a fire
of fiercer origin
                  you begin speaking out
and a great gust of freedom
                        rushes in with your words
yet still you speak
                  in the shattered language
                              of a partial vision
You draw your long skirts
                    deviant
                          across the nineteenth century
registering injustice
                failing to make it whole
How can I fail to love
                  your clarity and fury
how can I give you
              all your due
                        take courage from your courage
honor your exact
              legacy as it is
recognizing
          as well
              that it is not enough?

1980

GRANDMOTHERS

1. Mary Gravely Jones

We had no petnames, no diminutives for you,
always the formal guest under my father's roof:
you were "Grandmother Jones" and you visited rarely.
I see you walking up and down the garden,
restless, southern-accented, reserved, you did not seem
my mother's mother or anyone's grandmother.
You were Mary, widow of William, and no matriarch,
yet smoldering to the end with frustrate life,
ideas nobody listened to, least of all my father.
One summer night you sat with my sister and me
in the wooden glider long after twilight,
holding us there with streams of pent-up words.
You could quote every poet I had ever heard of,
had read *The Opium Eater,* Amiel and Bernard Shaw,
your green eyes looked clenched against opposition.
You married straight out of the convent school,
your background was country, you left an unperformed
typescript of a play about Burr and Hamilton,
you were impotent and brilliant, no one cared
about your mind, you might have ended
elsewhere than in that glider
reciting your unwritten novels to the children.

2. Hattie Rice Rich

Your sweetness of soul was a mystery to me,
you who slip-covered chairs, glued broken china,
lived out of a wardrobe trunk in our guestroom
summer and fall, then took the Pullman train
in your darkblue dress and straw hat, to Alabama,

shuttling half-yearly between your son and daughter.
Your sweetness of soul was a convenience for everyone,
how you rose with the birds and children, boiled your own egg,
fished for hours on a pier, your umbrella spread, took the street-car
downtown shopping
endlessly for your son's whims, the whims of genius,
kept your accounts in ledgers, wrote letters daily.
All through World War Two the forbidden word
Jewish was barely uttered in your son's house;
your anger flared over inscrutable things.
Once I saw you crouched on the guestroom bed,
knuckles blue-white around the bedpost, sobbing
your one brief memorable scene of rebellion:
you didn't want to go back South that year.
You were never "Grandmother Rich" but "Anana";
you had money of your own but you were homeless,
Hattie, widow of Samuel, and no matriarch,
dispersed among the children and grandchildren.

3. Granddaughter

Easier to encapsulate your lives
in a slide-show of impressions given and taken,
to play the child or victim, the projectionist,
easier to invent a script for each of you,
myself still at the center,
than to write words in which you might have found
yourselves, looked up at me and said
"Yes, I was like that; but I was something more. . . ."
Danville, Virginia; Vicksburg, Mississippi;
the "war between the states" a living memory
its aftermath the plague-town closing
its gates, trying to cure itself with poisons.
I can almost touch that little town. . . .
a little white town rimmed with Negroes,

making a deep shadow on the whiteness.
Born a white woman, Jewish or of curious mind
—twice an outsider, still believing in inclusion—
in those defended hamlets of half-truth
broken in two by one strange idea,
"blood" the all-powerful, awful theme—
what were the lessons to be learned? If I believe
the daughter of one of you—Amnesia was the answer.

1980

THE SPIRIT OF PLACE

For Michelle Cliff

I.

Over the hills in Shutesbury, Leverett
driving with you in spring   road
like a streambed unwinding downhill
fiddlehead ferns uncurling
spring peepers ringing sweet and cold

while we talk yet again
of dark and light, of blackness, whiteness, numbness
rammed through the heart like a stake
trying to pull apart the threads
from the dried blood of the old murderous uncaring

halting on bridges in bloodlight
where the freshets call out freedom
to frog-thrilling swamp, skunk-cabbage
trying to sense the conscience of these hills

knowing how the single-minded, pure
solutions bleached and dessicated
within their perfect flasks

for it was not enough to be New England
as every event since has testified:
New England's a shadow-country, always was

it was not enough to be for abolition
while the spirit of the masters
flickered in the abolitionist's heart

it was not enough to name ourselves anew
while the spirit of the masters
calls the freedwoman to forget the slave

With whom do you believe your lot is cast?
If there's a conscience in these hills
it hurls that question

unquenched, relentless, to our ears
wild and witchlike
ringing every swamp

II.

The mountain laurel in bloom
constructed like needlework
tiny half-pulled stitches piercing
flushed and stippled petals

here in these woods it grows wild
midsummer moonrise turns it opal
the night breathes with its clusters
protected species

meaning endangered
Here in these hills
this valley   we have felt
a kind of freedom

planting the soil   have known
hours of a calm, intense and mutual solitude
reading and writing
trying to clarify   connect

past and present   near and far
the Alabama quilt
the Botswana basket
history   the dark crumble

of last year's compost
filtering softly through your living hand
but here as well we face
instantaneous violence   ambush   male

dominion on a back road
to escape in a locked car   windows shut
skimming the ditch   your split-second
survival reflex taking on the world

as it is   not as we wish it
as it is   not as we work for it
to be

III.

Strangers are an endangered species

In Emily Dickinson's house in Amherst
cocktails are served   the scholars
gather in celebration

554

their pious or clinical legends
festoon the walls like imitations
of period patterns

(. . . *and, as I feared, my "life" was made a "victim"*)

The remnants pawed   the relics
the cult assembled in the bedroom
and you   whose teeth were set on edge by churches
resist your shine
                escape
                          are found
nowhere
          unless in words
                          (your own)

All we are strangers—dear—The world is not
acquainted with us, because we are not acquainted
with her. And Pilgrims!—Do you hesitate? and
Soldiers oft—some of us victors, but those I do
not see tonight owing to the smoke.—We are hungry,
and thirsty, sometimes—We are barefoot—and cold—

This place is large enough for both of us
the river-fog will do for privacy
this is my third and last address to you

with the hands of a daughter I would cover you
from all intrusion   even my own
saying   rest to your ghost

with the hands of a sister I would leave your hands
open or closed as they prefer to lie
and ask no more of who or why or wherefore

with the hands of a mother I would close the door
on the rooms you've left behind
and silently pick up my fallen work

IV

The river-fog will do for privacy
on the low road a breath
here, there, a cloudiness floating on the blacktop

sunflower heads turned black and bowed
the seas of corn a stubble
the old routes flowing north, if not to freedom

no human figure now in sight
(with whom do you believe your lot is cast?)
only the functional figure of the scarecrow

the cut corn, ground to shreds, heaped in a shape
like an Indian burial mound
a haunted-looking, ordinary thing

The work of winter starts fermenting in my head
how with the hands of a lover or a midwife
to hold back till the time is right

force nothing, be unforced
accept no giant miracles of growth
by counterfeit light

trust roots, allow the days to shrink
give credence to these slender means
wait without sadness and with grave impatience

here in the north where winter has a meaning
where the heaped colors suddenly go ashen
where nothing is promised

learn what an underground journey
has been, might have to be; speak in a winter code
let fog, sleet, translate; wind, carry them.

V.

Orion plunges like a drunken hunter
over the Mohawk Trail   a parallelogram
slashed with two cuts of steel

A night so clear that every constellation
stands out from an undifferentiated cloud
of stars, a kind of aura

All the figures up there look violent to me
as a pogrom on Christmas Eve in some old country
I want our own earth   not the satellites, our

world as it is   if not as it might be
then as it is: male dominion, gangrape, lynching, pogrom
the Mohawk wraiths in their tracts of leafless birch

watching: will we do better?
The tests I need to pass are prescribed by the spirits
of place   who understand travel but not amnesia

The world as it is: not as her users boast
damaged beyond reclamation by their using
Ourselves as we are   in these painful motions

of staying cognizant: some part of us always
out beyond ourselves
knowing   knowing   knowing

Are we all in training for something we don't name?
to exact reparation for things
done long ago to us and to those who did not

survive what was done to them   whom we ought to honor
with grief   with fury   with action
On a pure night   on a night when pollution

seems absurdity when the undamaged planet seems to turn
like a bowl of crystal in black ether
they are the piece of us that lies out there
knowing   knowing   knowing

1980

FRAME

Winter twilight. She comes out of the lab-
oratory, last class of the day
a pile of notebooks slung in her knapsack, coat
zipped high against the already swirling
evening sleet. The wind is wicked and the
busses slower than usual. On her mind
is organic chemistry and the issue
of next month's rent and will it be possible to
bypass the professor with the coldest eyes
to get a reference for graduate school,
and whether any of them, even those who smile
can see, looking at her, a biochemist

or a marine biologist, which of the faces
can she trust to see her at all, either today
or in any future. The busses are worm-slow in the
quickly gathering dark. *I don't know her. I am
standing though somewhere just outside the frame
of all this, trying to see.* At her back
the newly finished building suddenly looks
like shelter, it has glass doors, lighted halls
presumably heat. The wind is wicked. She throws a
glance down the street, sees no bus coming and runs
up the newly constructed steps into the newly
constructed hallway. *I am standing all this time
just beyond the frame, trying to see.* She runs
her hand through the crystals of sleet about to melt
on her hair. She shifts the weight of the books
on her back. It isn't warm here exactly but it's
out of that wind. Through the glass
door panels she can watch for the bus through the thickening
weather. Watching so, she is not
watching for the white man who watches the building
who has been watching her. This is Boston 1979.
*I am standing somewhere at the edge of the frame
watching the man, we are both white, who watches the building
telling her to move on, get out of the hallway.
I can hear nothing because I am not supposed to be
present but I can see her gesturing
out toward the street at the wind-raked curb
I see her drawing her small body up
against the implied charges.* The man
goes away. Her body is different now.
It is holding together with more than a hint of fury
and more than a hint of fear. She is smaller, thinner
more fragile-looking than I am. *But I am not supposed to be
there. I am just outside the frame
of this action when the anonymous white man
returns with a white police officer.* Then she starts

to leave into the wind-raked night but already
the policeman is going to work, the handcuffs are on her
wrists he is throwing her down his knee has gone into
her breast he is dragging her down the stairs *I am unable*
to hear a sound of all this all that I know is what
I can see from this position there is no soundtrack
to go with this and I understand at once
it is meant to be in silence that this happens
in silence that he pushes her into the car
banging her head in silence that she cries out
in silence that she tries to explain she was only
waiting for a bus
in silence that he twists the flesh of her thigh
with his nails in silence that her tears begin to flow
that she pleads with the other policeman as if
he could be trusted to see her at all
in silence that in the precinct she refuses to give her name
in silence that they throw her into the cell
in silence that she stares him
straight in the face in silence that he sprays her
in her eyes with Mace in silence that she sinks her teeth
into his hand in silence that she is charged
with trespass assault and battery in
silence that at the sleet-swept corner her bus
passes without stopping and goes on
in silence. *What I am telling you*
is told by a white woman who they will say
was never there. I say I am there.

1980

RIFT

I have in my head some images of you:
your face turned awkwardly from the kiss of greeting
the sparkle of your eyes in the dark car, driving
your beautiful fingers reaching for
a glass of water.
    Also your lip curling
at what displeases you, the sign of closure,
the fending-off, the clouding-over.
       Politics,
you'd say, *is an unworthy name*
for what we're after.
     What we're after
is not that clear to me, if politics
is an unworthy name.

When language fails us, when we fail each other
there is no exorcism. The hurt continues. Yes, your scorn
turns up the jet of my anger. Yes, I find you
overweening, obsessed, and even in your genius
narrow-minded—I could list much more—
and absolute loyalty was never in my line
once having left it in my father's house—
but as I go on sorting images of you
my hand trembles, and I try
to train it not to tremble.

1980

A VISION

(thinking of Simone Weil)

You. There, with your gazing eyes
Your blazing eyes

A hand or something passes across the sun. Your eyeballs slacken,
you are free for a moment. Then it comes back: this
test of the capacity to keep in focus
this
     unfair struggle with the forces of perception
this enforced
                 (but at that word your attention changes)
this enforced   loss of self
in a greater thing of course, who has ever
lost herself in something smaller?

You with your cornea and iris and their power
you with your stubborn lids that have stayed open
at the moment of pouring liquid steel
you with your fear of blinding

Here it is. I am writing this almost
involuntarily on a bad, a junky typewriter that skips
and slides the text
Still these are mechanical problems, writing to you
is another kind of problem
and even so the words create themselves

What is your own will that it
can so transfix you
why are you forced to take this test
over and over and call it God
why not call it you and get it over

you with your hatred of enforcement
and your fear of blinding?

1981

TURNING THE WHEEL

1. Location

No room for nostalgia here. What would it look like?
The imitation of a ghost mining town,
the movie-set façade of a false Spanish
arcade, the faceless pueblo
with the usual faceless old woman grinding corn?
It's all been done. Acre on acre
of film locations disguised as Sears,
Safeway, the Desert National Bank,
Fashion Mall, Sun Valley Waterbeds.
Old people, rich, pass on in cloistered stucco
tiled and with fountains; poor, at Golden Acres
Trailer Ranch for Adult Seniors, at the edge of town,
close by the Reassembled Church of Latter-Day
Saints and a dozen motels called Mountain View.
The mountains are on view from everywhere
in this desert: this poor, conquered, bulldozed desert
overridden like a hold-out
enemy village. Nostalgia for the desert
will soon draw you to the Desert Museum
or off on an unpaved track to stare at one saguaro
—velvety, pleated, from a distance graceful—
closer-on, shot through with bullet holes
and seeming to give the finger to it all.

2. Burden Baskets

False history gets made all day, any day,
the truth of the new is never on the news
False history gets written every day
and by some who should know better:
the lesbian archaeologist watches herself
sifting her own life out from the shards she's piecing,
asking the clay all questions but her own.
Yet suddenly for once the standard version
splits open to something shocking, unintentional.
In the elegant Southwest Museum, no trace of bloodshed
or broken treaty. But, behind glass, these baskets
woven for the young women's puberty dances
still performed among the still surviving
Apache people;   filled with offerings:
cans of diet Pepsi, peanut brittle,
Cracker Jack, Hershey bars
piled there, behind glass, without notation
in the anthropologist's typewritten text
which like a patient voice tired of explaining
goes on to explain a different method of weaving.

3. Hohokam

Nostalgia is only amnesia turned around.
I try to pierce through to a prehistoric culture
the museum says were known as *those who have ceased.*
I try to imagine them, before the Hopi
or Navaho, *those who have ceased*
but they draw back, an archetypal blur.
Did they leave behind for Pima or Navaho
something most precious, now archaic,
more than a faceless woman grinding corn?

Those who have ceased is amnesia-language:
no more to be said of them. Nobody wants
to see their faces or hear what they were about.
I try to imagine a desert-shamaness
bringing water to fields of squash, maize and cotton
but where the desert herself is half-eroded
half-flooded by a million jets of spray
to conjure a rich white man's paradise
the shamaness could well have withdrawn her ghost.

4. Self-hatred

In Colcha embroidery, I learn,
women use raveled yarn from old wool blankets
to trace out scenes on homespun woollen sacks—
our ancient art of making out of nothing—
or is it making the old life serve the new?
The impact of Christian culture, it is written,
and other influences, have changed the patterns.
(*Once they were birds perhaps,* I think; *or serpents.*)
Example: here we have a scene of flagellants,
each whip is accurately self-directed.
To understand colonization is taking me
years. I stuck my loaded needle
into the coarse squares of the sack, I smoothed
the stylized pattern on my knee with pride.
I also heard them say my own designs
were childlike, primitive, obscene.
What rivets me to history is seeing
arts of survival turned
to rituals of self-hatred. This
is colonization. Unborn sisters,
look back on us in mercy where we failed ourselves,
see us not one-dimensional but with
the past as your steadying and corrective lens.

5. Particularity

In search of the desert witch, the shamaness
forget the archetypes, forget the dark
and lithic profile, do not scan the clouds
massed on the horizon, violet and green,
for her icon, do not pursue
the ready-made abstraction, do not peer for symbols.
So long as you want her faceless, without smell
or voice, so long as she does not squat
to urinate, or scratch herself, so long
as she does not snore beneath her blanket
or grimace as she grasps the stone-cold
grinding stone at dawn
so long as she does not have her own peculiar
face, slightly wall-eyed or with a streak
of topaz lightning in the blackness
of one eye, so long as she does not limp
so long as you try to simplify her meaning
so long as she merely symbolizes power
she is kept helpless and conventional
her true power routed backward
into the past, we cannot touch or name her
and, barred from participation by those who need her
she stifles in unspeakable loneliness.

6. Apparition

If she appears, hands ringed with rings
you have dreamed about, if on her large fingers
jasper and sardonyx and agate smolder
if she is wearing shawls woven in fire
and blood, if she is wearing shawls
of undyed fiber, yellowish
if on her neck are hung

obsidian and silver, silver and turquoise
if she comes skirted like a Christian
her hair combed back by missionary fingers
if she sits offering her treasure by the road
to spare a brother's or an uncle's dignity
or if she sits pretending
to weave or grind or do some other thing
for the appeasement of the ignorant
if she is the famous potter
whose name confers honor on certain vessels
if she is wrist-deep in mud and shawled in dust
and wholly anonymous
look at her closely if you dare
do not assume you know those cheekbones
or those eye-sockets; or that still-bristling hair.

7. Mary Jane Colter, 1904

My dear Mother and Sister:
                              I have been asked
to design a building in the Hopi style
at the Grand Canyon. As you know
in all my travels for Mr. Harvey
and the Santa Fe Railroad, I have thought this the greatest
sight in the Southwest—in our land entire.
I am here already, trying to make a start.
I cannot tell you with what elation
this commission has filled me. I regret to say
it will mean I cannot come home to St. Paul
as I hoped, this spring. I am hoping this may lead
to other projects here, of equal grandeur.
(Do you understand? I want this glory,
I want to place my own conception
and that of the Indians whose land this was
at the edge of this incommensurable thing.)

I know my life seems shaky, unreliable
to you. When this is finished I promise you
to come home to St. Paul and teach. You will never lack
for what I can give you. Your affectionate
daughter and sister,

                Mary.

8. Turning the Wheel

The road to the great canyon always feels
like that road and no other
the highway to a fissure   to the female core
of a continent
Below Flagstaff even   the rock erosions wear
a famous handwriting
the river's still prevailing signature

Seeing those rocks   that road   in dreams   I know
it is happening again   as twice while waking
I am traveling to the edge   to meet the face
of annihilating and impersonal time
stained in the colors of a woman's genitals
outlasting every transient violation
a face that is strangely intimate to me

Today I turned the wheel   refused that journey
I was feeling too alone on the open plateau
of piñon juniper   world beyond time
of rockflank spread around me   too alone
and too filled with you   with whom I talked for hours
driving up from the desert   though you were far away
as I talk to you all day   whatever day

1981

YOUR NATIVE LAND,
YOUR LIFE
(1981–1985)

I

Sources

For Helen Smelser
—since 1949—

I

Sixteen years.   The narrow, rough-gullied backroads
almost the same.   The farms: almost the same,
a new barn here, a new roof there, a rusting car,
collapsed sugar-house, trailer, new young wife
trying to make a lawn instead of a dooryard,
new names, old kinds of names: Rocquette, Desmarais,
Clark, Pierce, Stone.   Gossier.   No names of mine.

The vixen I met at twilight on Route 5
south of Willoughby: long dead.   She was an omen
to me, surviving, herding her cubs
in the silvery bend of the road
in nineteen sixty-five.

Shapes of things: so much the same
they feel like eternal forms: the house and barn
on the rise above May Pond; the brow of Pisgah;
the face of milkweed blooming,
brookwater pleating over slanted granite,
boletus under pine, the half-composted needles
it broke through patterned on its skin.
Shape of queen anne's lace, with the drop of blood.
Bladder-campion veined with purple.
Multifoliate heal-all.

II

I refuse to become a seeker for cures.
Everything that has ever
helped me has come through what already
lay stored in me.   Old things, diffuse, unnamed, lie strong
across my heart.

This is from where
my strength comes, even when I miss my strength
even when it turns on me
like a violent master.

III

From where?   the voice asks coldly.

This is the voice in cold morning air
that pierces dreams.   *From where does your strength come?*

Old things . . .
                    From where does your strength come, you Southern Jew?
split at the root, raised in a castle of air?

Yes.   I expected this.   I have known for years
the question was coming.   *From where*

(not from these, surely,
Protestant separatists, Jew-baiters, nightriders

who fired in Irasburg in nineteen-sixty-eight
on a black family newly settled in these hills)
                                    From where

the dew grows thick late August on the fierce green grass
and on the wooden sill and on the stone

the mountains stand in an extraordinary
point of no return   though still are green

collapsed shed-boards gleam like pewter in the dew
the realms of touch-me-not   fiery with tiny tongues

cover the wild ground of the woods

IV

With whom do you believe your lot is cast?
From where does your strength come?

I think somehow, somewhere
every poem of mine must repeat those questions

which are not the same.   There is a *whom,* a *where*
that is not chosen   that is given   and sometimes falsely given

in the beginning we grasp whatever we can
to survive

V

All during World War II
I told myself I had some special destiny:
there had to be a reason
I was not living in a bombed-out house
or cellar   hiding out with rats

there had to be a reason
I was growing up safe, American
with sugar rationed in a Mason jar

split at the root   white-skinned social Christian
neither gentile nor Jew

through the immense silence
of the Holocaust

I had no idea of what I had been spared

still less of the women and men   my kin
the Jews of Vicksburg or Birmingham
whose lives must have been strategies no less
than the vixen's on Route 5

VI

If they had played the flute, or chess
I was told   I was not told what they told
their children when the Klan rode
how they might have seen themselves

                                        a chosen people

of shopkeepers
clinging by strategy to a way of life
that had its own uses for them

proud of their length of sojourn in America
deploring the late-comers   the peasants from Russia

I saw my father building
his rootless ideology

his private castle in air

in that most dangerous place, the family home
we were the chosen people

In the beginning we grasp whatever we can

VII

    For years I struggled with you: your categories, your theories,
your will, the cruelty which came inextricable from your love.   For

years all arguments I carried on in my head were with you.   I saw myself, the eldest daughter raised as a son, taught to study but not to pray, taught to hold reading and writing sacred: the eldest daughter in a house with no son, she who must overthrow the father, take what he taught her and use it against him.   All this in a castle of air, the floating world of the assimilated who know and deny they will always be aliens.

After your death I met you again as the face of patriarchy, could name at last precisely the principle you embodied, there was an ideology at last which let me dispose of you, identify the suffering you caused, hate you righteously as part of a system, the kingdom of the fathers.   I saw the power and arrogance of the male as your true watermark; I did not see beneath it the suffering of the Jew, the alien stamp you bore, because you had deliberately arranged that it should be invisible to me.   It is only now, under a powerful, womanly lens, that I can decipher your suffering and deny no part of my own.

VIII

Back there in Maryland the stars
showed liquescent, diffuse

in the breathless summer nights
the constellation melted

I thought I was leaving a place of enervation
heading north where the Drinking Gourd

stood cold and steady at last
pointing the way

I thought I was following a track of freedom
and for awhile it was

IX

Why has my imagination stayed
northeast with the ones who stayed

Are there spirits in me, diaspora-driven
that wanted to lodge somewhere

hooked into the "New" Englanders who hung on
here in this stringent space

believing their Biblical language
their harping on righteousness?

And, myself apart, what was this like for them,
this unlikely growing season

after each winter so mean, so mean
the trying-down of the spirit

and the endless rocks in the soil, the endless
purifications of self

there being no distance, no space around
to experiment with life?

X

These upland farms are the farms
of invaders, these villages

white with rectitude and death
are built on stolen ground

The persecuted, pale with anger
know how to persecute

those who feel destined, under god's eye
need never ponder difference

and if they kill others for being who they are
or where they are

is this a law of history
or simply, *what must change?*

XI

If I try to conjure their lives
—who are not my people by any definition—

Yankee Puritans, Québec Catholics
mingled within sight of the Northern Lights

I am forced to conjure a passion
like the tropism in certain plants

bred of a natural region's
repetitive events

beyond the numb of poverty
christian hypocrisy, isolation

—a passion so unexpected
there is no name for it

so quick, fierce, unconditional
short growing season is no explanation.

XII

And has any of this to do with how
Mohawk or Wampanoag knew it?.

is the passion I connect with in this air
trace of the original

existences that knew this place
is the region still trying to speak with them

is this light a language
the shudder of this aspen-grove a way

of sending messages
the white mind barely intercepts

are signals also coming back
from the vast diaspora

of the people who kept their promises
as a way of life?

XIII

Coming back after sixteen years
I stare anew at things

that steeple pure and righteous
that clapboard farmhouse

seeing what I hadn't seen before
through barnboards, crumbling plaster

decades of old wallpaper roses
clinging to certain studs

—into that dangerous place
the family home:

There are verbal brutalities
borne thereafter like any burn or scar

there are words pulled down from the walls
like dogwhips

the child backed silent against the wall
trying to keep her eyes dry;   haughty;   in panic

I will never let you know
I will never
let you know

XIV

And if my look becomes the bomb that rips
the family home apart

is this betrayal, that the walls
slice off, the staircase shows

torn-away above the street
that the closets where the clothes hung

hang naked, the room the old
grandmother had to sleep in

the toilet on the landing
the room with the books

where the father walks up and down
telling the child to *work, work*

harder than anyone has worked before?
—But I can't stop seeing like this

more and more I see like this everywhere.

XV

It's an oldfashioned, an outrageous thing
to believe one has a "destiny"

—a thought often peculiar to those
who possess privilege—

but there is something else: the faith
of those despised and endangered

that they are not merely the sum
of damages done to them:

have kept beyond violence the knowledge
arranged in patterns like kente-cloth

unexpected as in batik
recurrent as bitter herbs and unleavened bread

of being a connective link
in a long, continuous way

of ordering hunger, weather, death, desire
and the nearness of chaos.

XVI

The Jews I've felt rooted among
are those who were turned to smoke

Reading of the chimneys against the blear air
I think I have seen them myself

the fog of northern Europe licking its way
along the railroad tracks

to the place where all tracks end
You told me not to look there

to become
a citizen of the world

bound by no tribe or clan
yet dying you followed the Six Day War

with desperate attention
and this summer I lie awake at dawn

sweating the Middle East through my brain
wearing the star of David

on a thin chain at my breastbone

XVII

But there was also the other Jew. The one you most feared, the
one from the *shtetl*, from Brooklyn, from the wrong part of history,
the wrong accent, the wrong class. The one I left you for.   The
one both like and unlike you, who explained you to me for years,
who could not explain himself.   The one who said, as if he had

memorized the formula, *There's nothing left now but the food and the humor.* The one who, like you, ended isolate, who had tried to move in the floating world of the assimilated who know and deny they will always be aliens. Who drove to Vermont in a rented car at dawn and shot himself. For so many years I had thought you and he were in opposition. I needed your unlikeness then; now it's your likeness that stares me in the face. There is something more than food, humor, a turn of phrase, a gesture of the hands: there is something more.

XVIII

There is something more than self-hatred. That still outlives
these photos of the old Ashkenazi life:
we are gifted children at camp in the country
or orphaned children in kindergarten
we are hurrying along the rare book dealers' street
with the sunlight striking one side
we are walking the wards of the Jewish hospital
along diagonal squares   young serious nurses
we are part of a family group
formally taken in 1936
with tables, armchairs, ferns
(behind us, in our lives, the muddy street
and the ragged shames
the street-musician, the weavers lined for strike)
we are part of a family wearing white head-bandages
we were beaten in a pogrom

The place where all tracks end
is the place where history was meant to stop
but does not stop   where thinking
was meant to stop but does not stop
where the pattern was meant to give way at last
                                        but only

becomes a different pattern

                             terrible, threadbare

strained   familiar   on-going

XIX

They say such things are stored
in the genetic code—

half-chances, unresolved
possibilities, the life

passed on because unlived—
a mystic biology?—

I think of the women who sailed to Palestine
years before I was born—

halutzot, pioneers
believing in a new life

socialists, anarchists, jeered
as excitable, sharp of tongue

too filled with life
wanting equality in the promised land

carrying the broken promises
of Zionism in their hearts

along with the broken promises
of communism, anarchism—

makers of miracle who expected miracles
as stubbornly as any housewife does

that the life she gives her life to
shall not be cheap

that the life she gives her life to
shall not turn on her

that the life she gives her life to
shall want an end to suffering

Zion by itself is not enough.

XX

The faithful drudging child
the child at the oak desk whose penmanship,
hard work, style will win her prizes
becomes the woman with a mission, not to win prizes
but to change the laws of history.
How she gets this mission
is not clear, how the boundaries of perfection
explode, leaving her cheekbone grey with smoke
a piece of her hair singed off, her shirt
spattered with earth . . . Say that she grew up in a house
with talk of books, ideal societies—
she is gripped by a blue, a foreign air,
a desert absolute: dragged by the roots of her own will
into another scene of choices.

XXI

YERUSHALAYIM: a vault of golden heat
hard-pulsing from bare stones

the desert's hard-won, delicate green
the diaspora of the stars

thrilling like thousand-year-old locusts
audible yet unheard

a city on a hill
waking with first light to voices

piercing, original, intimate
as if my dreams mixed with the cries

of the oldest, earliest birds
and of all whose wrongs and rights

cry out for explication
as the night pales and one more day

breaks on this *Zion* of hope and fear
and broken promises
     this promised land

XXII

I have resisted this for years, writing to you as if you could hear me. It's been different with my father: he and I always had a kind of rhetoric going with each other, a battle between us, it didn't matter if one of us was alive or dead. But, you, I've had a sense of protecting your existence, not using it merely as a theme for poetry or tragic musings; letting you dwell in the minds of those who have reason to miss you, in your way, or their way, not mine. The living, writers especially, are terrible projectionists. I hate the way they use the dead.

Yet I can't finish this without speaking to you, not simply of you. You knew there was more left than food and humor. Even as you said that in 1953 I knew it was a formula you had found, to stand between you and pain. The deep crevices of black pumpernickel under the knife, the sweet butter and red onions we ate on those slices;

the lox and cream cheese on fresh onion rolls; bowls of sour cream mixed with cut radishes, cucumber, scallions; green tomatoes and kosher dill pickles in half-translucent paper; these, you said, were the remnants of the culture, along with the fresh *challah* which turned stale so fast but looked so beautiful.

That's why I want to speak to you now.   To say: no person, trying to take responsibility for her or his identity, should have to be so alone.   There must be those among whom we can sit down and weep, and still be counted as warriors.   (I make up this strange, angry packet for you, threaded with love.)   I think you thought there was no such place for you, and perhaps there was none then, and perhaps there is none now; but we will have to make it, we who want an end to suffering, who want to change the laws of history, if we are not to *give ourselves away.*

XXIII

Sixteen years ago I sat in this northeast kingdom
reading Gilbert White's *Natural History*
of Selborne   thinking
I can never know this land I walk upon
as that English priest knew his
—a comparable piece of earth—
rockledge   soil   insect   bird   weed   tree

I will never know it so well because . . .

Because you have chosen
something else: to know other things
even the cities which
create of this a myth

Because you grew up in a castle of air
disjunctured

Because without a faith
                    you are faithful

I have wished I could rest among the beautiful and common weeds I cán name, both here and in other tracts of the globe.   But there is no finite knowing, no such rest. Innocent birds, deserts, morning-glories, point to choices. leading away from the familiar. When I speak of an end to suffering I don't mean anesthesia. I mean knowing the world, and my place in it, not in order to stare with bitterness or detachment, but as a powerful and womanly series of choices: and here I write the words, in their fullness:
powerful;   womanly.

August 1981–
August 1982

II

North American Time

. . . traigo este calendario.
Sí; aquí se marca el tiempo.
Es almanaque por lo tanto, solo
que es tiempo injusto el que aparece . . .
— Georgina Herrera

(. . . I offer this calendar.
Yes; here time is marked.
It's an almanac therefore, but
only unjust time appears.)

FOR THE RECORD

The clouds and the stars didn't wage this war
the brooks gave no information
if the mountain spewed stones of fire into the river
it was not taking sides
the raindrop faintly swaying under the leaf
had no political opinions

and if here or there a house
filled with backed-up raw sewage
or poisoned those who lived there
with slow fumes, over years
the houses were not at war
nor did the tinned-up buildings

intend to refuse shelter
to homeless old women and roaming children
they had no policy to keep them roaming
or dying, no, the cities were not the problem
the bridges were non-partisan
the freeways burned, but not with hatred

Even the miles of barbed-wire
stretched around crouching temporary huts
designed to keep the unwanted
at a safe distance, out of sight
even the boards that had to absorb
year upon year, so many human sounds

so many depths of vomit, tears
slow-soaking blood
had not offered themselves for this

The trees didn't volunteer to be cut into boards
nor the thorns for tearing flesh
Look around at all of it

and ask whose signature
is stamped on the orders, traced
in the corner of the building plans
Ask where the illiterate, big-bellied
women were, the drunks and crazies,
the ones you fear most of all: ask where you were.

1983

NORTH AMERICAN TIME

I

When my dreams showed signs
of becoming
politically correct
no unruly images
escaping beyond borders
when walking in the street I found my
themes cut out for me
knew what I would not report
for fear of enemies' usage
then I began to wonder

II

Everything we write
will be used against us
or against those we love.
These are the terms,
take them or leave them.
Poetry never stood a chance
of standing outside history.
One line typed twenty years ago
can be blazed on a wall in spraypaint
to glorify art as detachment
or torture of those we
did not love but also
did not want to kill

We move   but our words stand
become responsible
for more than we intended

and this is verbal privilege

III

Try sitting at a typewriter
one calm summer evening
at a table by a window
in the country, try pretending
your time does not exist
that you are simply you
that the imagination simply strays
like a great moth, unintentional
try telling yourself
you are not accountable
to the life of your tribe
the breath of your planet

IV

It doesn't matter what you think.
Words are found responsible
all you can do is choose them
or choose
to remain silent.   Or, you never had a choice,
which is why the words that do stand
are responsible

and this is verbal privilege

V

Suppose you want to write
of a woman braiding
another woman's hair—
straight down, or with beads and shells
in three-stand plaits or corn-rows—
you had better know the thickness
the length   the pattern
why she decides to braid her hair
how it is done to her
what country it happens in
what else happens in that country

You have to know these things

VI

Poet, sister: words—
whether we like it or not—
stand in a time of their own.
No use protesting   *I wrote that*

before Kollontai was exiled
Rosa Luxemburg, Malcolm,
Anna Mae Aquash, murdered,
before Treblinka, Birkenau,
Hiroshima, before Sharpeville,
Biafra, Bangladesh, Boston,
Atlanta, Soweto, Beirut, Assam
—those faces, names of places
sheared from the almanac
of North American time

VII

I am thinking this in a country
where words are stolen out of mouths
as bread is stolen out of mouths
where poets don't go to jail
for being poets, but for being
dark-skinned, female, poor.
I am writing this in a time
when anything we write
can be used against those we love
where the context is never given
though we try to explain, over and over
For the sake of poetry at least
I need to know these things

VIII

Sometimes, gliding at night
in a plane over New York City
I have felt like some messenger
called to enter, called to engage
this field of light and darkness.

A grandiose idea, born of flying.
But underneath the grandiose idea
is the thought that what I must engage
after the plane has raged onto the tarmac
after climbing my old stairs, sitting down
at my old window
is meant to break my heart and reduce me to silence.

IX

In North America time stumbles on
without moving, only releasing
a certain North American pain.
Julia de Burgos wrote:
That my grandfather was a slave
is my grief;   had he been a master
that would have been my shame.
A poet's words, hung over a door
in North America, in the year
nineteen-eighty-three.
The almost-full moon rises
timelessly speaking of change
out of the Bronx, the Harlem River
the drowned towns of the Quabbin
the pilfered burial mounds
the toxic swamps, the testing-grounds

and I start to speak again

1983

EDUCATION OF A NOVELIST

(Italicized lines quoted from Ellen Glasgow's
autobiography, *The Woman Within*.)

I

Looking back   trying to decipher
yourself and Lizzie Jones:

>   *We were strange companions, but*
that everyone knew us: a dark
lean, eager colored woman
and a small, pale, eager little girl
roaming together, hand-in-hand

Waking early, Mammy and I
would be dressed before the family had risen
spurred on by an inborn love

>   *of adventure*
a vital curiosity

>   . . . visiting
the neighbors and the neighbors' cooks and *with the neighbors' maids*
>   *sweeping the brick pavement*

>   *and the apothecary*
and the friendly light-colored letter-carrier

But when you made one visit to the almshouse
"Mammy" was reprimanded

II

I revolted from sentimentality
less because it was false then because
it was cruel . . .

>   In the country, later
the Black artist spent her genius on the white children
Mammy was with us; we were all happy together

599

(I revolted from sentimentality   when it suited me)

She would dress us as gypsies, darken
our faces with burnt cork

                        We would start
on a long journey, telling fortunes
wherever we came to a farm or a Negro cabin
I was always the one who would
think up the most exciting fortunes

                              (I, too, was always the one)

III

Where or how I learned to read
(you boast so proudly)   *I could never*
remember   After supper
in front of the fire, undressing by candlelight
Mammy and I would take up and spin out
the story left from the evening before

Nobody ever taught me to read
                              (Nobody had to,
it was your birthright, Ellen.)

"As soon as I learn my letters,
Mammy, I'm going to teach you yours"

IV

Givens, Ellen. That we'd *pick out our way*
through the Waverly novels
that our childish, superior fire

was destined for fortune
even though female   deaf   or lame
dewomanized   The growing suspicion
haunting the growing life

the sense of exile in a hostile world
how do we use that?

and for what?

with whom?

Givens.   The pale skin, the eager look, the fact
of having been known
                              by everyone
our childish, superior fire, and all
I was always the one . . .
                              Deafness finally drives you
here, there, to specialists in Europe
for hardening of the Eustachian tube

Finding no cure you build
a wall of deceptive gaiety   to shield your pain:
That I, who was winged for flying, should be
wounded and caged!

V

Lizzie Jones vanishes.   Her trace is lost.
She, who was winged for flying

Where at the end
of the nineteenth century   you ask
could one find the Revolution?
In what mean streets and alleys of the South

was it then lying in ambush?   *Though I suffered*
with the world's suffering. . . .

                       "*As soon*

as I learn my letters, Mammy,
I'm going to teach you yours"
                  but by your own admission

you never did

Where at the end of the twentieth century
does the Revolution find us
in what streets and alleys, north or south
is it now lying in ambush?

                It's not enough
using your words to damn you, Ellen:
they could have been my own:
                 this criss-cross
map of kept and broken promises
                I was always the one

1983

VIRGINIA 1906

A white woman dreaming of innocence,
of a country childhood, apple-blossom driftings,
is held in a DC-10 above the purity
of a thick cloud ceiling in a vault of purest blue.
She feels safe.   Here, no one can reach her.
Neither men nor women have her in their power.

Because I have sometimes been her, because I am of her,
I watch her with eyes that blink away like a flash
cruelly, when she does what I don't want to see.
I am tired of innocence and its uselessness,
sometimes the dream of innocence beguiles me.
Nothing has told me how to think of her power.

Blurredly, apple-blossom drifts
across rough earth, small trees contort and twist
making their own shapes, wild.   Why should we love purity?
Can the woman in the DC-10 see this
and would she call this innocence?   If no one can reach her
she is drawing on unnamed, unaccountable power.

This woman I have been and recognize
must know that beneath the quilt of whiteness lies
a hated nation, hers,
earth whose wet places call to mind
still-open wounds: her country.
Do we love purity?   Where do we turn for power?

Knowing us as I do I cringe when she says
But I was not culpable,
I was the victim, the girl, the youngest,
the susceptible one, I was sick,
the one who simply had to get out, and did
: I am still trying how to think of her power.

And if she was forced, this woman, by the same
white Dixie boy who took for granted as prey
her ignored dark sisters?   What if at five years old
she was old to his fingers splaying her vulva open
what if forever after, in every record
she wants her name inscribed as *innocent*

and will not speak, refuses to know, can say
I have been numb for years
does not want to hear of any violation
like or unlike her own, as if the victim
can be innocent only in isolation
as if the victim dare not be intelligent

(I have been numb for years):   and if this woman
longs for an intact world, an intact soul,
longs for what we all long for, yet denies us all?
What has she smelled of power without once
tasting it in the mouth? For what protections
has she traded her wildness and the lives of others?

There is a porch in Salem, Virginia
that I have never seen, that may no longer stand,
honeysuckle vines twisting above the talk,
a driveway full of wheeltracks, paths going down
to the orchards, apple and peach,
divisions so deep a wild child lost her way.

A child climbing an apple-tree in Virginia
refuses to come down, at last comes down
for a neighbor's lying bribe.   Now, if that child, grown old
feels safe in a DC-10 above thick white clouds
and no one can reach her
and if that woman's child, another woman

chooses another way, yet finds the old vines
twisting across her path, the old wheeltracks
how does she stop dreaming the dream
of protection, how does she follow her own wildness
shedding the innocence, the childish power?
How does she keep from dreaming the old dreams?

1983

DREAMS BEFORE WAKING

Despair is the question.

> —Elie Wiesel

Hasta tu país cambió. Lo has cambiado tú mismo.

> —Nancy Morejón

Despair falls:
the shadow of a building
they are raising in the direct path
of your slender ray of sunlight
Slowly the steel girders grow
the skeletal framework rises
yet the western light still filters
through it all
still glances off the plastic sheeting
they wrap around it
for dead of winter

At the end of winter something changes
a faint subtraction
from consolations you expected
an innocent brilliance that does not come
though the flower shops set out
once again on the pavement
their pots of tight-budded sprays
the bunches of jonquils stiff with cold
and at such a price
though someone must buy them
you study those hues as if with hunger

Despair falls
like the day you come home
from work, a summer evening
transparent with rose-blue light
and see they are filling in
the framework
the girders are rising
beyond your window
that seriously you live
in a different place
though you have never moved

and will not move, not yet
but will give away
your potted plants to a friend
on the other side of town
along with the cut crystal flashing
in the window-frame
will forget the evenings
of watching the street, the sky
the planes in the feathered afterglow:
will learn to feel grateful simply for this foothold

where still you can manage
to go on paying rent
where still you can believe
it's the old neighborhood:
even the woman who sleeps at night
in the barred doorway—wasn't she always there?
and the man glancing, darting
for food in the supermarket trash—
when did his hunger come to this?
what made the difference?
what will make it for you?

What will make it for you?
You don't want to know the stages
and those who go through them don't want to tell
You have your four locks on the door
your savings, your respectable past
your strangely querulous body, suffering
sicknesses of the city no one can name
You have your pride, your bitterness
your memories of sunset
you think you can make it straight through
if you don't speak of despair.

What would it mean to live
in a city whose people were changing
each other's despair into hope?—
You yourself must change it.—
what would it feel like to know
your country was changing?—
You yourself must change it.—
Though your life felt arduous
new and unmapped and strange
what would it mean to stand on the first
page of the end of despair?

1983

WHEN/THEN

Tell us

        how we'll be together

                in that time

patch of sun on a gritty floor; an old newspaper, torn
for toilet paper and coughed-up scum   Don't talk, she said

when we still love but are no longer young

they bring you a raw purple stick and say
it is one of her fingers;   it could be

                    Tell us

about aging, what it costs, how women
have loved forty, fifty years

               enamel basin, scraped

down to the bare iron   some ashen hairs   red fluid
they say is her blood   how can you

Tell us about the gardens we will keep, the milk
we'll drink from our own goats

                  she needs

anti-biotics they say which will be given
when you name names   they show you her fever chart

Tell us about community   *the joy*
of coming to rest

         among women

             who will love us

you choose between your community
and her   later others

will come through the cell   not all of them will love you
whichever way you choose

Don't talk, she said   (you will learn to hear
only her voice when they close in on you)   Don't talk

Why are you telling us this?

                              patch of sun on a gritty
floor, bad dreams, a torn newspaper, someone's blood
in a scraped basin. . . .

1983

UPCOUNTRY

The silver shadow   where the line falls grey
and pearly   the unborn villages quivering
under the rock   the snail   traveling the crevice
the furred, flying white insect like a tiny
intelligence lacing the air
this woman whose lips lie parted
after long speech
her white hair unrestrained

All that you never paid
or have with difficulty paid
attention to

Change and be forgiven!   the roots of the forest
muttered   but you tramped through   guilty
unable to take forgiveness   neither do you
give mercy

She is asleep now   dangerous   her mind
slits the air like silk   travels faster than sound
like scissors flung into the next century

Even as you watch for the trout's hooked stagger
across the lake   the crack of light and the crumpling bear
her mind was on them first
                     when forgiveness ends
her love means danger

1983

ONE KIND OF TERROR: A LOVE POEM

1.

From 1964: a color snapshot: you
riding a camel past the Great Pyramid

its rough earthy diagonal shouldering
the blue triangle of sky

I know your white shirt   dark skirt   your age
thirty-five   as mine was then

your ignorance like mine
in those years   and your curious mind

throw of your head   bend of your gilt knees
the laugh exchanged with whoever took the picture

I don't know how you were talking to yourself
I know I was thinking

with a schoolgirl's ardent rectitude
this will be the deciding year

I am sick of drift
Weren't we always trying to do better?

Then the voices began to say: *Your plans*
are not in the book of plans

written, printed and bound while you
were absent
                    no, not here nor in Egypt
will you ever catch up

2.

So, then   as if by plan
I turn   and you are lost

How have I lived   knowing
that day of your laugh   so alive/so nothing

even the clothes you wore then
rotted away   How can I live believing

any year can be the deciding year
when I know the book of plans

how it disallows us
time for change   for growing older

truthfully   in our own way

3.

I used to think you ought to be
a woman   in charge   in a desperate time

of whole populations
such seemed the power of your restlessness

I saw you a rescuer
amid huge events   diasporas

scatterings and returnings
I needed this for us

I would have gone to help you
flinging myself into the fray

both of us treading free
of the roads we started on

4.

In the book of plans it is written
that our lifelines shall be episodic

faithless   frayed   lived out
under impure violent rains

and rare but violent sun
It is written there that we may reach

like wan vines across a window
trying to grasp each other

but shall lack care and tending
that water and air shall betray us

that the daughter born a poet
will die of dysentery

while the daughter born to organize
will die of cancer

5.

In the book of plans it says no one
will speak of the book of plans

the appearance will continue
that all this is natural

It says my grief for you is natural
but my anger for us is not

that the image of a white curtain trembling
across a stormy pane

is acceptable   but not
the image I make of you

arm raised hurling   signalling
the squatters   the refugees

storming the food supply
The book of plans says only that you must die

that we all, very soon, must die

6.

Well, I am studying a different book
taking notes wherever I go

the movement of the wrist does not change
but the pen plows deeper

my handwriting flows into words
I have not yet spoken

I'm the sole author of nothing
the book moves from field to field

of testimony   recording
how the wounded teach each other   the old

refuse to be organized
by fools   how the women say

in more than one language   *You have struck a rock—*
prepare to meet the unplanned

the ignored   the unforeseen   that which breaks
despair   which has always travelled

underground   or in the spaces
between the fixed stars

gazing full-faced   wild
and calm   on the Revolution

7.

Love: I am studying a different book
and yes, a book is a finite thing

In it your death will never be reversed
the deaths I have witnessed since   never undone

The light drained from the living eyes
can never flash again from those same eyes

I make you no promises
but something's breaking open here

there were certain extremes we had to know
before we could continue

Call it a book, or not
call it a map of constant travel

Call it a book, or not
call it a song   a ray

of images thrown on a screen
in open lots   in cellars

and among those images
one woman's meaning to another woman

long after death
in a different world

1983

IN THE WAKE OF HOME

1.

You sleep in a room with bluegreen curtains
posters   a pile of animals on the bed
A woman and a man who love you
and each other   slip the door ajar
you are almost asleep   they crouch in turn
to stroke your hair   you never wake

This happens every night for years.
This never happened.

2.

Your lips   steady   never say
It should have been this way
That's not what you say
You   so carefully not asking, *Why?*
Your eyes   looking straight in mine
remind me of a woman's
auburn hair   my mother's hair
but you never saw that hair

The family coil   so twisted, tight and loose
anyone trying to leave
has to strafe the field
burn the premises down

3.

The home houses
mirages   memory fogs the kitchen panes
the rush-hour traffic outside
has the same old ebb and flow
Out on the darkening block
somebody calls you home
night after night   then never again
Useless for you to know
they tried to do what they could
before they left for good

4.

The voice that used to call you home
has gone off on the wind
beaten into thinnest air
whirling down other streets
or maybe the mouth was burnt to ash
maybe the tongue was torn out
brownlung has stolen the breath
or fear has stolen the breath
maybe under another name
it sings on AM radio:
And if you knew, what would you know?

5.

But you will be drawn to places
where generations lie
side by side with each other:
fathers, mothers and children
in the family prayerbook

or the country burying-ground
You will hack your way through the bush
to the Jodensavanne
where the gravestones are black with mould
You will stare at old family albums
with their smiles   their resemblances
You will want to believe that nobody
wandered off   became strange
no woman dropped her baby and ran
no father took off for the hills
no axe splintered the door
—that once at least it was all in order
and nobody came to grief

6.

Anytime you go back
where absence began
the kitchen faucet sticks in a way you know
you have to pull the basement door
in before drawing the bolt
the last porch-step is still loose
the water from the tap
is the old drink of water
Any time you go back
the familiar underpulse
will start its throbbing: *Home, home!*
and the hole torn and patched over
will gape unseen again

7.

Even where love has run thin
the child's soul musters strength

calling on dust-motes   song on the radio
closet-floor of galoshes
stray cat   piles of autumn leaves
whatever comes along
—the rush of purpose to make a life
worth living past abandonment
building the layers up again
over the torn hole   filling in

8.

And what of the stern and faithful aunt
the fierce grandmother   the anxious sister
the good teacher   the one
who stood at the crossing when you had to cross
the woman hired to love you
the skeleton who held out a crust
the breaker of rules   the one
who is neither a man nor a woman   the one
who warmed the liquid vein of life
and day after day whatever the need
handed it on to you?
You who did and had to do
so much for yourself   this was done for you
by someone who did what they could
when others left for good

9.

You imagine an alley   a little kingdom
where the mother-tongue is spoken
a village of shelters   woven
or sewn of hides   in a long-ago way
a shanty standing up

at the edge of sharecropped fields
a tenement where life is seized by the teeth
a farm battened down on snowswept plains
a porch with rubber-plant and glider
on a steep city street
You imagine the people would all be there
fathers mothers and children
the ones you were promised would all be there
eating   arguing   working
trying to get on with life
you imagine this used to be
for everyone   everywhere

10.

What if I told you your home
is this continent of the homeless
of children sold   taken by force
driven from their mothers' land
killed by their mothers to save from capture
—this continent of changed names and mixed-up blood
of languages tabooed
diasporas unrecorded
undocumented refugees
underground railroads   trails of tears
What if I tell you your home
is this planet of warworn children
women and children standing in line or milling
endlessly calling each others' names
What if I tell you, you are not different
it's the family albums that lie
—will any of this comfort you
and how should this comfort you

11.

The child's soul carries on
in the wake of home
building a complicated house
a tree-house without a tree
finding places for everything
the song   the stray cat   the skeleton
The child's soul musters strength
where the holes were torn
but there are no miracles:
even children become exhausted
And how shall they comfort each other
who have come young to grief?
Who will number the grains of loss
and what would comfort be?

1983

WHAT WAS, IS;
WHAT MIGHT HAVE BEEN, MIGHT BE

What's kept.   What's lost.   A snap decision.
Burn the archives.   Let them rot.
Begin by going ten years back.

A woman walks downstairs in a brownstone
in Brooklyn.   Late that night, some other night
snow crystals swarm in her hair
at the place we say, So long.

I've lost something.   I'm not sure what it is.
I'm going through my files.

Jewel-weed flashing
blue fire against an iron fence
Her head bent to a mailbox
long fingers ringed in gold   in red-eyed
golden serpents

the autumn sun
burns like a beak off the cars
parked along Riverside   we so deep in talk
in burnt September grass

I'm trying for exactitude
in the files I handle worn and faded labels
And how she drove, and danced, and fought, and worked
and loved, and sang, and hated
dashed into the record store   then out
with the Stevie Wonder   back in the car
flew on

Worn and faded label . . . This was
our glamour for each other
underlined in bravado

Could it have been another way:
could we have been respectful comrades
parallel warriors   none of that
fast-falling

could we have kept a clean
and decent slate

1984

FOR AN OCCUPANT

Did the fox speak to you?
Did the small brush-fires on the hillside
smoke her out?
Were you standing on the porch
not the kitchen porch   the front
one of poured concrete   full in the rising moon
and did she appear   wholly on her own
asking no quarter   wandering by
on impulse   up the drive   and on
into the pine-woods
but were you standing there
at the moment of moon and burnished light
leading your own life   till she caught your eye
asking no charity
but did she speak to you?

1983

EMILY CARR

I try to conjure the kind of joy
you tracked through the wildwoods where the tribes
had set up their poles   what brought you
how by boat, water, wind, you found
yourself facing the one great art
of your native land, your life

All I know is, it is here
even postcard-size can't diminish
the great eye, nostril, tongue
the wave of the green hills

the darkblue crest of sky   the white
and yellow fog bundled behind the green

You were alone in this
Nobody knew or cared
how to paint the way you saw
or what you saw   Alone
you walked up to the sacred and disregarded
with your canvas, your box of colors

saying *Wait for me* and the crumbling
totem poles held still
while you sat down on your stool, your knees
spread wide, and let the mist
roll in past your shoulders
bead your rough shawl, your lashes

Wait for me, I have waited so long for you
But you never said that   I
am ashamed to have thought it
You had no personal leanings
You brushed in the final storm-blue stroke
and gave its name: *Skidegate Pole*

1984

POETRY: I

Someone at a table under a brown metal lamp
is studying the history of poetry.
Someone in the library at closing-time
has learned to say *modernism,*
trope, vatic, text.

She is listening for shreds of music.
He is searching for his name
back in the old country.
They cannot learn without teachers.
They are like us   what we were
if you remember.

In a corner of night a voice
Is crying in a kind of whisper:
More!

Can you remember?   when we thought
the poets taught   how to live?
That is not the voice of a critic
nor a common reader
it is someone young   in anger
hardly knowing what to ask
who finds our lines   our glosses
wanting   in this world.

1985

POETRY: II, CHICAGO

Whatever a poet is
at the point of conception   is
conceived in these projects
of beige and grey bricks   Yes, poets are born
in wasted tracts like these   whatever color, sex
comes to term in this winter's driving nights
And the child pushes like a spear
a cry   through cracked cement   through zero air
a spear, a cry of green   Yes, poets endure

these schools of fear   balked yet unbroken
where so much gets broken: trust
windows   pride   the mothertongue

Wherever a poet is born   enduring
depends on the frailest of chances:
Who listened to your murmuring
over your little rubbish   who let you be
who gave you the books
who let you know you were not
alone   showed you the twist
of old strands   raffia, hemp or silk
the beaded threads   the fiery lines
saying: *This belongs to you   you have the right*
you belong to the song
of your mothers and fathers   You have a people

1984

POETRY: III

Even if we knew the children were all asleep
and healthy   the ledgers balanced   the water running
clear in the pipes
                    and all the prisoners free

Even if every word we wrote by then
were honest   the sheer heft
of our living behind it
                    not these sometimes
lax, indolent lines
                    these litanies

Even if we were told   not just by friends
that this was honest work

Even if each of us didn't wear
a brass locket with a picture
of a strangled woman   a girlchild sewn through the crotch

Even if someone had told us, young: *This is not a key*
nor a peacock feather

                              not a kite nor a telephone
This is the kitchen sink   *the grinding-stone*

would we give ourselves
more calmly over   feel less criminal joy
when the thing comes   as it does come
clarifying grammar
and the fixed and mutable stars—?

1984

BALTIMORE: A FRAGMENT FROM THE THIRTIES

Medical textbooks propped in a dusty window.
Outside, it's summer. Heat
swamping stretched awnings, battering dark-green shades.
The Depression, Monument Street,
ice-wagons trailing melt, the Hospital
with its segregated morgues . . .
I'm five years old and trying to be perfect
walking hand-in-hand with my father.
A Black man halts beside us
croaks in a terrible voice, *I'm hungry* . . .

I'm a lucky child but I've read about beggars—
how the good give, the evil turn away.
But I want to turn away.   My father gives.
We walk in silence.   Why did he sound like that?
Is it evil to be frightened?   I want to ask.
He has no roof in his mouth,

                                        my father says at last.

1985

NEW YORK

For B. and C.

                    at your table
telephone rings
                            every four minutes
                                                talk
of terrible things
                        the papers bringing
no good news
                    and burying the worst

Cut-up fruit in cutglass bowls
good for you
                        French Market coffee
cut with hot milk
                            crying together
wanting to save this
                            how we are when we meet
all our banners out
                        do we deceive each other
do we speak of the dead we sit with
do we mourn in secret

                    do we taste the sweetness
of life in the center of pain

I wanted to say to you
until the revolution this is happiness
yet was afraid to praise
                         even with such skeptic turn
of phrase   so shrugged a smile

1985

HOMAGE TO WINTER

You: a woman too old
for passive contemplation
caught staring out a window
at bird-of-paradise spikes
jewelled with rain, across an alley
It's winter in this land
of roses, roses   sometimes
the fog lies thicker around you than your past
sometimes the Pacific radiance
scours the air to lapis
In this new world you feel
backward along the hem of your whole life
questioning every breadth
Nights you can watch the moon shed skin after skin
over and over, always a shape
of imbalance except
at birth and in the full
You, still trying to learn
how to live, what must be done
though in death you will be complete
whatever you do

But death is not the answer.

On these flat green leaves
light skates like a golden blade
high in the dull-green pine
sit two mushroom-colored doves
afterglow overflows
across the bungalow roof
between the signs for the three-way stop
over everything that is:
the cotton pants stirring on the line, the
empty Coke can by the fence
onto the still unflowering
mysterious acacia
and a sudden chill takes the air

Backward you dream to a porch
you stood on a year ago
snow flying quick as thought
sticking to your shoulder   gone
Blue shadows, ridged and fading
on a snow-swept road
the shortest day of the year
Backward you dream to glare ice
and ice-wet pussywillows
to Riverside Drive, the wind
cut loose from Hudson's Bay
driving tatters into your face
And back you come at last to that room
without a view, where webs of frost
blinded the panes at noon
where already you had begun
to make the visible world your conscience
asking things: *What can you tell me?*
what am I doing?   what must I do?

1985

BLUE ROCK

For Myriam Díaz-Diocaretz

Your chunk of lapis-lazuli shoots its stain
blue into the wineglass on the table

the full moon moving up the sky is plain
as the dead rose and the live buds on one stem

No, this isn't Persian poetry I'm quoting:
all this is here in North America

where I sit trying to kindle fire
from what's already on fire:

the light of a blue rock from Chile swimming
in the apricot liquid called "eye of the swan".

This is a chunk of your world, a piece of its heart:
split from the rest, does it suffer?

You needn't tell me.   Sometimes I hear it singing
by the waters of Babylon, in a strange land

sometimes it just lies heavy in my hand
with the heaviness of silent seismic knowledge

a blue rock in a foreign land, an exile
excised but never separated

from the gashed heart, its mountains,
winter rains, language, native sorrow.

At the end of the twentieth century
cardiac graphs of torture reply to poetry

line by line: in North America
the strokes of the stylus continue

the figures of terror are reinvented
all night, after I turn the lamp off, blotting

wineglass, rock and roses, leaving pages
like this scrawled with mistakes and love,

falling asleep; but the stylus does not sleep,
cruelly the drum revolves, cruelty writes its name.

Once when I wrote poems they did not change
left overnight on the page

they stayed as they were and daylight broke
on the lines, as on the clotheslines in the yard

heavy with clothes forgotten or left out
for a better sun next day

But now I know what happens while I sleep
and when I wake the poem has changed:

the facts have dilated it, or cancelled it;
and in every morning's light, your rock is there.

1985

YOM KIPPUR 1984

I drew solitude over me, on the lone shore.

> —Robinson Jeffers, "Prelude"

For whoever does not afflict his soul throughout this day, shall be
cut off from his people.

> —Leviticus 23:29

What is a Jew in solitude?
What would it mean not to feel lonely or afraid
far from your own or those you have called your own?
What is a woman in solitude: a queer woman or man?
In the empty street, on the empty beach, in the desert
what in this world as it is can solitude mean?

The glassy, concrete octagon suspended from the cliffs
with its electric gate, its perfected privacy
is not what I mean
the pick-up with a gun parked at a turn-out in Utah or the Golan
                    Heights
is not what I mean
the poet's tower facing the western ocean, acres of forest planted to
                    the east, the woman reading in the cabin, her
                    attack dog suddenly risen
is not what I mean

Three thousand miles from what I once called home
I open a book searching for some lines I remember
about flowers, something to bind me to this coast as lilacs in the
                    dooryard once
bound me back there—yes, lupines on a burnt mountainside,
something that bloomed and faded and was written down
in the poet's book, forever:

Opening the poet's book
I find the hatred in the poet's heart: . . . *the hateful-eyed*
and human-bodied are all about me: you that love multitude may have
> *them*

Robinson Jeffers, multitude
is the blur flung by distinct forms against these landward valleys
and the farms that run down to the sea; the lupines
are multitude, and the torched poppies, the grey Pacific unrolling
> its scrolls of surf,
and the separate persons, stooped
over sewing machines in denim dust, bent under the shattering
> skies of harvest
who sleep by shifts in never-empty beds have their various dreams
Hands that pick, pack, steam, stitch, strip, stuff, shell, scrape,
> scour, belong to a brain like no other
Must I argue the love of multitude in the blur or defend
a solitude of barbed-wire and searchlights, the survivalist's final
> solution, have I a choice?

To wander far from your own or those you have called your own
to hear strangeness calling you from far away
and walk in that direction, long and far, not calculating risk
to go to meet the Stranger without fear or weapon, protection
> nowhere on your mind
(the Jew on the icy, rutted road on Christmas Eve prays for another
> Jew
the woman in the ungainly twisting shadows of the street: *Make*
> *those be a woman's footsteps;* as if she could believe in a
> woman's god)

Find someone like yourself.   Find others.
Agree you will never desert each other.
Understand that any rift among you
means power to those who want to do you in.

Close to the center, safety; toward the edges, danger.
But I have a nightmare to tell: I am trying to say
that to be with my people is my dearest wish
but that I also love strangers
that I crave separateness
I hear myself stuttering these words
to my worst friends and my best enemies
who watch for my mistakes in grammar
my mistakes in love.
This is the day of atonement; but do my people forgive me?
If a cloud knew loneliness and fear, I would be that cloud.

To love the Stranger, to love solitude—am I writing merely about
                    privilege
about drifting from the center, drawn to edges,
a privilege we can't afford in the world that is,
who are hated as being of our kind: faggot kicked into the icy
                    river, woman dragged from her stalled car
into the mist-struck mountains, used and hacked to death
young scholar shot at the university gates on a summer evening
                    walk, his prizes and studies nothing, nothing
                    availing his Blackness
Jew deluded that she's escaped the tribe, the laws of her exclusion,
                    the men too holy to touch her hand;   Jew who has
                    turned her back
on *midrash* and *mitzvah* (yet wears the *chai* on a thong between her
                    breasts) hiking alone
found with a swastika carved in her back at the foot of the cliffs
                    (did she die as queer or as Jew?)

Solitude, O taboo, endangered species
on the mist-struck spur of the mountain, I want a gun to defend
                    you
In the desert, on the deserted street, I want what I can't have:
your elder sister, Justice, her great peasant's hand outspread

her eye, half-hooded, sharp and true
And I ask myself, have I thrown courage away?

have I traded off something I don't name?
To what extreme will I go to meet the extremist?
What will I do to defend my want or anyone's want to search for
                her spirit-vision
far from the protection of those she has called her own?
Will I find O solitude
your plumes, your breasts, your hair
against my face, as in childhood, your voice like the mockingbird's
singing *Yes, you are loved, why else this song?*
in the old places, anywhere?

What is a Jew in solitude?
What is a woman in solitude, a queer woman or man?
When the winter flood-tides wrench the tower from the rock,
              crumble the prophet's headland, and the farms slide
              into the sea
when leviathan is endangered and Jonah becomes revenger
when center and edges are crushed together, the extremities
              crushed together on which the world was founded
when our souls crash together, Arab and Jew, howling our
              loneliness within the tribes
when the refugee child and the exile's child re-open the blasted and
              forbidden city
when we who refuse to be women and men as women and men are
              chartered, tell our stories of solitude spent in
              multitude
in that world as it may be, newborn and haunted, what will
              solitude mean?

1984–1985

EDGES

In the sleepless sleep of dawn, in the dreamless dream
the kingfisher cuts through   flashing
spirit-fire from his wings   bluer than violet's edge
the slice of those wings

5 a.m., first light, hoboes of the past
are leaning through the window, what freightcars
did they hop here   I thought I'd left behind?
Their hands are stretched out but not for bread
they are past charity, they want me to hear   their names

Outside in the world where so much is possible
sunrise rekindles and the kingfisher—
the living kingfisher, not that flash of vision—
darts where the creek drags her wetness over stump and stone
where poison oak reddens   acacia pods collect
curled and secretive against the bulkhead

and the firstlight ghosts go transparent
while the homeless line for bread

1985

III

Contradictions:
Tracking Poems

1.

Look: this is January   the worst onslaught
is ahead of us   Don't be lured
by these soft grey afternoons   these sunsets cut
from pink and violet tissue-paper   by the thought
the days are lengthening
Don't let the solstice fool you:
our lives will always be
a stew of contradictions
the worst moment of winter can come in April
when the peepers are stubbornly still   and our bodies
plod on without conviction
and our thoughts cramp down before the sheer
arsenal of everything that tries us:
this battering, blunt-edged life

2.

Heart of cold.   Bones of cold.   Scalp of cold.
the grey   the black   the blond   the red
hairs on a skull of cold.   Within that skull
the thought of war   the sovereign thought
the coldest of all thought.   Dreaming shut down
everything kneeling down to cold   intelligence
smirking with cold   memory
squashed and frozen cold   breath
half held-in for cold.   The freezing people
of a freezing nation   eating
luxury food or garbage
frozen tongues licking the luxury meat
or the pizza-crust   the frozen eyes
welded to other eyes   also frozen
the cold hands trying to stroke   the coldest sex.
Heart of cold   Sex of cold   Intelligence of cold

My country   wedged fast in history
stuck in the ice

3.

My mouth hovers across your breasts
in the short grey winter afternoon
in this bed   we are delicate
and tough   so hot with joy we amaze ourselves
tough   and delicate   we play rings
around each other   our daytime candle burns
with its peculiar light   and if the snow
begins to fall outside   filling the branches
and if the night falls   without announcement
these are the pleasures of winter
sudden, wild and delicate   your fingers
exact   my tongue exact at the same moment
stopping to laugh at a joke
my love   hot on your scent   on the cusp of winter

4.

He slammed his hand across my face   and I
let him do that until   I stopped letting him do it
so I'm in for life.

. . . . he kept saying I was crazy, he'd lock me up
until I went to Women's Lib and they
told me he'd been abusing me as much
as if he'd hit me: emotional abuse.
They told me how to answer back.   That I could
answer back.   But my brother-in-law's a shrink
with the State.   I have to watch my step.

If I stay just within bounds they can't come and get me.
Women's Lib taught me the words to say
to remind myself and him I'm a person with rights
like anyone.   But answering back's no answer.

5.

She is carrying my madness   and I dread her
avoid her when I can
She walks along I.S. 93   howling
in her bare feet
She is number 6375411
in a cellblock in Arkansas
and I dread what she is paying for   that is mine
She has fallen asleep at last in the battered
women's safe-house   and I dread
her dreams   that I also dream
If never I become exposed or confined like this
what am I hiding
O sister of nausea   of broken ribs   of isolation
what is this freedom I protect   how is it mine

6.

Dear Adrienne:

                  I'm calling you up tonight
as I might call up a friend   as I might call up a ghost
to ask what you intend to do
with the rest of your life.   Sometimes you act
as if you have all the time there is.
I worry about you when I see this.
The prime of life, old age
aren't what they used to be;
making a good death isn't either,

now you can walk around the corner of a wall
and see a light
that already has blown your past away.
Somewhere in Boston   beautiful literature
is being read around the clock
by writers   to signify
their dislike of this.
I hope you've got something in mind.
I hope you have some idea
about the rest of your life.

In sisterhood,

Adrienne

7.

Dear Adrienne,
I feel signified by pain

from my breastbone through my left shoulder down
through my elbow into my wrist is a thread of pain
I am typing this instead of writing by hand
because my wrist on the right side
blooms and rushes with pain
like a neon bulb
You ask me how I'm going to live
the rest of my life
Well, nothing is predictable with pain
Did the old poets write of this?
—in its odd spaces, free,
many have sung and battled—
But I'm already living the rest of my life
not under conditions of my choosing
wired   into pain
rider on the slow train

Yours, Adrienne

8.

I'm afraid of prison.   Have been all these years.
Afraid they'll take my aspirin away
and of other things as well:
beatings   damp and cold   I have my fears.
Unable one day to get up and walk
to do what must be done
Prison as idea   it fills me
with fear   this exposure to my own weakness
at someone else's whim
I watched that woman go over the barbed-wire fence
at the peace encampment
                              the wheelchair rider
I didn't want to do what she did
I thought, They'll get her for this
I thought, We are not such victims.

9.

Tearing but not yet torn: this page
The long late-winter rage
wild rain on the windshield
clenched stems   unyielding sticks
of maple, birch   bleached grass   the range
of things resisting change
And this is how I am
and this is how you are
when we resist the charmer's open sesame
the thief's light-fingered touch
staying closed because we will
not give ourselves away
until the agent   the manipulator   the false toucher
has left   and it is May

10.

Night   over the great and the little worlds
of Brooklyn   the shredded communities
in Chicago   Argentina   Poland
in Holyoke Massachusetts   Amsterdam   Manchester England
Night falls   the day of atonement begins
in how many divided hearts   how many defiant lives
Toronto   Managua   St. Johnsbury
and the great and little worlds of the women
Something ancient passes across the earth
lifting the dust of the blasted ghettos
You ask if I will eat and I say, Yes,
I have never fasted
but something crosses my life
not a shadow   the reflection of a fire

11.

I came out of the hospital like a woman
who'd watched a massacre
not knowing how to tell
my adhesions   the lingering infections
from the pain on the streets
In my room on Yom Kippur they took me off morphine
I saw shadows on the wall   the dying and the dead
They said Christian Phalangists did it
then Kol Nidre on the radio   and my own
unhoused spirit   trying to find a home
Was it then or another day
in what order did it happen
I thought   *They call this elective surgery*
but we all have died of this.

12.

Violence as purification: the one idea.
One massacre great enough to undo another
one last-ditch operation to solve the problem
of the old operation that was bungled
Look: I have lain on their tables under their tools
under their drugs   from the center of my body
a voice bursts   against these methods
(wherever you made a mistake
batter with radiation   defoliate   cut away)
and yes, there are merciful debridements
but burns turn into rotting flesh
for reasons of vengeance and neglect.
I have been too close to septic too many times
to play with either violence or non-violence.

13.

Trapped in one idea, you can't have your feelings,
feelings are always about more than one thing.
You drag yourself back home and it is autumn
you can't concentrate, you can't lie on the couch
so you drive yourself for hours on the quiet roads
crying at the wheel   watching the colors
deepening, fading   and winter is coming
and you long for one idea
one simple, huge idea to take this weight
and you know you will never find it, never
because you don't want to find it
You will drive and cry and come home and eat
and listen to the news
and slowly even at winter's edge
the feelings come back in their shapes
and colors   conflicting   they come back
   they are changed

14.

Lately in my dreams I hear long sentences
meaningless in ordinary American
like, *Your mother, too, was a missionary of poets*
and in another dream one of my old teachers
shows me a letter of reference
he has written for me, in a language
I know to be English but cannot understand,
telling me it's in "transformational grammar"
and that the student who typed the letter
does not understand this grammar either.
Lately I dreamed about my father,
how I found him, alive, seated on an old chair.
I think what he said to me was,
You don't know how lonely I am.

15.

You who think I find words for everything,
and you for whom I write this,
how can I show you what I'm barely
coming into possession of, invisible luggage
of more than fifty years, looking at first
glance like everyone else's, turning up
at the airport carousel
and the waiting for it, knowing what nobody
would steal must eventually come round—
feeling obsessed, peculiar, longing?

16.

It's true, these last few years I've lived
watching myself in the act of loss—the art of losing,
Elizabeth Bishop called it, but for me no art
only badly-done exercises
acts of the heart forced to question
its presumptions in this world   its mere excitements
acts of the body forced to measure
all instincts against pain
acts of parting   trying to let go
without giving up   yes   Elizabeth   a city here
a village there   a sister, comrade, cat
and more   no art to this but anger

17.

I have backroads I take   to places
like the hospital where night pain
is never tended enough but I can drive
under the overlacing boughs
of wineglass elm, oak, maple
from Mosquitoville to Wells River
along the double track with the greened hump
the slope with the great sugar-grove
New Age talk calls it "visualizing"   but I know
under torture I would travel
from the West Barnet burying-ground
to Joe's Brook   by heart   I know
all of those roads by heart
by heart I know what, and all, I have left behind

18.

The problem, unstated till now, is how
to live in a damaged body
in a world where pain is meant to be gagged
uncured   un-grieved-over   The problem is
to connect, without hysteria, the pain
of any one's body with the pain of the body's world
For it is the body's world
they are trying to destroy forever
The best world is the body's world
filled with creatures   filled with dread
misshapen so   yet the best we have
our raft among the abstract worlds
and how I longed to live on this earth
walking her boundaries   never counting the cost

19.

If to feel is to be unreliable
don't listen to us
if to be in pain is to be predictable
embittered   bullying
then don't listen to us
If we're in danger of mistaking
our personal trouble for the pain on the streets
don't listen to us
if my fury at being grounded frightens you
take off on your racing skis
in your beautiful tinted masks
Trapped in one idea, you can't have feelings
Without feelings perhaps you can feel like a god

20.

The tobacco fields lie fallow   the migrant pickers
no longer visible
where undocumented intelligences travailed
on earth they had no stake in
though the dark leaves growing beneath white veils
were beautiful   and the barns opened out like fans
All this of course could have been done differently
This valley itself: one more contradiction
the paradise fields   the brute skyscrapers
the pesticidal wells

I have been wanting for years
to write a poem   equal to these
material forces
and I have always failed
I wasn't looking for a muse
only a reader by whom   I could not be mistaken

21.

The cat-tails blaze in the corner   sunflowers
shed their pale fiery dust   on the dark stove-lid
others stand guard   heads bowed   over the garden
the fierce and flaring garden you have made
out of your woes and expectations
tilled into the earth   I circle close to your mind
crash into it sometimes   as you crash into mine
Given this strip of earth   given mere love
should we not be happy?
but happiness comes and goes as it comes and goes
the safe-house is temporary   the garden
lies open to vandals

this whole valley is one more contradiction
and more will be asked of us   we will ask more

22.

In a bald skull sits our friend   in a helmet
of third-degree burns
her quizzical melancholy grace
her irreplaceable self   in utter peril
In the radioactive desert walks a woman
in a black dress   white-haired   steady
as the luminous hand of a clock
in circles she walks   knitting
and unknitting her scabbed fingers
Her face is expressionless   shall we pray to her
shall we speak of the loose pine-needles   how they shook
like the pith of country summers
from the sacks of pitchblende ore in the tin-roofed shack
where it all began
Shall we accuse her of denial
first of the self   then of the mixed virtue
of the purest science   shall we be wise for her
in hindsight   shall we scream *It has come to this*
Shall we praise her   shall we let her wander
the atomic desert   in peace?

23.

You know the Government must have pushed them to settle,
the chemical industries   and pay
that hush-money to the men
who landed out there at twenty   not for belief
but because of who they were   and were called psychos

when they said their bodies contained dioxin
like memories they didn't want to keep
whose kids came out deformed
You know nothing has changed   no respect or grief
for the losers of a lost war everyone hated
nobody sent them to school like heroes
if they started suing for everything that was done
there would be no end   there would be a beginning
My country   wedged fast in history
stuck in the ice

24.

Someone said to me: *It's just that we don't*
know how to cope with the loss of memory.
When your own grandfather doesn't know you
when your mother thinks you're somebody else
it's a terrible thing.
Now just like that is this idea
that the universe will forget us, everything we've done
will go nowhere
no one will know who we were.
No one will know who we were!

Not the young who will never   Nor even the old folk
who knew us when we were young   insatiable
for recognition from them
trying so fiercely not to be them
counting on them to know us   anywhere

25.

Did anyone ever know who we were
if *we* means more than a handful?

flower of a generation   young white men
cut off in the named, commemorated wars
I stare   Jewish   into that loss
for which all names become unspeakable
not ever just the best and brightest
but the most wretched and bedeviled
the obscure   the strange   the driven
the twins   the dwarfs   the geniuses   the gay
But ours was not the only loss
(to whom does annihilation speak
as if for the first time?)

26.

You: air-driven   reft   from the tuber-bitten soil
that was your portion   from the torched-out village
the Marxist study-group   the Zionist cell
café or *cheder*   Zaddik or Freudian   straight or gay
woman or man   O you
stripped   bared   appalled
stretched to mere spirit   yet still physical
your irreplaceable knowledge   lost
at the mud-slick bottom of the world
how you held fast   with your bone-meal fingers
to yourselves   each other   and strangers
how you touched   held-up from falling
what was already half-cadaver
how your life-cry taunted extinction
with its wild, crude   *so what?*
Grief for you has rebellion at its heart
it cannot simply mourn
You: air-driven: reft: are yet our teachers
trying to speak to us in sleep
trying to help us wake

27.

The Tolstoyans   the Afro-American slaves
knew this: you could be killed
for teaching people to read and write
I used to think the worst affliction
was to be forbidden pencil and paper
well, Ding Ling recited poems to prison walls
for years of the Cultural Revolution
and truly, the magic of written characters
looms and dwindles   shrinks small   grows swollen
depending on where you stand
and what is in your hand
and who can read and why
I think now the worst affliction
is not to know who you are or have been
I have learned this in part
from writers   Reading and writing
aren't sacred   yet people have been killed
as if they were

28.

This high summer we love will pour its light
the fields grown rich and ragged in one strong moment
then before we're ready will crash into autumn
with a violence we can't accept
a bounty we can't forgive
Night frost will strike when the noons are warm
the pumpkins wildly glowing   the green tomatoes
straining huge on the vines
queen anne and blackeyed susan will straggle rusty
as the milkweed stakes her claim
she who will stand at last   dark sticks barely rising
up through the snow   her testament of continuation

We'll dream of a longer summer
but this is the one we have:
I lay my sunburnt hand
on your table: this is the time we have

29.

You who think I find words for everything
this is enough for now
cut it short   cut loose from my words
You for whom I write this
in the night hours when the wrecked cartilage
sifts round the mystical jointure of the bones
when the insect of detritus crawls
from shoulder to elbow to wristbone
remember: the body's pain and the pain on the streets
are not the same   but you can learn
from the edges that blur   O you who love clear edges
more than anything   watch the edges that blur

1983–1985

TIME'S POWER

(1985–1988)

For Michelle

SOLFEGGIETTO

1.

Your windfall at fifteen   your Steinway grand
paid for by fire insurance
came to me as birthright   a black cave
with teeth of ebony and ivory
twanging and thundering over the head
of the crawling child   until
that child was set on the big book on the chair
to face the keyboard world of black and white
—already knowing the world was black and white
The child's hands   smaller than a sand-dollar
set on the keys   wired to their mysteries
the child's wits facing the ruled and ruling staves

2.

For years we battled over music lessons
mine, taught by you   Nor did I wonder
what that keyboard meant to you
the hours of solitude   the practising
your life of prize-recitals   lifted hopes
Piatti's nephew praising you at sixteen
scholarships to the North
Or what it was to teach
boarding-school girls what won't be used
shelving ambition   beating time
to "On the Ice at Sweet Briar" or
"The Sunken Cathedral" for a child
counting the minutes and the scales to freedom

3.

Freedom: what could that mean, for you or me?
—Summers of '36, '37, Europe untuned
what I remember isn't lessons
not Bach or Brahms or Mozart
but the rented upright in the summer rental
One Hundred Best-Loved Songs on the piano rack
And so you played, evenings and so we sang
"Steal Away" and "Swanee River,"
"Swing Low," and most of all
"Mine Eyes Have Seen the Glory of the Coming of the Lord"
How we sang out the chorus   how I loved
the watchfires of the hundred circling camps
and *truth is marching on* and *let us die to make men free*

4.

Piano lessons   The mother and the daughter
Their doomed exhaustion   their common mystery
worked out in finger-exercises   Czerny, Hanon
The yellow Schirmer albums   quarter-rests   double-holds
glyphs of an astronomy   the mother cannot teach
the daughter because this is not the story
of a mother teaching magic to her daughter
Side by side I see us locked
My wrists   your voice   are tightened
Passion lives in old songs   in the kitchen
where another woman cooks   teaches   and sings
He shall feed his flock like a shepherd
and in the booklined room
where the Jewish father reads and smokes and teaches
Ecclesiastes, Proverbs, the Song of Songs
The daughter struggles with the strange notations
—dark chart of music's ocean flowers and flags

but would rather learn by ear and heart   The mother
says she must learn to read by sight   not ear and heart

5.

Daughter who fought her mother's lessons—
even today a scrip of music balks me—
I feel illiterate in this
your mother-tongue   Had it been Greek or Slovak
no more could your native alphabet have baffled
your daughter   whom you taught for years
held by a tether   over the ivory
and ebony teeth of the Steinway

                                        It is
the three hundredth anniversary of Johann
Sebastian Bach   My earliest life
woke to his English Suites   under your fingers
I understand a language I can't read
Music you played streams on the car radio
in the freeway night
You kept your passions deep   You have them still
I ask you, both of us
—Did you think mine was a virtuoso's hand?
Did I see power in yours?
What was worth fighting for?   What did you want?
What did I want from you?

1985–1988

THIS

Face flashing free   child-arms
lifting the collie pup
torn paper on the path
Central Park   April '72
behind you   minimal
those benches and that shade
that brilliant light in which
you laughed longhaired
and I'm the keeper of
this little piece of paper
this little piece of truth

I wanted this from you—
laughter   a child turning
into a boy   at ease
in the spring light   with friends
I wanted this for you

I could mutter   *Give back*
that day   give me again
that child   with the chance
of making it all right
I could yell   *Give back that light*
on the dog's teeth   the child's hair
but no rough drafts are granted
—Do you think I don't remember?
did you think I was all-powerful
unimpaired   unappalled?
yes   you needed that from me
I wanted this from you

1985

LOVE POEM

Tell me, bristler, where
do you get such hair
so quick a flare   so strong a tongue

Green eyes   fierce curls
there and here a mole
a girl's
dimples   a warrior's mind

dark blood under gold skin
testing, testing the world
the word

and so to write for you
a pretty sonnet
would be untrue

to your mud-river flashing
over rocks   your delicate
coffee-bushes

and more I cannot know
and some I labor with
and I mean to stay true

even in poems, to you
But there's something more

Beauty, when you were young
we both thought we were young
now that's all done

we're serious now
about death   we talk to her
daily, as to a neighbor

we're learning to be true
with her   she has the keys
to this house   if she must

she can sleep over

1986

NEGOTIATIONS

Someday if someday comes we will agree
that trust is not about safety
that keeping faith is not about deciding
to clip our fingernails exactly
to the same length or wearing
a uniform that boasts our unanimity

Someday if someday comes we'll know
the difference between liberal laissez-faire
pluralism and the way you cut your hair
and the way I clench my hand
against my cheekbone
both being possible gestures of defiance

Someday if there's a someday we will
bring food, you'll say I can't eat what you've brought
I'll say Have some in the name of our
trying to be friends, you'll say What about you?
We'll taste strange meat and we'll admit
we've tasted stranger

Someday if someday ever comes we'll go
back and reread those poems and manifestos
that so enraged us in each other's hand
I'll say, But damn, you wrote it so I
couldn't write it off   You'll say
I read you always, even when I hated you

1986

IN A CLASSROOM

Talking of poetry, hauling the books
arm-full to the table where the heads
bend or gaze upward, listening, reading aloud,
talking of consonants, elision,
caught in the how, oblivious of why:
I look in your face, Jude,
neither frowning nor nodding,
opaque in the slant of dust-motes over the table:
a presence like a stone, if a stone were thinking
What I cannot say, is me. For that I came.

1986

THE NOVEL

All winter you went to bed early, drugging yourself on *War and
                    Peace*
Prince Andrei's cold eyes taking in the sky from the battlefield
were your eyes, you went walking wrapped in his wound

like a padded coat against the winds from the two rivers
You went walking in the streets as if you were ordinary
as if you hadn't been pulling with your raw mittened hand
on the slight strand that held your tattered mind
blown like an old stocking from a wire
on the wind between two rivers.

                                        All winter you asked nothing
of that book though it lay heavy on your knees
you asked only for a shed skin, many skins in which to walk
you were old woman, child, commander
you watched Natasha grow into a neutered thing
you felt your heart go still while your eyes swept the pages
you felt the pages thickening to the left and on the right-
hand growing few, you knew the end was coming
you knew beyond the ending lay
your own, unwritten life

1986

A STORY

Absence is homesick. Absence wants a home.
but Absence left without a glance at Home.
Home tried to hold in Absence's despite,
Home caved, shuddered, yet held
without Absence's consent. Home took a walk
in several parks, Home shivered
in outlying boroughs, slept on strange floors,
cried many riffs of music, many words.
Home went out to teach school, Home studied pain control
Home learned to dive and came up blind with blood
Home learned to live on each location
but whenever Absence called, called, Home had to answer

in the grammar of Absence.

                        Home would hitch-hike
through flying snow, Home would roast meat,
light candles, to withstand the cold. Home washed the dishes
faithfully. But Absence
always knew when to call.

                       What if Absence calls
and a voice answers

               in the accent of Home?

1986

IN MEMORIAM: D.K.

A man walking on the street
feels unwell   has felt unwell
all week, a little   Yet the flowers crammed
in pots on the corner: furled anemones:
he knows they open
burgundy, violet, pink, Amarillo
all the way to their velvet cores
The flowers hanging over the fence: fuchsias:
each tongued, staring,   all of a fire:
the flowers   He who has
been happy oftener than sad
carelessly happy   well oftener than sick
one of the lucky   is thinking about death
and its music   about poetry
its translations of his life

And what good will it do you
to go home and put on the Mozart Requiem?
Read Keats?   How will culture cure you?

                              Poor, unhappy

unwell culture   what can it sing or say
six weeks from now, to you?

Give me your living hand   If I could take the hour
death moved into you   undeclared, unnamed
—even if sweet, if I could take that hour

between my forceps   tear at it like a monster
wrench it out of your flesh   dissolve its shape in quicklime
and make you well again
                              no, not again
but still. . . .

1986

CHILDREN PLAYING CHECKERS
AT THE EDGE OF THE FOREST

Two green-webbed chairs
                         a three-legged stool between
Your tripod
              Spears of grass
                              longer than your bare legs
cast shadows on your legs
                         drawn up
                                   from the red-and-black
cardboard squares
                    the board of play
                                   the board of rules
But you're not playing, you're talking
                                   It's midsummer
and greater rules are breaking

                        It's the last
innocent summer you will know
                        and I
will go on awhile pretending that's not true

When I have done pretending
                    I can see this:
the depth of the background
                    shadows
                            not of one moment only
erased and charcoaled in again
                        year after year
how the tree looms back behind you
the first tree of the forest
                    the last tree
from which the deer step out
                    from protection
                            the first tree
into dreadfulness
                The last and the first tree

1987

SLEEPWALKING   NEXT TO DEATH

Sleep   horns of a snail
                    protruding, retracting
What we choose to know
                or not know
                        all these years
sleepwalking
            next to death

I

This snail could have been eaten
This snail could have been crushed
This snail could have dreamed it was a painter or a poet
This snail could have driven fast at night
putting up graffiti with a spray-gun:

This snail could have ridden
in the back of the pick-up, handing guns

II

Knows, chooses not to know
                              It has always
been about death and chances
                              The Dutch artist wrote and painted
one or more strange and usable things
For I mean to meet you
in any land   in any language
This is my promise:
I will be there
if you are there

III

In between this and that there are different places
of waiting, airports mostly where the air
is hungover, visibility low   boarding passes not guaranteed
If you wrote me, *I sat next to Naomi*
I would read that, *someone who felt like Ruth*
I would begin reading you like a dream
That's how extreme it feels
                              that's what I have to do

IV

Every stone around your neck you know the reason for
at this time in your life   Relentlessly
you tell me their names and furiously I
forget their names   Forgetting the names of the stones
you love, you lover of stones
what is it I do?

V

What is it I do? I refuse to take your place
in the world   I refuse to make myself
your courier   I refuse so much
I might ask, what is it I do?
I will not be the dreamer for whom
you are the only dream
I will not be your channel
I will wrestle you to the end
for our difference (as you have wrestled me)
I will change your name and confuse
the Angel

VI

I am stupid with you and practical with you
I remind you to take a poultice   forget a quarrel
I am a snail in the back of the pick-up handing you
vitamins you hate to take

VII

Calmly you look over my shoulder   at this page   and say
It's all about you   *None of this*
tells my story

VIII

Yesterday noon I stood by a river
and many waited to cross over
from the Juarez barrio
              to El Paso del Norte
First day of spring   a stand of trees
in Mexico were in palegreen leaf
a man casting a net
             into the Rio Grande
and women, in pairs, strolling
                across the border
as if taking a simple walk
             Many thousands go

I stood by the river and thought of you
young   in Mexico in a time of hope

IX

The practical nurse is the only nurse
with her plastic valise of poultices and salves
her hands of glove leather and ebony
her ledgers of pain
The practical nurse goes down to the river
in her runover shoes and her dollar necklace

eating a burrito in hand
                                it will be a long day
a long labor
                the midwife will be glad to see her
it will be a long night   someone bleeding
from a botched abortion   a beating   Will you let her touch you
                       now?
Will you tell her you're fine?

X

I'm afraid of the border patrol
                             Not those men
of La Migra who could have run us
into the irrigation canal with their van
                                  I'm afraid
of the patrollers
the sleepwalker in me
                the loner in you

XI

I want five hours with you
in a train running south
                      maybe ten hours
in a Greyhound bound for the border
the two seats side-by-side that become a home
an island of light in the continental dark
the time that takes the place of a lifetime
I promise I won't fall asleep when the lights go down
I will not be lulled
Promise you won't jump the train

vanish into the bus depot at three a.m.
that you won't defect
                    that we'll travel
like two snails
                    our four horns erect

1987

LETTERS IN THE FAMILY

I: Catalonia 1936

Dear Parents:
                    I'm the daughter
you didn't bless when she left,
an unmarried woman wearing a khaki knapsack
with a poor mark in Spanish.
                    I'm writing now
from a plaster-dusted desk in a town
pocked street by street with hand grenades,
some of them, dear ones, thrown by me.
This is a school: the children are at war.
You don't need honors in schoolroom Spanish here
to be of use and my right arm
's as strong as anyone's. I sometimes think
all languages are spoken here,
even mine, which you got zero in.
Don't worry. Don't try to write. I'm happy,
if you could know it.
                    Rochelle.

II: Yugoslavia, 1944

Dear Chana,
           where are you now?
Am sending this pocket-to-pocket
(though we both know pockets we'd hate to lie in).
They showed me that poem you gave Reuven,
about the match:
Chana, you know, I never was
for martyrdom. I thought we'd try our best,
ragtag mission that we were,
then clear out if the signals looked too bad.
Something in you drives things ahead for me
but if I can I mean to stay alive.
We're none of us giants, you know,
just small, frail, inexperienced romantic people.
But there are things we learn.
You know the sudden suck of empty space
between the jump and the ripcord pull?
I hate it. I hate it so,
I've hated you for your dropping
ecstatically in free-fall, in the training,
your look, dragged on the ground, of knowing
precisely why you were there.
                 My mother's
still in Palestine. And yours
still there in Hungary. Well, there we are.
When this is over—
           I'm
your earthbound friend to the end, still yours—
                       Esther.

III: Southern Africa, 1986

Dear children:
                    We've been walking nights
a long time over rough terrain,
sometimes through marshes. Days we hide
under what bushes we can find.
Our stars steer us. I write
on my knee by a river with a weary hand,
and the weariness will come through
this letter that should tell you
nothing but love. I can't say where we are,
what weeds are in bloom, what birds cry at dawn.
The less you know the safer.

But not to know how you are going on—
Matile's earache, Emma's lessons, those tell-tale
eyes and tongues, so quick—are you remembering
to be brave and wise and strong?
At the end of this hard road
we'll sit all together at one meal
and I'll tell you everything: the names
of our comrades, how the letters
were routed to you, why I left.
And I'll stop and say, "Now you,
grown so big, how was it for you, those times?
Look, I know you in detail, every inch of each
sweet body, haven't I washed and dried you
a thousand times?"
                    And we'll eat and tell our stories
together. That is my reason.
                              Ma.

1987

THE DESERT AS GARDEN OF PARADISE

1.

Guard the knowledge
from the knowledgeable,
those who gobble:
make it unpalatable.

Stars in this place
might look
distant to me as you,
to you as me.

Monotheism. Where it began.
But all the spirits, too.
Desert says: What you believe
I can prove. I: amaranth flower,
I: metamorphic rock, I: burrow,
I: water-drop in tilted catchment,
I: vulture, I: driest thorn.

Rocks in a trance. Escaped
from the arms of other rocks.
Roads leading to gold and to false gold.

2.

I ask you to sing, Chavela, in the desert
on tapes pirated from smuggled LP's
I bring you here with me: I ask you to sing

It's not for me, your snarling contralto
caught on a backdrop of bitter guitar
not for me   yet I pray let me listen

I don't pray often   Never to male or female
sometimes to music or the flask of sunset
quick winter evenings   draining into the ground

our blood is mixed in, borderland magenta
and vermilion, never to become one
yet what we're singing, dying in, that color

two-worlded, never one   Where from bars
lit by candle and earthquake your music finds me
whom it didn't look for   This is why I ask you,

when the singing escapes the listener and goes
from the throat to where the mountains hang in chains
as if they never listened   why the song

wants so much to go where no song has ever gone.

3.

In this pale clear light where all mistakes are bathed
this afterglow of westernness
I write to you, head wrapped in your darkred scarf

framed by the sharp spines of the cholla
you love, the cruel blonde
spirit of the Mohave blossoming

in the spring twilights
of much earlier ages
Off at this distance I'm safe

to conjure the danger
you undergo daily, chin outthrust
eyelid lowered against the storm

that takes in an inkling whole ranches down
with the women the men and the children
the horses and cattle

—that much, flash-flood, lightning
all that had been done right, gone to hell
all crimes washed down the gulch

of independence, lost horse trail
Well, this was your country, Malinche,
and is, where you choose to speak

4.

Every drought-resistant plant has its own story
each had to learn to live
with less and less water, each would have loved

to laze in long soft rains, in the quiet drip
after the thunderstorm
each could do without deprivation

but where drought is the epic then there must be some
who persist, not by species-betrayal
but by changing themselves

minutely, by a constant study
of the price of continuity
a steady bargain with the way things are

5.

Then there were those, white-skinned
riding on camels

fast under scorching skies
their lives a tome of meaning
holding all this in fief:
star-dragged heavens, embroidered saddle-bags
coffee boiled up in slim urns
the salt, the oil, the roads
linking Europe with Asia
Crusaders, Legionnaires
desert-rats of empire
sucking the kid's bones, drunk with meaning
fucking the Arab, killing the Jew

6.

Deutsches Blut, Ahmad the Arab
tells Arnold the Jew
tapping the blue
veins of his own brown wrist
in his own walled garden
spread with figured carpets
summer, starlight, 1925
Was it the Crusader line?
Did they think it made them brothers?
Arnold the Jew my father
told me the story, showed me
his photograph of Ahmad: *Deutsches Blut*

7.

Then there were those, black-robed
on horseback, tracing the great plateaus
cut by arroyos, cleft by ravines
facing Sierra San Pedro San Mártir
a fixed bar welding Baja California
to the mainland north:

a land the most unfortunate
ungrateful and miserable of this world
Padre Miguel Venegas wrote
yet they ordered the missions raised
from fragile ramadas
the thin stream drawn from the watering-hole
into gardens of fig, palm, sugarcane
tried to will what cannot be willed
killed many in the trying:
unpacked smallpox, measles, typhus
from the chests with the linens and chalices
packed the sufferers in plague-ridden rooms
baptized in one village walk
all the children, who then died.
(San Ignacio!   Soledad!)
There were those: convinced the material
was base, the humanity less
—*Out of what can I bring forth a Christian soul?*
For these, naked and dark
I come to do the work of Cross and Crown?
winning hearts and minds
peeling the prickly pear
and dousing it in wine

8.

What would it mean to think
you are part of a generation
that simply must pass on?
What would it mean to live
in the desert, try to live
a human life, something
to hand on to the children
to take up to the Land?
What would it mean to think
you were born in chains and only time,

nothing you can do
could redeem the slavery
you were born into?

9.

Out of a knot of deadwood
on ghostly grey-green stems
the nightblooming cereus opens
On a still night, under Ursa Major
the tallest saguaro cracks with cold
The eaters of herbs are eaten
the carnivores' bones fall down
and scavengers pick them clean
This is not for us, or if it is
with whom, and where, is the covenant?

10.

When it all stands clear you come to love
the place you are:
the bundle of bare sticks soaked
with resin
always, and never, a bush on fire
the blue sky without tale or text
and without meaning
the great swing of the horizontal circle
Miriam, Aaron, Moses
are somewhere else, marching
You learn to live without prophets
without legends
to live just where you are
your burning bush, your seven-branched candlestick
the ocotillo in bloom

11.

What's sacred is nameless
moves in the eyeflash
holds still in the circle
of the great arid basin
once watered and fertile
probes outward through twigbark
a green ghost inhabiting
dormant stick, abstract thorn
What's sacred is singular:
out of this dry fork, this
wreck of perspective
what's sacred tries itself
one more time

1987–1988

DELTA

If you have taken this rubble for my past
raking through it for fragments you could sell
know that I long ago moved on
deeper into the heart of the matter

If you think you can grasp me, think again:
my story flows in more than one direction
a delta springing from the riverbed
with its five fingers spread.

1987

6/21

It's June and summer's height
the longest bridge of light
leaps from all the rivets
of the sky
Yet it's of earth
and nowhere else I have to speak
Only on earth has this light taken on
these swiveled meanings, only on this earth
where we are dying befouled, gritting our teeth
losing our guiding stars
                                      has this light
found an alphabet   a mouth

1987

FOR AN ALBUM

Our story isn't a file of photographs
faces laughing under green leaves
or snowlit doorways, on the verge of driving
away, our story is not about women
victoriously perched on the one
sunny day of the conference,
nor lovers displaying love:

Our story is of moments
when even slow motion moved too fast
for the shutter of the camera:
words that blew our lives apart, like so,
eyes that cut and caught each other,
mime of the operating room
where gas and knives quote each other

684

moments before the telephone
starts ringing: our story is
how still we stood,
how fast.

1987

DREAMWOOD

In the old, scratched, cheap wood of the typing stand
there is a landscape, veined, which only a child can see
or the child's older self,
a woman dreaming when she should be typing
the last report of the day.   If this were a map,
she thinks, a map laid down to memorize
because she might be walking it, it shows
ridge upon ridge fading into hazed desert,
here and there a sign of aquifers
and one possible watering-hole.   If this were a map
it would be the map of the last age of her life,
not a map of choices but a map of variations
on the one great choice. It would be the map by which
she could see the end of touristic choices,
of distances blued and purpled by romance,
by which she would recognize that poetry
isn't revolution but a way of knowing
why it must come.   If this cheap, massproduced
wooden stand from the Brooklyn Union Gas Co.,
massproduced yet durable, being here now,
is what it is yet a dream-map
so obdurate, so plain,
she thinks, the material and the dream can join
and that is the poem and that is the late report.

1987

WALKING DOWN THE ROAD

On a clear night in Live Oak you can see
the stars glittering low as from the deck
of a frigate.
In Live Oak without pavements you can walk
the fronts of old homesteads, past tattered palms,
original rosebushes, thick walnut trees
ghosts of the liveoak groves
the whitemen cleared.   On a night like this
the old California thickens and bends
the Baja streams out like lava-melt
we are no longer the United States
we're a lost piece of Mexico
maybe dreaming the destruction
of the Indians, reading the headlines,
how the gringos marched into Mexico City
forcing California into the hand
of Manifest Destiny, law following greed.
And the pale lies trapped in the flickering boxes
here in Live Oak tonight, they too follow.
One thing follows on another, that is time:
Carmel in its death-infested prettiness,
thousands of skeletons stacked in the *campo santo*:
the spring fouled by the pickaxe:
the flag dragged on to the moon:
the crystal goblet smashed: grains of the universe
flashing their angry tears, here in Live Oak.

1988

THE SLIDES

Three dozen squares of light-inflicted glass
lie in a quarter-century's dust
under the skylight. I can show you this:
also a sprung couch spewing
dessicated mouse-havens, a revolving bookstand
rusted on its pivot, leaning
with books of an era: *Roosevelt vs Recovery*
The Mystery & Lure of Perfume   *My Brother Was Mozart*
I've had this attic in mind for years
                         Now you
who keep a lookout for
places like this, make your living
off things like this: You see, the books are rotting,
sunbleached, unfashionable
the furniture neglected past waste
but the lantern-slides—their story
could be sold, they could be a prize
                        I want to see
your face when you start to sort them. You want
cloched hats of the Thirties, engagement portraits
with marcelled hair, maillots daring the waves,
my family album:
               This is the razing of the spinal cord
by the polio virus
this, the lung-tissue kissed by the tubercle bacillus
this with the hooked shape is
the cell that leaks anemia to the next generation
Enlarged on a screen
they won't be quaint; they go on working; they still kill.

1987

HARPERS FERRY

Where do I get this landscape? Two river-roads
glittering at each other's throats, the Virginia mountains fading
across the gorge, the October-shortened sun, the wooden town,
rebellion sprouting encampments in the hills
and a white girl running away from home
who will have to see it all. But where do I get this, how
do I know how the light quails from the trembling
waters, autumn goes to ash from ridge to ridge
how behind the gunmetal pines the guns
are piled, the sun drops, and the watchfires burn?

I know the men's faces tremble like smoky
crevices in a cave where candle-stumps have been stuck
on ledges by fugitives. The men are dark and sometimes pale
like her, their eyes pouched or blank or squinting, all by now
are queer, outside, and out of bounds and have no membership
in any brotherhood but this: where power is handed from
the ones who can get it to the ones
who have been refused. It's a simple act,
to steal guns and hand them to the slaves. Who would have thought
                it.

Running away from home is slower than her quick feet thought
and this is not the vague and lowering North, ghostland of deeper
                snows
than she has ever pictured
but this is one exact and definite place,
a wooden village at the junction of two rivers
two trestle bridges hinged and splayed,
low houses crawling up the mountains.

Suppose she slashes her leg on a slashed pine's tooth, ties the leg
                in a kerchief

knocks on the door of a house, the first on the edge of town
has to beg water, won't tell her family name, afraid someone will
                    know her family face
lies with her throbbing leg on the vined verandah where the woman
                    of the house
wanted her out of there, that was clear
yet with a stern and courteous patience leaned above her
with cold tea, water from the sweetest spring, mint from the same
                    source
later with rags wrung from a boiling kettle
and studying, staring eyes. Eyes ringed with watching. A peachtree
                    shedding yellowy leaves
and a houseful of men who keep off. So great a family of men, and
                    then this woman
who wanted her gone yet stayed by her, watched over her.
But this girl is expert in overhearing
and one word leaps off the windowpanes like the crack of dawn,
the translation of the babble of two rivers. What does this girl
with her little family quarrel, know about arsenals?
Everything she knows is wrapped up in her leg
without which she won't get past Virginia, though she's running
                    north.

Whatever gave the girl the idea you could run away
from a family quarrel? Displace yourself, when nothing else
would change? It wasn't books:

it was half-overheard, a wisp of talk:
escape   flight   free soil
softing past her shoulder

She has never dreamed of arsenals, though
she's a good rifle-shot, taken at ten
by her brothers, hunting

and though they've climbed her over and over
leaving their wet clots in her sheets
on her new-started maidenhair

she has never reached for a gun to hold them off
for guns are the language of the strong to the weak
—How many squirrels have crashed between her sights

what vertebrae cracked at her finger's signal
what wings staggered through the boughs
whose eyes, ringed and treed, has she eyed as prey?

There is a strategy of mass flight
a strategy of arming
questions of how, of when, of where:

the arguments soak through the walls
of the houseful of men where running from home
the white girl lies in her trouble.

There are things overheard and things unworded, never sung
or pictured, things that happen silently
as the peachtree's galactic blossoms open in mist, the frost-star
hangs in the stubble, the decanter of moonlight pours its mournless
                    liquid down
steadily on the solstice fields
the cotton swells in its boll and you feel yourself engorged,
                    unnameable
you yourself feel encased and picked-open, you feel yourself
                    unenvisaged

There is no quarrel possible in this silence
You stop yourself listening for a word that will not be spoken:
                    listening instead to the overheard
fragments, phrases melting on air: *No more   Many thousand go*

And you know they are leaving as fast as they can, you whose child's
                    eye followed each face wondering
not how could they leave but when: you knew they would leave
and so could you but not with them, you were not their child, they
                    had their own children
you could leave the house where you were daughter, sister, prey
picked open and left to silence, you could leave alone

This would be my scenario of course: that the white girl understands
what I understand and more, that the leg torn in flight
had not betrayed her, had brought her to another point of struggle
that when she takes her place she is clear in mind and her anger
true with the training of her hand and eye, her leg cured on the
                    porch of history
ready for more than solitary defiance. That when the General passes
                    through
in her blazing headrag, this girl knows her for Moses, pleads to
                    stand with the others in the shortened light
accepts the scrutiny, the steel-black gaze; but Moses passes and is
                    gone to her business elsewhere
leaving the men to theirs, the girl to her own.
But who would she take as leader?
would she fade into the woods
will she die in an *indefensible position,* a *miscarried raid*
does she lose the family face at last
pressed into a gully above two rivers, does Shenandoah or Potomac
                    carry her
north or south, will she wake in the mining camps to stoke the
                    stoves
and sleep at night with her rifle blue and loyal under her hand
does she ever forget how they left, how they taught her leaving?

1988

ONE LIFE

A woman walking in a walker on the cliffs
recalls great bodily joys, much pain.
Nothing in her is apt to say
My heart aches, though she read those words
in a battered college text, this morning
as the sun rose. It is all too
mixed, the heart too mixed with laughter
raucousing the grief, her life
too mixed, she shakes her heavy
silvered hair at all the fixed
declarations of baggage. I should be dead and I'm alive
don't ask me how; I don't eat like I should
and still I like how the drop of vodka
hits the tongue. I was a worker and a mother,
that means a worker and a worker
but for one you don't pay union dues
or get a pension; for the other
the men ran the union, we ran the home.
It was terrible and good, we had more than half a life,
I had four lives at least, one out of marriage
when I kicked up all the dust I could
before I knew what I was doing.
One life with the girls on the line during the war,
yes, painting our legs and jitterbugging together
one life with a husband, not the worst,
one with your children, none of it just what you'd thought.
None of it what it could have been, if we'd known.
We took what we could.
But even this is a life, I'm reading a lot of books
I never read, my daughter brought home from school,
plays where you can almost hear them talking,

Romantic poets, Isaac Babel. A lot of lives
worse and better than what I knew. I'm walking again.
My heart doesn't ache; sometimes though it rages.

1988

DIVISIONS OF LABOR

The revolutions wheel, compromise, utter their statements:
a new magazine appears, mastheaded with old names,
an old magazine polishes up its act
with deconstructions of the prose of Malcolm X
The women in the back rows of politics
are still licking thread to slip into the needle's
eye, trading bones for plastic, splitting pods
for necklaces to sell to the cruise-ships
producing immaculate First Communion dresses
with flatiron and irresolute hot water
still fitting the microscopic golden wires
into the silicon chips
still teaching, watching the children
quenched in the crossfire alleys, the flashflood gullies
the kerosene flashfires
—the women whose labor remakes the world
each and every morning
                              I have seen a woman sitting
between the stove and the stars
her fingers singed from snuffing out the candles
of pure theory   Finger and thumb: both scorched:
I have felt that sacred wax blister my hand

1988

LIVING MEMORY

Open the book of tales you knew by heart,
begin driving the old roads again,
repeating the old sentences, which have changed
minutely from the wordings you remembered.
A full moon on the first of May
drags silver film on the Winooski River.
The villages are shut
for the night, the woods are open
and soon you arrive at a crossroads
where late, late in time you recognize
part of yourself is buried.   Call it Danville,
village of water-witches.

From here on instinct is uncompromised and clear:
the tales come crowding like the Kalevala
longing to burst from the tongue.   Under the trees
of the backroad you rumor the dark
with houses, sheds, the long barn
moored like a barge on the hillside.
Chapter and verse.   A mailbox.   A dooryard.
A drink of springwater from the kitchen tap.
An old bed, old wallpaper.   Falling asleep like a child
in the heart of the story.

Reopen the book.   A light mist soaks the page,
blunt naked buds tip the wild lilac scribbled
at the margin of the road, no one knows when.
Broken stones of drywall mark the onset
of familiar paragraphs slanting up and away
each with its own version, nothing ever
has looked the same from anywhere.

We came like others to a country of farmers—
Puritans, Catholics, Scotch Irish, Québecois:

bought a failed Yankee's empty house and barn
from a prospering Yankee,
Jews following Yankee footprints,
prey to many myths but most of all
that Nature makes us free.   That the land can save us.
Pioneer, indigenous; we were neither.

You whose stories these farms secrete,
you whose absence these fields publish,
all you whose lifelong travail
took as given this place and weather
who did what you could with the means you had—
it was pick and shovel work
done with a pair of horses, a stone boat
a strong back, and an iron bar: clearing pasture—
Your memories crouched, foreshortened in our text.
Pages torn.   New words crowding the old.

I knew a woman whose clavicle was smashed
inside a white clapboard house with an apple tree
and a row of tulips by the door.   I had a friend
with six children and a tumor like a seventh
who drove me to my driver's test and in exchange
wanted to see Goddard College, in Plainfield.   She'd heard
women without diplomas could study there.
I knew a woman who walked
straight across cut stubble in her bare feet away,
women who said, *He's a good man, never*
laid a hand to me as living proof.
A man they said fought death
to keep fire for his wife for one more winter, leave
a woodpile to outlast him.

I was left the legacy of a pile of stovewood
split by a man in the mute chains of rage.
The land he loved as landscape

could not unchain him.   There are many,
Gentile and Jew, it has not saved.   Many hearts have burst
over these rocks, in the shacks
on the failure sides of these hills.   Many guns
turned on brains already splitting
in silence.   Where are those versions?
Written-across like nineteenth-century letters
or secrets penned in vinegar, invisible
till the page is held over flame.

I was left the legacy of three sons
—as if in an old legend of three brothers
where one changes into a rufous hawk
one into a snowy owl
one into a whistling swan
and each flies to the mother's side
as she travels, bringing something she has lost,
and she sees their eyes are the eyes of her children
and speaks their names and they become her sons.
But there is no one legend and one legend only.

This month the land still leafless, out from snow
opens in all directions, the transparent woods
with sugar-house, pond, cellar-hole unscreened.
Winter and summer cover the closed roads
but for a few weeks they lie exposed,
the old nervous-system of the land.   It's the time
when history speaks in a row of crazy fence-poles
a blackened chimney, houseless, a spring
soon to be choked in second growth
a stack of rusting buckets, a rotting sledge.

It's the time when your own living
laid open between seasons
ponders clues like the *One Way* sign defaced
to *Bone Way,* the stones

of a graveyard in Vermont, a Jewish cemetery
in Birmingham, Alabama.
How you have needed these places,
as a tall gaunt woman used to need to sit
at the knees of bronze-hooded *Grief*
by Clover Adams' grave.
But you will end somewhere else, a sift of ashes
awkwardly flung by hands you have held and loved
or, nothing so individual, bones reduced
with, among, other bones, anonymous,
or wherever the Jewish dead
have to be sought in the wild grass overwhelming
the cracked stones. Hebrew spelled in wilderness.

All we can read is life.   Death is invisible.
A yahrzeit candle belongs
to life.   The sugar skulls
eaten on graves for the Day of the Dead
belong to life.   To the living.   The Kaddish is to the living,
the Day of the Dead, for the living.   Only the living
invent these plumes, tombs, mounds, funeral ships,
living hands turn the mirrors to the walls,
tear the boughs of yew to lay on the casket,
rip the clothes of mourning.   Only the living
decide death's color: is it white or black?
The granite bulkhead
incised with names, the quilt of names, were made
by the living, for the living.
                              I have watched
films from a Pathé camera, a picnic
in sepia, I have seen my mother
tossing an acorn into the air;
my grandfather, alone in the heart of his family;
my father, young, dark, theatrical;
myself, a six-month child.
Watching the dead we see them living

their moments, they were at play, nobody thought
they would be watched so.
                              When Selma threw
her husband's ashes into the Hudson
and they blew back on her and on us, her friends,
it was life.   Our blood raced in that gritty wind.

Such details get bunched, packed, stored
in these cellar-holes of memory
so little is needed
to call on the power, though you can't name its name:
It has its ways of coming back:
a truck going into gear on the crown of the road
the white-throat sparrow's notes
the moon in her fullness standing
right over the concrete steps the way
she stood the night they landed there.
                              From here

nothing has changed, and everything.

The scratched and treasured photograph Richard showed me
taken in '29, the year I was born:
it's the same road I saw
strewn with the Perseids one August night,
looking older, steeper than now
and rougher, yet I knew it.   Time's
power, the only just power—would you
give it away?

1988

TURNING

1.

Deadstillness over droughtlands.
Parched, the heart of the matter.
Panic among smaller animals
used to licking water from cool stones.
Over the great farms, a burning-glass
one-eyed and wild as a jack,
the corn snatched in a single afternoon
of the one-eyed jack's impassive stare.

And in that other country
of choices made by others
that country I never chose
that country of terrible leavings and returnings
in that country whose map I carry on my palm
the forests are on fire: history is on fire.

My foot drags in the foothills of two lands;
At the turn the spirit pauses
and faces the high passes:
bloodred granite, sandstone steeped in blood.
At the turn the spirit turns,
looks back—if any follow—
squints ahead—if any lead—
What would you bring along on a trek like this?
What is bringing you along?

2.

In a time of broken hands
in a broken-promised land
something happens to the right hand

Remembering a city, it forgets
flexion, gestures that danced like flames
the lifeline buried in the fist

forgets the pedlar's trinket, fine to finger and lay forth,
the scalpel's path, the tracing of the pulse
the sprinkle of salt and rip of chicken feathers

forgets the wrist's light swivel breaking bread
the matzoh crumb
fingered to secret lips in stinking fog

forgets its own ache, lying
work-stiffened, mute
on the day most like Paradise

Becomes the handle of a club
an enemy of hands
emptied of all memories but one

When the right hand forgets its cunning, what of the other?
Shall we invent its story?
Has it simply lain in trance

disowned, written-off, unemployed?
Does it twitch now, finger and thumb,
does the prickle of memory race through?

When the right hand becomes the enemy of hands
what does the left hand make of their old collaboration?
Pick up the book, the pinch of salt, the matzoh crumb,

hand, and begin to teach.

3.

Finally, we will make change. This eyeflash,
this touch, handling the drenched flyers,
these glances back at history—

riverside where harps hang from the trees,
cracked riverbed with grounded hulks,
unhealed water to cross—

leaving superstition behind—
first our own, then other's—
that barrier, that stream

where swimming against the current will become
no metaphor: this is how you land, unpurified,
winded, shivering, on the further shore

where there are only new kinds of tasks, and old:
writing with others that open letter or brief
that might—if only—we know it happens:

no sudden revelation but the slow
turn of consciousness, while every day
climbs on the back of the days before:

no new day, only a list of days,
no task you expect to see finished, but
you can't hold back from the task.

4.

A public meeting.   I glance at a woman's face:
strong lines and soft, listening, a little on guard:
we have come separately, are sitting apart,
know each other in the room, have slept twelve years
in the same bed, attend now to the speaker.

Her subject is occupation, a promised land,
displacement, deracination, two peoples called Semites,
humiliation, force, women trying to speak with women,
the subject is how to break a mold of discourse,
how little by little minds change
but that they do change.   We two have fought
our own battles side by side, at dawn, over supper,
our changes of mind have come
with the stir of hairs, the sound of a cracked phrase:
we have depended on something.
What then?   Sex isn't enough, merely to trust
each other's inarticulate sounds,
—what then?   call it mutual recognition.

5.

Whatever you are that has tracked us this far,
I never thought you were on our side,
I only thought you did not judge us.

Yet as a cell might hallucinate
the eye—intent, impassioned—
behind the lens of the microscope

so I have thought of you,
whatever you are—a mindfulness—
whatever you are: the place beyond all places,

beyond boundaries, green lines,
wire-netted walls
the place beyond documents.

Unnameable by choice.
So why am I out here, trying
to read your name in the illegible air?

—vowel washed from a stone,
solitude of no absence,
forbidden face-to-face

—trying to hang these wraiths
of syllables, breath
without echo, why?

1988

AN ATLAS OF THE DIFFICULT WORLD

(1988–1991)

—For John Benedict, in memory—

I

*An Atlas of the
Difficult World*

I

A dark woman, head bent, listening for something
—a woman's voice, a man's voice or
voice of the freeway, night after night, metal streaming downcoast
past eucalyptus, cypress, agribusiness empires
THE SALAD BOWL OF THE WORLD, gurr of small planes
dusting the strawberries, each berry picked by a hand
in close communion, strawberry blood on the wrist,
Malathion in the throat, communion,
the hospital at the edge of the fields,
prematures slipping from unsafe wombs,
the labor and delivery nurse on her break watching
planes dusting rows of pickers.
Elsewhere declarations are made: at the sink
rinsing strawberries flocked and gleaming, fresh from market
one says: "On the pond this evening is a light
finer than my mother's handkerchief
received from her mother, hemmed and initialed
by the nuns in Belgium."
One says: "I can lie for hours
reading and listening to music. But sleep comes hard.
I'd rather lie awake and read."   One writes:
"Mosquitoes pour through the cracks
in this cabin's walls, the road
in winter is often impassable,
I live here so I don't have to go out and act,
I'm trying to hold onto my life, it feels like nothing."
One says: "I never knew from one day to the next
where it was coming from: I had to make my life happen
from day to day.   Every day an emergency.
Now I have a house, a job from year to year.
What does that make me?"
In the writing workshop a young man's tears
wet the frugal beard he's grown to go with his poems
hoping they have redemption stored

in their lines, maybe will get him home free.   In the classroom
eight-year-old faces are grey.   The teacher knows which children
have not broken fast that day,
remembers the Black Panthers spooning cereal.

•

I don't want to hear how he beat her after the earthquake,
tore up her writing, threw the kerosene
lantern into her face waiting
like an unbearable mirror of his own.   I don't
want to hear how she finally ran from the trailer
how he tore the keys from her hands, jumped into the truck
and backed it into her.   I don't want to think
how her guesses betrayed her—that he meant well, that she
was really the stronger and ought not to leave him
to his own apparent devastation.   I don't want to know
wreckage, dreck and waste, but these are the materials
and so are the slow lift of the moon's belly
over wreckage, dreck, and waste, wild treefrogs calling in
another season, light and music still pouring over
our fissured, cracked terrain.

•

Within two miles of the Pacific rounding
this long bay, sheening the light for miles
inland, floating its fog through redwood rifts and over
strawberry and artichoke fields, its bottomless mind
returning always to the same rocks, the same cliffs, with
ever-changing words, always the same language
—this is where I live now.   If you had known me
once, you'd still know me now though in a different
light and life.   This is no place you ever knew me.

But it would not surprise you
to find me here, walking in fog, the sweep of the great ocean
eluding me, even the curve of the bay, because as always

I fix on the land.   I am stuck to earth.   What I love here
is old ranches, leaning seaward, lowroofed spreads between rocks
small canyons running through pitched hillsides
liveoaks twisted on steepness, the eucalyptus avenue leading
to the wrecked homestead, the fogwreathed heavy-chested cattle
on their blond hills.   I drive inland over roads
closed in wet weather, past shacks hunched in the canyons
roads that crawl down into darkness and wind into light
where trucks have crashed and riders of horses tangled
to death with lowstruck boughs.   These are not the roads
you knew me by.   But the woman driving, walking, watching
for life and death, is the same.

II

Here is a map of our country:
here is the Sea of Indifference, glazed with salt
This is the haunted river flowing from brow to groin
we dare not taste its water
This is the desert where missiles are planted like corms
This is the breadbasket of foreclosed farms
This is the birthplace of the rockabilly boy
This is the cemetery of the poor
who died for democracy   This is a battlefield
from a nineteenth-century war   the shrine is famous
This is the sea-town of myth and story   when the fishing fleets
went bankrupt   here is where the jobs were   on the pier
processing frozen fishsticks   hourly wages and no shares
These are other battlefields   Centralia   Detroit
here are the forests primeval   the copper   the silver lodes
These are the suburbs of acquiescence   silence rising fumelike
            from the streets
This is the capital of money and dolor whose spires
flare up through air inversions whose bridges are crumbling

whose children are drifting blind alleys pent
between coiled rolls of razor wire
I promised to show you a map you say but this is a mural
then yes let it be   these are small distinctions
where do we see it from is the question

III

Two five-pointed star-shaped glass candleholders, bought at the
                    Ben Franklin, Barton, twenty-three years ago, one
                    chipped
—now they hold half-burnt darkred candles, and in between
a spider is working, the third point of her filamental passage
a wicker basket-handle.   All afternoon I've sat
at this table in Vermont, reading, writing, cutting an apple in
                    slivers
and eating them, but mostly gazing down through the windows
at the long scribble of lake due south
where the wind and weather come from.   There are bottles set in
                    the windows
that children dug up in summer woods or bought for nickels and
                    dimes
in dark shops that are no more, gold-brown, foam-green or cobalt
                    glass, blue that gave way to the cobalt
                    bomb.   The woods
are still on the hill behind the difficult unknowable
incommensurable barn.   The wind's been working itself up
in low gusts gnashing the leaves left chattering on branches
or drifting over still-green grass;   but it's been a warm wind.
An autumn without a killing frost so far, still warm
feels like a time of self-deception, a memory of pushing
limits in youth, that intricate losing game of innocence long
                    overdue

Frost is expected tonight, gardens are gleaned, potplants taken in,
    there is talk of withering, of wintering-over.

•

North of Willoughby the back road to Barton
turns a right-hand corner on a high plateau
bitten by wind now and rimed grey-white
—farms of rust and stripping paint, the shortest growing season
south of Quebec, a place of sheer unpretentious hardship, dark
            pines stretching away
toward Canada.   There was a one-room schoolhouse
by a brook where we used to picnic, summers, a little world
of clear bubbling water, cowturds, moss, wild mint, wild mush-
            rooms under the pines.
One hot afternoon I sat there reading Gaskell's *Life of Charlotte
            Brontë*—the remote
upland village where snow lay long and late, the deep-rutted
            roads, the dun and grey moorland
—trying to enfigure such a life, how genius
unfurled in the shortlit days, the meagre means of that house. I
            never thought
of lives at that moment around me, what girl dreamed
and was extinguished in the remote back-country I had come to
            love,
reader reading under a summer tree in the landscape
of the rural working poor.

Now the panes are black and from the south the wind still stag-
            gers, creaking the house:
brown milkweeds toss in darkness below but I cannot see them
the room has lost the window and turned into itself: two corner
            shelves of things
both useful and unused, things arrived here by chance or choice,
            two teapots, one broken-spouted, red and blue
came to me with some books from my mother's mother, my

                        grandmother Mary
who travelled little, loved the far and strange, bits of India, Asia
and this teapot of hers was Chinese or she thought it was
—the other given by a German Jew, a refugee who killed herself
Midlands flowered ware, and this too cannot be used because
                coated inside—why?—with flaking paint:
"You will always use it for flowers," she instructed when she
                        gave it.
In a small frame, under glass, my father's bookplate, engraved in
                his ardent youth, the cleft tree-trunk and the win-
                tering ants:
Without labor, no sweetness—motto I breathed in from him and
                learned in grief and rebellion to take and use
—and later learned that not all labor ends in sweetness.
A little handwrought iron candlestick, given by another German
                woman
who hidden survived the Russian soldiers beating the walls in
        1945,
emigrated, married a poet.   I sat many times at their table.
                They are now long apart.
Some odd glasses for wine or brandy, from an ignorant, passion-
                ate time—we were in our twenties—
with the father of the children who dug for old medicine bottles
                in the woods
—afternoons listening to records, reading Karl Shapiro's *Poems
                of a Jew* and Auden's "In Sickness and in Health"
                aloud, using the poems to talk to each other
—now it's twenty years since last I heard that intake
of living breath, as if language were too much to bear,
that voice overcast like klezmer with echoes, uneven, edged,
                torn, Brooklyn street crowding Harvard Yard
—I'd have known any syllable anywhere.

Stepped out onto the night-porch.   That wind has changed,
                though still from the south
it's blowing up hard now, no longer close to earth but driving

into the crowns of the maples, into my face
almost slamming the stormdoor into me.   But it's warm, warm,
pneumonia wind, death of innocence wind, unwinding wind,
time-hurtling wind.   And it has a voice in the house.   I hear
conversations that can't be happening, overhead in the bedrooms
and I'm not talking of ghosts.   The ghosts are here of course but
                      they speak plainly
—haven't I offered food and wine, listened well for them all
                      these years,
not only those known in life but those before our time
of self-deception, our intricate losing game of innocence long
                      overdue?

•

The spider's decision is made, her path cast, candle-wick to
                      wicker handle to candle,
in the air, under the lamp, she comes swimming toward me
(have I been sitting here so long?)   she will use everything,
                      nothing comes without labor, she is working so
                      hard and I know
nothing all winter can enter this house or this web, not all labor
                      ends in sweetness.
But how do I know what she needs?   Maybe simply
to spin herself a house within a house, on her own terms
in cold, in silence.

IV

Late summers, early autumns, you can see something that binds
the map of this country together: the girasol, orange gold-
                      petalled
with her black eye, laces the roadsides from Vermont to
                      California
runs the edges of orchards, chain-link fences

milo fields and malls, schoolyards and reservations
truckstops and quarries, grazing ranges, graveyards
of veterans, graveyards of cars hulked and sunk, her tubers the
                jerusalem artichoke
that has fed the Indians, fed the hobos, could feed us all.
Is there anything in the soil, cross-country, that makes for
a plant so generous?   *Spendtbrift* we say, as if
accounting nature's waste.   Ours darkens
the states to their strict borders, flushes
down borderless streams, leaches from lakes to the curdled foam
down by the riverside.

Waste.   Waste.   The watcher's eye put out, hands of the
                builder severed, brain of the maker starved
those who could bind, join, reweave, cohere, replenish
now at risk in this segregate republic
locked away out of sight and hearing, out of mind, shunted aside
those needed to teach, advise, persuade, weigh arguments
those urgently needed for the work of perception
work of the poet, the astronomer, the historian, the architect of
                new streets
work of the speaker who also listens
meticulous delicate work of reaching the heart of the desperate
                woman, the desperate man
—never-to-be-finished, still unbegun work of repair—it cannot
                be done without them
and where are they now?

V

Catch if you can your country's moment, begin
where any calendar's ripped-off: Appomattox
Wounded Knee, Los Alamos, Selma, the last airlift from Saigon
the ex-Army nurse hitch-hiking from the debriefing center; medal

of spit on the veteran's shoulder
—catch if you can this unbound land these states without a cause
earth of despoiled graves and grazing these embittered brooks
these pilgrim ants pouring out from the bronze eyes, ears,
        nostrils,
the mouth of Liberty

        over the chained bay waters

                San Quentin:
once we lost our way and drove in under the searchlights to the
        gates
end of visiting hours, women piling into cars
the bleak glare aching over all

        Where are we moored?   What
        are the bindings?   What be-
        hooves us?

Driving the San Francisco–Oakland Bay Bridge
no monument's in sight but fog
prowling Angel Island muffling Alcatraz
poems in Cantonese inscribed on fog
no icon lifts a lamp here
history's breath blotting the air
over Gold Mountain   a transfer
of patterns like the transfer of African appliqué
to rural Alabama   voices alive in legends, curses
tongue-lashings
        poems on a weary wall
And when light swivels off Angel Island and Alcatraz
when the bays leap into life
        views of the Palace of Fine Arts,
        TransAmerica
when sunset bathes the three bridges
            still
old ghosts crouch hoarsely whispering
under Gold Mountain

•

North and east of the romantic headlands there are roads into tule
                fog
places where life is cheap poor quick unmonumented
Rukeyser would have guessed it coming West for the opening
of the great red bridge   *There are roads to take* she wrote
when you think of your country   driving south
to West Virginia Gauley Bridge silicon mines the flakes of it
                heaped like snow, death-angel white
—poet journalist pioneer mother
uncovering her country: *there are roads to take*

•

I don't want to know how he tracked them
along the Appalachian Trail, hid close
by their tent, pitched as they thought in seclusion
killing one woman, the other
dragging herself into town   his defense they had teased his
                loathing
of what they were   I don't want to know
but this is not a bad dream of mine   these are the materials
and so are the smell of wild mint and coursing water remembered
and the sweet salt darkred tissue I lay my face
upon, my tongue within.
                A crosshair against the pupil of an eye
could blow my life from hers
a cell dividing without maps, sliver of ice beneath a wheel
could do the job.   Faithfulness isn't the problem.

VI

A potato explodes in the oven.   Poetry and famine:
the poets who never starved, whose names we know
the famished nameless taking ship with their hoard of poetry

Annie Sullivan half-blind in the workhouse enthralling her child-
        mates
with lore her father had borne in his head from Limerick along
        with the dream of work
and *hatred of England smouldering like a turf-fire.* But a poetry older
        than hatred. Poetry
in the workhouse, laying of the rails, a potato splattering oven
        walls
poetry of cursing and silence, bitter and deep, shallow and
        drunken
poetry of priest-talk, of I.R.A.-talk, kitchen-talk, dream-talk,
        tongues despised
in cities where in a mere fifty years language has rotted to jargon,
        lingua franca of inclusion
from turns of speech ancient as the potato, muttered at the coals
        by women and men
rack-rented, harshened, numbed by labor ending
in root-harvest rotted in field. 1847. No relief. No succour.
America. Meat three times a day, they said.   Slaves—You would
        not be that.

VII (The Dream-Site)

Some rooftop, water-tank looming, street-racket strangely quelled
and others known and unknown there, long sweet summer eve-
        ning on the tarred roof:
leaned back your head to the nightvault swarming with stars
the Pleiades broken loose, not seven but thousands
every known constellation flinging out fiery threads
and you could distinguish all
—cobwebs, tendrils, anatomies of stars
coherently hammocked, blueblack avenues between
—you knew your way among them, knew you were part of them
until, neck aching, you sat straight up and saw:

It was New York, the dream-site
the lost city the city of dreadful light
where once as the sacks of garbage rose
like barricades around us we
stood listening to riffs from Pharaoh Sanders' window
on the brownstone steps
went striding the avenues in our fiery hair
in our bodies young and ordinary riding the subways reading
or pressed against other bodies
feeling in them the maps of Brooklyn Queens Manhattan
The Bronx unscrolling in the long breakneck
express plunges
                    as darkly we felt our own blood
streaming   a living city overhead
coherently webbed and knotted   bristling
we and all the others
                  known and unknown

living its life

VIII

He thought there would be a limit and that it would stop him.
                He depended on that:
the cuts would be made by someone else, the direction
come from somewhere else, arrows flashing on the freeway.
That he'd end somewhere gazing
straight into It was what he imagined and nothing beyond.
That he'd end facing as limit a thing without limits and so he
              flung
and burned and hacked and bled himself toward that (if I
              understand
this story at all). What he found: FOR SALE: DO NOT
              DISTURB
OCCUPANT on some cliffs;   some ill-marked, ill-kept roads

ending in warnings about shellfish in Vietnamese, Spanish and
           English.
But the spray was any color he could have dreamed
—gold, ash, azure, smoke, moonstone—
and from time to time the ocean swirled up through the eye of a
           rock and taught him
limits.   Throwing itself backward, singing and sucking, no
           teacher, only its violent
self, the Pacific, dialectical waters rearing
their wild calm constructs, momentary, ancient.

•

If your voice could overwhelm those waters, what would it say?
What would it cry of the child swept under, the mother
on the beach then, in her black bathing suit, walking straight
           out
into the glazed lace as if she never noticed, what would it say of
           the father
facing inland in his shoes and socks at the edge of the tide,
what of the lost necklace glittering twisted in foam?

•

If your voice could crack in the wind hold its breath still as the
           rocks
what would it say to the daughter searching the tidelines for a
           bottled message
from the sunken slaveships?   what of the huge sun slowly de-
           faulting into the clouds
what of the picnic stored in the dunes at high tide, full of the
           moon, the basket
with sandwiches, eggs, paper napkins, can-opener, the meal
packed for a family feast, excavated now by scuttling
ants, sandcrabs, dune-rats, because no one understood
all picnics are eaten on the grave?

IX

On this earth, in this life, as I read your story, you're lonely.
Lonely in the bar, on the shore of the coastal river
with your best friend, his wife, and your wife, fishing
lonely in the prairie classroom with all the students who love
                   you. You know some ghosts
come everywhere with you yet leave them unaddressed
for years.   You spend weeks in a house
with a drunk, you sober, whom you love, feeling lonely.
You grieve in loneliness, and if I understand you fuck in
                   loneliness.

I wonder if this is a white man's madness.
I honor your truth and refuse to leave it at that.

What have I learned from stories of the hunt, of lonely men in
                   gangs?
But there were other stories:
one man riding the Mohave Desert
another man walking the Grand Canyon.
I thought those solitary men were happy, as ever they had been.

Indio's long avenues
of Medjool date-palm and lemon sweep to the Salton Sea
in Yucca Flats the high desert reaches higher, bleached and spare
                   of talk.
At Twentynine Palms I found the grave
of Maria Eleanor Whallon, eighteen years, dead at the watering-
                   hole in 1903, under the now fire-branded palms
Her mother traveled on alone to cook in the mining camps.

X

Soledad. = f. Solitude, loneliness, homesickness; lonely retreat.
Winter sun in the rosetrees.

An old Mexican with a white moustache prunes them back
                spraying
the cut branches with dormant oil.   The old paper-bag-brown
                adobe walls
stretch apart from the rebuilt mission, in their own time.   It is
                lonely here
in the curve of the road winding through vast brown fields
                machine-engraved in furrows
of relentless precision.   In the small chapel
La Nuestra Señora de la Soledad dwells in her shallow arch
painted on either side with columns.   She is in black lace crisp as
                cinders
from head to foot.   Alone, solitary, homesick
in her lonely retreat.   Outside black olives fall and smash
littering and staining the beaten path.   The gravestones of the
                padres
are weights pressing down on the Indian artisans.   It is the sixth
                day of another war.

•

Across the freeway stands another structure
from the other side of the mirror   *it destroys*
the logical processes of the mind, a man's thoughts
become completely disorganized, madness streaming from every throat
frustrated sounds from the bars, metallic sounds from the walls
the steel trays, iron beds bolted to the wall, the smells, the human waste.
To determine how men will behave once they enter prison
it is of first importance to know that prison.   (From the freeway
gun-turrets planted like water-towers in another garden, out-
                buildings spaced in winter sun
and the concrete mass beyond: who now writes letters deep in-
                side that cave?)

If my instructor tells me that the world and its affairs
are run as well as they possibly can be, that I am governed
by wise and judicious men, that I am free and should be happy,
and if when I leave the instructor's presence and encounter

the exact opposite, if I actually sense or see confusion, war,
recession, depression, death and decay, is it not reasonable
that I should become perplexed?

From eighteen to twenty-eight
of his years

a young man schools himself, argues,
debates, trains, lectures to himself,
teaches himself Swahili, Spanish, learns
five new words of English every day,
chainsmokes, reads, writes letters.
In this college of force he wrestles bitterness,
self-hatred, sexual anger, cures his own nature.
Seven of these years in solitary.   Soledad.

But the significant feature of the desperate man reveals itself
when he meets other desperate men, directly or vicariously;
and he experiences his first kindness, someone to strain with him,
to strain to see him as he strains to see himself,
someone to understand, someone to accept the regard,
the love, that desperation forces into hiding.
Those feelings that find no expression in desperate times
store themselves up in great abundance, ripen, strengthen,
and strain the walls of their repository to the utmost;
where the kindred spirit touches this wall it crumbles—
no one responds to kindness, no one is more sensitive to it
than the desperate man.

XI

One night on Monterey Bay the death-freeze of the century:
a precise, detached caliper-grip holds the stars and the quarter-
            moon
in arrest: the hardiest plants crouch shrunken, a "killing frost"
on bougainvillea, Pride of Madeira, roseate black-purple succu-
            lents bowed

juices sucked awry in one orgy of freezing
slumped on their stems like old faces evicted from cheap hotels
—*into the streets of the universe, now!*

Earthquake and drought followed by freezing followed by war
Flags are blossoming now where little else is blossoming
and I am bent on fathoming what it means to love my country.
The history of this earth and the bones within it?
Soils and cities, promises made and mocked, plowed contours of
                shame and of hope?
Loyalties, symbols, murmurs extinguished and echoing?
Grids of states stretching westward, underground waters?
Minerals, traces, rumors I am made from, morsel, minuscule
                fibre, one woman
like and unlike so many, fooled as to her destiny, the scope of
                her task?
One citizen like and unlike so many, touched and untouched in
                passing
—each of us now a driven grain, a nucleus, a city in crisis
some busy constructing enclosures, bunkers, to escape the com-
                mon fate
some trying to revive dead statues to lead us, breathing their
                breath against marble lips
some who try to teach the moment, some who preach the
                moment
some who aggrandize, some who diminish themselves in the face
                of half-grasped events
—power and powerlessness run amuck, a tape reeling backward
                in jeering, screeching syllables—
some for whom war is new, others for whom it merely continues
                the old paroxysms of time
some marching for peace who for twenty years did not march for
                justice
some for whom peace is a white man's word and a white man's
                privilege
some who have learned to handle and contemplate the shapes of
                powerlessness and power

as the nurse learns hip and thigh and weight of the body he has
          to lift and sponge, day upon day
as she blows with her every skill on the spirit's embers still burn-
          ing by their own laws in the bed of death.
A patriot is not a weapon.   A patriot is one who wrestles for the
          soul of her country
as she wrestles for her own being, for the soul of his country
(gazing through the great circle at Window Rock into the sheen
          of the Viet Nam Wall)
as he wrestles for his own being.   A patriot is a citizen trying to
          wake
from the burnt-out dream of innocence, the nightmare
of the white general and the Black general posed in their
          camouflage,
to remember her true country, remember his suffering land:
          remember
that blessing and cursing are born as twins and separated at birth
to meet again in mourning
that the internal emigrant is the most homesick of all women and
          of all men
that every flag that flies today is a cry of pain.
                    Where are we moored?
                    What are the bindings?
                    What behooves us?

XII

What homage will be paid to a beauty built to last
from inside out, executing the blueprints of resistance and mercy
drawn up in childhood, in that little girl, round-faced with
                    clenched fists, already acquainted with mourning
in the creased snapshot you gave me?   What homage will be
                    paid to beauty
that insists on speaking truth, knows the two are not always the
                    same,

beauty that won't deny, is itself an eye, will not rest under
       contemplation?
Those low long clouds we were driving under a month ago in
       New Mexico, clouds an arm's reach away
were beautiful and we spoke of it but I didn't speak then
of your beauty at the wheel beside me, dark head steady, eyes
       drinking the spaces
of crimson, indigo, Indian distance, Indian presence,
your spirit's gaze informing your body, impatient to mark what's
       possible, impatient to mark
what's lost, deliberately destroyed, can never any way be
       returned,
your back arched against all icons, simulations, dead letters
your woman's hands turning the wheel or working with shears,
       torque wrench, knives with salt pork, onions, ink
       and fire
your providing sensate hands, your hands of oak and silk, of
       blackberry juice and drums
—I speak of them now.

For M.

XIII (Dedications)

I know you are reading this poem
late, before leaving your office
of the one intense yellow lamp-spot and the darkening window
in the lassitude of a building faded to quiet
long after rush-hour.   I know you are reading this poem
standing up in a bookstore far from the ocean
on a grey day of early spring, faint flakes driven
across the plains' enormous spaces around you.
I know you are reading this poem
in a room where too much has happened for you to bear
where the bedclothes lie in stagnant coils on the bed
and the open valise speaks of flight

but you cannot leave yet.   I know you are reading this poem
as the underground train loses momentum and before running
                    up the stairs
toward a new kind of love
your life has never allowed.
I know you are reading this poem by the light
of the television screen where soundless images jerk and slide
while you wait for the newscast from the *intifada.*
I know you are reading this poem in a waiting-room
of eyes met and unmeeting, of identity with strangers.
I know you are reading this poem by fluorescent light
in the boredom and fatigue of the young who are counted out,
count themselves out, at too early an age.   I know
you are reading this poem through your failing sight, the thick
lens enlarging these letters beyond all meaning yet you read on
because even the alphabet is precious.
I know you are reading this poem as you pace beside the stove
warming milk, a crying child on your shoulder, a book in your
                    hand
because life is short and you too are thirsty.
I know you are reading this poem which is not in your language
guessing at some words while others keep you reading
and I want to know which words they are.
I know you are reading this poem listening for something, torn
                    between bitterness and hope
turning back once again to the task you cannot refuse.
I know you are reading this poem because there is nothing else
                    left to read
there where you have landed, stripped as you are.

1990–1991

II

SHE

goes through what must be gone through:
that catalogue she is pitching out
mildew spores   velvet between the tiles
soft hairs, nests, webs
in corners, edges of basins, in the teeth
of her very comb.   All that rots or rusts
in a night, a century.
Balances memory, training, sits in her chair
hairbrush in hand, breathing the scent of her own hair
and thinks: *I have been the weir*
where disintegration stopped.
Lifts her brush once like a thrown thing
lays it down at her side like a stockpiled weapon
crushes out the light.   Elsewhere
dust chokes the filters, dead leaves rasp in the grate.
Clogged, the fine nets bulge
and she is not there.

1988

THAT MOUTH

This is the girl's mouth, the taste
daughters, not sons, obtain:
These are the lips, powerful rudders
pushing through groves of kelp,
the girl's terrible, unsweetened taste
of the whole ocean, its fathoms: this is that taste.

This is not the father's kiss, the mother's:
a father can try to choke you,
a mother drown you to save you:
all the transactions have long been enacted.
This is neither a sister's tale nor a brother's:
strange trade-offs have long been made.

This is the swallow, the splash
of krill and plankton, that mouth
described as a girl's—
enough to give you a taste:
Are you a daughter, are you a son?
Strange trade-offs have long been made.

1988

MARGHANITA

at the oak table under the ceiling fan
Marghanita at the table counting up
a dead woman's debts.
Kicks off a sandal, sips
soda from a can, wedges the last bills
under the candelabrum.   She is here
because no one else was there when worn-to-skeleton
her enemy died.   Her love.   Her twin.
Marghanita dreamed the intravenous, the intensive
the stainless steel
before she ever saw them.   She's not practical,
you know, they used to say.
She's the artist, she got away.

In her own place Marghanita glues bronze
feathers into wings, smashes green and clear
bottles into bloodletting particles
crushed into templates of sand
scores mirrors till they fall apart and sticks them up
in driftwood boughs, drinks golden
liquid with a worm's name, forgets
her main enemy, her twin;
scores her wrist on a birthday
dreams the hospital dream.

When they were girl and boy together, boy and girl
she pinned his arm against his back
for a box containing false
lashes and fingernails, a set of veils, a string of pearls,
she let go and listened to his tales
she breathed their breath, he hers,
they each had names only the other knew.

Marghanita in the apartment everyone has left:
not a nephew, not a niece,
nobody from the parish
—gone into hiding, emigrated, lost?
where are the others?
Marghanita comes back because she does,
adding up what's left:
a rainsoaked checkbook, snapshots
razed from an album,
colors ground into powder, brushes, wands
for eyelids, lashes, brows,
beads of bath-oil, tubes of glycerin
—a dead woman's luxuries.

Marghanita will
take care of it all.   Pay if nothing else
the last month's rent.   The wings of the fan

stir corners of loose paper,
light ebbs from the window-lace,
she needs to go out and eat.   And so
hating and loving come down
to a few columns of figures,
an aching stomach, a care taken: something done.

1989

OLIVIA

Among fundamentalist Christians, she was one of them;
in our anti-apartheid groups, she was the
most militant. . . . She was a chameleon.
—White South African student activist interviewed on National Public Radio,
10/11/88

Yes, I saw you, see you, come
into the meetings, out of the rain
with your wan cheek and your thin waist—
did anyone see you eat?

Did anyone see you eat, did you wear
a woman's body, were you air
to their purpose, liquid at their call
when you stood, spine against the wall?

And I know your stance, back to the wall,
overlooking the others, your bent head
your sense of timing, your outraged tongue
the notes you take when you get home.

I see the white joints of your wrist
moving across the yellow pad
the exhausted theatre of your sleep:
I know the power you thought you had—

to know them all, better than they
knew you, than they knew you knew,
to know better than those who paid
you—paid by them, to move

at some pure point of mastery
as if, in your slight outline, moon
you could dwell above them, light and shade,
travel forever to and fro

above both sides, all sides, none,
gliding the edges, knapsack crammed
—was that it? to lift above
loyalty, love and all that trash

higher than power and its fields of force?
—never so much as a woman friend?
You were a woman walked on a leash.
And they dropped you in the end.

1988

EASTERN WAR TIME

1

Memory lifts her smoky mirror: 1943,
single isinglass window   kerosene
stove in the streetcar barn   halfset moon
8:15 a.m. Eastern War Time dark
Number 29 clanging in and turning
looseleaf notebook   *Latin for Americans*
Breasted's *History of the Ancient World*
on the girl's lap
money for lunch and war-stamps in her pocket
darkblue wool wet acrid on her hands
three pools of light   weak ceiling bulbs
a schoolgirl's hope-spilt terrified
sensations wired to smells
of kerosene wool and snow
and the sound of the dead language
praised as key   torchlight of the great dead
Grey spreading   behind still-flying snow
the lean and sway of the streetcar she must ride
to become one   of a hundred girls
rising white-cuffed and collared in a study hall
to sing *For those in peril on the sea*
under plaster casts of the classic frescoes
chariots horses draperies certitudes.

2

Girl between home and school   what is that girl
Swinging her plaid linen bookbag   what's an American girl
in wartime   her permed friz of hair
her glasses for school and movies

between school and home   ignorantly Jewish
trying to grasp the world
through books: *Jude the Obscure   The Ballad*
of Reading Gaol   Eleanor Roosevelt's *My Story*

NV15   CABLE-LIVERPOOL   122   1/63NFD
HEADQUARTERS PLAN DISCUSSED AND UNDER
               CONSIDERATION
ALL JEWS IN COUNTRIES OCCUPIED OR CONTROLLED
               GERMANY
NUMBER 3 1/2 – TO 4 MILLION SHOULD AFTER
               DEPORTATION
AND CONCENTRATION IN EAST
AT ONE BLOW EXTERMINATED TO RESOLVE
ONCE AND FOR ALL JEWISH QUESTION IN EUROPE

3

How telegrams used to come: ring
of the doorbell   serious messenger
bicycling with his sheaf   enveloped pasted strips
yellow on yellow   the stripped messages
DELAYED STOP MEET 2:27 THURSDAY
DAUGHTER BORN LAST NIGHT STOP BOTH DOING
               WELL
THE WAR DEPARTMENT REGRETS TO INFORM YOU
also: PARENTS DEPORTED UNKNOWN DESTINATION
               EAST
SITUATION DIFFICULT   ether of messages
in capital letters   silence

4

What the grown-ups can't speak of   would you push
onto children?   and the deadweight of Leo Frank
thirty years lynched   hangs heavy
:   "this is what our parents were trying to spare us"   :
here in America   but in terrible Europe
anything was possible   surely?
:   "But this is the twentieth century"   :
what the grown-ups can't teach   children must learn
how do you teach a child what you won't believe?
how do you say   *unfold, my flower, shine, my star*
and *we are hated, being what we are?*

5

A young girl knows she is young and meant to live
taken on the closed journey
her pockets drained of meaning
her ankles greased in vomit and diarrhea
driven naked across the yard
a young girl remembers her youth:
anything   textbooks   forbidden novels
school songs   petnames
the single time she bled and never since
having her hair done   its pale friz
clipped and shaped   still friz   pale Jewish hair
over her green Jewish eyes
thinking she was pretty and that others would see it
and not to bleed again and not to die
in the gas   but on the operating table
of the famous doctor
who plays string quartets with his staff in the laboratory

6

A girl wanders with a boy into the woods
a romantic walk   a couple in a poem
hand-in-hand   but you're not watching each other
for signs of desire   you're watching the woods
for signs of the secret bases   lines
converging toward the resistance   where the guns
are cached   the precious tools
the strategies argued   you're fourteen, fifteen
classmates from Vilna   walking away from Vilna
your best marks were in history and geometry   his
in chemistry   you don't intend to die
too much you think is waiting in you   for you
you never knew the forest outside Vilna
could hide so many   would have to
you'd dreamed of living in the forest
as in a folksong   lying on loose pine-needles
light ribboning from sky cross-hatched with needles
you and one dearest friend   now you will meet the others

7

A woman of sixty   driving
the great grades   sea-level to high desert
a century slipping from her shoulders
a blink in geological time
though heavy to those who had to wear it
Knowledge has entered her connective tissue and
into sand dissolved her cartilage
If her skeleton is found this will be clear
or was it knowledge   maybe a dangerous questioning
At night she lies   eyes open   seeing
the young who do not wander in the moonlight
as in a poem   faces seen

for thirty years   under the fire-hoses
walking through mobs to school
dragged singing from the buses
following the coffins
and here   brows knotted under knotted scarfs
dark eyes   searching armed streets
for the end of degradation

8

A woman wired in memories
stands by a house   collapsed in dust
her son beaten in prison   grandson
shot in the stomach   daughter
organizing the camps   an aunt's unpublished poems
grandparents' photographs   a bridal veil
phased into smoke   up the obliterate air
With whom shall she let down and tell her story
Who shall hear her to the end
standing if need be for hours   in wind
that swirls the leveled dust
in sun that beats through their scarfed hair
at the lost gate by the shattered prickly pear
Who must hear her to the end
but the woman   forbidden to forget
the blunt groats freezing in the wooden ladle
old winds   dusting the ovens with light snow?

9

Streets closed, emptied by force   Guns at corners
with open mouths and eyes   Memory speaks:
You cannot live on me alone

you cannot live without me
I'm nothing if I'm just a roll of film
stills from a vanished world
fixed lightstreaked mute
left for another generation's
restoration and framing   I can't be restored or framed
I can't be still   I'm here
in your mirror   pressed leg to leg beside you
intrusive inappropriate bitter flashing
with what makes me unkillable though killed

10

Memory says: Want to do right? Don't count on me.
I'm a canal in Europe where bodies are floating
I'm a mass grave   I'm the life that returns
I'm a table set with room for the Stranger
I'm a field with corners left for the landless
I'm accused of child-death   of drinking blood
I'm a man-child praising God he's a man
I'm a woman bargaining for a chicken
I'm a woman who sells for a boat ticket
I'm a family dispersed between night and fog
I'm an immigrant tailor who says *A coat
is not a piece of cloth only*   I sway
in the learnings of the master-mystics
I have dreamed of Zion   I've dreamed of world revolution
I have dreamed my children could live at last like others
I have walked the children of others through ranks of hatred
I'm a corpse dredged from a canal in Berlin
a river in Mississippi   I'm a woman standing
with other women dressed in black
on the streets of Haifa, Tel Aviv, Jerusalem
there is spit on my sleeve there are phonecalls in the night

I am a woman standing in line for gasmasks
I stand on a road in Ramallah   with naked face   listening
I am standing here in your poem   unsatisfied
lifting my smoky mirror

1989–1990

TATTERED KADDISH

Taurean reaper of the wild apple field
messenger from earthmire gleaning
transcripts of fog
in the nineteenth year and the eleventh month
speak your tattered Kaddish for all suicides:

Praise to life though it crumbled in like a tunnel
on ones we knew and loved

      Praise to life though its windows blew shut
      on the breathing-room of ones we knew and loved

Praise to life though ones we knew and loved
loved it badly, too well, and not enough

      Praise to life though it tightened like a knot
      on the hearts of ones we thought we knew loved us

Praise to life giving room and reason
to ones we knew and loved who felt unpraisable

      Praise to them, how they loved it, when they could.

1989

THROUGH CORRALITOS UNDER ROLLS OF CLOUD

I

Through Corralitos under rolls of cloud
between winter-stiff, ranged apple-trees
each netted in transparent air,
thin sinking light, heartsick within and filmed
in heartsickness around you, gelatin cocoon
invisible yet impervious—to the hawk
steering against the cloudbank, to the clear
oranges burning at the rancher's gate
rosetree, agave, stiff beauties holding fast
with or without your passion,
the pruners freeing up the boughs
in the unsearched faith these strange stiff shapes will bear.

II

Showering after 'flu;   stripping the bed;
running the shrouds of sickness through the wash;
airing the rooms;   emptying the trash;
it's as if part of you had died in the house
sometime in that last low-lit afternoon
when your dreams ebbed salt-thick into the sheets
and now this other's left to wash the corpse,
burn eucalyptus, turn the mirrors over—
this is other who herself barely came back,
whose breath was fog to your mist, whose stubborn shadow
covered you as you lay freezing, she survived
uncertain who she is or will be without you.

III

If you know who died in that bed, do you know
who has survived   If you say, *she was weaker,*
held life less dear, expected others
to fight for her   if pride lets you name her
victim   and the one who got up and threw
the windows open, stripped the bed, *survivor*
—what have you said, what do you know
of the survivor when you know her
only in opposition to the lost?
What does it mean to say *I have survived*
until you take the mirrors and turn them outward
and read your own face in their outraged light?

IV

That light of outrage is the light of history
springing upon us when we're least prepared,
thinking maybe a little glade of time
leaf-thick and with clear water
is ours, is promised us, for all we've hacked
and tracked our way through: to this:
What will it be?   Your wish or mine?   your
prayers or my wish then: that those we love
be well, whatever that means, to be well.
Outrage: who dare claim protection for their own
amid such unprotection?   What kind of prayer
is that?   To what kind of god?   What kind of wish?

V

She who died on that bed sees it her way:
She who went under peers through the translucent shell
cupping her death and sees her other well,

through a long lens, in silvered outline, well
she sees her other and she cannot tell
why when the boom of surf struck at them both
she felt the undertow and heard the bell,
thought death would be their twinning, till the swell
smashed her against the reef, her other still
fighting the pull, struggling somewhere away
further and further, calling her all the while:
she who went under summons her other still.

1989–1990

FOR A FRIEND IN TRAVAIL

Waking from violence: the surgeon's probe left in the foot
paralyzing the body from the waist down.
Dark before dawn: wrapped in a shawl, to walk the house
the Drinking-Gourd slung in the northwest,
half-slice of moon to the south
through dark panes.   A time to speak to you.

What are you going through? she said, is the great question.
Philosopher of oppression, theorist
of the victories of force.

We write from the marrow of our bones.   What she did not
ask, or tell: how victims save their own lives.

That crawl along the ledge, then the raveling span of fibre
                strung
from one side to the other, I've dreamed that too.
Waking, not sure we made it.   Relief, appallment, of waking.
Consciousness.   O, no.   To sleep again.
O to sleep without dreaming.

How day breaks, when it breaks, how clear and light the moon
melting into moon-colored air
moist and sweet, here on the western edge.
Love for the world, and we are part of it.
How the poppies break from their sealed envelopes
she did not tell.

What are you going through, there on the other edge?

1990

1948: JEWS

A mother's letter, torn open
in a college mailroom:
. . . *Some of them will be*
the most brilliant, fascinating
you'll ever meet
but don't get taken up by any clique
trying to claim you

—*Marry out, like your father*
she didn't write   She wrote for   wrote
against   him

It was a burden for anyone
to be fascinating, brilliant
after the six million
Never mind just coming home
and trying to get some sleep
like an ordinary person

1990

TWO ARTS

1

I've redone you by daylight.
Squatted before your gauntness
chipping away.   Slivers of rock
piling up like petals.
All night I'd worked to illuminate the skull.
By dawn you were pure electric.   You pulsed like a star.
You awoke in the last darkness
before the light poured in.
I've redone you by daylight.

Now I can submit you to the arts administrator
and the council of patrons
who could never take your measure.
This time they will love you,
standing on the glass table, fluent and robed at last,
and all your origins countered.
I wrap you in pure white sheets to mail you,
I brush you off my apron,
the charged filings crunch like cinders on the floor.

2

Raise it up there and it will
loom, the gaunt original thing
gristle and membrane of your life
mortared with shells of trilobites
it will hold between the cracks
of lightning, in the deadpan face of before and after
it will stick on up there as you left it

pieced together by starlight
it will hang by the flying buttresses you gave it
—hulk of mist, rafter of air, suspension bridge of mica
helm of sweat and dew—
but you have to raise it up there, you
have a brutal thing to do.

1990

DARKLIGHT

I

Early day.   Grey the air.
Grey the boards of the house, the bench,
red the dilated potflower's petals
blue the sky that will rend through
this fog.
                Dark summer's outer reaches:
thrown husk of a moon
sharpening
in the last dark blue.
I think of your eye
                        (dark the light
that washes into a deeper dark).

An eye, coming in closer.
                        Under the lens
lashes and veins grow huge
and huge the tear that washes out the eye,
the tear that clears the eye.

II

When heat leaves the walls at last
and the breeze comes
or seems to come, off water
or off the half-finished moon
her silver roughened by a darkblue rag
this is the ancient hour
between light and dark, work and rest
earthly tracks and star-trails
the last willed act of the day
and the night's first dream

If you could have this hour
for the last hour of your life.

1988–1990

FINAL NOTATIONS

it will not be simple, it will not be long
it will take little time, it will take all your thought
it will take all your heart, it will take all your breath
it will be short, it will not be simple

it will touch through your ribs, it will take all your heart
it will not be long, it will occupy your thought
as a city is occupied, as a bed is occupied
it will take all your flesh, it will not be simple

You are coming into us who cannot withstand you
you are coming into us who never wanted to withstand you

you are taking parts of us into places never planned
you are going far away with pieces of our lives

it will be short, it will take all your breath
it will not be simple, it will become your will

1991

DARK FIELDS OF
THE REPUBLIC
(1991–1995)

He had come a long way to this blue lawn, and his dream must have seemed so close that he could hardly fail to grasp it. He did not know that it was already behind him, somewhere back in that vast obscurity beyond the city, where the dark fields of the republic rolled on under the night.

—*The Great Gatsby*

What Kind of Times
Are These

WHAT KIND OF TIMES ARE THESE

There's a place between two stands of trees where the grass grows
        uphill
and the old revolutionary road breaks off into shadows
near a meeting-house abandoned by the persecuted
who disappeared into those shadows.

I've walked there picking mushrooms at the edge of dread, but
        don't be fooled,
this isn't a Russian poem, this is not somewhere else but here,
our country moving closer to its own truth and dread,
its own ways of making people disappear.

I won't tell you where the place is, the dark mesh of the woods
meeting the unmarked strip of light—
ghost-ridden crossroads, leafmold paradise:
I know already who wants to buy it, sell it, make it disappear.

And I won't tell you where it is, so why do I tell you
anything? Because you still listen, because in times like these
to have you listen at all, it's necessary
to talk about trees.

1991

IN THOSE YEARS

In those years, people will say, we lost track
of the meaning of *we*, of *you*
we found ourselves
reduced to *I*
and the whole thing became
silly, ironic, terrible:

we were trying to live a personal life and, yes, that was the only life
we could bear witness to

But the great dark birds of history screamed and plunged
into our personal weather
They were headed somewhere else but their beaks and pinions drove
along the shore, through the rags of fog
where we stood, saying *I*

1991

TO THE DAYS

From you I want more than I've ever asked,
all of it—the newscasts' terrible stories
of life in my time, the knowing it's worse than that,
much worse—the knowing what it means to be lied to.

Fog in the mornings, hunger for clarity,
coffee and bread with sour plum jam.
Numbness of soul in placid neighborhoods.
Lives ticking on as if.

A typewriter's torrent, suddenly still.
Blue soaking through fog, two dragonflies wheeling.
Acceptable levels of cruelty, steadily rising.
Whatever you bring in your hands, I need to see it.

Suddenly I understand the verb without tenses.
To smell another woman's hair, to taste her skin.
To know the bodies drifting underwater.
To be human, said Rosa—I can't teach you that.

A cat drinks from a bowl of marigolds—his moment.
Surely the love of life is never-ending,
the failure of nerve, a charred fuse?
I want more from you than I ever knew to ask.

Wild pink lilies erupting, tasseled stalks of corn
in the Mexican gardens, corn and roses.
Shortening days, strawberry fields in ferment
with tossed-aside, bruised fruit.

1991

MIRACLE ICE CREAM

Miracle's truck comes down the little avenue,
Scott Joplin ragtime strewn behind it like pearls,
and, yes, you can feel happy
with one piece of your heart.

Take what's still given: in a room's rich shadow
a woman's breasts swinging lightly as she bends.
Early now the pearl of dusk dissolves.
Late, you sit weighing the evening news,
fast-food miracles, ghostly revolutions,
the rest of your heart.

1992

RACHEL

There's a girl born in abrupt August light
far north, a light soon to be peeled
like an onion, down to nothing. Around her ions are falling
in torrents, glacial eyes are staring, the monster's body
trapped in the bay goes through its spasms.
What she opens her gray eyes on
is drastic. Even the man and woman gazing
into her unfocused gaze, searching for focus,
are drastic.
                It's the end of a century.
If she gets to grow old, if there's anything
: anyone to speak, will they say of her,
She grew up to see it, she was our mother, but
she was born one of them?

1992

AMENDS

Nights like this: on the cold apple-bough
a white star, then another
exploding out of the bark:
on the ground, moonlight picking at small stones

as it picks at greater stones, as it rises with the surf
laying its cheek for moments on the sand
as it licks the broken ledge, as it flows up the cliffs,
as it flicks across the tracks

as it unavailing pours into the gash
of the sand-and-gravel quarry

as it leans across the hangared fuselage
of the crop-dusting plane

as it soaks through cracks into the trailers
tremulous with sleep
as it dwells upon the eyelids of the sleepers
as if to make amends

1992

CALLE VISIÓN

1

Not what you thought: just a turn-off
leading downhill not up

narrow, doesn't waste itself
has a house at the far end

scrub oak and cactus in the yard
some cats   some snakes

in the house there is a room
in the room there is a bed

on the bed there is a blanket
that tells the coming of the railroad

under the blanket there are sheets
scrubbed transparent here and there

under the sheets there's a mattress
the old rough kind, with buttons and ticking

under the mattress is a frame
of rusting iron   still strong

the whole bed smells of soap and rust
the window smells of old tobacco-dust and rain

this is your room
in Calle Visión

if you took the turn-off
it was for you

2

Calle Visión   sand in your teeth
granules of cartilage in your wrists

Calle Visión   firestorm behind
shuttered eyelids   fire in your foot

Calle Visión   rocking the gates
of your locked bones

Calle Visión   dreamnet dropped
over your porous sleep

3

Lodged in the difficult hotel
all help withheld

a place not to live but to die in
not an inn but a hospital

a friend's love came to me
touched and took me away

in a car   love
of a curmudgeon, a short-fuse

and as he drove   eyes on the road
I felt his love

and that was simply the case   the way things were
unstated and apparent

and like the rest of it
clear as a dream

4

Calle Visión   your heart beats on unbroken
    how is this possible

Calle Visión   wounded knee
    wounded spine   wounded eye

        Have you ever worked around metal?
        Are there particles under your skin?

Calle Visión   but your heart is still whole
    how is this possible

since what can be   will be taken
    when not offered in trust and faith

by the collectors of collectibles
  the professors of what-has-been-suffered

    The world is falling down   hold my hand
    It's a lonely sound   hold my hand

Calle Visión   never forget
  the body's pain

never divide it

5

Ammonia
            carbon dioxide
                        carbon monoxide
                                    methane
                        hydrogen sulfide
:   the gasses that rise from urine and feces

in the pig confinement units known as nurseries
can eat a metal doorknob off in half a year

pig-dander
            dust from dry manure
—lung-scar: breath-shortedness an early symptom

And the fire shall try
every man's work   :Calle Visión:
and every woman's

if you took the turn-off
this is your revelation   this the source

6

The repetitive motions of slaughtering
    —fire in wrists   in elbows—
the dead birds coming at you along the line
    —how you smell them in your sleep—
fire in your wrist   blood packed
    under your fingernails   heavy air
doors padlocked on the outside
    —you might steal a chicken—
fire in the chicken factory fire
    in the carpal tunnel   leaping the frying vats
yellow smoke from soybean oil
    and wasted parts and insulating wire
—some fleeing to the freezer some
    found "stuck in poses of escape"—

7

You can call on beauty still and it will leap
from all directions

you can write beauty into the cruel file
of things done   things left undone   but

once we were dissimilar
yet unseparate   that's beauty   that's what you catch

in the newborn's midnight gaze
the fog that melts the falling stars

the virus from the smashed lianas driven
searching now for us

8

In the room   in the house
in Calle Visión

all you want   is to lie down
alone on your back   let your hands

slide lightly over your hipbones
But she's there with her remnants her cross-sections

trying to distract you
with her childhood her recipes her

cargo of charred pages her
carved and freckled neck-stones

her crying-out-for-witness her
backward-forward timescapes

her suitcase in Berlin
and the one lost and found

in her island go-and-come
—is she terrified you will forget her?

9

In the black net
of her orange wing

the angry nightblown butterfly
hangs on a piece of lilac in the sun

carried overland like her
from a long way off

She has travelled hard and far
and her interrogation goes:

—*Hands dripping with wet earth*
head full of shocking dreams

O what have you buried all these years
what have you dug up?

•

This place is alive with the dead and with the living
I have never been alone here

I wear my triple eye as I walk along the road
past, present, future all are at my side

Storm-beaten, tough-winged passenger
there is nothing I have buried that can die

10

On the road there is a house
scrub oak and cactus in the yard

lilac carried overland
from a long way off

in the house there is a bed
on the bed there is a blanket

telling the coming of the railroad
under the mattress there's a frame

of rusting iron   still strong
the window smells of old tobacco-dust and rain

the window smells of old
tobacco-dust and rain

1992–1993

REVERSION

This woman/   the heart of the matter.
This woman flung into solitary by the prayers of her tribe.
This woman waking/   reaching for scissors/   starting to cut
        her hair
Hair long shaven/   growing out.
To snip to snip to snip/   creak of sharpness meeting itself against
        the roughness of her hair.

This woman whose voices drive her into exile.
(Exile, exile.)
Drive her toward the other side.
By train and foot and ship, to the other side.
Other side.   Of a narrow sea.

This woman/   the heart of the matter.
Heart of the law/   heart of the prophets.
Their voices buzzing like raspsaws in her brain.
Taking ship without a passport.
How does she do it. Even the ships have eyes.
Are painted like birds.
This woman has no address book.
This woman perhaps has a toothbrush.
Somewhere dealing for red/blue dyes to crest her
        rough-clipped hair.

On the other side: stranger to women and to children.
Setting her bare footsole in the print of the stranger's bare foot in
     the sand.
Feeding the stranger's dog from the sack of her exhaustion.
Hearing the male prayers of the stranger's tribe/   rustle of the
     stranger's river.
Lying down asleep and dreamless in one of their doorways.

She has long shed the coverings.
On the other side she walks bare-armed, bare-legged, clothed
     in voices.
Here or there picks up a scarf/   a remnant.
Day breaks cold on her legs and in her sexual hair.
Her punk hair/   her religious hair.

Passing the blue rectangles of the stranger's doors.
Not one opens to her.
Threading herself into declining alleys/   black on white plaster/
     olive on violet.
To walk to walk to walk.
To lie on a warm stone listening to familiar insects.
(Exile, exile.)

This woman/   the heart of the matter.
Circling back to the city where her name crackles behind
     creviced stones.
This woman who left alone and returns alone.
Whose hair again is covered/   whose arms and neck are covered/
     according to the law.
Underneath her skin has darkened/   her footsoles roughened.
Sand from the stranger's doorway sifting from her plastic
     carry-all/   drifting into the sand
          whirling around in her old quarter.

1993

REVOLUTION IN PERMANENCE (1953, 1993)

Through a barn window, three-quartered
the profile of Ethel Rosenberg
stares down past a shattered apple-orchard
into speechless firs.
Speechless this evening.   Last night
the whole countryside thrashed in lowgrade fever
under low swollen clouds
the mist advanced and the wind
tore into one thing then another
—you could think *random* but you know
the patterns are there—
a sick time, and the human body
feeling it, a loss of pressure,
an agitation without purpose . . .
Purpose?   Do you believe
all agitation has an outcome
like revolt, like Bread and Freedom?
—or do you hang on to the picture
of the State as a human body
—some people being heads or hearts
and others only hands or guts or legs?
But she—how did she end up here
in this of all places?
What she is seeing I cannot see,
what I see has her shape.
There's an old scythe propped
in an upper window of the barn—
—does it call up marches of peasants?
what is it with you and this barn?
And, no, it's not an old scythe,
it's an old rag, you see how it twitches.

And Ethel Rosenberg? I've worried about her
through the liquid window in that damp place.
I've thought she was coughing, like me,
but her profile stayed still watching
what held her in that position.

1993

Then or Now

Is it necessary for me to write obliquely
about the situation? Is that what
you would have me do?

FOOD PACKAGES: 1947

Powdered milk, chocolate bars, canned fruit, tea,
salamis, aspirin:
Four packages a month to her old professor in Heidelberg
and his Jewish wife:
Europe is trying to revive an intellectual life
and the widow of the great sociologist needs flour.

Europe is trying/to revive/
with the Jews somewhere else.

The young ex-philosopher tries to feed her teachers
all the way from New York, with orders for butter from Denmark,
sending dispatches into the fog
of the European spirit:
I am no longer German. I am a Jew and the German language
was once my home.

1993

INNOCENCE: 1945

"The beauty of it was the guilt.
It entered us, quick *schnapps,*
forked tongue of ice.   The guilt
made us feel innocent again.
We had done nothing while some
extreme measures were taken.   We drifted.   In the
Snow Queen's huge ballroom had dreamed
of the whole world and a new pair of skates.
But we had suffered too.

The miracle was: felt
nothing.   Felt we had done
nothing.   Nothing to do.   Felt free.
And we had suffered, too.
It was that freedom we craved,
cold needle in the bloodstream.
Guilt after all was a feeling."

1993

SUNSET, DECEMBER, 1993

Dangerous of course to draw
Parallels   Yet more dangerous to write

as if there were a steady course, we and our poems
protected: the individual life, protected

poems, ideas, gliding
in mid-air, innocent

I walked out on the deck and every board
was luminous with cold dew   It could freeze tonight

Each board is different of course but each does gleam
wet, under a complicated sky: mounds of swollen ink

heavy gray unloading up the coast
a rainbow suddenly and casually

unfolding its span
Dangerous not to think

how the earth still was   in places
while the chimneys shuddered with the first dischargements

1993

DEPORTATIONS

It's happened already while we were still
searching for patterns   A turn of the head
toward a long horizontal window overlooking the city
to see people being taken
neighbors, vendors, paramedicals
hurried from their porches, their tomato stalls
their auto-mechanic arguments
and children from schoolyards
There are far more of the takers-away than the taken
at this point anyway

Then: dream-cut: our house:
four men walk through the unlatched door
One in light summer wool and silken tie
One in work clothes browned with blood
One with open shirt, a thin
thong necklace hasped with silver around his neck
One in shorts naked up from the navel

And they have come for us, two of us and four of them
and I think, perhaps they are still human
and I ask them   *When do you think this all began?*

as if trying to distract them from their purpose
as if trying to appeal to a common bond
as if one of them might be you
as if I were practicing for something
yet to come

1994

AND NOW

And now as you read these poems
—you whose eyes and hands I love
—you whose mouth and eyes I love
—you whose words and minds I love—
don't think I was trying to state a case
or construct a scenery:
I tried to listen to
the public voice of our time
tried to survey our public space
as best I could
—tried to remember and stay
faithful to details, note
precisely how the air moved
and where the clock's hands stood
and who was in charge of definitions
and who stood by receiving them
when the name of compassion
was changed to the name of guilt
when to feel with a human stranger
was declared obsolete.

1994

SENDING LOVE

Voice
from the grain

of the forest bought
and condemned

sketched bond
in the rockmass

the earthquake sought
and threw

•

Sending love: Molly sends it
Ivan sends it, Kaori

sends it to Brian, Irina sends it
on pale green aerograms Abena sends it

to Charlie and to Joséphine
Arturo sends it, Naomi sends it

Lourdes sends it to Naoual
Walter sends it to Arlene

Habib sends it, Vashti
floats it to Eqbal in a paper plane

Bored in the meeting, on a postcard
Yoel scribbles it to Gerhard

Reza on his e-mail
finds it waiting from Patricia

Mario and Elsie
send it to Francísco

Karolina sends it monthly
home with a money order

June seals it with a kiss to Dahlia
Mai sends it, Montserrat

scrawls it to Faíz on a memo
Lenny wires it with roses

to Lew who takes it on his
whispery breath, Julia sends it

loud and clear, Dagmar brailles it
to Maureen, María Christina

sends it, Meena and Moshe send it
Patrick and Max are always

sending it back and forth
and even Shirley, even George

are found late after closing
sending it, sending it

•

Sending love is harmless
doesn't bind you   can't make you sick

sending love's expected
precipitous   and wary

sending love can be carefree
Joaquín knew it, Eira knows it

sending love without heart
—well, people do that daily

•

Terrence years ago
closed the window, wordless

Grace who always laughed is leaning
her cheek against bullet-proof glass

her tears enlarged
like scars on a planet

Vivian hangs her raincoat
on a hook, turns to the classroom

her love entirely
there, supreme

Victor fixes his lens
on disappearing faces

—caught now or who will ever
see them again?

1992–1994

TAKE

At the head of this poem I have laid out
a boning knife a paring knife a wooden spoon a pair of tongs.
Oaken grain beneath them olive and rusty light
around them.
And you looming: This is not your scene
this is the first frame of a film
I have in mind to make: move on, get out.
And you here telling me: What will be done
with these four objects will be done
through my lens not your words.

The poet shrugs: I was only in the kitchen
looking at the chopping board.   (Not the whole story.)
And you telling me: Awful is the scope
of what I have in mind, awful the music I shall deploy, most
awful the witness of the camera moving
out from the chopping board to the grains of snow
whirling against the windowglass to the rotating
searchlights of the tower.   The humped snow-shrouded tanks
laboring toward the border.   This is not your bookish art.

But say the poet picks up the boning knife and thinks *my bones*
if she touching the paring knife thinks *carrot, onion, celery*
if staring at the wooden spoon I see the wood is split
as if from five winters of war
when neither celery, onion, carrot could be found
or picking up the tongs I whisper *What this was for*

And did you say *get on, get out* or just *look out?*
Were you speaking from exhaustion from disaster from your last
          assignment were you afraid.
for the vision in the kitchen, that it could not be saved
—no time to unload the heavy
cases to adjust

the sensitive equipment
to seize the olive rusty light to scan the hand that reaches
          hovering
over a boning knife a paring knife a wooden spoon a pair
          of tongs
to cull the snow before it blows away across the border's blacked-
          out sheds
and the moon swims in a bluish bubble dimmed
by the rotating searchlights of the tower?   Here
it is in my shorthand, do what you have in mind.

1994

LATE GHAZAL

Footsole to scalp alive facing the window's black mirror.
First rains of the winter   morning's smallest hour.

Go back to the ghazal then   what will you do there?
Life always pulsed harder than the lines.

Do you remember the strands that ran from eye to eye?
The tongue that reached everywhere, speaking all the parts?

Everything there was cast in an image of desire.
The imagination's cry is a sexual cry.

I took my body anyplace with me.
In the thickets of abstraction my skin ran with blood.

Life was always stronger . . . the critics couldn't get it.
Memory says the music always ran ahead of the words.

1994

SIX NARRATIVES

1

You drew up the story of your life   I was in that story
Nights on the coast I'd meet you flashlight in hand
curving my soles over musseled rocks   cracked and raw we'd lick
        inside the shells for danger
You'd drop into the bar   I'd sit upstairs at my desk writing
        the pages
you hoped would make us famous   then in the face of my
        turned back
you went to teach at the freedom school as if
you were teaching someone else to get free from me   this was
        your story
Like a fogsmeared planet over the coast
I'd walked into, served, your purposeful longings   I knew, I did
        not stop   till I turned my back

2

You drew up a story about me   I fled that story
Aching in mind I noticed names on the helms of busses:
        COP CITY   SHEEPSHEAD BAY
I thought I saw the city where the cops came home
to lay kitchen linoleum   barbecue on balconies
I saw the bloodied head of the great sheep dragged through
        the underpasses
trucked to the bay where the waters would not touch it
left on the beach in its shroud of flies
On the bus to La Guardia my arms ached with all my findings
anchored under my breasts with all my will

I cried *sick day, O sick day, this is my day and I, for this I will*
          not pay
as the green rushed bleeding out through the snarled cracks of
          the expressway

3

You were telling a story about women to young men   It was
          not my story
it was not a story about women it was a story about men
Your hunger a spear gripped in hand a tale unspun in your
          rented campground
clothed in captured whale-songs tracked with synthesized
          Andes flutes
it was all about you   beaded and bearded   misfeathered and
          miscloaked
where the TV cameras found you in your sadness

4

You were telling a story about love   it was your story
I came and stood outside
listening :   : death was in the doorway
death was in the air but the story
had its own life   no pretenses
about women in that lovesong for a man
Listening I went inside the bow scraping the bass-string
inside the horn's heartbroken cry
I was the breath's intake the bow's rough mutter:
Vigil for boy of responding kisses, (never again on earth responding,)
Vigil for comrade swiftly slain . . .

5.

I was telling you a story about love
how even in war it goes on speaking its own language

Yes you said but the larynx is bloodied
the knife was well-aimed into the throat

Well I said love is hated   it has no price

No you said   you are talking about feelings
Have you ever felt nothing?   that is what war is now

Then a shadow skimmed your face
Go on talking in a normal voice   you murmured
Nothing is listening

6.

You were telling a story about war   it is our story
an old story   and still it must be told
the story of the new that fled the old
how the big dream strained and shifted
the ship of hope shuddered on the iceberg's breast
the private affections swayed and staggered
So we are thrown together   so we are racked apart
in a republic shivering on   its glassy lips
parted   as if the fundamental rift
had not been calculated from the first into the mighty scaffold.

1994

FROM PIERCÉD DARKNESS

New York/December

Taking the least griefcrusted avenue the last worst bridge away
somewhere beyond her Lost & Found we stopped in our flight to
        check backward
in the rearview mirror into her piercéd darkness.   A mirror is
        either flat or deep
and ours was deep to the vanishing point: we saw showroom
        mannequins draped and trundled
—black lace across blackening ice—
false pearls knotted by nervous fingers, backribs lacquered in
        sauce.
Narrow waters rocking in spasms.   The torch hand-held and the
        poem of entrance.
Topless towers turned red and green.
Dripping faucet icicled radiator.
Eyes turned inward.   Births arced into dumpsters.
Eyes blazing under knitted caps,
hands gripped on taxi-wheels, steering.
Fir bough propped in a cardboard doorway, bitter tinsel.
The House of the Jewish Book, the Chinese Dumpling House.
Swaddled limbs dreaming on stacked shelves of sleep   opening
        like knives.

•

Her piercéd darkness.   Dragqueen dressed to kill in beauty
drawing her bridgelit shawls
over her shoulders.   Her caves ghosted by foxes.   Her tracked
        arms.
Who climbs the subway stairs at the end of night

lugging a throwaway banquet.   Her
Man Who Lived Underground and all his children.
Nightcrews uncapping her streets wildlamps strung up on high.

•

Fairy lights charming stunted trees.
Hurt eyes awake to the glamor.
I've walked this zone
gripping my nightstick, worked these rooms
in silver silk charmeuse and laid my offerings
next to the sexless swathed form lying in the doorway.
I've preached for justice rubbing crumbs
from sticky fingers for the birds.
Picked up a pretty chain of baubles
in the drugstore, bitten them to see if they were real.
I've boiled a stocking and called it Christmas pudding.
Bought freeborn eggs to cook
with sugar, milk and pears.

•

Altogether the angels arrive for the chorus
in rapidly grabbed robes they snatch scores of hallelujahs
complicit with television cameras they bend down their eyes.
However they sing their voices will glisten
in the soundmix.   All of it good enough for us.
Altogether children will wake before the end of night
("not good dawn" my Jewish grandmother called it) will stand
            as we did
handheld in cold dark before the parents' door
singing for glimpsed gilt and green
packages, the drama, the power of the hour.

•

Black lace, blackening ice.   To give on one designated day—
a window bangs shut on an entire
forcefield of chances, connections.   A window flies open
on the churning of birds in flight going surely somewhere else.
A snowflake like no other flies past, we will not hear of it
                    again, we will surely
                    hear of it
                    again.

1994–1995

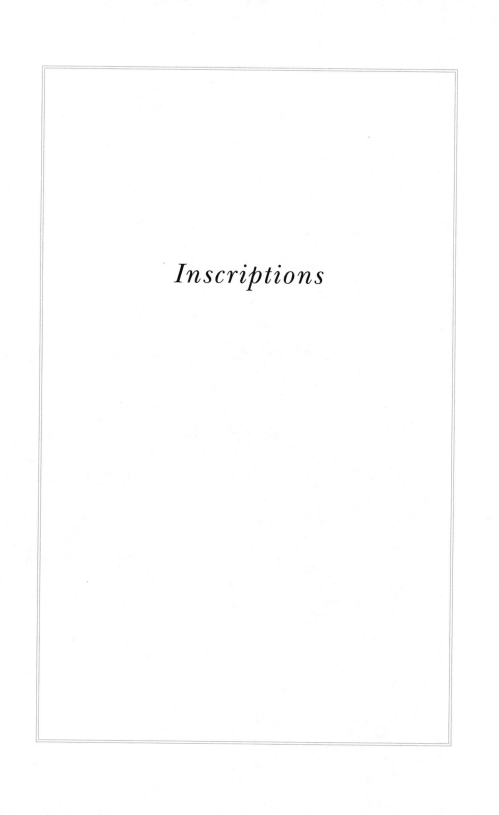

Inscriptions

ONE: COMRADE

Little as I knew you I know you: little as you knew me you
            know me
—that's the light we stand under when we meet.
I've looked into flecked jaws
walked injured beaches footslick in oil
watching licked birds stumble in flight
while you drawn through the pupil of your eye
across your own oceans in visionary pain and in relief
headlong and by choice took on the work of charting
your city's wounds ancient and fertile
listening for voices within and against.
My testimony: yours: Trying to keep faith
not with each other exactly yet it's the one known and unknown
who stands for, imagines the other   with whom faith could
            be kept.

In city your mind burns wanes waxes with hope
(no stranger to bleakness you: worms have toothed at
            your truths
but you were honest regarding that).
You conspired to compile the illegal discography
of songs forbidden to sing or to be heard.
If there were ethical flowers one would surely be yours
and I'd hand it to you headlong across landmines
across city's whyless sleeplight I'd hand it
purposefully, with love, a hand trying to keep beauty afloat
on the bacterial waters.

When a voice learns to sing it can be heard as dangerous
when a voice learns to listen it can be heard as desperate.
The self unlocked to many selves.
A mirror handed to one who just released
from the locked ward from solitary from preventive detention
sees in her thicket of hair her lost eyebrows

whole populations.

One who discharged from war stares in the looking-glass of home

at what he finds there, sees in the undischarged tumult of his

own eye

how thickskinned peace is, and those who claim to promote it.

TWO: MOVEMENT

Old backswitching road bent toward the ocean's light

Talking of angles of vision   movements   a black or a red tulip

opening

Times of walking across a street   thinking

not *I have joined a movement* but   *I am stepping in this deep current*

Part of my life washing behind me   terror I couldn't swim with

part of my life waiting for me   a part I had no words for

I need to live each day through   have them and know them all

though I can see from here where I'll be standing at the end.

•

When does a life bend toward freedom?   grasp its direction?

How do you know you're not circling in pale dreams, nostalgia,

stagnation

but entering that deep current   malachite, colorado

requiring all your strength wherever found

your patience and your labor

desire pitted against desire's inversion

all your mind's fortitude?

Maybe through a teacher: someone with facts with numbers

with poetry

who wrote on the board: IN EVERY GENERATION ACTION FREES

OUR DREAMS.

Maybe a student: one mind unfurling like a redblack peony

quenched into percentile, dropout, stubbed-out bud
—Your journals Patricia: Douglas your poems: but the repeti-
          tive blows
on spines whose hope you were, on yours:
to see that quenching and decide.

—And now she turns her face brightly on the new morning in
          the new classroom
new in her beauty her skin her lashes her lively body:
Race, class . . . all that . . . but isn't all that just history?
Aren't people bored with it all?

She could be
myself at nineteen   but free of reverence of past ideas
ignorant of hopes piled on her   She's a mermaid
momentarily precipitated from a solution
which could stop her heart   She could swim or sink
like a beautiful crystal.

THREE: ORIGINS

Turning points.   We all like to hear about those.   Points
          on a graph
Sudden conversions.   Historical swings.   Some kind of
          dramatic structure.
But a life doesn't unfold that way   it moves
in loops   by switchbacks loosely strung
around the swelling of one hillside toward another
one island toward another
A child's knowing   a child's forgetting   remain childish
till you meet them   mirrored and echoing   somewhere else
Don't ask me when I learned love
Don't ask me when I learned fear
Ask about the size of rooms   how many lived in them

what else the rooms contained
what whispers of the histories of skin

Should I simplify my life for you?
The Confederate Women of Maryland
on their dried-blood granite pedestal incised
                    IN DIFFICULTY AND IN DANGER . . .
                        "BRAVE AT HOME"
—words a child could spell out
standing in wetgreen grass stuck full of yellow leaves
monumental women bandaging wounded men
Joan of Arc in a book   a peasant in armor
Mussolini   Amelia Earhart   the President on the radio
     —what's taught, what's overheard

FOUR: HISTORY

Should I simplify my life for you?
Don't ask how I began to love men.
Don't ask how I began to love women.
Remember the forties songs, the slowdance numbers
the small sex-filled gas-rationed Chevrolet?
Remember walking in the snow and who was gay?
Cigarette smoke of the movies, silver-and-gray
profiles, dreaming the dreams of he-and-she
breathing the dissolution of the wisping silver plume?
Dreaming that dream we leaned applying lipstick
by the gravestone's mirror when we found ourselves
playing in the cemetery.   In Current Events she said
the war in Europe is over, the Allies
and she wore no lipstick have won the war
and we raced screaming out of Sixth Period.

Dreaming that dream
we had to maze our ways through a wood
where lips were knives breasts razor and I hid
in the cage of my mind scribbling
this map stops where it all begins
into a red-and-black notebook.
Remember after the war when peace came down
as plenty for some and they said we were saved
in an eternal present and we knew the world could end?
—remember after the war when peace rained down
on the winds from Hiroshima Nagasaki Utah Nevada?
and the socialist queer Christian teacher jumps from the
             hotel window?
and L.G. saying *I want to sleep with you but not for sex*
and the red-and-black enamelled coffee-pot dripped slow through
             the dark grounds
—appetite terror power tenderness
the long kiss in the stairwell the switch thrown
on two Jewish Communists married to each other
the definitive crunch of glass at the end of the wedding?
(When shall we learn, what should be clear as day,
We cannot choose what we are free to love?)

FIVE: VOICES

"That year I began to understand the words *burden of proof*
—how the free market of ideas depended
on certain lives laboring under that burden.
I started feeling in my body
how that burden was bound to our backs
keeping us cramped in old repetitive motions
crouched in the same mineshaft year on year
or like children in school striving to prove

proofs already proven over and over
to get into the next grade
but there is no next grade no movement onward only this

and the talk goes on, the laws, the jokes, the deaths, the way of
                life goes on
as if you had proven nothing as if this burden were what
                you are."

•

(Knotted crowns of asparagus lowered by human hands
into long silver trenches fogblanched mornings
the human spine translated into fog's
almost unbearable rheumatic beauty flattering pain
into a daze a mystic text of white and white's
absolute faceless romance : : the photographer's
darkroom thrill discerning two phantoms caught
trenchside deep in the delicate power
of fog : : phantoms who nonetheless have to know
the length of the silvery trenches how many plants how long
this bending can go on and for what wage and what
that wage will buy in the Great Central Valley 1983.)

•

"Desire disconnected   meetings and marches
for justice and peace   the sex of the woman
the bleached green-and-gold   of the cotton print bedspread
in the distance the sound   of the week's demonstration
July sun louvered shutters   off Riverside Drive
shattered glass in the courtyard   the sex of the woman
her body entire aroused to the hair
the sex of the women our bodies entire
molten in purpose each body a tongue
each body a river and over and over

and after to walk   in the streets still unchanging
a stormy light, evening   tattered emblems, horse-droppings
DO NOT CROSS POLICE BARRIER   yellow boards kicked awry
the scattering crowds   at the mouth of the subway

A thumbprint on a glass of icy water
memory that scours and fogs

night when I threw my face
on a sheet of lithic scatter
wrapped myself in a sack of tears"

•

"My thief   my counsellor
    tell me how it was then under the bridge
    in the long cashmere scarf
    the opera-lover left
silken length rough flesh violet light meandering
the splash that trickled down the wall
O tell me what you hissed to him and how he groaned to you
tell me the opera-lover's body limb by limb and touch by touch
how his long arms arched dazzling under the abutment
    as he played himself to the hilt
    cloak flocked with light
My thief   my counsellor
tell me was it good or bad, was it good and bad, in the
    unbefriended archway of your first ardor?
was it an oilstain's thumbprint on moving water?
the final drench and fizzle on the wall?
was it freedom from names from rank from color?
Thieving the leather trenchcoat of the night, my counsellor?
Breathing the sex of night of water never having to guess its
    source, my thief?

O thief
I stand at your bedside   feed you segments of orange
O counsellor
you have too many vanishing children to attend
There were things I was meant to learn from you   they wail out
     like a train leaving the city
Desire the locomotive   death the tracks   under the bridge
the silken roughness drench of freedom the abruptly
     floodlit parapet
LOVE CONQUERS ALL spelled out in flickering graffiti
—my counsellor, my thief"

•

"In the heart of the capital of Capital
against banked radiations of azalea
I found a faux-marble sarcophagus inscribed
          HERE LIES THE WILL OF THE PEOPLE
I had been wondering why for so long so little
had been heard from that quarter.
I found myself there by deepest accident
wandering among white monuments
looking for the Museum of Lost Causes.
A strangely focused many-lumened glare
was swallowing alive the noon.
I saw the reviewing stand the podium draped and swagged
the huge screen all-enhancing and all-heightening
I heard the martial bands the choirs the speeches
amplified in the vacant plaza
swearing to the satellites it had been a natural death."

SIX: EDGELIT

Living under fire in the raincolored opal of your love
I could have forgotten other women I desired
so much I wanted to love them but
here are some reasons love would not let me:
One had a trick of dropping her lashes along her cheekbone
in an amazing screen so she saw nothing.
Another would stand in summer arms rounded and warm
catching wild apricots that fell
either side of a broken fence but she caught them on one
            side only.
One, ambitious, flushed
to the collarbone, a shapely coward.
One keen as mica, glittering,
full at the lips, absent at the core.
One who flirted with danger
had her escape route planned when others had none
and disappeared.
One sleepwalking on the trestle
of privilege dreaming of innocence
tossing her cigarette into the dry gully
—an innocent gesture.

•

Medbh's postcard from Belfast:
               one's poetry seems aimless
covered in the blood and lies
               oozing corrupt & artificial
but of course one will continue . . .

This week I've dredged my pages
for anything usable
              head, heart, perforated

by raw disgust and fear
If I dredge up anything it's suffused
by what it works in, "like the dyer's hand"
I name it unsteady, slick, unworthy

and I go on

In my sixty-fifth year I know something about language:
it can eat or be eaten by experience
Medbh, poetry means refusing
the choice to kill or die

but this life of continuing is for the sane mad
and the bravest monsters

•

The bright planet that plies her crescent shape
in the western air   that through the screendoor gazes
with her curved eye now speaks: *The beauty of darkness*
is how it lets you see.   Through the screendoor
she told me this and half-awake I scrawled
her words on a piece of paper.
She is called Venus but I call her You
You   who sees me   You   who calls me to see
You   who has other errands far away in space and time
You   in your fiery skin   acetylene
scorching the claims of the false mystics
You   who like the moon arrives in crescent
changeable changer   speaking truth from darkness

•

Edgelit: firegreen yucca under fire-ribbed clouds
blue-green agave   grown huge in flower
cries of birds streaming over

The night of the eclipse the full
moon
swims clear between flying clouds until

the hour of the occlusion   It's not of aging
anymore and its desire
which is of course unending

it's of dying   young or old
in full desire

Remember me . . . . O, O, O,
O, remember me

these vivid stricken cells
precarious living marrow
this my labyrinthine filmic brain
this my dreaded blood
this my irreplaceable
footprint vanishing from the air

dying in full desire
thirsting for the coldest water
hungering for hottest food
gazing into the wildest light

edgelight from the high desert
where shadows drip from tiniest stones
sunklight of bloody afterglow

torque of the Joshua tree
flinging itself forth in winter
factoring freeze into its liquid consciousness

These are the extremes I stoke
into the updraft of this life
still roaring

                    into thinnest air

1993–1994

MIDNIGHT SALVAGE

(1995–1998)

I don't know how to measure happiness. The issue is happiness,
there is no other issue, or no other issue one has a right to think
about for other people, to think about politically, but I don't
know how to measure happiness.

> —George Oppen, letter to June Oppen Degnan,
> August 5, 1970

THE ART OF TRANSLATION

1

To have seen you exactly, once:
red hair over cold cheeks fresh from the freeway
your lingo, your daunting and dauntless
eyes. But then to lift toward home, mile upon mile
back where they'd barely heard your name
—neither as terrorist nor as genius would they detain you—

to wing it back to my country bearing
your war-flecked protocols—

that was a mission, surely: my art's pouch
crammed with your bristling juices
sweet dark drops of your spirit
that streaked the pouch, the shirt I wore
and the bench on which I leaned.

2

It's only a branch like any other
green with the flare of life in it
and if I hold this end, you the other
that means it's broken

broken between us, broken despite us
broken and therefore dying
broken by force, broken by lying
green, with the flare of life in it

3

But say we're crouching on the ground like children
over a mess of marbles, soda caps, foil, old foreign coins
—the first truly precious objects. Rusty hooks, glass.

Say I saw the earring first but you wanted it.
Then you wanted the words I'd found. I'd give you
the earring, crushed lapis if it were,

I would look long at the beach glass and the sharded self
of the lightbulb. Long I'd look into your hand
at the obsolete copper profile, the cat's-eye, the lapis.

Like a thief I would deny the words, deny they ever
existed, were spoken, or could be spoken,
like a thief I'd bury them and remember where.

4

The trade names follow trade
the translators stopped at passport control:
Occupation: no such designation—
Journalist, maybe spy?

That the books are for personal use
only—could I swear it?
That not a word of them
is contraband—how could I prove it?

1995

FOR AN ANNIVERSARY

The wing of the osprey lifted
over the nest on Tomales Bay
into fog and difficult gust
raking treetops from Inverness Ridge on over
The left wing shouldered into protective
gesture the left wing we thought broken

and the young beneath in the windy nest
creaking there in their hunger
and the tides beseeching, besieging
the bay in its ruined languor

1996

MIDNIGHT SALVAGE

1

Up skyward through a glazed rectangle I
sought the light of a so-called heavenly body
: : a planet or our moon in some event and caught

nothing nothing but a late wind
pushing around some Monterey pines
themselves in trouble and rust-limbed

Nine o'clock : : July : the light
undrained : : that blotted blue
that lets has let will let

thought's blood ebb between life- and death-time
darkred behind darkblue
bad news pulsing back and forth of "us" and "them"

And all I wanted was to find an old
friend an old figure an old trigonometry
still true to our story in orbits flaming or cold

2

Under the conditions of my hiring
I could profess or declare anything at all
since in that place nothing would change
So many fountains, such guitars at sunset

Did not want any more to sit under such a window's
deep embrasure, wisteria bulging on spring air
in that borrowed chair
with its collegiate shield at a borrowed desk

under photographs of the spanish steps, Keats' death mask
and the English cemetery all so under control and so eternal
in burnished frames : : or occupy the office
of the marxist-on-sabbatical

with Gramsci's fast-fading eyes
thumbtacked on one wall opposite a fading print
of the same cemetery : : had memories
and death masks of my own : : could not any more

peruse young faces already straining for
the production of slender testaments
to swift reading and current thinking : : would not wait
for the stroke of noon to declare all passions obsolete

Could not play by the rules
in that palmy place : : nor stand at lectern professing
anything at all
                    in their hire

3

Had never expected hope would form itself
completely in my time : : was never so sanguine
as to believe old injuries could transmute easily
through any singular event or idea : : never
so feckless as to ignore the managed contagion
of ignorance the contrived discontinuities
the felling of leaders and future leaders
the pathetic erections of soothsayers

But thought I was conspiring, breathing-along
with history's systole-diastole
twenty thousand leagues under the sea a mammal heartbeat
sheltering another heartbeat
plunging from the Farallons all the way to Baja
sending up here or there a blowhole signal
and sometimes beached
making for warmer waters
where the new would be delivered : : though I would not see it

4

But neither was expecting in my time
to witness this : : wasn't deep
lucid or mindful you might say enough
to look through history's bloodshot eyes
into this commerce this dreadnought wreck cut loose
from all vows, oaths, patents, compacts, promises : :
                                    To see

not O my Captain
fallen cold & dead by the assassin's hand

but cold alive & cringing : : drinking with the assassins
in suit of noir Hong Kong silk
pushing his daughter in her famine-
waisted flamingo gown
out on the dance floor with the traffickers
in nerve gas saying to them *Go for it*
and to the girl *Get with it*

5

When I ate and drank liberation once I walked
arm-in-arm with someone who said she had something to teach me
It was the avenue and the dwellers
free of home : roofless : : women
without pots to scour or beds to make
or combs to run through hair
or hot water for lifting grease or cans
to open or soap to slip in that way
under arms then beneath breasts then downward to thighs

Oil-drums were alight under the freeway
and bottles reached from pallets of cardboard corrugate
and piles of lost and found to be traded back and forth
and figures arranging themselves from the wind
Through all this she walked me : : And said
My name is Liberation and I come from here
Of what are you afraid?

We've hung late in the bars like bats
kissed goodnight at the stoplights
—did you think I wore this city without pain?
did you think I had no family?

6

Past the curve where the old craftsman was run down
there's a yard called Midnight Salvage
He was walking in the road which was always safe
The young driver did not know that road
its curves or that people walked there
or that you could speed yet hold the curve
watching for those who walked there
such skills he did not have being in life unpracticed

but I have driven that road in madness and driving rain
thirty years in love and pleasure and grief-blind
on ice I have driven it and in the vague haze of summer
between clumps of daisies and sting of fresh cowflop odors
lucky I am I hit nobody old or young
killed nobody left no trace
practiced in life as I am

7

This horrible patience which is part of the work
This patience which waits for language for meaning for the
                    least sign
This encumbered plodding state doggedly dragging
the IV up and down the corridor
with the plastic sack of bloodstained urine

Only so can you start living again
waking to take the temperature of the soul
when the black irises lean at dawn
from the mouth of the bedside pitcher
This condition in which you swear *I will*
submit to whatever poetry is
I accept no limits   Horrible patience

8

You cannot eat an egg   You don't know where it's been
The ordinary body of the hen
vouchsafes no safety   The countryside refuses to supply
Milk is powdered   meat's in both senses high

Old walls the pride of architects   collapsing
find us in crazed niches   sleeping like foxes
we wanters we unwanted we
wanted for the crime of being ourselves

Fame slides on its belly like any other animal after food
Ruins are disruptions of system leaking in
weeds and light   redrawing
the City of Expectations

You cannot eat an egg   Unstupefied not unhappy
we braise wild greens and garlic   feed the feral cats
and when the fog's irregular documents break open
scan its fissures for young stars
                in the belt of Orion

1996

CHAR

1

There is bracken there is the dark mulberry
there is the village where no villager survived
there are the hitlerians there are the foresters
feeding the partisans from frugal larders

there is the moon ablaze in every quarter
there is the moon "of tin and sage" and unseen pilots dropping
explosive gifts into meadows of fog and crickets
there is the cuckoo and the tiny snake

there is the table set at every meal
for freedom whose chair stays vacant
the young men in their newfound passions
(*Love along with them the ones they love*)

Obscurity, code, the invisible existence
of a thrush in the reeds, the poet watching
as the blood washes off the revolver in the bucket
Redbreast, your song shakes loose a ruin of memories

A horrible day . . . Perhaps he knew, at that final instant?
The village had to be spared at any price . . .
How can you hear me? I speak from so far . . .
The flowering broom hid us in a blazing yellow mist . . .

2

This war will prolong itself beyond any platonic armistice. The implanting
of political concepts will go on amid upheavals and under cover of self-
confident hypocrisy. Don't smile. Thrust aside both skepticism and
resignation and prepare your soul to face an intramural confrontation with
demons as cold-blooded as microbes.

The poet in wartime, the Surréalistes' younger brother
turned realist (*the village had to be spared at any price*)
all eyes on him in the woods crammed with maquisards ex-
pecting him to signal to fire and save their comrade
shook his head and watched Bernard's execution
knowing that *the random shooting of a revolver*
may be the simplest surreal act but never

changes the balance of power and that real acts are not simple
The poet, prone to exaggerate, thinks clearly under torture

knowing the end of the war
would mean no end to the microbes frozen in each soul
the young freedom fighters
in love with the Resistance
fed by a thrill for violence
familiar as his own jaw under the razor

3

Insoluble riverrain conscience echo of the future
I keep vigil for you here by the reeds of Elkhorn Slough
and the brown mouth of the Salinas River going green
where the white egret fishes the fragile margins
Hermetic guide in resistance I've found you and lost you
several times in my life   You were never just
the poet appalled and transfixed by war you were the maker
of terrible delicate decisions and that did not smudge
your sense of limits   You saw squirrels crashing
from the tops of burning pines when the canister exploded
and worse and worse and you were in charge of every risk
the incendiary motives of others were in your charge
and the need for a courage wrapped in absolute tact
and you decided and lived like that and you
held poetry at your lips a piece of wild thyme ripped
from a burning meadow a mimosa twig
from still unravaged country   You kept your senses
about you like that and like this I keep vigil for you.

1996

MODOTTI

Your footprints of light on sensitive paper
that typewriter you made famous
my footsteps following you up stair-
wells of scarred oak and shredded newsprint
these windowpanes smeared with stifled breaths
corridors of tile and jaundiced plaster
if this is where I must look for you
then this is where I'll find you

From a streetlamp's wet lozenge bent
on a curb plastered with newsprint
the headlines aiming straight at your eyes
to a room's dark breath-smeared light
these footsteps I'm following you with
down tiles of a red corridor
if this is a way to find you
of course this is how I'll find you

Your negatives pegged to dry in a darkroom
rigged up over a bathtub's lozenge
your footprints of light on sensitive paper
stacked curling under blackened panes
the always upstairs of your hideout
the stern exposure of your brows
—these footsteps I'm following you with
aren't to arrest you

The bristling hairs of your eyeflash
that typewriter you made famous
your enormous will to arrest and frame
what was, what is, still liquid, flowing
your exposure of manifestos, your
lightbulb in a scarred ceiling
well if this is how I find you

Modotti so I find you

In the red wash of your darkroom
from your neighborhood of volcanoes
to the geranium nailed in a can
on the wall of your upstairs hideout
in the rush of breath a window
of revolution allowed you
on this jaundiced stair in this huge lashed eye

                                                    these

footsteps I'm following you with

1996

SHATTERED HEAD

A life hauls itself uphill
        through hoar-mist steaming
the sun's tongue licking
        leaf upon leaf into stricken liquid
When?   *When?* cry the soothseekers
        but time is a bloodshot eye
seeing its last of beauty its own
        foreclosure
                                a bloodshot mind
finding itself unspeakable
        What is the last thought?
Now I will let you know?
        or, *Now I know?*
(porridge of skull-splinters, brain tissue
        mouth and throat membrane, cranial fluid)

Shattered head on the breast
        of a wooded hill

laid down there endlessly so
  tendrils soaked into matted compost
become a root
  torqued over the faint springhead
groin whence illegible
  matter leaches: worm-borings, spurts of silt
volumes of sporic changes
  hair long blown into far follicles
blasted into a chosen place

Revenge on the head (genitals, breast, untouched)
  revenge on the mouth
packed with its inarticulate confessions
  revenge on the eyes
green-gray and restless
  revenge on the big and searching lips
              the tender tongue
revenge on the sensual, on the nose the
  carrier of history
revenge on the life devoured
in another incineration

You can walk by such a place, the earth is made of them
where the stretched tissue of a field or woods is humid
              with belovéd matter
the soothseekers have withdrawn
you feel no ghost, only a sporic chorus
when that place utters its worn sigh
  let us have peace

And the shattered head answers back
  I believed I was loved, I believed I loved,
      who did this to us?

1996–97

1941

In the heart of pain where mind is broken
and consumed by body, I sit like you
on the rocky shore   (like you, not with you)

A windmill shudders, great blades cleave the air and corn is ground
for a peasant century's bread and fear of hunger
(like that, but not like that)

Pewter sails drive down green water
barges shoulder fallowing fields
(Like then, not then)

If upstairs in the mill sunrise fell low and thin
on the pierced sleep of children hidden in straw
where the mauled hen had thrashed itself away

if some lost their heads and ran
if some were dragged

if some lived and grew old remembering
how the place by itself was not evil
had water, spiders, a cat

if anyone asked me—

How did you get here anyway?
Are you the amateur of drought? the collector
of rains? are you poetry's inadmissible
untimely messenger?

By what right?
In whose name?
Do you

1997

LETTERS TO A YOUNG POET

1

Your photograph won't do you justice
those wetted anthill mounds won't let you focus
that lens on the wetlands

five swans chanting overhead
distract your thirst for closure
and quick escape

2

Let me turn you around in your frozen nightgown and say
one word to you: Ineluctable

—meaning, you won't get quit
of this: the worst of the new news

history running back and forth
panic in the labyrinth

—I will not touch you further:
your choice to freeze or not

to say, you and I are caught in
a laboratory without a science

3

Would it gladden you to think
poetry could purely

take its place beneath lightning sheets
or fogdrip   live its own life

screamed at, howled down
by a torn bowel of dripping names

—composers visit Terezin, film-makers Sarajevo
Cabrini-Green or Edenwald Houses

    ineluctable

if a woman as vivid as any artist
can fling any day herself from the 14th floor

would it relieve you to decide   *Poetry*
doesn't make this happen?

4

From the edges of your own distraction turn
the cloth-weave up, its undersea-fold venous

with sorrow's wash and suck, pull and release,
    annihilating rush

to and fro, fabric of caves, the onset of your fear
kicking away their lush and slippery flora nurseried
    in liquid glass

trying to stand fast in rootsuck, in distraction,
    trying to wade this
undertow of utter repetition

Look: with all my fear I'm here with you, trying what it
    means, to stand fast; what it means to move

5

Beneaped. Rowboat, pirogue, caught between the lowest
and highest tides of spring. Beneaped. Befallen,
becalmed, benighted, yes, begotten.
—*Be*—infernal prefix of the actionless.
—*Be*—as in Sit, Stand, Lie, Obey.
The dog's awful desire that takes his brain
and lays it at the boot-heel.

You can be like this forever—*Be*
as without movement.

6

But this is how
I come, anyway, pushing up from below
my head wrapped in a chequered scarf a lanterned helmet on this
                head
pushing up out of the ore
this sheeted face this lanterned head facing the seep of death
my lips having swum through silt
        clearly pronouncing
Hello and farewell

Who, anyway, wants to know
this pale mouth, this stick
of crimson lipsalve Who my
dragqueen's vocal chords my bitter beat
my overshoulder backglance flung
at the great strophes and antistrophes
my chant my ululation my sacred parings
nails, hair my dysentery my hilarious throat
my penal colony's birdstarved ledge my face downtown
in films by Sappho and Artaud?

Everyone.   For a moment.

7

It's not the déjà vu that kills
it's the foreseeing
the head that speaks from the crater

I wanted to go somewhere
the brain had not yet gone
I wanted not to be
there so alone.

1997

CAMINO REAL

Hot stink of skunk
crushed at the vineyards' edge

hawk-skied, carrion-clean
clouds ranging themselves
over enormous autumn

that scribble   edged and skunky
as the great road winds on
toward my son's house seven hours south

Walls of the underpass
smudged and blistered eyes gazing from armpits
THE WANTER WANTED   ARMED IN LOVE AND
          DANGEROUS
WANTED FOR WANTING

To become the scholar of : :
: : to list compare contrast events to footnote lesser evils
calmly to note "bedsprings"
describe how they were wired
to which parts of the body
to make clear-eyed assessments of the burnt-out eye: : investigate
the mouth-bit and the mouth
the half-swole slippery flesh the enforced throat
the whip they played you with the backroad games the beatings by
            the river
O to list collate commensurate to quantify:
I was the one, I suffered, I was there

never
to trust to memory only

to go back   notebook in hand
dressed as no one there was dressed

over and over to quantify
on a gridded notebook page

The difficulty of proving
such things were done for no reason
that every night
"in those years"
people invented reasons for torture

Asleep now,   head in hands
hands over ears   O you
Who do this work
every one of you
every night

Driving south: santabarbara's barbarous
landscaped mind: lest it be forgotten
in the long sweep downcoast

let it not be exonerated

but O the light
on the raw Pacific silks

Charles Olson: "Can you afford not to make
                            the magical study
                                    which happiness is?"

I take him to mean
that happiness is in itself a magical study
a glimpse of the *unhandicapped life*
as it might be for anyone, somewhere

a kind of alchemy, a study of transformation
else it withers, wilts

—that happiness is not to be
mistrusted or wasted
though it ferment in grief

George Oppen to June Degnan: "I don't know how
to measure happiness"
—Why measure? in itself it's the measure—
at the end of a day
        of great happiness if there be such a day

drawn by love's unprovable pull

I write this, sign it
                        Adrienne

1997

PLAZA STREET AND FLATBUSH

1

On a notepad on a table
tagged for the Goodwill
the word   *Brooklyn*

on the frayed luggage label
the matchbox cover
the name   *Brooklyn*

in steel-cut script on a watermarked form
on a postcard postmarked 1961
the word   *Brooklyn*

on the medal for elocution
on the ashtray with the bridge
the inscription   *Brooklyn*

in the beige notebook
of the dead student's pride
in her new language

on the union card   the love letter
the mortgaged insurance policy
somewhere it would say,   *Brooklyn*

on the shear of the gull
on the ramp that sweeps
to the great cable-work

on the map of the five boroughs
the death certificate
the last phone bill

in the painter's sighting
of light unseen
till now, in Brooklyn

2

If you had been required
to make inventory
of everything in the apartment

if you had had to list
the acquisitions of a modest life
punctuated with fevers of shopping

—a kind of excitement for her
but also a bandage
over bewilderment

and for him, the provider
the bandage of providing
for everyone

if you had had to cram the bags
with unworn clothing unused linens
bought by a woman

who but just remembered
being handed through the window
of a train in Russia

if you had had to haul
the bags to the freight elevator
if you had been forced to sign

a declaration of all
possessions kept or given away

in all the old apartments

in one building say
at Plaza and Flatbush
or on Eastern Parkway?

Art doesn't keep accounts
though artists
do as they must

to stay alive
and tend their work
art is a register of light

3

The painter taking her moment
—a rift in the clouds—
and pulling it out

—mucous strand, hairy rootlet
sticky clew to the labyrinth
pulling and pulling

forever or as long
as this grain of this universe
will be tested

the painter seizing the light
of creation
giving it back to its creatures

headed under the earth

1997

SEVEN SKINS

1

Walk along back of the library
in 1952
someone's there to catch your eye
Vic Greenberg in his wheelchair
paraplegic GI—
Bill of Rights Jew
graduate student going in
by the only elevator route
up into the great stacks where
all knowledge should and is
and shall be stored like sacred grain
while the loneliest of lonely
American decades goes aground
on the postwar rock
and some unlikely
shipmates found ourselves
stuck amid so many smiles

Dating Vic Greenberg you date
crutches and a chair
a cool wit an outrageous form:
"—just back from a paraplegics' conference,
guess what the biggest meeting was about—
Sex with a Paraplegic!—for the wives—"
In and out of cabs his chair
opening and closing round his
electrical monologue the air
furiously calm around him
as he transfers to the crutches

But first you go for cocktails
in his room at Harvard
he mixes the usual martinis, plays Billie Holiday
talks about Melville's vision of evil
and the question of the postwar moment:
Is there an American civilization?
In the bathroom huge
grips and suction-cupped
rubber mats long-handled sponges
the reaching tools a veteran's benefits
in plainest sight

And this is only memory, no more
so this is how you remember

Vic Greenberg takes you to the best restaurant
which happens to have no stairs
for talk about movies, professors, food
Vic orders wine and tastes it
you have lobster, he Beef Wellington
the famous dessert is baked Alaska
ice cream singed in a flowerpot
from the oven, a live tulip inserted there

Chair to crutches, crutches to cab
chair in the cab and back to Cambridge
memory shooting its handheld frames
Shall I drop you, he says, or shall
we go back to the room for a drink?
It's the usual question
a man has to ask it
a woman has to answer
you don't even think

2

What a girl I was then what a body
ready for breaking open like a lobster
what a little provincial village
what a hermit crab seeking nobler shells
what a beach of rattling stones what an offshore raincloud
what a gone-and-come tidepool

what a look into eternity I took and did not return it
what a book I made myself
what a quicksilver study
bright little bloodstain
liquid pouches escaping

What a girl pelican-skimming over fear what a mica lump
                splitting
into tiny sharp-edged mirrors through which
the sun's eclipse could seem normal
what a sac of eggs what a drifting flask
eager to sink   to be found
to disembody   what a mass of swimmy legs

3

Vic into what shoulder could I have pushed your face
laying hands first on your head
onto whose thighs pulled down your head
which fear of mine would have wound itself
around which of yours   could we have taken it   nakedness
without sperm   in what insurrectionary
convulsion would we have done it   mouth to mouth
mouth-tongue to vulva-tongue to anus   earlobe to nipple
what seven skins each have to molt what seven shifts
what tears boil up through sweat to bathe
what humiliatoriums   what layers of imposture

What heroic tremor
released into pure moisture
might have soaked our shape   two-headed   avid
into your heretic
linen-service
sheets?

1997

"THE NIGHT HAS A THOUSAND EYES"

1

The taxi meter clicking up
loose change who can afford to pay

basalt blurring spectral headlights
darkblue stabbed with platinum

raincoats glassy with evening wet
the city gathering

itself for darkness
into a bitter-chocolate vein

the east side with its trinkets
the west side with its memories

2

Wherever you had to connect:
question of passport, glances, bag

dumped late on the emptied carousel
departure zones

where all could become mislaid, disinvented
undocumented, unverified

all but the footprint of your soul
in the cool neutral air

till the jumbo jet groaned and gathered
itself over Long Island

gathered you into your earth-craving
belly-self, that desire

3

Gaze through the sliced-glass window
nothing is foreign here

nothing you haven't thought or taught
nothing your thumbnail doesn't know

your old poets and painters knew it
knocking back their wine

you're just in a cab driven wild
on the FDR by a Russian Jew

who can't afford to care if he lives or dies
you rode with him long ago

4

Between two silvered glass urns an expensive
textile is shouldered

it's after dark now, floodlight
pours into the wired boutique

there are live roses in the urns
there are security codes

in the wall   there are children, dead, near death
whose fingers worked this

intricate
desirable thing

—nothing you haven't seen on your palm
nothing your thumbnail doesn't know

5

After one stroke she looks at the river
remembers her name—Muriel

writes it in her breath
on the big windowpane

never again perhaps
to walk in the city freely

but here is her landscape this old
industrial building converted

for artists
her river   *the Lordly Hudson*

Paul named it   *which has no peer*
in Europe or the East

her mind on that water   widening

6

Among five men walks a woman
tall as the tallest man, taller than several

a mixed creature
from country poverty   good schooling

and from that position seeing
further than many

beauty, fame, notwithstanding   standing
for something else

—*Where do you come from?*—
—*Como tú, like you, from nothing*—

Julia de Burgos, of herself, fallen
in Puerto Rican Harlem

7

Sometime tonight you'll fall down
on a bed far from your heart's desire

in the city as it is
for you now: her face or his

private across an aisle
throttling uptown

bent over clasped hands or
staring off then suddenly glaring:

Back off! Don't ask!   you will meet those eyes
(none of them meeting)

8

The wrapped candies from Cleveland
The acclaim of East St. Louis

deadweight trophies borne
through *interboro fissures of the mind*

in search of Charlie Parker
—Where are you sleeping tonight? with whom?

in crippled Roebling's harbor room
where he watched his bridge transpire?—

Hart   Miles   Muriel   Julia   Paul
you will meet the eyes you were searching for

and the day will break

as we say, it breaks
as we don't say, of the night

as we don't say of the night

1997

RUSTED LEGACY

Imagine a city where nothing's
forgiven   your deed adheres
to you like a scar, a tattoo   but almost everything's
forgotten   deer flattened leaping a highway for food
the precise reason for the shaving of the confused girl's head
the small boys' punishing of the frogs
—a city memory-starved but intent on retributions
Imagine the architecture   the governance
the men and the women in power
—tell me if it is not true you still
        live in that city.

Imagine a city partitioned   divorced from its hills
where temples and telescopes used to probe the stormy codices
a city brailling through fog
thicket and twisted wire
into dark's velvet dialectic
sewers which are also rivers
art's unchartered aquifers   the springhead
sprung open in civic gardens left unlocked at night
I finger the glass beads I strung and wore
under the pines while the arrests were going on
(transfixed from neck to groin I wanted to save what I could)
They brought trays with little glasses of cold water
into the dark park   a final village gesture
before the villages were gutted.
They were trying to save what they could
—tell me if this is not the same city.

I have forced myself to come back like a daughter
required to put her mother's house in order
whose hands need terrible gloves to handle
the medicinals   the disease packed in those linens
Accomplished criminal I've been but

can I accomplish justice here? Tear the old wedding sheets
into cleaning rags? Faithless daughter
like stone   but with water pleating across
Let water be water let stone be stone
Tell me is this the same city.

This *I*—must she, must she lie scabbed with rust
crammed with memory in a place
of little anecdotes   no one left
to go around gathering the full dissident story?
Rusting her hands and shoulders stone her lips
yet leaching down from her eyesockets tears
—for one self only? each encysts a city.

1997

A LONG CONVERSATION

—warm bloom of blood in the child's arterial tree
could you forget?   do you
remember?   not to
know you were cold?   Altercations
from porches   color still high in your cheeks
the leap for the catch
the game getting wilder as the lights come on
catching your death it was said

                              your death of cold
something you couldn't see ahead, you couldn't see

                         (energy: Eternal Delight)

•

a long conversation

      between persistence and impatience
      between the bench of forced confessions
          hip from groin swiveled
          apart
          young tongues torn in the webbing
          the order of the cities
          founded on disorder

      and intimate resistance
      desire exposed and shameless
      as the flags go by

•

Sometime looking backward
into this future, straining
neck and eyes I'll meet your shadow
with its enormous eyes
     you who will want to know
     what this was all about

             Maybe this is the beginning of madness
             Maybe it's your conscience . . .

as you, straining neck and eyes
gaze forward into this past:
what did it mean to you?
     —to receive "full human rights"
     or the blue aperture of hope?

•

      Mrs. Bartender, will you tell us dear
      who came in when the nights were
      cold and drear and who sat where

well helmeted and who
was showing off his greasy hair
Mrs. Bartender tell me quickly
who spoke thickly or not at all
how you decided what you'd abide
what was proud and thus allowed
how you knew what to do
with all the city threw at you
Mrs. Bartender tell me true
we've been keeping an eye on you
and this could be a long conversation
we could have a long accommodation

•

On the oilcloth of a certain table, in the motel room of a certain time and country, a white plastic saucer of cheese and hard salami, winter radishes, cold cuts, a chunk of bread, a bottle of red wine, another of water proclaimed drinkable. Someone has brought pills for the infection that is ransacking this region. Someone else came to clean birds salvaged from the oil spill. Here we eat, drink from thick tumblers, try to pierce this thicket with mere words.

Like a little cell. Let's not aggrandize ourselves; we are not a little cell, but we are like a little cell.

Music arrives, searching for us. What hope or memory without it. Whatever we may think. After so many words.

•

A long conversation
              pierced, jammed, scratched out:
                    bans, preventive detention, broken mouths
                    and on the scarred bench sequestered
                          a human creature with bloody wings
                                its private parts

reamed

still trying to speak

A hundred and fifty years. In 1848 a pamphlet was published, one of many but the longest-read. One chapter in the long book of memories and expectations. A chapter described to us as evil; if not evil out-of-date, naïve and mildewed. Even the book they say is out of print, lacking popular demand.

So we have to find out what in fact that manifesto said. Evil, we can judge. Mildew doesn't worry us. We don't want to be more naïve or out-of-date than necessary. Some old books are probably more useful than others.

The bourgeoisie cannot exist without constantly revolutionizing the instruments of production, thereby the relations of production, and with them the whole relations of society . . . it creates a world after its own image.

In proportion as the bourgeoisie, i.e., capital, is developed, in the same proportion is the proletariat, the modern working class developed—a class of laborers who live only so long as they find work, and who find work only so long as their labor increases capital. These laborers, who must *sell themselves piecemeal, are a commodity, like every other article of commerce, and are consequently exposed to all the vicissitudes of competition, to all the fluctuations of the market.*

—Can we say if or how we find this true in our lives today?

She stands before us as if we are a class, in school, but we are long out of school. Still, there's that way she has of holding the book in her hands, as if she knew it contained the answer to her question.

Someone: —Technology's changing the most ordinary forms of human contact—who can't see that, in their own life?

—But technology is nothing but a means.

—Someone, I say, makes a killing off war. You: —I've been telling you, that's the engine driving the free market. Not information, militarization. Arsenals spawning wealth.

Another woman: —But surely then patriarchal nationalism is the key?

He comes in late, as usual he's been listening to sounds outside, the tide scraping the stones, the voices in nearby cottages, the way he used to listen at the beach, as a child. He doesn't speak like a teacher, more like a journalist come back from war to report to us. —It isn't nations anymore, look at the civil wars in all the cities. Is there a proletariat that can act effectively on this collusion, between the state and the armed and murderous splinter groups roaming at large? How could all these private arsenals exist without the export of increasingly sophisticated arms approved by the metropolitan bourgeoisie?

Now someone gets up and leaves, cloud-faced: —I can't stand that kind of language. I still care about poetry.

All kinds of language fly into poetry, like it or not, or even if you're only
> as we were   trying
>   to keep an eye
>   on the weapons on the street
>   and under the street

Just here, our friend L.: bony, nerve-driven, closeted, working as a nurse when he can't get teaching jobs. Jew from a dynasty of converts, philosopher trained as an engineer, he can't fit in where his brilliant and privileged childhood pointed him. He too is losing patience: *What is the use of studying philosophy if all that it does for you is enable you to talk with some plausibility about some abstruse questions of logic, etc . . . & if it does not improve your thinking about the important question of everyday life, if it does not make you more conscientious than any journalist in the use of the dangerous phrases such people use for their own ends?*

You see, I know that it's difficult to think well about "certainty," "probability," perception, etc. But it is, if possible, still more difficult to think, or try to think, really honestly about your life and other people's lives. And thinking about these things is NOT THRILLING, but often downright nasty. And when it's nasty then it's MOST important.

His high-pitched voice with its darker, hoarser undertone.

At least he didn't walk out, he stayed, long fingers drumming.

•

So now your paledark face thrown up
into pre-rain silver light your white shirt takes
on the hurl and flutter of the gull's wings
over your dark leggings their leathery legs
flash past your hurling arm one hand
snatching crusts from the bowl another hand holds close

You, barefoot on that narrow strand
with the iceplant edges and the long spindly pier
you just as the rain starts leaping into the bay
in your cloud of black, bronze and silvering hair

•

Later by the window on a fast-gathering winter evening
my eyes on the page then catch your face your breasts that light

                              . . . small tradespeople,
shopkeepers, retired tradesmen, handicraftsmen and peasants—
all these sink gradually into the proletariat

                              partly because their
diminutive capital does not suffice for the scale on which
modern industry is carried on, and is swamped in the
competition with the large capitalists

842

partly because their specialized
skill is rendered worthless by new methods of production.

        Thus, the proletariat is recruited
from all classes of the population. . . .

pelicans and cormorants stumbling up the bay
the last gash of light abruptly bandaged in darkness

•

1799, Coleridge to Wordsworth: *I wish*
you would write a poem
addressed to those who, in consequence
of the complete failure of the French Revolution
have thrown up all hopes
of the amelioration of mankind
and are sinking into an almost epicurean
selfishness, disguising the same
under the soft titles of domestic attachment
and contempt for visionary philosophes

A generation later, revolutions scorching Europe:
the visionaries having survived despite
rumors of complete failure

the words have barely begun   to match the desire

when the cold fog blows back in
organized and disordering
muffling words and faces

Your lashes, visionary! screening
in sudden rushes this
shocked, abraded crystal

•

I can imagine a sentence that might someday end with the word, love.
Like the one written by that asthmatic young man, which begins, *At
the risk of appearing ridiculous* . . . It would have to contain losses, resil-
iencies, histories faced; it would have to contain a face—his yours hers
mine—by which I could do well, embracing it like water in my hands,
because by then we could be sure that "doing well" by one, or some,
was immiserating nobody. A true sentence then, for greeting the new-
born. (—Someplace else. In our hopes.)

But where ordinary collective affections carry a price (swamped, or
accounted worthless) I'm one of those driven seabirds stamping oil-
distempered waters   maimed "by natural causes."

The music's pirated from somewhere else: Catalan songs reaching
us after fifty years. Old *nuevos canciones,* after twenty years? In them,
something about the sweetness of life, the memory of traditions of
mercy, struggles for justice. A long throat, casting memory forward.

•

"it's the layers of history
we have to choose, along
with our own practice: what must be tried again
over and over and
what must not be repeated
and at what depth   which layer
will we meet others"

        the words barely begin
        to match the desire

and the mouth crammed with dollars doesn't testify

            . . . the eye has become a human eye
        when its object has become a human, social object

BRECHT BECOMES GERMAN ICON ANEW
FORGIVEN MARXIST IDEAS

. . . the Arts, you know—they're Jews, they're left-wing,
in other words, stay away . . .

•

> So, Bo Kunstelaar, tell us true
> how you still do what you do
> your old theories forgiven
> —the public understands
> it was one thing then but now is now
> and everyone says your lungs are bad
> and your liver very sad
> and the force of your imagination
> has no present destination
> though subversive has a certain charm
> and art can really do no harm
> but still they say you get up and go
> every morning to the studio
> Is it still a thrill?
> or an act of will?
> Mr. Kunstelaar?

•

—After so long, to be asked an opinion? Most of that time, the opinions unwelcome. But opinion anyway was never art. Along the way I was dropped by some; others could say I had dropped them. I tried to make in my studio what I could not make outside it. Even to have a studio, or a separate room to sleep in, was a point in fact. In case you miss the point: I come from hod-carriers, lint-pickers, people who hauled cables through half-dug tunnels. Their bodies created the possibility of my existence. I come from the kind of family where loss means not just grief but utter ruin—adults and children dispersed into prostitution, orphanages, juvenile prisons, emigration—never to meet again. I wanted to show those lives—designated insignificant—as beauty, as terror. They were significant to me and what they had endured terrified me. I knew such a life could have been my own. I also knew they had saved me from it.

—I tried to show all this and as well to make an art as impersonal as it demanded.

—I have no theories. I don't know what I am being forgiven. I am my art: I make it from my body and the bodies that produced mine. I am still trying to find the pictorial language for this anger and fear rotating on an axle of love. If I still get up and go to the studio—it's there I find the company I need to go on working.

•

"This is for you
this little song
without much style
because your smile
fell like a red leaf
through my tears
in those fogbound years
when without ado
you gave me a bundle of fuel to burn
when my body was utterly cold
This is for you
who would not applaud
when with a kick to the breast or groin
they dragged us into the van
when flushed faces cheered
at our disgrace
or looked away   this is
for you who stayed
to see us through

delivered our bail and disappeared
This little song
without much style
may it find you
somewhere   well."

•

In the dark windowglass
a blurred face
—is it still mine?

Who out there hoped to change me—
what out there has tried?

What sways and presses against the pane
what can't I see beyond or through—

charred, crumpled, ever-changing human language
is that still *you?*

1997–98

FOX

(1998–2000)

For Michelle, again,
after twenty-five years

Y in alto cielo, su fondo estrellado
Y en las multitudes, la mujer que amo

VICTORY

Something spreading underground won't speak to us
under skin won't declare itself
not all life-forms want dialogue with the
machine-gods in their drama   hogging down
the deep bush   clear-cutting refugees
from ancient or transient villages into
our opportunistic fervor   to search
                    crazily for a host   a lifeboat

Suddenly instead of art we're eyeing
organisms traced and stained on cathedral transparencies
cruel blues   embroidered purples   succinct yellows
a beautiful tumor

•

I guess you're not alone   I fear you're alone
There's, of course, poetry:
awful bridge rising over naked air: I first
took it as just a continuation of the road:
"a masterpiece of engineering
praised, etc."   then on the radio:
"incline too steep for ease of, etc."
Drove it nonetheless because I had to
this being how—   So this is how
I find you: alive and more

•

As if (how many conditionals must we suffer?)
I'm driving to your side
—an intimate collusion—
packed in the trunk my bag of foils for fencing with pain
glasses of varying spectrum for sun or fog or sun-struck

                    rain or bitterest night my sack of hidden
poetries, old glue shredding from their spines

my time exposure of the Leonids
                                    over Joshua Tree

As if we're going to win this   O because

•

If you have a sister I am not she
nor your mother nor you my daughter
nor are we lovers or any kind of couple
          except in the intensive care
                              of poetry and
death's master plan   architecture-in-progress
draft elevations of a black-and-white mosaic dome
the master left on your doorstep
with a white card in black calligraphy:
          Make what you will of this
          As if leaving purple roses

•

If (how many conditionals must we suffer?)
I tell you a letter from the master
is lying on my own doorstep
glued there with leaves and rain
and I haven't bent to it yet
                    if I tell you I surmise
          he writes differently to me:

> *Do as you will, you have had your life*
>   *many have not*

signing it in his olden script:

>   *Meister aus Deutschland*

•

In coldest Europe   end of that war
frozen domes   iron railings frozen   stoves lit in the
    streets
memory banks of cold

the Nike of Samothrace
on a staircase   wings in blazing
backdraft   said to me
: : to everyone she met
        Displaced, amputated   never discount me

Victory
        indented in disaster   striding
            at the head of stairs

For Tory Dent

1998

VETERANS DAY

1

No flag heavy or full enough to hide this face
this body swung home from home   sewn into its skin

Let you   entrusted to close the box
for final draping   take care

what might be due
to the citizen wounded

by no foreign blast nor shell   (*is this*
body a child's?   if?   why?)

eyes hooded in refusal—
over these to lower the nation's pall, thick flutter

this body shriveled into itself
—a normal process they have said

The face?   another story, a flag
hung upside down against glory's orders

2

Trying to think about
something else—what?—when?

the story broke
the scissor-fingered prestidigitators

snipped the links of concentration
State vs memory

State vs unarmed citizen
wounded by no foreign blast nor shell

forced into the sick-field
brains-out coughing downwind

backing into the alley   hands shielding eyes
under glare-lit choppers coming through   low

3

In the dream you—is it?—set down
two packages in brown paper

saying, *Without such means
there can be no end*

*to the wrenching of mind
from body, the degradation*

*no end to everything you hate
and have exposed, lie upon lie*

I think: *We've been dying slowly
now we'll be blown to bits*

I think you're testing me
"how vitally we desired disaster"

You say, *there can be no poetry
without the demolition*

of language, no end to everything you hate
lies upon lies

I think: you're testing me
testing us both

but isn't this what it means to live—
pushing further the conditions in which we breathe?

4

In the college parlor by the fireplace
ankled and waisted with bells

he, inclined by nature toward tragic themes
chants of the eradication of tribal life

in a blue-eyed trance
shaking his neckbent silvering hair

Afterward, wine and cake at the Provost's house

and this is surely no dream, how the beneficiary
of atrocities yearns toward innocence

and this is surely a theme, the vengeful rupture
of prized familiar ways

and calculated methods
for those who were there   But for those elsewhere

it's something else, not herds hunted down cliffs
maybe a buffalo burger in the

tribal college cafeteria
and computer skills after lunch Who wants to be tragic?

The college coheres out of old quonset huts
demolition-scavenged doors, donated labor

used textbooks, no waste, passion

5

Horned blazing fronds of Sierra ice
grow hidden rivulets, last evening's raindrop pulses

in the echeveria's cup next morning, fogdrip darkens the
    road
under fire-naked bishop pines

thick sweats form on skins
of pitched-out nectarines, dumpster shrine

of miracles of truths of mold
Rain streaming, stroking

a broken windowpane
When the story broke I thought

I was thinking about water
how it is most of what we are

and became bottled chic
such thoughts are soon interrupted

6

When the story broke we were trying to think
about history   went on stubbornly thinking

though history plunged
with muddy spurs   screamed at us for trying

to plunder its nest   seize its nestlings
capture tame and sell them or something

after the manner of our kind
Well, was it our secret hope?

—a history you could seize
(as in old folios of "natural history"

each type and order pictured in its place?)
—Back to the shambles, comrades.

where the story is always breaking
down   having to be repaired

7

Under the small plane's fast shadow an autumn
afternoon bends sharply

—swathes of golden membrane, occult blood
seeping up through the great groves

where the intestinal the intestate
blood-cords of the stags are strung from tree to tree

I know already where we're landing
what cargo we'll take on

boxed for the final draping
coming home from home   sewn into its skin

eyes hooded in refusal

—what might be due—

1998–1999

FOR THIS

If I've reached for your lines   (I have)
    like letters from the dead that stir the nerves
dowsed you for a springhead
    to water my thirst
dug into my compost skeletons and petals
    you surely meant to catch the light:

—at work in my wormeaten wormwood-raftered
    stateless underground
        have I a plea?

If I've touched your finger
    with a ravenous tongue
        licked from your palm a rift of salt
if I've dreamt or thought you
    a pack of blood   fresh-drawn
        hanging darkred from a hook
higher than my heart
    (you who understand transfusion)
        where else should I appeal?

A pilot light lies low
    while the gas jets sleep
        (a cat getting toed from stove
into nocturnal ice)

language uncommon and agile as truth
    melts down the most intractable silence

A lighthouse keeper's ethics:
    you tend for all or none
        for this you might set your furniture on fire
A *this* we have blundered over
    as if the lamp could be shut off at will
        rescue denied for some

and still a lighthouse be

1999

REGARDLESS

An idea declared itself between us
clear as a washed wineglass
that we'd love
regardless of manifestos I wrote or signed
my optimism of the will
regardless
your wincing at manifestos
your practice of despair you named
anarchism
: : an idea we could meet
somewhere else   a road
straggling unmarked through ice-plant
toward an ocean   heartless as eternity

Still hungry for freedom   I walked off
from glazed documents   becalmed
passions   time of splintering and sawdust

pieces lying still   I was not myself but
I found a road like that   it straggled
The ocean still
looked like eternity
I drew it on a
napkin mailed it to you

On your hands you wear work gloves stiffened
in liquids your own body has expressed
: : what stiffens hardest?   tears? blood? urine? sweat? the first
        drops from the penis?
Your glove then meets my hand   this is our meeting
Which of us has gone furthest?

To meet you like this I've had to rise
from love in a room
of green leaves larger than my clitoris or my brain
in a climate where winter never precisely
does or does not engrave its name on the windowpane
while the Pacific lays down its right of way
to the other side of the world

: : to a table where singed manifestos
curl back crying to be reread

but can I even provoke you
joking or
in tears
you   in long-stiffened gloves   still
protector of despair?

For H.C.

1998–1999

SIGNATURES

It would have made no difference who commanded us in
those first hours. . . .

      —veteran, invasion of Normandy, 1944

That was no country for old women . . . Someone from D-Day
at the redgold turn of the party
recites his line of Yeats with a sex-change
someone already stricken
in his urethra   rising four times nightly

Went through *that* and still despises . . .

Here an old woman's best country is her art
or it's not her country
Here the old don't pity the old
As when young we scale our rock face
relentless, avid

looking sometimes back at the whole terrain:

—those scrapings on the rocks
are they a poet's signature?
a mother's who tried for all her worth to cling
to the steep   with the small soft claws gripping her back?

1998

NORA'S GAZE

Clayton, we can't
    have it both ways:
        Nora's art

was erotic
    not sensual
        yet how can that be?

Mostly, she handled
    the body in a bleak light
        —surely that was her right

to make such paintings, drawings more
    than paintings anyway—
        grey-brown, black, white-grey

—not the usual hues encoding
    sensual encounter
        but how she figured it
          and stained it

And had she painted
    the deep-dyed swollen shaft
        the balls' magenta shadow

in dark dominion
    that
        might have "done well"

But to paint and paint again
    the penis as a workaday
        routine

wintry morning thing
    under a gaze
        expert and merciful as hers

that was heinous
    and her genius
        still lies chained

till that is told

  You a man
    I a woman tell it
none of it lessens her

For Clayton Eshleman

1998

ARCHITECT

Nothing he had done before
    or would try for later
        will explain or atone
this facile suggestion of crossbeams
languid elevations traced on water
his stake in white colonnades cramping his talent
                showing up in
facsimile mansions overbearing the neighborhood
his leaving the steel rods out of the plinths
    (bronze raptors gazing from the boxwood)

You could say he spread himself too thin   a plasterer's term
      you could say he was then
skating thin ice   his stake in white colonnades against the
    thinness of

ice itself   a slickened ground
        Could say he did not then love
his art enough to love anything more

Could say he wanted the commission so
badly betrayed those who hired him   an artist
    who in dreams followed
        the crowds who followed him

Imagine commandeering those oversize those prized
        hardwood columns to be hoisted and hung
by hands expert and steady on powerful machines
        his knowledge using theirs as the one kind does the
                                other (as it did in Egypt)

        —while devising the little fountain to run all night
            outside the master bedroom

1998–1999

FOX

I needed fox   Badly I needed
a vixen for the long time none had come near me
I needed recognition from a
triangulated face   burnt-yellow eyes
fronting the long body the fierce and sacrificial tail
I needed history of fox   briars of legend it was said she had run through
I was in want of fox

And the truth of briars she had to have run through
I craved to feel on her pelt   if my hands could even slide
past or her body slide between them   sharp truth distressing surfaces

of fur
lacerated skin calling legend to account
a vixen's courage in vixen terms

For a human animal to call for help
on another animal
is the most riven the most revolted cry on earth
come a long way down
Go back far enough it means tearing and torn   endless and sudden
back far enough it blurts
into the birth-yell of the yet-to-be human child
pushed out of a female   the yet-to-be woman

1998

MESSAGES

I love the infinity of these silent spaces
Darkblue shot with deathrays but only a short distance
Keep of course water and batteries, antibiotics
Always look at California for the last time

We weren't birds, were we, to flutter past each other
But what were we meant to do, standing or lying down
Together on the bare slope where we were driven
The most personal feelings become historical

Keep your hands knotted deep inside your sweater
While the instruments of force are more credible than beauty
Inside a glass paperweight dust swirls and settles (Manzanar)
Where was the beauty anyway when we shouldered past each other

Where is it now in the hollow lounge
Of the grounded airline where the cameras

For the desouling project are being handed out
Each of us instructed to shoot the others naked

If you want to feel the true time of our universe
Put your hands over mine on the stainless pelvic rudder
No, here   (sometimes the most impassive ones will shudder)
The infinity of these spaces comforts me
Simple textures falling open like a sweater

1999

FIRE

      in the old city   incendiaries abound
who hate this place stuck to their foot soles
Michael Burnhard is being held and I
can tell you about him   pushed-out and living
across the river   low-ground given to flooding
in a shotgun house
his mother working for a hospital
or restaurant   dumpsters   she said a restaurant
hospital cafeteria who cares
what story
you bring home with the food

I can tell you Michael knows beauty
from the frog-iris in mud
the squelch of ankles
stalking the waterlily
the blues beat flung across water from the old city

Michael Burnhard in Black History Month
not his month only he was born there

not black and almost without birthday one
February 29 Michael Burnhard
on the other side of the river
glancing any night at his mother's wrists
crosshatched raw
beside the black-opal stream

Michael Burnhard still beside himself
when fire took the old city
lying like a black spider on its back
under the satellites and a few true stars

1999

TWILIGHT

Mudseason dusk schoolmaster: pressed out of rain my spine
on your grey dormitory
chiseled from Barre

caught now in your blurred story
hauling my jacket overshoulder
against your rectilinear stones

Out of the rain I waited
in a damp parlor ghosted
with little gifts and candy toys
pitting my brain against your will

Could rays from my pupils dissect
mortar   pry boards from floor
probe the magnetic field of your
granitic clarity

Schoolmaster: could swear I've caught your upper-window profile
bent down on this little kingdom   dreamed your advice:
Always read with the dark falling over your left shoulder

                                   —seen you

calculate volume of blocks required
                          inspect the glazing
pay the week's wages
       blueprints scrolled under arm

treading home over snow
driven virgin then cow-pied
five o'clock's blue eyeballs
strung open day after day
a few seconds longer

an ascendant planet
following in your footprints possibly

1999

OCTOBRISH

—it is to have these dreams

still married/where
   you tell me *In those days*
        instead of working
        I was playing on the shore with a wolf

coming to a changed
house/you
glad of the changes

but still almost
transparent
and bound to disappear

    A life thrashes/half unlived/its passions
        don't desist/displaced from their own habitat
           like other life-forms take up other dwellings

so in my body's head
so in the stormy spaces
that life
leads itself which could not be led

1999

SECOND SIGHT

1

Tonight I could write many verses
beginning   Let this not happen
for a woman leaning over a thirtieth story railing
in hot July   worn webbed-plastic
chairs aglare on the nickel-colored balcony
foreseeing in tracked patterns
of a project landscape
the hammer brought
down by one child upon another's skull

Not moved yet   she   and hers
her child inside   gazing
at a screen
and she a reader once   now a woman foreseeing

elbows sore with the weight
she has placed on them
a woman on a balcony with a child inside
gazing at a screen

2

A woman   neither architect nor engineer   construes the dustmotes
of a space primed for neglect
Indoor, outdoor exhausted air

Paths that have failed as paths   trees
that have failed as trees

Practiced in urban literacy she
traverses and assesses streets and bridges
tilting the cumbrous ornamental sewer lids ajar
in search of reasons underground
              which there why this must be

1999–2000

GRATING

I

Not having worn
    the pearly choker
          of innocence around my throat
willed by a woman
    whose leavings I can't afford
          Not having curled up like that girl

in maternal gauze
                              Not
                  having in great joy gazing
on another woman's thick fur
        believed I was unsexed for that

Now let me not
        you   not I   but who ought to be
hang like a leaf twisting
              endlessly toward the past
              nor reach for a woman's skinned-off mask
        to hide behind
                          You
                              not I but who ought to be
get me out of this, human
                                  through some
        air vent, grating

II

There's a place where beauty names itself:
"I am beauty," and becomes irreproachable
to the girl transfixed beside the mother
the artist and her mother

There must be a color for the mother's
Otherness   must be some gate of chalk some slit or stain
through which the daughter sees outside that otherness
Long ago must have been burnt a bunch of rags
still smelling of umbrage
that can be crushed into a color
there must be such a color
if, lying full length
on the studio floor

the artist were to paint herself
in monochrome
from a mirror in the ceiling
an elongated figure suspended across the room
first horizontal

then straight up and naked
free of beauty
ordinary in fact

III

The task is to row a strong-boned, legally blind
hundred-and-one-year-old woman
across the Yangtze River

An emergency or not, depending
Others will have settled her in the boat with pillows but the arms
wielding the oars will be yours
crepitus of the shoulders yours
the conversation still hers

Three days' labor
*with you . . . **that** was torture*

—to pilot through current and countercurrent
requiring silence and concentration

There is a dreadfulness that charm o'erlies
—as might have been said
in an older diction

Try to row deadweight someone without
death skills

Shouldering the river a pilot figures
how

The great rock shoulders overlook
in their immensity all decisions

1999–2000

NOCTILUCENT CLOUDS

Late night on the underside   a spectral glare
abnormal   Everything below
must and will betray itself
as a floodlit truckstop out here
on the North American continent stands revealed
and we're glad because it's late evening and no town
but this, diesel, regular, soda, coffee, chips, beer and video
no government no laws but LIGHT in the continental dark
and then   and then   what smallness the soul endures
rolling out on the ramp from such an isle
onto the harborless Usonian plateau

Dear Stranger   can I raise a poem
to justice   you not here
with your sheet-lightning apprehension
of nocturne
your surveyor's eye for distance
as if any forest's fallen tree were for you
a possible hypotenuse

Can I wake as I once woke with no thought of you
into the bad light of a futureless motel

This thing I am calling justice:
I could slide my hands into your leather gloves
but my feet would not fit into your boots

Every art leans on some other: yours
on mine in spasm retching
last shreds of vanity
We swayed together like cripples when the wind
suddenly turned a corner   or was it we who turned

Once more I invite you into this
in retrospect it will be clear

1999

IF YOUR NAME IS ON THE LIST

If your name is on the list of judges
you're one of them
though you fought their hardening
assumptions   went and stood
alone by the window while they
concurred
It wasn't enough to hold your singular
minority opinion
You had to face the three bridges
down the river
your old ambitions
flamboyant in bloodstained mist

You had to carry off under arm
and write up in perfect loneliness
your soul-splitting dissent

Yes, I know a soul can be partitioned like a country
In all the new inhere old judgments
loyalties crumbling send up sparks and smoke
We want to be part of the future   dragging in
what pure futurity can't use

Suddenly a narrow street a little beach a little century
screams   *Don't let me go*

Don't let me die   Do you forget
what we were to each other

1999

1999

Before the acute
point of the severing
I wanted to see into my century's
hinged and beveled mirror
clear of smoke
eyes of coal and ruby
stunned neck the carrier of bricks and diamonds
brow of moonlit oyster shells
barbed wire lacework disgracing
the famous monument

Behind it spread the old
indigenous map   landscape
before conquerors   horizon ownless

TERZA RIMA

1

Hail-spurting sky   sun
splashing off persimmons left
in the quit garden

of the quit house   The realtor's swaying name
against this cloudheap this
surrendered acre

I would   so help me   tell you if I could
how some great teacher
came to my side and said:

Let's go down   *into the underworld*
—the earth already crazed
Let me take your hand

—but who would that be?
already trembling on the broken crust
who would I trust?

I become the default derailed memory-raided
limping
teacher I never had   I lead and   I follow

2

Call it the earthquake trail:
I lead through live-oak meadows
to the hillside   where the plates shuddered

rewind the seismic story
point to the sundered
fence of 1906   the unmatching rocks

trace the loop under dark bay branches
blurred with moss
behaving like a guide

Like a novice I lag
behind with the little snake
dead on the beaten path

This will never happen again

3

At the end of the beaten path we're sold free
tickets for the celebration
of the death of history

The last page of the calendar
will go up   a sheet of flame
(no one will be permitted on the bridge)

We'll assemble by letters
alphabetical
each ticket a letter

to view ourselves as giants
on screen-surround
in the parking lot

figures of men and women firmly pushing
babies in thickly padded prams
through disintegrating malls

into the new era

4

I have lost our way   the fault is mine
ours   the fault belongs
to us   I become   the guide

who should have defaulted
who should have remained the novice
I   as guide   failed

I as novice   trembled
I should have been stronger   held us
together

5

I thought I was
stronger   my will the ice-sail
speeding my runners

along frozen rivers
bloodied by sunset
thought I could be forever

will-ful   my sail filled
with perfect ozone   my blades
flashing clean into the ice

6

Was that youth?   that clear
sapphire on snow
a distinct hour

in Central Park   that smell
on sidewalk and windowsill
fresh and unmixt

the blizzard's peace and drama
over the city
a public privacy

                    waiting
in the small steamed-up copy shop
slush tracked in across a wooden floor

then shivering   elated
in twilight
at the bus stop   with others   a public happiness

7

Not simple is it to do
a guide's work   the novices
irrupting hourly with their own bad vigor

knowing not who they are
every phase of moon an excuse
for fibrillating

besides the need   in today's world
to consider
outreach   the new thinking

—Or: love will strongly move you
or commerce will
You want a priest?   go to the altar

where eternal bargains are struck
want love?
go down inside your destructible heart

8

In Almodóvar's film
we go for truth to the prostitutes' field
to find past and future

elegant   beaten-up and knifed
sex without gender
preyed-on and preying

transactions   zones of play
the circling drivers
in search of their desires

theater of love   Ninth Circle
there are so many teachers
here   no fire can shrink them

Do you understand?   you could get your face
slashed in such a place
Do you think this is a movie?

9

She says: I gave my name and it was taken
I no longer have my name
I gave my word and it was broken

My words are learning
to walk on crutches
through traffic

without stammering
My name is a prisoner
who will not name names

She says: I gave my tongue
to love   and this
makes it hard to speak

She says: When my life depended
on one of two
opposite terms

I dared mix beauty with courage
they were my lovers
together they were tortured

10

Sick of my own old poems   caught
on rainshower Fifth Avenue
in a bookstore

I reach to a shelf
and there you are   Pier Paolo
speaking to Gramsci's ashes

in the old encircling rhyme
Vivo nel non volere
del tramontato dopoguerra:

                    amando

il mondo che odio . . .
that vernacular voice
intimately political

and that was how you died
so I clasp my book to my heart
as the shop closes

11

Under the blackened dull-metal corners
of the small espresso pot
a jet flares blue

a smell tinctures the room
—some sniff or prescience of
a life that actually could be

lived   a grain of hope
a bite of bitter chocolate in the subway
to pull on our senses

without them we're prey
to the failed will
its science of despair

12

How I hate it when you ascribe to me
a "woman's vision"
cozy with coffeepots   drawn curtains

or   leaning in black leather dress
over your chair
black fingernail tracing your lines

overspent Sibyl drifting in a bottle

How I've hated speaking "as a woman"
for mere continuation
when the broken is what I saw

As a woman   do I love
and hate?   as a woman
do I munch my bitter chocolate underground?

Yes.   No.   You too
sexed as you are   hating
this whole thing   you keep on   it remaking

13

Where the novice pulls the guide
across frozen air
where the guide suddenly grips   the shoulder

of the novice   where the moss is golden
the sky sponged with pink at sunset
where the urine of reindeer barely vanished

stings the air like a sharp herb
where the throat of the clear-cut opens
across the surrendered forest

I'm most difficultly
with you   I lead
and I follow

our shadows   reindeer-huge
slip onto the map
of chance and purpose   figures

on the broken crust
exchanging places   bites to eat
a glance

2000

FOUR SHORT POEMS

1

(driving home from Robin Blaser's reading)

The moon
is not romantic.   No.   It's
a fact of life and still
we aren't inured. You would think, it reflects
the waves not draws them.   So
I'd compel you as I
have been compelled by you.   On the coast road
between drafts of fog
that face (and yes, it is
expressioned) breaking in and out
doth speak to us
as he did in his courtliness
and operatic mystery.

2

We're not yet out of the everglades
    of the last century
        our body parts are still there

though we would have our minds careen and swoop
    over the new ocean
        with a wild surmise

the bloody strings
    tangled and stuck between
        become our lyre

3

Beethoven's "Appassionata" played on a parlor grand piano
in a small California town by a boy from Prague
here for a month to learn American
This is not "The Work of Art in the Age of Mechanical Reproduction"
This is one who startles the neighbors with his owning
of the transmissible heritage one evening
then for the whole month droops over the Internet.

4

From the new crudities, from the old
apartheid spraying ruin on revolution,
back to Du Bois of Great Barrington and Africa

or Kafka of the intransmissible
tradition
the stolen secrets in the cleft

reside   and this, beloved poets
is where our hearts, livers and lights still
dwell unbeknownst and vital

For Elizabeth Willis and for Peter Gizzi

2000

RAUSCHENBERG'S BED

How a bed once dressed with a kindly quilt becomes
unsleepable site of anarchy   What body holes expressed
their exaltation loathing exhaustion
what horse of night has pawed those sheets
what talk under the blanket raveled
what clitoris lain very still in her own subversion
what traveler homeward reached for familiar bedding
and felt stiff tatters under his fingers
How a bed is horizontal yet this is vertical
inarticulate liquids spent from a spectral pillow

How on a summer night someone drives out on the roads
while another one lies ice-packed in dreams of freezing

Sometimes this bed has eyes, sometimes breasts
sometimes eking forth from its laden springs
pity compassion pity again for all they have worn and borne
Sometimes it howls for penis sometimes vagina sometimes
for the nether hole the everywhere

How the children sleep and wake
the children   sleep awake upstairs

How on a single night the driver of roads comes back
into the sweat-cold bed of the dreamer

leans toward what's there for warmth
human limbs   human crust

2000

WAITING FOR YOU AT THE MYSTERY SPOT

I sat down facing the steep place where
tours clambered upward and others straggled down, the redwoods
    outstanding all
A family, East Asian, holding a picnic at their van:
"We are always hungry," the older sister said laughing, "and we
    always bring our food"
Roses clambered a rough fence in the slanting sun that speared
    the redwoods
We'd gone into the gift shop while waiting for your tour
found Davy Crockett coonskin caps, deerskin coin purses
scorpions embedded in plastic, MYSTERY SPOT bumper stickers
and postcards of men you wouldn't be left alone with
a moment if you could help it, illustrating
the Mystery Spot and its tricks with gravity and horizon
Your tour was called and you started upward.   I went back
to my redwood bench
                "The *mystai* streamed"
                          toward the

          mystery

But if anything up there was occult
nothing at ground level was: tiny beings flashing around
in the sun secure knowing their people were nearby
grandfathers, aunts, elder brothers or sisters, parents and loved friends
You could see how it was when each tour was called and gathered itself
who rode on what shoulders, ran alongside, held hands
the languages all different, English the least of these
I sat listening to voices watching the miraculous migration
of sunshafts through the redwoods   the great spears folding up
into letters from the sun deposited through dark green slots
each one saying
           I love you but
I must draw away   *Believe, I will return*

Then: happiness! your particular figures
in the descending crowd: Anne, Jacob, Charlie!
Anne with her sandals off
in late day warmth and odor and odd wonder

2000

ENDS OF THE EARTH

All that can be unknown is stored in the black screen of a broken
    television set.
Coarse-frosted karst crumbling as foam, eel eyes piercing the rivers.
Dark or light, leaving or landfall, male or female demarcations
    dissolve
into the O of time and solitude. I found here: no inter/
ruption to a version of earth so abandoned and abandoning
I read it my own acedia lashed by the winds
questing shredmeal toward the Great Plains, that ocean. My fear.

Call it Galisteo but that's not the name of what happened here.

If indoors in an eyeflash (perhaps) I caught the gazer of spaces
lighting the two wax candles in black iron holders
against the white wall after work and after dark
but never saw the hand

how inhale the faint mist of another's gazing, pacing, dozing
words muttered aloud in utter silence, gesture unaware
thought that has suffered and borne itself to the ends of the earth
web agitating between my life and another's?
Other whose bed I have shared but never at once together?

2000

THE SCHOOL AMONG THE RUINS

(2000–2004)

For Jean Valentine

I

CENTAUR'S REQUIEM

Your hooves drawn together underbelly
shoulders in mud   your mane
of wisp and soil deporting all the horse of you

your longhaired neck
eyes   jaw yes   and ears
unforgivably human on such a creature
unforgivably what you are
deposited in the grit-kicked field of a champion

tender neck and nostrils   teacher   water-lily suction-spot
what you were   marvelous   we could not stand

Night drops   an awaited storm
driving in to wreck your path
Foam on your hide like flowers
where you fell   or fall   desire

2001

EQUINOX

Time split like a fruit between dark and light
and a usual fog drags
over this landfall
I've walked September end to end
barefoot room to room
carrying in hand a knife well honed for cutting stem or root
                         or wick   eyes open
to abalone shells   memorial candle flames
split lemons   roses laid

along charring logs   Gorgeous things
: : dull acres of developed land as we had named it: Nowhere
wetland   burnt garbage looming at its heart
gunmetal thicket   midnightblue blood and
                    tricking masks   I thought I knew
history was not a novel

So can I say it was not I   listed as Innocence
betrayed you   serving (and protesting always)
the motives of my government
thinking we'd scratch out a place
where poetry   old subversive shape
grew out of Nowhere   here?
where skin could lie on skin
a place "outside the limits"

                    Can say I was mistaken?

To be so bruised: in the soft organs   skeins of consciousness
Over and over have let it be
damage to others   crushing of the animate core
that tone-deaf cutloose ego swarming the world

so bruised: heart   spleen   long inflamed ribbons of the guts
the spine's vertical necklace swaying

Have let it swarm
through us   let it happen
as it must, inmost

but before this: long before this   those other eyes
frontally exposed themselves and spoke

2001

TELL ME

1

Tell me, why way toward dawn the body
close to a body familiar as itself
chills—tell me, is this the hour
                            remembered if outlived
as freezing—no, don't tell me

Dreams spiral birdwinged overhead
a peculiar hour   the silver mirror-frame's
quick laugh the caught light-lattice on the wall
as a truck drives off before dawn
headlights on

Not wanting
to *write this up*   for the public   not wanting
to *write it down*   in secret

just to lie here in this cold story
feeling it   trying to feel it through

2

Blink and smoke, flicking with absent nail
                            at the mica bar
where she refills without asking
Crouch into your raingarb   this will be a night
unauthorized shock troops are abroad

this will be a night
the face-ghosts lean
                  over the banister

declaring the old stories all
froze like beards or frozen margaritas
all the new stories taste of lukewarm
margaritas, lukewarm kisses

3

From whence I draw this: *harrowed in defeats of language*
in history to my barest marrow
This: one syllable then another
gropes upward
one stroke laid on another
sound from one throat then another
never in the making
making beauty or sense

always mis-taken, draft, roughed-in
only to be struck out
is blurt is roughed-up
hot   keeps body
in leaden hour
simmering

2001

FOR JUNE, IN THE YEAR 2001

The world's quiver and shine
I'd clasp for you forever
jetty vanishing into pearlwhite mist
western sunstruck water-light

Touch food to the lips
let taste never betray you
cinnamon vanilla melting
on apple tart

but what you really craved:
a potency of words
Driving back from Berkeley
880's brute dystopia

I was at war with words
Later on C-SPAN: Tallahassee:
words straight to the point:
One person, one vote

No justice, no peace
it could lift you by the hair
it could move you like a wind
it could take you by surprise

as sudden Canada geese
took us by the marina
poised necks and alert
attitudes of pause

Almost home I wanted
you to smell the budding acacias
tangled with eucalyptus
on the road to Santa Cruz

2002

THE SCHOOL AMONG THE RUINS

Beirut.Baghdad.Sarajevo.Bethlehem.Kabul. Not of course here.

1

Teaching the first lesson and the last
—great falling light of summer will you last
longer than schooltime?
When children flow
in columns at the doors
BOYS GIRLS and the busy teachers

open or close high windows
with hooked poles   drawing darkgreen shades

closets unlocked, locked
questions unasked, asked, when

love of the fresh impeccable
sharp-pencilled   yes
order without cruelty

a street on earth   neither heaven nor hell
busy with commerce and worship
young teachers walking to school

fresh bread and early-open foodstalls

2

When the offensive rocks the sky when nightglare
misconstrues day and night when lived-in
rooms from the upper city
tumble cratering lower streets

cornices of olden ornament   human debris
when fear vacuums out the streets

When the whole town flinches
blood on the undersole thickening to glass

Whoever crosses   hunched   knees bent   a contested zone
knows why she does this suicidal thing

School's now in session day and night
children sleep
in the classrooms   teachers rolled close

3

How the good teacher loved
his school   the students
the lunchroom with fresh sandwiches

lemonade and milk
the classroom   glass cages
of moss and turtles
teaching responsibility

A morning breaks without bread or fresh-poured milk
parents or lesson plans

diarrhea first question of the day
children shivering   it's September
Second question: where is my mother?

4

One: I don't know where your mother
is   Two: I don't know
why they are trying to hurt us
Three: or the latitude and longitude
of their hatred   Four: I don't know if we
hate them as much   I think there's more toilet paper
in the supply closet   I'm going to break it open

Today this is your lesson:
write as clearly as you can
your name   home street   and number
down on this page
No you can't go home yet
but you aren't lost
this is our school

I'm not sure what we'll eat
we'll look for healthy roots and greens
searching for water though the pipes are broken

5

There's a young cat sticking
her head through window bars
she's hungry like us
but can feed on mice
her bronze erupting fur
speaks of a life already wild

her golden eyes
don't give quarter   She'll teach us   Let's call her
Sister
when we get milk we'll give her some

6

I've told you, let's try to sleep in this funny camp
All night pitiless pilotless things go shrieking
above us to somewhere

Don't let your faces turn to stone
Don't stop asking me why
Let's pay attention to our cat   she needs us

Maybe tomorrow the bakers can fix their ovens

7

"We sang them to naps   told stories   made
shadow-animals with our hands

wiped human debris off boots and coats
sat learning by heart the names
some were too young to write
some had forgotten how"

2001

THIS EVENING LET'S

not talk

about my country   How
I'm from an optimistic culture

that speaks louder than my passport
Don't double-agent-contra my

invincible innocence   I've
got my own

suspicions   Let's
order retsina

cracked olives and bread
I've got questions of my own but

let's give a little
let's let a little be

If *friendship is not a tragedy*
if it's a mercy

we can be merciful
if it's just escape

we're neither of us running
why otherwise be here

Too many reasons not
to waste a rainy evening

in a backroom of bouzouki
and kitchen Greek

I've got questions of my own but
let's let it be a little

There's a beat in my head
song of my country

called Happiness, U.S.A.
Drowns out bouzouki

drowns out world and fusion
with its *Get—get—get*

into your happiness before
happiness pulls away

hangs a left along the piney shore
weaves a hand at you—"one I adore"—

Don't be proud, run hard for that
enchantment boat

tear up the shore if you must but
get into your happiness because

before
and otherwise
it's going to pull away

So tell me later
what I know already

and what I don't get
yet   save for another day

Tell me this time
what you are going through

travelling the Metropolitan
Express

break out of that style
give me your smile
awhile

2001

VARIATIONS ON LINES FROM A CANADIAN POET

> I needed a genre for the times I go phantom. I needed a genre to
> rampage Liberty, haunt the foul freedom of silence. I needed a
> genre to pry loose Liberty from an impacted marriage with the soil.
> I needed a genre to gloss my ancestress' complicity. . . .
>
> —Lisa Robertson, *XEclogue* (1993)

I need a gloss for the silence implicit in my legacy
for phantom Liberty standing bridal at my harbor
I need a gauze to slow the hemorrhaging of my history
I need an ancestor complicit in my undercover prying

I need soil that whirls and spirals upward somewhere else
I need dustbowl, sand dune, dustdevils for roots
I need the border-crossing eye of a tornado
I need an ancestor fleeing into Canada

to rampage freedom there or keep on fleeing
to keep on fleeing or invent a genre
to distemper ideology

2002

DELIVERED CLEAN

You've got to separate what they signify from what
they are   distinguish
their claimed intentions from the stuff coming
out from their hands and heads   The professor of cultural dynamics
taught us this   They're disasters   in absentia
really   when supposedly working
Look at the record:
lost their minds wrote bad checks and smoked in bed
and if they were men were bad with women and if they were women
picked men like that or would go with women
and talked too much and burnt the toast and abused all
known substances   Anyone who says
they were generous to a fault putting change
in whoever's cup if they had it on them   always room for the friend
with no place to sleep   refused to make what they made
in the image of the going thing
cooked up stews that could keep you alive with
gizzards and onions and splashes of raw
red wine   were
loyal where they loved and wouldn't name names
should remember   said the professor of cultural
dynamics   what
messes they made

The building will be delivered vacant
of street actors   so-called artists in residence
fast-order cooks on minimum wage
who dreamed up a life where space was cheap
muralists doubling as rabble-rousers
cross-dressing pavement poets
delivered clean
of those who harbor feral cats illegals illicit ideas
selling their blood to buy old vinyls
living at night and sleeping by day

with huge green plants in their windows
and huge eyes painted on their doors.

For Jack Foley

2002

THE EYE

A balcony, violet shade on stucco   fruit in a plastic bowl on the iron
     raggedy legged table, grapes and sliced melon, saucers, a knife, wine
in a couple of thick short tumblers cream cheese once came in: our snack
     in the eye of the war   There are places where fruit is implausible, even
rest is implausible, places where wine if any should be poured into wounds
     but we're not yet there or it's not here yet   it's the war
not us, that moves, pauses and hurtles forward into the neck
     and groin of the city, the soft indefensible places but not here yet

Behind the balcony an apartment, papers, pillows, green vines still watered
     there are waterless places but not here yet, there's a bureau topped
                                        with marble
and combs and brushes on it, little tubes for lips and eyebrows, a dish
                                        of coins and keys
     there's a bed a desk a stove a cane rocker a bookcase civilization
cage with a skittery bird, there are birdless places but not
     here yet, this bird must creak and flutter in the name of all
uprooted orchards, limbless groves
     this bird standing for wings and song that here can't fly

Our bed quilted   wine poured   future uncertain   you'd think
     people like us would have it scanned and planned   tickets to somewhere
would be in the drawer   with all our education you'd think we'd
                                        have taken measures

908

soon as ash started turning up on the edges of everything ash
in the leaves of books ash on the leaves of trees and in the veins of
                                        the passive
    innocent life we were leading calling it hope
you'd think that and we thought this   it's the war not us that's moving
    like shade on a balcony

2002

THERE IS NO ONE STORY AND ONE STORY ONLY

The engineer's story of hauling coal
to Davenport for the cement factory, sitting on the bluffs
between runs looking for whales, hauling concrete
back to Gilroy, he and his wife renewing vows
in the glass chapel in Arkansas after 25 years
The flight attendant's story murmured
to the flight steward in the dark galley
of her fifth-month loss of nerve
about carrying the baby she'd seen on the screen
The story of the forensic medical team's
small plane landing on an Alaska icefield
of the body in the bag they had to drag
over the ice like the whole life of that body
The story of the man driving
600 miles to be with a friend in another country   seeming
easy when leaving but afterward
writing in a letter difficult truths
Of the friend watching him leave remembering
the story of her body
with his once and the stories of their children
made with other people and how his mind went on

pressing hers like a body
There is the story of the mind's
temperature neither cold nor celibate
Ardent   The story of
not one thing only.

2002

II

USonian Journals 2000

[*Usionian*: the term used by Frank Lloyd Wright for his prairie-inspired architecture. Here, *of the United States of North America*.]

Citizen/Alien/Night/Mare

A country I was born and lived in undergoes rapid and flagrant change. I return here as a stranger. In fact I've lived here all along. At a certain point I realized I was no longer connected along any continuous strand to the nature of the change. I can't find my passport. Nobody asks me to show it.

Day/Job/Mare

. . . to lunch with K., USonian but recently from a British university. Described as "our Marxist." Dark and pretty, already she's got half the department classified: *She's crazy . . . He's carrying the chip of race on his shoulder . . . she's here because he is, isn't she? . . . He's not likely to make it through . . .* Ask her about current Brit. labor scene; she talks about the influence of the industrial revolution on Victorian prose. My aim: get clear of this, find another day job.

As we left the dark publike restaurant the street—ordinary enough couple of blocks between a parking lot and an office complex—broke into spitting, popping sounds and sudden running. I held back against the wall, she beside me. Something happened then everything. A man's voice screamed, then whined: a police siren starting up seemed miles away but then right there. I didn't see any blood. We ran in different directions, she toward, I away from, the police.

Document Window

Could I just show what's happening. Not that shooting, civil disturbance, whatever it was. I'd like you to see how differently we're all moving, how the time allowed to let things become known grows shorter and shorter, how quickly things and people get replaced. How interchangeable it all could get to seem. *Could get to seem* . . . the kind of phrase we use now, avoiding the verb *to be*. *There's a sense in which*, we say, dismissing other senses.

Rimbaud called for the rational derangement of all the senses in the name of poetry. Marx: capitalism deranges all the senses save the sense of property.

Keeping my back against unimportant walls I moved out of range of the confusion, away from the protection of the police. Having seen nothing I could swear to I felt at peace with my default. I would, at least, not be engaged in some mess not my own.

This is what I mean though: how differently we move now, rapidly deciding what is and isn't ours. Indifferently.

Voices

Wreathed around the entrance to a shopping mall, a student dining hall, don't pause for a word, or to articulate an idea. What hangs a moment in the air is already dead: *That's history.*

The moment—Edwin Denby describes it—when a dancer, leaping, stands still in the air. Pause in conversation when time would stop, an idea hang suspended, then get taken up and carried on. (Then that other great style of conversation: everyone at once, each possessed with an idea.) This newer conversation: *I am here and talking, talking, here and talking* . . . Television the first great lesson: against silence. "I thought she'd never call and I went aaah! to my friend and she went give it a week, she'll call you all right and you did"—" And you went waowh! and I went, right, I went O.K., it's only I was clueless? so now can we grab something nearby, cause I'm due on in forty-five?"

A neighbor painting his garage yelling in cell phone from the driveway: voice that penetrates kitchen-window glass. "Fucking worst day of my fucking life, fucking wife left me for another man, both on coke and, you know? I don't CARE! thought it was only maryjane she was, do you KNOW the prison term for coke? Fucking dealer, leaves me for him because she's HOOKED and I'm supposed to CARE? Do they know what they'll GET?"

Private urgencies made public, not collective, speaker within a bubble. In the new restaurant: "Marty? Thought I'd never get through to you. We need to move quickly with SZ-02, there are hounds on the trail. Barney won't block you at all. Just give him what we talked about."

USonian speech. Men of the upwardly mobilizing class needing to sound boyish, an asset in all the newness of the new: upstart, startup, adventurist, pirate lad's nasal bravado in the male vocal cords. Voices of girls and women screeking to an excitable edge of brightness. In an excessively powerful country, grown women sound like girls without authority or experience. Male, female voices alike pitched fastforward commercial, one timbre, tempo, intonation.

Mirrors

Possible tones of the human voice, their own possible physical beauty—no recognition. The fish-eye lens bobbles faces back.

Bodies heavy with sad or enraged feminine or macho brooding mimic stand-up comics, celebrities; grimace, gesticulate. The nakedest generation of young USonians with little intuition of the human history of nakedness, luminous inventions of skin and musculature. Their surfaces needlepointed with conventionally outrageous emblems, what mirror to render justly their original beauty back to them?

You touched me in places so deep I wanted to ignore you.

Artworks (I)

Painting on a gallery wall: people dwelling on opposite sides of a pane of glass. None of their eyes exchanging looks. Yellow flashes off the rug in the room and from the orchard beyond. Houses of people whose eyes do not meet.

White people doing and seeing no evil.

(Photograph of family reunion, eyes on the wide-lens camera unmeeting.) "In fact I've lived here all along."

That was them not us. We were at the time in the time of our displacement, being torn from a false integrity. We stared at the pictures in the gallery knowing they were not us, we were being driven further for something else and who knew how far and for how long and what we were to do.

Stranger

Isolation begins to form, moves in like fog on a clear afternoon. Arrives with the mail, leaves its messages on the phone machine. If you hadn't undergone this so often it could take you by surprise, but its rime-white structure is the simple blueprint of your displacement. You: who pride yourself on not giving in, keep discovering in dreams new rooms in an old house, drawing new plans: living with strangers, enough for all, wild tomato plants along the road, redness for hunger and thirst. (Unrest, too, in the house of dreams: the underworld lashing back.)

But this fog blanks echoes, blots reciprocal sounds. The padded cell of a moribund democracy, or just your individual case?

Artworks (II)

Early summer lunch with friends, talk rises: poetry, urban design and planning, film. Strands of interest and affection binding us differently around the table. If an uneasy political theme rears up—the meaning of a show of lynching photographs in New York, after Mapplethorpe's photos, of sociopathic evil inside the California prison industry— talk fades. Not a pause but: a suppression. No one is monitoring this conversation but us. We know the air is bad in here, maybe want not to push that knowledge, ask *what is to be done?* How to breathe? *What will suffice?* Draft new structures or simply be aware? If art is our only resistance, what does that make us? If we're collaborators, what's our offering to corruption—an aesthetic, anaesthetic, dye of silence, with-drawal, intellectual disgust?

This fade-out/suspension of conversation: a syndrome of the past decades? our companionate immune systems under siege, viral spread of social impotence producing social silence?

Imagine written language that walks away from human conversation. A written literature, back turned to oral traditions, estranged from music and body. So what might reanimate, rearticulate, becomes less and less available.

Incline

Dreamroad rising steeply uphill; David is driving. I see it turning into a perpendicular structure salvaged from a long metal billboard: we will have to traverse this at a ninety-degree angle, then at the top go over and down the other side. There are no exits. Around is the Mojave Desert: open space. D.'s car begins to lose momentum as the incline increases; he tries shifting into a lower gear and gun-ning the engine. There is no way off this incline now, we're forced into a situation we hadn't reckoned on—a road now become something that is no road, something designated as "commercial space." I suggest rolling (ourselves in) the car down the steep dusty shoulder into the desert below, and out. For both of us, the desert isn't vacancy or fear, it's life, a million forms of witness. The fake road, its cruel deception, is what we have to abandon.

Mission Statement

The Organization for the Abolition of Cruelty has an air deployment with bases on every continent and on obscurer tracts of land. Airstrips and hangars have been constructed to accommodate large and small aircraft for reconnoiter and rescue missions whether on polar ice or in desert or rainforest conditions. Many types of craft are of course deployed to urban clusters. The mission of the Organization is not to the First, Third, or any other World. It is directed toward the investigation and abrogation of cruelty in every direction, including present and future extraterrestrial locations.

It is obvious that the destruction of despair is still our most urgent task. In this regard, we employ paramilitary methods with great care and watchfulness.

The personnel dedicated to this new program are responsible to the mission, not to any national body. We are apprised of all new technologies as soon as available. Hence we have a unique fusion of policy and technology, unique in that its purpose is the abolition of cruelty.

Ours is the first project of its kind to be fully empowered through the new paranational charters. In principle, it is now recognized that both agents and objects of cruelty must be rescued and transformed, and that they sometimes merge into each other.

In response to your inquiry: this is a complex operation. We have a wide range of specializations and concerns. Some are especially calibrated toward language

because of its known and unknown powers
  to bind and to dissociate

because of its capacity
  to ostracize the speechless

because of its capacity
  to nourish self-deception

because of its capacity
  for rebirth and subversion

because of the history
  of torture
    against human speech

2000–2002

III

Territory Shared

ADDRESS

Orientation of the word toward its addressee has an extremely high
significance. In point of fact, word is a two-sided act. It is determined
equally by *whose* word it is and *for whom* it is meant. . . . Each and
every word expresses the "one" in relation to the "other." . . . A word
is territory shared by both addressor and addressee, by the speaker
and his interlocutor.

—V. N. Voloshinov, *Marxism and the Philosophy of Language*

If all we would speak is ideology
believable walking past pent-up Christmas trees
in a California parking lot   day before Thanksgiving   hot sun
                                on faint
scent of spruce   in the supermarket
mixed metaphors of food
faces expectant, baffled, bitter, distracted
wandering aisles or like me and the man ahead of me buying
                            only milk
my car door grabbed open by a woman
thinking it her husband's car honking for her somewhere else

—and I think it true indeed I know
I who came only for milk am speaking it   :   though
would stand somewhere beyond
this civic nausea

: desiring not to stand apart
like Jeffers giving up on his kind   loving only unhuman creatures
because they transcend ideology   in eternity as he thought
but he wasn't writing to them
nor today's gull perched on the traffic light

Nor can this be about remorse
staring over its shopping cart

feeling its vague ideological thoughts

nor about lines of credit
blanketing shame and fear

nor being conscripted for violence
from without   beckoning at rage within

I know what it cannot be

But who   at the checkout this one day
do I address   who is addressing me
what's the approach whose the manners
whose dignity whose truth
when the change purse is tipped into the palm
for an exact amount without which

2002

TRANSPARENCIES

That the meek word like the righteous word can bully
that an Israeli soldier interviewed years
after the first Intifada could mourn on camera
what under orders he did, saw done, did not refuse
that another leaving Beit Jala could scrawl
on a wall: *We are truely sorry for the mess we made*
is merely routine   word that would cancel deed
That human equals innocent and guilty

That we grasp for innocence whether or no
is elementary   That words can translate into broken bones
That the power to hurl words is a weapon
That the body can be a weapon
any child on playground knows   That asked your favorite word
                                               in a game
you always named a thing, a quality, *freedom* or *river*
(never a pronoun never *God* or *War*)
is taken for granted   That word and body
are all we have to lay on the line
That words are windowpanes in a ransacked hut, smeared
by time's dirty rains, we might argue
likewise that words are clear as glass till the sun strikes it blinding

But that in a dark windowpane you have seen your face
That when you wipe your glasses the text grows clearer
That the sound of crunching glass comes at the height of the
                                                  wedding
That I can look through glass
into my neighbor's house
but not my neighbor's life
That glass is sometimes broken to save lives

That a word can be crushed like a goblet underfoot
is only what it seems, part question, part answer: how
                                    you live it

2002

LIVRESQUE

There hangs a space between the man
and his words

    like the space around a few snowflakes
    just languidly beginning

    space
    where an oil rig has dissolved in fog

man in self-arrest
between word and act

writing *agape, agape*
with a silver fountain pen

2002

COLLABORATIONS

I

Thought of this "our" nation : : thought of war
                                 ghosts of war fugitive
    in labyrinths of amnesia
veterans   out-of-date textbooks in a library basement
evidence trundled off   plutonium   under tarps after dark
        didn't realize it until I wrote it

August now   apples have started
                            severing from the tree

over the deck   by night their dim impact

                                        thuds into dreams

by daylight bruised   starting to stew in sun

saying "apple" to nose and tongue

                           to memory

    Word following sense, the way it should be

and if you don't speak the word

                        do you lose your senses

And isn't this just one speck, one atom

               on the glazed surface we call

America

    from which I write

       the war ghosts treading in their shredded

                      disguises above the clouds

and the price we pay here still opaque as the fog

these mornings

       we always say will break open?

II

Try this on your tongue: "the poetry of the enemy"

If you read it will you succumb

Will the enemy's wren fly through your window

and circle your room

Will you smell the herbs hung to dry in the house

he has had to rebuild in words

Would it weaken your will to hear

riffs of the instruments he loves

rustling of rivers remembered

where faucets are dry

"The enemy's water"   is there a phrase
for that in your language?

And you   what do you write
now in your borrowed house   tuned in

to the broadcasts of horror
under a sagging arbor, *dimdumim*

do you grope for poetry
to embrace all this

—not describe, embrace   staggering
in its arms, Jacob-and-angel-wise?

III

Do you understand why I want your voice?
At the seder table it's said

you reclined and said nothing
now in the month of Elul is your throat so dry

your dreams so stony
you wake with their grit in your mouth?

There was a beautiful life here once
Our enemies poisoned it?

Make a list of what's lost but don't
call it a poem

that's for the scriptors of nostalgia
bent to their copying-desks

Make a list of what you love well
twist it   insert it

into a bottle of old Roman glass
go to the edge of the sea

at Haifa where the refugee ships lurched in
and the ships of deportation wrenched away

IV

For Giora Leshem

Drove upcoast   first day of another year   no rain
oxalis gold lakes floating
on January green

Can winter tides off the Levant
churn up wilder spume?

Think Crusades, remember Acre
wind driving at fortress walls

everything returns in time except the
utterly disappeared
What thou lovest well can well be reft from thee

What does not change / is the will
to vanquish
the fascination with what's easiest
see it in any video arcade

is this what the wind is driving at?

Where are you Giora?   whose hands
lay across mine a moment
Can you still believe that afternoon
talking   you smoking   light and shade
on the deck, here in California
our laughter, your questions of translation
your daughter's flute?

2002–2003

RITUAL ACTS

i

We are asking for books
No, not—but a list of books
to be given to young people
Well, to young poets
to guide them in their work
He gestures impatiently
They won't read he says
My time is precious
If they want to they'll find
whatever they need
I'm going for a walk after lunch
After that I lie down
Then and only then do I read the papers
Mornings are for work
the proofs of the second volume
—my trilogy, and he nods
And we too nod recognition

ii

The buses—packed
since the subways are forbidden
and the highways forsaken
so people bring everything on—
what they can't do without—
Air conditioners, sculpture
Double baskets of babies
Fruit platters, crematory urns
Sacks of laundry, of books
Inflated hearts, bass fiddles
Bridal gowns in plastic bags
Pet iguanas, oxygen tanks
The tablets of Moses

iii

After all—to have loved, wasn't that the object?
Love is the only thing in life
but then you can love too much
or the wrong way, you lose
yourself or you lose
the person
or you strangle each other
Maybe the object of love is
    to have loved
    greatly
    at one time or another
Like a cinema trailer
watched long ago

iv

You need to turn yourself around
face in another direction
She wrapped herself in a flag
soaked it in gasoline and lit a match
This is for the murdered babies
they say she said
Others heard
for the honor of my country
Others remember
the smell and how she screamed
Others say, This was just theater

v

This will not be a love scene
but an act between two humans
Now please let us see you
tenderly scoop his balls
into your hand
You will hold them
under your face
There will be tears on your face
That will be all
the director said
We will not see his face
He wants to do the scene
but not to show
his face

vi

A goat devouring a flowering plant
A child squeezing through a fence to school
A woman slicing an onion
A bare foot sticking out
A wash line tied to a torn-up tree
A dog's leg lifted at a standpipe
An old man kneeling to drink there
A hand on the remote

We would like to show but to not be obvious
except to the oblivious
We want to show ordinary life
We are dying to show it

2003

POINT IN TIME

If she's writing a letter on a sheet of mica
to be left on the shelf of the cave
with the century's other letters each
stained with its own DNA expressed
in love's naked dark or the dawn
of a day of stone:
it's a fact like a town crosshaired on a map
But we are not keeping archives here
where all can be blown away
nor raking the graves in Père-Lachaise
nor is she beholden or dutiful
as her pen pushes its final stroke
into the mineral page

molecule speaking to molecule
for just this moment

This is the point in time when
she must re-condense her purpose
like ink, like rain, like winter light
like foolishness and hatred
like the blood her hand first knew
as a wet patch on the staircase wall
she was feeling her way down in the dark.

2003

IV

Alternating Current

Sometimes I'm back in that city
in its/   not my/   autumn
                    crossing a white bridge
over a dun-green river
eating shellfish with young poets
under the wrought-iron roof of the great market
drinking with the dead poet's friend
                    to music struck
from odd small instruments

walking arm in arm with the cinematographer
through the whitelight gardens of Villa Grimaldi
earth and air stretched
to splitting still
                    his question:
have you ever been in a place like this?

•

No bad dreams.   Night, the bed, the faint clockface.
No bad dreams.   Her arm or leg or hair.
No bad dreams.   A wheelchair unit screaming
off the block.   No bad dreams.   Pouches of blood: red cells,
plasma.   Not here.   No, none.   Not yet.

•

Take one, take two
—camera out of focus   delirium swims
across the lens   Don't get me wrong   I'm not
critiquing your direction
but I was there   saw what you didn't

take   the care
you didn't   first of yourself then
of the child   Don't get me wrong I'm on
your side but standing off
where it rains   not on the set where it's
not raining yet
take three

•

What's suffered in laughter   in aroused afternoons
in nightly yearlong back-to-back
wandering each others' nerves and pulses
O changing love that doesn't change

•

A deluxe blending machine
A chair with truth's coat of arms
A murderous code of manners
A silver cocktail reflecting a tiny severed hand
A small bird stuffed with print and roasted
A row of Lucite chessmen filled with shaving lotion
A bloodred valentine to power
A watered-silk innocence
A microwaved foie gras
A dry-ice carrier for conscience donations
A used set of satin sheets folded to go
A box at the opera of suffering
A fellowship at the villa, all expenses
A Caterpillar's tracks gashing the environment
A bad day for students of the environment
A breakdown of the blending machine
A rush to put it in order
A song in the chapel a speech a press release

As finally by wind or grass
   drive-ins
           where romance always was
   an after-dark phenomenon
                 lie crazed and still
   great panoramas lost to air
      this time this site of power shall pass
         and we remain or not but not remain
   as now we think we are

•

For J.J.

             When we are shaken out

when we are shaken out to the last vestige
when history is done with us
   when our late grains glitter
               salt swept into shadow
   indignant and importunate strife-fractured crystals
will it matter if our tenderness (our solidarity)
            abides in residue
   long as there's tenderness and solidarity

Could the tempos and attunements of my voice
   in a poem or yours   or yours and mine
in telephonic high hilarity
             cresting above some stupefied inanity
   be more than personal

(and—as you once said—what's wrong with that?)

2002–2003

V

If some long unborn friend
looks at photos in pity,
we say, sure we were happy,
but it was not in the wind.

MEMORIZE THIS

i

Love for twenty-six years, you can't stop
A withered petunia's crisp   the bud sticky   both are dark
The flower engulfed in its own purple   So common, nothing
                                        like it
The old woodstove gone to the dump
Sun plunges through the new skylight
This morning's clouds piled like autumn in Massachusetts
This afternoon's far-flung like the Mojave
Night melts one body into another
One drives fast the other maps a route
Thought new it becomes familiar
From thirteen years back maybe
One oils the hinges one edges the knives
One loses an earring the other finds it
One says I'd rather make love
Than go to the Greek Festival
The other, I agree.

ii

Take a strand of your hair
on my fingers let it fall
across the pillow   lift to my nostrils
inhale your body entire

Sleeping with you after
weeks apart   how normal
yet   after midnight
to turn and slide my arm

along your thigh
drawn up in sleep
what delicate amaze

2002–2003

THE PAINTER'S HOUSE

Nineteen-thirties Midwestern
—the painter long gone to the sea—
plutonic sycamore by the shed
a mailbox open mouthed
in garden loam a chip
of veiny china   turned
up there where he might have stood

eyeing the dim lip of grass
beyond, the spring stars sharpening
above

Well since there's still light   walk around
stand on the porch
cup hands around eyes peering in

Is this the kitchen where she worked and thought
Is that the loft where their bodies fell
into each other   The nail where the mirror
hung   the shelf where her college books
eyed her aslant
Those stairs would her bare feet have felt?

In the mute shed no trace
of masterworks   occult
fury of pigment   no

downslash of provocation
no whirled hands at the doorjamb
no lightning streak   no stab in the dark
no   sex   no   face

2003

AFTER APOLLINAIRE & BRASSENS

When the bridge of lovers bends
over the oilblack river
and we see our own endings
through eyes aching and blearing
when the assault begins
and we're thrown apart still longing

when the Bridge of Arts trembles
under the streaked sky
when words of the poets tumble
into the shuddering stream
where who knew what joy
would leap after what pain

what flows under the Seine
Mississippi Jordan Tigris
Elbe Amazon Indus Nile

and all the tributaries
who knows where song goes
now and from whom
toward what longings

2003

SLASHES

Years pass   and two   who once
don't know each other at all
dark strokes gouge a white wall   as lives
and customs slashed by dates :   October '17/May '68
                              /September '73
Slash across lives   memory pursues its errands
    a lent linen shirt pulled unabashedly over her naked shoulders
      cardamom seed bitten in her teeth
                            watching him chop onions
    words in the air   *segregation/partition/apartheid*
    vodka/cigarette smoke   a time
                    vertigo on subway stairs
Years pass   she pressing the time into a box
not to be opened   a box
quelling pleasure and pain

You could describe something like this
in gossip   write a novel   get it wrong

    In wolf-tree, see the former field
The river's muscle :   greater than its length
the lake's light-blistered blue :   scorning
           circumference
A map inscribes relation
                only when
underground aquifers are fathomed in
water table rising or falling
    beneath apparently
      imperturbable earth

    music from a basement session overheard

2002

TRACE ELEMENTS

Back to the shallow pond   sharp rotting scatter
leaf-skinned edge there   where the ring
couldn't be sunk far out enough
                    (far enough from shore)

back out the rock-toothed logging road
to the dark brook where it's dropped   mudsucked gold
                    (sucked under stones)
that's another marriage   lucid and decisive
to say at last: I did, I do, I will
                    (I did not, I will not)

Snow-whirled streetlamps under a window
                    (a bedroom and a window)
icy inch of the raised sash   blizzard clearing to calm
outlined furniture: figured mirror: bedded bodies:
              warm blood: eyes in the dark:
                      no contradiction:

              She was there
and they were there: her only   now   seeing it   (only now)

Bow season: then gun season
Apricot leaves bloodsprinkled: soaked: case closed

Memory: echo in time

All's widescreen now   lurid inchoate century
Vast disappearing acts   *the greatest show on earth*

    but here are small clear refractions
    from an unclear season

blood on a leaf
gold trace element in water
light from the eye behind the eye

2003

BRACT

Stories of three islands
you've told me, over years
over meals, after quarrels,
light changing the spectrum of your hair
your green eyes, lying on our backs
naked or clothed, driving
through wind, eighteen-wheeler trucks
of produce crates ahead and behind
you saying, I couldn't live long
far from the ocean

Spring of new and continuing
war, harpsichord crashing
under Verlet's fingers
I tell you I could not live long
far from your anger
lunar reefed and tidal
bloodred bract from spiked stem
tossing on the ocean

2003

VI

Dislocations:
Seven Scenarios

1

Still learning the word
"home"   or what it could mean
                    say, to relinquish

   a backdrop of Japanese maples turning
   color of rusted wheelbarrow bottom
   where the dahlia tubers were thrown

You must go live in the city now
over the subway though not on
                    its grating

must endure the foreign music
of the block party

finger in useless anger
the dangling cords of the window blind

2

In a vast dystopic space the small things
multiply

when all the pills run out the pain
grows more general

flies find the many eyes
quarrels thicken then
                    weaken

tiny mandibles of rumor open and close
blame has a name that will not be spoken

you grasp or share a clot of food
according to your nature
                              or your strength

love's ferocity snarls
from under the drenched blanket's hood

3

City and world: this infection drinks like a drinker
whatever it can

casual salutations first
little rivulets of thought

then wanting stronger stuff
sucks at the marrow of selves

the nurse's long knowledge of wounds
the rabbi's scroll of ethics
the young worker's defiance

only the solipsist seems intact
in her prewar building

4

For recalcitrancy of attitude
the surgeon is transferred
to the V.A. hospital   where poverty
is the administrator
of necessity and her
orders don't necessarily
get obeyed
because

the government
is paying
and the
used-to-be
warriors
are patients

5

Faces in the mesh: defiance or disdain
      remember Paul Nizan?
            You thought you were innocent if you said

"I love this woman and I want to live
      in accordance with my love"
          but you were beginning the revolution

maybe so, maybe not
      look at her now
          pale lips papery flesh

at your creased belly   wrinkled sac
      look at the scars
          reality's autographs

along your ribs across her haunches
look at the collarbone's reverberant line

      how in a body can defiance
          still embrace its likeness

6

Not to get up and go back to the drafting table
where failure crouches accusing

like the math test you bluffed and flunked
so early on
not to drag into the window's
cruel and truthful light   your blunder
not to start over

but to turn your back, saying
all anyway is compromise
impotence and collusion
from here on I will be no part of it

is one way could you afford it

7

Tonight someone will sleep in a stripped apartment
the last domestic traces, cup and towel
awaiting final disposal

—has ironed his shirt for travel
left an envelope for the cleaning woman
on the counter under the iron

internationalist turning toward home
three continents to cross   documents declarations
searches queues

and home no simple matter
of hearth or harbor
bleeding from internal wounds

he diagnosed   physician
without frontiers

2002

VII

FIVE O'CLOCK, JANUARY 2003

Tonight as cargoes of my young
fellow countrymen and women are being hauled
into positions aimed at death, positions
they who did not will it suddenly
have to assume
I am thinking of Ed Azevedo
half-awake in recovery
if he has his arm whole
and how much pain he must bear
under the drugs
On cliffs above a beach
luxuriant in low tide after storms
littered with driftwood hurled and piled and
humanly arranged in fantastic
installations and beyond
silk-blue and onion-silver-skinned
Jeffers' "most glorious creature on earth"
we passed, greeting, I saw his arm
bandaged to the elbow
asked and he told me: It was just
a small cut, nothing, on the hand he'd
washed in peroxide thinking
that was it until the pain began
traveling up his arm
and then the antibiotics the splint the
numbing drugs the sick sensation
and this evening at five o'clock the emergency
surgery and last summer
the train from Czechoslovakia to Spain
with his girl, cheap wine, bread and cheese
room with a balcony, ocean like this
nobody asking for pay in advance
kindness of foreigners
in that country, sick sensation now
needing to sit in his brother's truck again

even the accident on the motorcycle
was nothing like this
I'll be thinking of you at five
this evening I said
afterward you'll feel better, your body
will be clean of this poison
I didn't say Your war is here
but could you have believed
that from a small thing infection
would crawl through the blood
and the enormous ruffled shine
of an ocean wouldn't tell you.

2003

WAIT

In paradise every
the desert wind is rising
third thought
in hell there are no thoughts
is of earth
sand screams against your government
issued tent   hell's noise
in your nostrils   crawl
into your ear-shell
wrap yourself in no-thought
wait   no place for the little lyric
wedding-ring glint the reason why
on earth
they never told you

2003

DON'T TAKE ME

too seriously   please
    take the December goodness
       of my neighbors' light-strung eaves
    take the struggle helping with the tree
       for the children's sake
          don't take me seriously
  on questionnaires about faith and fault
     and country   Don't
        take me for a loner don't take me for a foreigner don't
take me in the public
     library checking definitions
        of freedom in the dictionary or
   tracing satellites after curfew
or in my Goodwill truck delivering a repaired TV
    to the house of the foil'd revolutionary

2002

TO HAVE WRITTEN THE TRUTH

To have spent hours stalking the whine of an insect
have smashed its body in blood on a door
then lain sleepless with rage

to have played in the ship's orchestra crossing
the triangle route
dissonant arpeggios under cocktail clatter

to have written the truth in a lightning flash
then crushed those words in your hand
balled-up and smoking

when self-absolution
easygoing pal of youth
leans in the doorframe

Kid, you always
                            took yourself so hard!

2003

SCREEN DOOR

Metallic slam on a moonless night
A short visit and so we departed.
A short year with many long
                              days
A long phone call with many   pauses.
                      It was gesture's code
we were used to using, we were
                          awkward without it.

Over the phone: knocking heard
at a door in another country.
Here it's tonight: there tomorrow.
A vast world we used to think small.
That we knew everyone who mattered.

Firefly flicker.   Metallic slam.   A moonless night.   Too dark
                         for gesture.
But it was gesture's code we were used to.
                        Might need again.   Urgent
                        hold-off or beckon.

Fierce supplication. One finger pointing: "Thither."
Palms flung upward: "What now?"
Hand slicing the air or across the throat.
A long wave to the departing.

2003

VIII

Tendril

TENDRIL

1

Why does the outstretched finger of home
probe the dark hotel room like a flashlight beam

on the traveller, half-packed, sitting on the bed
face in hands, wishing her bag emptied again at home

Why does the young security guard
pray to keep standing watch forever, never to fly

Why does he wish he were boarding
as the passengers file past him into the plane

What are they carrying in their bundles
what vanities, superstitions, little talismans

What have the authorities intercepted
who will get to keep it

2

Half-asleep in the dimmed cabin
she configures a gecko

aslant the overhead bin   tendrils of vine
curling up through the cabin floor

buried here in night as in a valley
remote from rescue

Unfound, confounded, vain, superstitious, whatever we were
                                                    before
now we are still, outstretched, curled, however we were

Unwatched the gecko, the inching of green
through the cracks in the fused imperious shell

3

Dreaming a womb's languor valleyed in death
among fellow strangers

she has merely slept through the night
a nose nearby rasps, everyone in fact is breathing

the gecko has dashed into some crevice
of her brain, the tendrils retract

orange juice is passed on trays
declarations filled out in the sudden dawn

4

She can't go on dreaming of mass death
this was not to have been her métier

she says to the mirror in the toilet
a bad light any way you judge yourself

and she's judge, prosecutor, witness, perpetrator
of her time

's conspiracies of the ignorant
with the ruthless   She's the one she's looking at

5

This confessional reeks of sweet antiseptic
and besides she's not confessing

her mind balks   craving wild onions
nostril-chill of eucalyptus

that seventh sense of what's missing
against what's supplied

She walks at thirty thousand feet into the cabin
sunrise crashing through the windows

Cut the harping she tells herself
You're human, porous like all the rest

6

She was to have sat in a vaulted
library   heavy scrolls wheeled to a desk

for sieving, sifting, translating
all morning   then a quick lunch   thick coffee

then light descending slowly
on earthen-colored texts

but that's a dream of dust
frail are thy tents   humanity

facing thy monologues of force
She must have fallen asleep reading

7

She must have fallen asleep reading
The woman who mopped the tiles

is deliquescent   a scarlet gel
her ligaments and lungs

her wrought brain   her belly's pulse
disrupt among others mangled there

the chief librarian the beggar
the man with the list of questions

the scrolls never to be translated
and the man who wheeled the scrolls

8

She had wanted to find meaning in the past but the future drove
a vagrant tank a rogue bulldozer

rearranging the past in a blip
coherence smashed into vestige

not for her even the thought
of her children's children picking up

one shard of tile then another laying
blue against green seeing words

in three scripts flowing through vines and flowers
guessing at what it was

the levantine debris
Not for her but still for someone?

2003

TELEPHONE RINGING
IN THE LABYRINTH

(2004–2006)

For Aijaz Ahmad
and
in memory of
F. O. Matthiessen
1902–1950

Poetry isn't easy to come by.
You have to write it like you owe a debt to the world.
In that way poetry is how the world comes to be in you.

—Alan Davies

Poetry is not self-expression, the I is a dramatic I.

—Michael S. Harper,
quoting Sterling A. Brown

To which I would add: and so, unless
otherwise indicated, is the You.

—A.R.

I

VOYAGE TO THE DENOUEMENT

A child's hand smears a wall   the reproof is bitter
     wall contrives to linger   child, punisher, gone in smoke
An artisan lays on hues: lemon, saffron, gold
     stare hard before you start covering the whole room
Inside the thigh a sweet mole   on the balding
     skull an irregular island   what comes next
After the burnt forests   silhouettes wade
     liquid hibiscus air
Velvet rubs down to scrim   iron utensils
     discolor unseasoned
Secret codes of skin and hair
     go dim   left from the light too long

Because my wish was to have things simpler
     than they were   memory too became
a smudge   sediment from a hand
     repeatedly lying on the same surface
Call it a willful optimism
     from when old ownerships unpeeled   curled out
into the still nameless   new imperium   Call it
     haplessness of a creature   not yet ready
for her world-citizen's papers
     (Across the schoolroom mural   bravely
small ships did under sail traverse great oceans)
     Rain rededicates the exhumed
African burial ground
     traffic lashes its edges
the city a scar a fragment floating
     on tidal dissolution
The opal on my finger
     fiercely flashed till the hour it started to crumble

2004

CALIBRATIONS

She tunes her guitar for Landstuhl
where she will sit on beds and sing
ballads from when Romany
roamed Spain

•

A prosthetic hand calibrates perfectly
the stem of a glass
or how to stroke a face
is this how far we have come
to make love easy

Ghost limbs go into spasm in the night
You come back from war with the body you have

•

What you can't bear
carry endure lift
you'll have to drag

it'll come with you the ghostlimb

the shadow   blind
echo of your body spectre of your soul

•

Let's not talk yet of making love
nor of ingenious devices
replacing touch

And this is not theoretical:
A poem with calipers to hold a heart
so it will want to go on beating

2004

SKELETON KEY

In the marina an allegro creaking
boats on the tide
each with its own sway
                                        rise and fall
acceptance and refusal
La Barqueta, My Pelican

barometer in the body
rising and falling

•

A small wound, swallow-shaped, on my wrist
ripped by a thorn
exacerbated by ash and salt

And this is how I came to be
protector of the private
and enemy of the personal

•

Then I slept, and had a dream
No more
No màs

From now on, only
reason's drugged and dreamless sleep

•

Creeps down the rockface   shadow cast
from an opposite crag exactly at that moment
you needed light on the trail   These are the shortening days
you forgot about   bent on your own design

•

Cut me a skeleton key
to that other time, that city
talk starting up, deals and poetry

Tense with elation, exiles
walking old neighborhoods
calm journeys of streetcars

revived boldness of cats
locked eyes of couples
music playing full blast again

Exhuming the dead   Their questions

2004

WALLPAPER

1

A room papered with clippings:
newsprint in bulging patches
none of them mentions our names
none from that history then   O red

kite snarled in a cloud
small plane melted in fog: no matter:
I worked to keep it current
and meaningful: a job of living I thought

history as wallpaper
urgently selected clipped and pasted
but the room itself   nowhere

gone the address   the house
golden-oak banisters zigzagging
upward, stained glass on the landings
streaked porcelain in the bathrooms

loose floorboards quitting in haste we pried
up to secrete the rash imagination
of a time to come

What we said then, our breath   remains
otherwhere: in me   in you

2

Sonata for Unaccompanied Minor
Fugitive Variations
discs we played over and over

on the one-armed phonograph
Childish we were in our adoration
of the dead composer

who'd ignored the weather signs
trying to cross the Andes
stupidly   I'd say now

and you'd agree   seasoned
as we are   working stretched
weeks   eating food bought

with ordinary grudging wages
keeping up with rent, utilities

a job of living as I said

3

Clocks are set back   quick dark
snow filters past my lashes
this is the common ground

white-crusted sidewalks   windshield wipers
licking, creaking
to and *fro   to* and *fro*

If the word gets out if the word
escapes if the word

flies if it dies
it has its way of coming back

The handwritings on the walls
are vast and coded

the music blizzards past

2004

IN PLAIN SIGHT

My neighbor moving
in a doorframe   moment's
reach of her hand   then

withdrawn   As from some old
                    guilty pleasure

Smile etched like a scar
which must be borne
                    Smile
in a photograph taken against one's will

Her son up on a ladder stringing
along the gutter
electric icicles in a temperate zone

If the suffering hidden in plain sight
is of her past her future
or the thin-ice present where
we're balancing here
                    or how she sees it
I can't presume

. . . Ice-thin.   Cold and precarious
the land I live in and have argued not to leave
Cold on the verge of crease
                              crack without notice

ice-green disjuncture   treasoning us
to flounder cursing each other
Cold and grotesque the sex
the grimaces the grab

A privilege   you say
to live here   *A luxury*
Everyone still wants to come here!
You want a Christmas card, a greeting
to tide us over
with pictures of the children

then you demand a valentine
an easterlily   anything for the grab
a mothersday menu   wedding invitation

It's not as in a museum that I
observe
and mark in every Face I meet

            under crazed surfaces
traces of feeling   locked in shadow

Not as in a museum of history
do I pace here   nor as one who in a show
of bland paintings shrugs and walks on   I gaze
through faces   not as an X-ray
                              nor

as paparazzo shooting
the compromised celebrity

nor archaeologist filming
the looted site
nor as the lover tearing out of its frame
the snapshot to be held to a flame

but as if a mirror
forced to reflect a room
                              the figures

standing   the figures crouching

2004

BEHIND THE MOTEL

A man lies under a car half bare
a child plays bullfight with a torn cloth
hemlocks grieve in wraps of mist
a woman talks on the phone, looks in a mirror
fiddling with the metal pull of a drawer

She has seen her world wiped clean, the cloth
that wiped it disintegrate in mist
or dying breath on the skin of a mirror
She has felt her life close like a drawer
has awoken somewhere else, bare

He feels his skin as if it were mist
as if his face would show in no mirror
He needs some bolts he left in a vanished drawer
crawls out into the hemlocked world with his bare
hands, wipes his wrench on an oil-soaked cloth

stares at the woman talking into a mirror
who has shut the phone into the drawer
while over and over with a torn cloth
at the edge of hemlocks behind the bare
motel a child taunts a horned beast made from mist

2004

PIANO MÉLANCOLIQUE (extraits)

par Élise Turcotte

N'emporte rien avec toi.
Essayons de croire
qu'il n'y a rien dans mes poumons.
Qu'aucune maladie ne noircit
tes yeux.
Que je t'écris de la mangrove
pour te parler des palétuviers
qui sont les personnages
les plus mystérieux que j'aie vu.

Fantomatique, comme les
arbres, je reviens aux paysages.

Vapeurs et reflets.
Et petites racines aériennes
fixées au bas de ma robe.

MELANCHOLY PIANO (extracts)

from the French of Élise Turcotte

Take nothing with you
Let's try believing
there's nothing in my lungs.
That no sickness clouds
your eyes.
That I write you from the swamp
to tell you about the mangroves
the most mysterious
presences I've seen.

Spectral as the
trees, I return to landscape.

Fumes and reflections.
And little airy roots
stuck to the hem of my skirt.

Je me décris comme un animal
à plumes.
Je décris. Tu regardes.
Tandis que poussent mes plumes.

La nuit, tu cherches un motif fragile,
un relief aussi précis qu'un visage
aimé.

Des insectes occupent la chapelle cachée
sous le sable.

Beaucoup d'années ont passé
jusqu'ici.

I describe myself as a feathered
animal.
I describe.   You watch.
While my plumes grow.

Nights, you search for a fragile cause
set in relief, precise as a loved
face.

Insects dwell in the chapel hidden
in sand.

Many years have gone by
until this moment.

C'est la nuit qui parle,
dis-tu.
Mon poème sans mot.
Ma fuite en terre sauvage.

Le corps est léger quand
il est pris pour ce qu'il est.
Composé de murs et de
fenêtres.
Prêt à brûler.
Avec des petits drapeaux
flottant au centre.

Je te caresse avec le secours
du vide.
Une ode à la survie.
Un dictionnaire d'herbes folles.
Pour guérir, nous sommes prêts
à tout.

Night is speaking
you say.
My poem without words.
My flight into wild country.

The body is light when
taken for what it is.
Formed of walls and
windows.
Ready to burn.
With little flags
fluttering   in the center.

I touch you with the help
of the void.
An ode to survival.
A dictionary of wild grasses.
We'll do anything
for a cure.

2004

II

ARCHAIC

Cold wit leaves me cold
this time of the world   Multifoliate disorders
straiten my gait   Minuets don't become me
Been wanting to get out   see the sights
but the exits are slick with people
going somewhere fast
every one with a shared past
and a mot juste   And me so out of step
with my late-night staircase inspirations   my
utopian slant

Still, I'm alive here
in this village drawn in a tightening noose
of ramps and cloverleafs
but the old directions I drew up
for you
are obsolete

Here's how
to get to me
I wrote
Don't misconstrue the distance
take along something for the road
everything might be closed
this isn't a modern place

You arrived starving at midnight
I gave you warmed-up food
poured tumblers of brandy
put on Les Barricades Mystérieuses
—the only jazz in the house
We talked for hours   of barricades
lesser and greater sorrows

ended up laughing in the thicksilver
birdstruck light

2005

LONG AFTER STEVENS

A locomotive pushing through snow in the mountains
more modern than the will

to be modern   The mountain's profile
in undefiled snow disdains

definitions of poetry   It was always
indefinite, task and destruction

the laser eye of the poet   her blind eye
her moment-stricken eye   her unblinking eye

She had to get down from the blocked train
lick snow from bare cupped hands

taste what had soared into that air
—local cinders, steam of the fast machine

clear her plate with a breath   distinguish
through tumbling whiteness   figures

frozen   figures advancing
weapons at the ready
for the new password

She had to feel her tongue
freeze and burn at once

instrument searching, probing
toward a foreign tongue

2005

IMPROVISATION ON LINES FROM EDWIN MUIR'S "VARIATIONS ON A TIME THEME"

Packed in my skin from head to toe
Is one I know and do not know

He never speaks to me yet is at home
More snug than embryo in the womb . . .

His name's Indifference
Nothing offending he is all offence . . .

Can note with a lack-lustre eye
Victim and murderer go by . . .

If I could drive this demon out
I'd put all Time's display to rout . . .

Or so I dream when at my door
I hear my Soul, my Visitor.

He comes but seldom, and I cannot tell
If he's myself or one who loves me well
And comes in pity, for he pities all . . .

Victim and murderer . . . Vision's
bloodshot wandering eye engages and

the whetted tool moves toward the hand
scrapes down an impassive sky   debrides

the panicked face   erases or redresses
with understrokes and slashes

in smeared roughed-over surfaces
false moves bad guesses

pausing to gauge its own
guilty innocence, desire

to make it clear yet leave the field
still dark and dialectical

This is unpitying yet not cold

—And Muir I wonder, standing under
the bruised eye-socket of late-winter sun

about your circling double-bind
between indifference and pity

your dream of history as Eden's
loss, all else as repetition

—Wonder at your old opposite
number, Hugh MacDiarmid

his populated outraged joy
his ear for Lenin and for Rilke

for the particular and vast
the thistle's bony elegance

the just, the wild, the urge, the cry for
what must change what be demolished
what secreted for the future

bardic or technological
together dialectical

2005–2006

RHYME

Walking by the fence but the house
 not there

going to the river but the
 river looking spare

bones of the river spread out
 everywhere

O tell me this is home

Crossing the bridge but
 some planks not there

looking at the shore but only
 getting back the glare

dare you trust the river when there's
 no water there

O tell me is this home

Getting into town seeing
   nobody I know

folks standing around
   nowhere to go

staring into the air like
   they saw a show

O tell me was this my home

Come to the railroad no train
   on the tracks

switchman in his shanty
   with a great big axe

so what happened here so what
   are the facts

So tell me where is my home

2005

HOTEL

I dreamed the Finnish Hotel founded by Finns in an olden time
It was in New York had been there a long time
Finnish sea-captains had stayed there in their time
It had fallen on one then another bad time
Now restored it wished to be or seem of the olden time
The Finnish Hotel founded by Finns in an olden time

There was a perpendicular lighted sign along its spine:
THE FINNISH HOTEL and on the desk aligned
two lamps like white globes and a blond
wood lounge with curved chairs and a bar beyond
serving a clear icy liquor of which the captains had been fond
reputedly in the olden time

In the Finnish Hotel I slept on a mattress stuffed with straw
after drinking with a Finnish captain who regarded me with awe
saying, Woman who could put away that much I never saw
but I did not lie with him on the mattress, his major flaw
being he was a phantom of the olden time
and I a woman still almost in my prime

dreaming the Finnish Hotel founded by Finns in the olden time

2005

THREE ELEGIES

i. LATE STYLE

Propped on elbow in stony light
Green lawns of entitlement
out the window you can neither
open nor close

man crouched in den flung trembling
back on failed gifts
lapsed desire   A falling
star   Dim, trapped
in the narrow place of fame

And beneath the skin of boredom
indecipherable fear

ii. AS EVER

As ever, death.   Whenever, where.   But it's
the drawn-together life we're finally
muted by.   Must stand, regard as whole
what was still partial   still
under revision.   So it felt, so we thought.

Then to hear sweep
the scythe on grass
still witherless and sweet

iii. FALLEN FIGURE

The stone walls will recede and the needs that laid them
scar of winter sun stretch low
behind the advancing junipers

darkness rise up from the whitening pond

Crusted silver your breath in this ditch
the pitchfork in your hand
still stuck to your hand

The northern lights
will float, probe, vacillate

the yellow eye
of the snowplow you used to drive
will seek and find you

2005

HUBBLE PHOTOGRAPHS: AFTER
SAPPHO

It should be the most desired sight of all
the person with whom you hope to live and die

walking into a room, turning to look at you, sight for sight
Should be yet I say there is something

more desirable: the ex-stasis of galaxies
so out from us there's no vocabulary

but mathematics and optics
equations letting sight pierce through time

into liberations, lacerations of light and dust
exposed like a body's cavity, violet green livid and venous,
    gorgeous

beyond good and evil as ever stained into dream
beyond remorse, disillusion, fear of death

or life, rage
for order, rage for destruction

—beyond this love which stirs
the air every time she walks into the room

These impersonae, however we call them
won't invade us as on movie screens

they are so old, so new, we are not to them
we look at them or don't from within the milky gauze

of our tilted gazing
but they don't look back and we cannot hurt them

For Jack Litewka

2005

THIS IS NOT THE ROOM

of polished tables lit with medalled
torsos bent toward microphones
where ears lean hands scribble
"working the dark side"

—glazed eye meeting frozen eye—

This is not the room where tears down carven
cheeks track rivulets in the scars
left by the gouging tool
where wood itself is weeping

where the ancient painted eye speaks to the living eye

This is the room
where truth scrubs around the pedestal of the toilet
flings her rag into the bucket
straightens up   spits at the mirror

2005

UNKNOWN QUANTITY

Spring nights you pillow your head on a sack
of rich compost   Charcoal, your hair

sheds sparks through your muttered dreams
Deep is your sleep in the starless dark

and you wake in your live skin to show me
a tulip   Not the prizewinning Queen of the Night

furled in her jade wrappings
but the Prince of Darkness, the not-yet, the X

crouched in his pale bulb
held out in the palm of your hand

Shall we bury him wait and see what happens
will there be time for waiting and to see

2005

TACTILE VALUE

from crush and splinter
death in the market

jeering robotic
dry-ice disrupt

to conjure this:
perishing
persistent script

scratched-up smeared
and torn

> *let hair, nail cuttings*
> *nourish the vine and fig tree*

> *let man, woman*
> *eat, be sheltered*

•

Marx the physician laid his ear
on the arhythmic heart

felt the belly
diagnosed the pain

did not precisely write
of lips roaming damp skin

hand plunged in hair   bed-laughter
mouth clasping mouth

> *(what we light with this coalspark*
> *living instantly in us*
> *if it continue*

2005–2006

MIDNIGHT, THE SAME DAY

i

When the sun seals my eyes the emblem
of failure will still be standing
motionless at this intersection
between family restaurant
and medical clinic
wearing his cardboard necklace lettered
H ARD LU CK

until his sister
the Fury of reparations
descends
curdling the air in whirlwind
tears it from his neck
picks him up and hurls on

ii

Try to rest now, says a voice.
Another: *Give yourself time.*
But rest is no act of will
and gifts to the self come back unopened
Milk will boil down in the iron pot
blistering into black sugar,
scalded vinegar lift
crispened layers
pages of a codex
in a library blown away

2005

EVEN THEN MAYBE

Not spent   those bloodshot friendships   those
soul-marriages sealed and torn
those smiles of pain
I told her a mouthful
I shut my mouth against him
Throat thick with tears
how words sound when you swallow
—and under the roof
of the mouth   long stroke
reaching from the tongue's root

No, I was not living with her at the time
At the time I was not living
with him, at the time we were living together
I was living with neither of them
—was dwelling you could say
But as for living at that time
we were all living together with many others
for whom living was precisely the question

Haven't seen evenings like that since
vesuvian emerald to brass dissolving
—a sentence you'd waited for
taken back half-spoken—
Luxury even then maybe
evenings like those

2005

DIRECTOR'S NOTES

You don't want a harsh outcry here
not to violate the beauty yet
dawn unveiling ochre village
but to show coercion
within that beauty, endurance required
Begin with girl
pulling hand over hand on chain
only sound drag and creak
in time it becomes monotonous

then must begin sense of unease produced by monotony
repetitive motion, repetitive sound
resistance, irritation
increasing for the viewers
sense of what are they here for, anyway
dislike of the whole thing how boring to watch

(they aren't used to duration
this was a test)

Keep that dislike that boredom as a value
also as risk
so when bucket finally tinks at rim
they breathe a sigh, not so much relief
as finally grasping
what all this was for

dissolve as she dips from bucket

2005

REREADING *THE DEAD LECTURER*

Overthrow.   And make new.

An idea.   And we felt it.
A meaning.   And we caught it
as the dimensions spread, gathering
in pre-utopian basements   figured shadows
scrawled with smoke and music.
                    Shed the dead hand,
let sound be sense.   A world
echoing everywhere, Fanon, Freire, thin pamphlets lining
raincoat pockets, poetry on walls, damp purple mimeos cranking
—the feeling of an idea.   An idea of feeling.

That love could be so resolute

And the past?   Overthrow of systems, forms
could not overthrow the past
                  nor our
                      neglect of consequences.
Nor that cold will we misnamed.

There were consequences.   A world
repeating everywhere: the obliterations.
What's surreal, hyperreal, virtual,
what's poetry what's verse what's new.   What is
a political art.   If we
(who?) ever were conned
into mere definitions.
                If we
                    accept

(book of a soul contending

2005

III

LETTERS CENSORED
SHREDDED
RETURNED TO SENDER
OR JUDGED UNFIT TO SEND

Unless in quotation marks (for which see Notes on the Poems), the
letter fragments are written by various imaginary persons.

"We must prevent this mind from functioning . . .": words of the
prosecutor sentencing Antonio Gramsci to prison, June 2, 1928.

—Could you see me laboring over this
right arm in sling, typing left-handed with one finger—

{*On a scale of one to ten what is your pain today*}

•

—shall I measure the split atoms
of pleasure flying outward from the core—

•

—To think of her naked every day unfreezes me—

•

Banditry, rapes, burning the woods
"a kind of primitive class struggle
with no lasting or effective results"

—The bakers strike, the needleworkers strike, the mechanics strike,
the miners strike

the great machine coughs out the pieces and hurtles on—

•

—then there are days all thought comes down to sound:
Rust.   August.   Mattress.   Must.
Chains . . .

—when consciousness + sensation feels like/ = suffering—

•

—the people, yes, as yet unformed—deformed—no: disinformed—

•

—What's realistic fantasy?—Call it hope—

•

—heard your voice on the news tonight, its minor key
your old-fashioned mindfulness—could have loved you again—

•

—Autumn invades my body, anger
wrapped in forgiving sunlight, fear of the cold—

•

—Words gather like flies above this carcass of meaning—

•

"this void, this vacuum"

•

—You think you are helpless because you are empty-handed
of concepts that could become your strength—

•

—we're told it's almost over, but we see no sign of it yet—

•

"caught between a feeling of immense tenderness for you
which seems . . . a weakness
that could only be consoled
by an immediate physical caress . . ."

   [*We must prevent this mind from functioning for twenty years*]

". . . and these inadequate, cold and colorless words"

•

—What I meant to write, belov'd critic, then struck it out
thinking you might accuse me of
whatever you would:
I wanted a sensual materialism to utter pleasure

Something beyond a cry that could sound like a groan—

•

—Vocalizing forbidden syllables—

•

—our mythologies choke us, we have enthralled ourselves—

•

   [*Writing like this for the censors
   but I won't hide behind words*]

•

"my body cells revolve in unison
with the whole universe

    The cycle of the seasons, the progression of the solstices
    and equinoxes
    I feel them as flesh of my flesh
    and under the snow the first violets are already trembling
        In short, time has seemed to me a thing of flesh
        ever since space
        ceased to exist for me"

•

—History = bodies in time—

or, in your language:

$$H = \frac{T}{b}$$

•

—to think of the one asleep
in that field beside the chimney
of the burnt-out house
a thing of flesh, exhausted—

•

—this flash is all we know. . . . can we shut our eyes to it . . . ?—

•

—more and more I dread futility—

"The struggle, whose normal external expressions
have been choked,
attaches itself to the structure
of the old class like a destructive gangrene . . .
it takes on morbid forms of mysticism,
sensualism, moral indifference,
physical and psychic pathological depravations . . .
The old structure does not contain and is unable
to satisfy the new needs . . ."

•

—Trying to hold an inner focus while hoarse laughter
ricochets from the guardroom—

•

—*liquefaction*   is a word I might use for how I would take you—

•

—the daunted river finally
undammed?—

　　　　[*prevent this mind*]

2005

IV

IF/AS THOUGH

you'd spin out on your pirate platter
chords I'd receive on my crystal set
blues purpling burgundy goblets
Lorca's piano spuming up champagne flutes
could drop over any night at will
with that bottle of Oregon Pinot to watch *Alexander Nevsky*
If no curfews no blackouts no
no-fly lists no profiling racial genital mental
If all necessary illicits blew in
like time-release capsules or spores in the mulch
up-rising as morels, creviced and wild-delicious   If
Gerard Manley Hopkins were here to make welsh rarebit
reciting *The Wreck of the Deutschland* to Hart Crane in his high tenor
guessing him captive audience to sprung rhythm   as we in lóst lóve
sequences   hearing it
                         skim uncurfewed, uncowled
pelicans over spindrift beating agnostic wings

For Ed Pavlić

2006

TIME EXPOSURES

i

Glance into glittering moisture
webbed in lashes   unshed tears
I'd guess as yours
Known odor inhaled years later
in a brief social kiss   sudden conjuncture
soap, sweat, breath, hair   other embraces
diffused   once, again, time's exhilarations

ii

Is there a doctor in the house
who in his plain mindful way
cared for his patients through
pain rain and snow

who at each and every grave
side knew
what could be done
he'd done

And where have all the patients gone
who wanted (more than one)
a tending hand
across the forehead   at the end

And what's the house?

iii

They'd say she was humorless
didn't go to the parties
giggle   show white teeth

So would suspend her in
their drained
definitions

Her body had nipples, eyes
a tongue and other parts

mirthful
obscene

which rose from love   quite often
hilarious into daylight
even forgetting why

iv

When I stretched out my legs beyond your wishful thinking
into the long history they were made for running
caught the train you missed sought you eye-level
at the next station   You having run the whole way
to seize my face between your hands   your kind
of victory or benediction   then
we swerved down-tunnel
in separate cars   What is it to
catch yourself mirror-twinned
in an underwater window   what
about speed   matching
technology and desire   getting off
at the last stop: dispersed

v

You've got ocean through sheet glass brandy and firelog
ocean in its shaking
looks back at you with a blurred eye

Who's that reflected
naked and sundered

reaching a hand

Go
down to the beach, walk in the wind
Pick up the washed-in shell
at your foot

Shell castle built on sand
your body and what's your soul?

Is there a ghost-in-waiting?
time to bring that one in

2006

THE UNIVERSITY REOPENS AS THE
FLOODS RECEDE

Should blue air in its purity let you disdain
the stink of artificial pine

the gaunt architecture
of cheap political solutions

if there are philosophies to argue
the moment when you would

or wouldn't spring to shield
a friend's body or jump

into scummed waters after
a stranger caught submerging

or walk off to your parked
car your sandwich your possible orange

if theories rage or dance
about this if in the event   any

can be sure who did
or did not act on principle or impulse

and what's most virtuous

can we not be nodding smiling
taking down notes like this

and of all places
in a place like this

I'll work with you on this bad matter   I can
but won't give you the time of day

if you think it's hypothetical

2006

VIA INSOMNIA

Called up in sleep: your   voice:
I don't know where I am . . .

A hand, mine, stroking a white fur surface
you as a white fur hat unstitched, outspread

white as your cold brancusian marble head
what animal's pelt resembles you?
but these are my navigations: *you don't know where you are*

Is this how it is to be newly dead?   unbelieving
the personal soul, electricity unsheathing
from the cortex, light-waves fleeing
into the black universe

to lie awake half-sleeping, wondering
Where, when will I sleep

For Tory Dent

2006

A BURNING KANGAROO

leaping forward   escaping
out of rock reamed
on sky
in violet shadow

leaping   scorched to the skin

toward water
(none for miles)

Who did
             (and can you see
this thing
             not as a dream

a kangaroo
and not in profile either

Frontal
in flame   no halo
no aura   burning meat in movement

Can
you see with me
                   (unverified
otherwise

(whoever   did this thing

2006

EVER, AGAIN

Mockingbird shouts *Escape! Escape!*
and would I could   I'd

fly, drive back to that house
up the long hill between queen

anne's lace and common daisyface
shoulder open stuck door

run springwater from kitchen
tap   drench tongue

palate and throat
throw window sashes up screens down

breathe in   mown grass
pine-needle heat

manure, lilac   unpack
brown sacks from the store:

ground meat, buns, tomatoes, one
big onion, milk and orange juice

iceberg lettuce, ranch dressing
potato chips, dill pickles

the *Caledonian-Record*
Portuguese rosé in round-hipped flask

open the box of newspapers by the stove
reread: (Vietnam Vietnam)

Set again on the table
the Olivetti, the stack

of rough yellow typing paper
mark the crashed instant

of one summer's mosquito
on a bedroom door

voices of boys outside
proclaiming twilight and hunger

Pour iced vodka into a shotglass
get food on the table

sitting with those wild heads
over hamburgers, fireflies, music

staying up late with the typewriter
falling asleep with the dead

2006

V

DRAFT #2006

i

Suppose we came back as ghosts asking the unasked questions.

(What were you there for? Why did you walk out? What
would have made you stay? Why wouldn't you listen?)

—Couldn't you show us what you meant, can't we get it right
this time? Can't you put it another way?—

(You were looking for openings where they'd been walled up—)

—But you were supposed to be our teacher—

(One-armed, I was trying to get you, one by one, out of that
cellar.   It wasn't enough)

ii

Dreamfaces blurring horrorlands: border of poetry.

Ebb tide sucks out clinging rockpool creatures, no swimming
back into sleep.

Clockface says too early, body prideful and humble shambles
into another day, reclaiming itself piecemeal in private ritual
acts.

Reassembling the anagram scattered nightly, rebuilding daily
the sand city.

iii

What's concrete for me: from there I cast out further.

But need to be there. On the stone causeway. Baffled and
obstinate.

Eyes probing the dusk. Foot-slippage possible.

iv

Sleeping that time at the philosopher's house.   Not lovers,
friends from the past.

Music the vertex of our triangle.   Bach our hypotenuse
strung between philosophy and poetry.

Sun loosening fog on the hillside, cantata spun on the
turntable: *Wie schön leuchtet der Morgenstern.*

Feeling again, in our mid-forties, the old contrapuntal ten-
sion between our natures.   The future as if still open, like
when we were classmates.

He'd met Heidegger in the Black Forest, corresponded
with Foucault.   We talked about Wittgenstein.

I was on my way to meet the one who said *Philosophers have
interpreted the world: the point is to change it.*

v

On a street known for beautiful shops she buys a piece of
antique Japanese silk, a white porcelain egg.

Had abandoned her child, later went after him, found the
child had run away.

Hurt and angry, joined a group to chant through the pain.
They said, you must love yourself, give yourself gifts.

Whatever eases you someone says, lets you forgive yourself,
let go.

America, someone says.

Orphaning, orphaned here, don't even know it.

vi

Silent limousines meet jets descending over the Rockies.
Steam rooms, pure thick towels, vases of tuberose and jas-
mine, old vintages await the après-skiers.

Rooms of mahogany and leather, conversations open in
international code.   Thighs and buttocks to open later by
arrangement.

Out of sight, out of mind, she solitary wrestles a huge
duvet, resheathes heavy tasseled bolsters.   Bed after bed.
Nights, in her room, ices strained arms.   Rests her legs.

Elsewhere, in Andhra Pradesh, another farmer swallows
pesticide.

vii

Condemned, a clinic coughs up its detritus.

Emergency exit, gurneys lined double, mercy draining
down exhausted tubes.

Drills and cranes clearing way for the new premises.

As if I already stood at their unglazed windows, eyeing
the distressed site through skeletal angles.

Tenant already of the disensoulment projects.

Had thought I deserved nothing better than these stark
towers named for conglomerates?—a line of credit, a give-
away?

viii

They asked me, is this time worse than another.

I said, for whom?

Wanted to show them something.   While I wrote on the
chalkboard they drifted out. I turned back to an empty room.

Maybe I couldn't write fast enough.   Maybe it was too soon.

ix

The sheer mass of the thing, its thereness, stuns thought.
Since it exists, it must have existed.   Will exist.   It says so
here.

Excruciating contempt for love.   For the strained fibre of
common affections, mutual assistance

sifted up from landfill, closed tunnels, drought-sheared
riverbeds, street beds named in old census books, choked
under the expressway.

Teachers bricolating scattered schools of trust.   Rootlets
watered by fugitives.

Contraband packets, hummed messages.   Dreams of the
descendants, surfacing.

Hand reaching for its like exposes a scarred wrist.
Numerals.   A bracelet of rust.

In a desert observatory, under plaster dust, smashed lenses
left by the bombardments,

star maps crackle, unscrolling.

2006

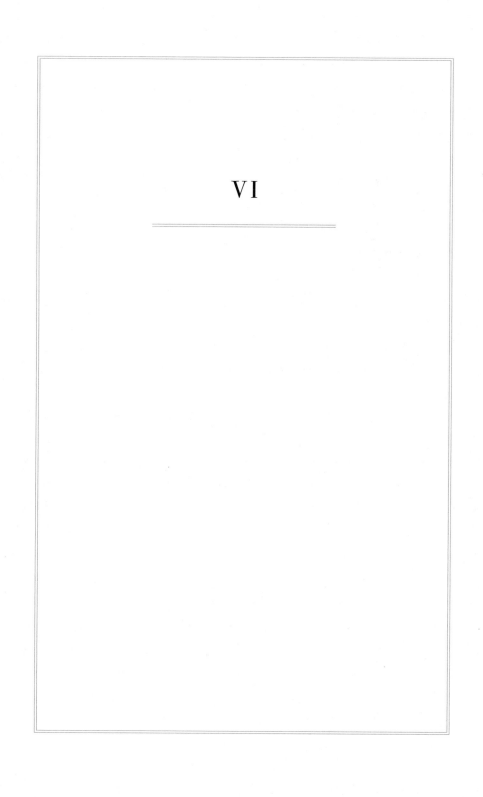

VI

TELEPHONE RINGING IN THE LABYRINTH

i

You who can be silent in twelve languages
trying to crease again in paling light
the map you unfurled that morning   if

you in your rearview mirror sighted me
rinsing a green glass bowl
by midsummer nightsun in, say, Reykjavík

if at that moment my hand slipped
and that bowl cracked to pieces
and one piece stared at me like a gibbous moon

if its convex reflection caught you walking
the slurried highway shoulder after the car broke down
if such refractions matter

ii

Well, I've held on   peninsula
to continent, climber
to rockface

Sensual peninsula attached so   stroked
by the tides' pensive and moody hands
Scaler into thin air

seen from below as weed or lichen
improvidently fastened
a mat of hair webbed in a bush

A bush ignited   then
consumed
Violent lithography

smolder's legacy on a boulder traced

iii

Image erupts from image
atlas from vagrancy
articulation from mammal howl

strangeness from repetition
even this   default location
surveyed again   one more poem

one more Troy or Tyre or burning tire
seared eyeball genitals
charred cradle

but a different turn   working
this passage of the labyrinth
as laboratory

I'd have entered, searched before
but that ball of thread   that clew
offering an exit choice was no gift at all

iv

I found you by design or
was it your design
or: we were drawn, we drew

Midway in this delicate
negotiation   telephone rings
(Don't stop! . . . they'll call again . . .)

Offstage the fabulous creature scrapes and shuffles
we breathe its heavy dander
I don't care how, if it dies   this is not the myth

No ex/interior: compressed
between my throat
and yours, hilarious oxygen

And, for the record, each did sign
our true names on the register
at the mouth of this hotel

v

I would have wanted to say it
without falling back
on words   Desired not

you so much as your life,
your prevailing   Not for me
but for furtherance   how

you would move
on the horizon   You, the person, you
the particle   fierce and furthering

2006

TONIGHT NO POETRY WILL SERVE

WILL SERVE

(2007–2010)

SERVE (v.t.):

to work for, be a servant to;

to give obedience and reverent honor to;

to fight for; do military or naval service for;

to go through or spend (a term of imprisonment);

to meet the needs of or satisfy the requirements of, be used by;

to deliver (a legal document) as a summons

—Webster's New World Dictionary
of the American Language (1964)

I

WAITING FOR RAIN, FOR MUSIC

Burn me some music   *Send my roots rain*   I'm swept
dry from inside   Hard winds rack my core

A struggle at the roots of the mind   Whoever said
it would go on and on like this

Straphanger swaying inside a runaway car
palming a notebook scribbled in

contraband calligraphy   against the war
poetry wages against itself

•

Once under a shed's eaves
thunder drumming membrane of afternoon
electric scissors slitting the air

thick drops spattering few and far
we could smell it then a long way off

But where's the rain coming to soak this soil

•

Burn me some music   There's a tune
"Neglect of Sorrow"
I've heard it hummed or strummed
my whole life long
in many a corridor

waiting for tomorrow
long after tomorrow
should've come

on many an ear it should have fallen
but the bands were playing so loud

2007

READING THE *ILIAD* (AS IF) FOR THE FIRST TIME

Lurid, garish, gash
rended creature struggles to rise, to
    run with dripping belly
Blood making everything more real
    pounds in the spearthruster's arm as in
the gunman's neck the offhand
moment—Now!—before he
    takes the bastards out

  •

Splendor in black and ochre on a grecian urn
    Beauty as truth
The sea as background
    stricken with black long-oared ships
on shore chariots shields greaved muscled legs
    horses rearing   Beauty!   flesh before gangrene

  •

Mind-shifting gods rush back and forth   Delusion
a daughter seized by the hair   swung out to bewilder men
Everything here is conflictual and is called man's fate

  •

Ugly glory: open-eyed wounds
feed enormous flies
Hoofs slicken on bloodglaze

Horses turn away their heads
weeping equine tears
                              Beauty?
a wall with names of the fallen
from both sides   passionate objectivity

2009

BENJAMIN REVISITED

The angel
   of history is
flown

         now meet the janitor
                  down
in the basement   who
         shirtless   smoking

has the job of stoking
   the so-called past
         into the so-called present

2007

INNOCENCE

. . . thought, think, I did

some terrible
thing back then

—thing that left traces
all over you
your work / how your figure
pressed into the world   ?

     Had you murdered
     —or not—something if not
     someone   Had blindly—or not—
     followed custom needing to be
     broken   Broken
     —or not—with custom
     needing to be kept   ?

     Something—a body—still
     spins in air   a weaving weight
     a scorching

However it was done

And the folks disassembling
   from under the tree

   after you snapped the picture

       saliva thick in your mouth

  •

Disfigured sequel:

confederations of the progeny
cottaged along these roads

front-center colonials
shrubbery lights in blue
and silver

crèche on the judge's lawn   O the dear baby

People craving   in their mouths
warm milk over soft white bread

2007

DOMAIN

i

A girl looks through a microscope   her father's
showing her life
in a drop of water or
finger blood smeared onto a glass wafer

Later leaning head on hand
while the sound of scales being practiced
clambers bleakly, adamantly up the stairs
she reads her own handwriting

Neighbors don't meet on the corner here
the child whose parents aren't home is not offered a meal
the congressman's wife who wears nothing but green

tramples through unraked oak leaves yelling
　　　　　　　to her strayed dogs *Hey Rex! Hey Roy!*
Husband in Washington:　　1944

The girl finding her method:　　you want friends
you're going to have to write
letters to strangers

ii

A coffee stain splashed on a desk:　　her accident her
mistake her true
country:　　wavy brown coastline　　upland
silken reeds swayed by long lectures of the wind

From the shore small boats reach, depart, return
the never-leavers tie nets of dried seaweed weighted
with tumbled-down stones
instructing young fingers through difficult knots
guiding, scraping some young fingers
No sound carries far from here

Rebuked, utopian projection

she visits rarely trying to keep
interior root systems, milky
nipples of stars, airborne wings rushing over

refuge of missing parts

intact

2008

FRACTURE

When on that transatlantic call into the unseen
ear of a hack through whiskey film you blabbed
your misanthrope's
misremembered remnant of a story
given years back in trust

a rearview mirror
cracked /
shock of an ice-cube biting liquid

Heard the sound / didn't know yet
where it was coming from

That mirror / gave up our ghosts

This fine clear summer morning / a line from Chekhov:
it would be strange not to forgive

(I in body now alive)

All are human / give / forgive
drop the charges / let go / put away

Rage for the trusting
it would be strange not to say

Love? yes
in this lifted hand / behind
these eyes
upon you / now

2007

TURBULENCE

There'll be turbulence.   You'll drop
your book to hold your
water bottle steady.   Your
mind, mind has mountains, cliffs of fall
may who ne'er hung there let him
watch the movie.   The plane's
supposed to shudder, shoulder on
like this.   It's built to do that.   You're
designed to tremble too.   Else break
Higher you climb, trouble in mind
lungs labor, heights hurl vistas
Oxygen hangs ready
overhead.   In the event put on
the child's mask first.   Breathe normally

2007

TONIGHT NO POETRY WILL SERVE

Saw you walking barefoot
taking a long look
at the new moon's eyelid

later spread
sleep-fallen, naked in your dark hair
asleep but not oblivious
of the unslept unsleeping
elsewhere

Tonight I think
no poetry
will serve

Syntax of rendition:

verb pilots the plane
adverb modifies action

verb force-feeds noun
submerges the subject
noun is choking
verb   disgraced   goes on doing

now diagram the sentence

2007

II

SCENES OF NEGOTIATION

Z: I hated that job but   You'd have taken it too if you'd had a family
Y: Pretty filthy and dangerous though wasn't it?
Z: Those years, one bad move, you were down on your knees begging
     for work

*Zz: If you'd had a family! Who'd you think we were, just people standing
     around?*
Yy: Filthy and dangerous like the streets I worked before you ever met me?
*Zz: Those years you never looked at any of us. Staring into your own eyelids.
     Like you saw a light there. Can you see me now?*

•

Hired guards shove metal barriers through plate glass, then prod
the first line of protestors in through the fanged opening. Video and
cellphone cameras devouring it all. Sucked in and blurted worldwide:
"Peace" Rally Turns Violent

Protestors, a mixed bunch, end up in different holding cells where
they won't see each other again

Being or doing: you're taken in for either, or both. Who you were born
as, what or who you chose or became. Facing moral disorder head-on,
some for the first time, on behalf of others. Delusion of inalienable
rights. Others who've known the score all along

Some bailed-out go back to the scene. Some go home to sleep. Others, it's months in solitary mouthing dialogues with nobody. Imagining social presence. Fending off, getting ready for the social absence
called death

•

This isn't much more than a shed on two-by-fours over the water. Uncaulked. Someone's romantic hideaway. We've been here awhile, like it well enough. The tide retches over rocks below. Wind coming up now. We liked it better when the others were still here. They went off in different directions. Patrol boats gathered some in, we saw the lights and heard the megaphones. Tomorrow I'll take the raggedy path up to the road, walk into town, buy a stamp and mail this. Town is a mini-mart, church, oyster-bar-dance-hall, fishing access, roadside cabins. Weekenders, locals, we can blend in. They couldn't so well. We were trying to stay with the one thing most people agree on. They said there was no such one thing without everything else, you couldn't make it so simple

Have books, tapes here, and this typewriter voice telling you what I'm telling you in the language we used to share. Everyone still sends love

•

There are no illusions at this table, she said to me

Room up under the roof. Men and women, a resistance cell   ? I thought. Reaching hungrily for trays of folded bread, rice with lentils, brown jugs of water and pale beer. Joking across the table along with alertness, a kind of close mutual attention. One or two picking on small stringed instruments taken down from a wall

I by many decades the oldest person there. However I was there

Meal finished, dishes rinsed under a tap, we climbed down a kind of stair-ladder to the floor below. There were camouflage-patterned outfits packed in cartons; each person shook out and put on a pair of pants and a shirt, still creased from the packing. They wore them like work clothes. Packed underneath were weapons

Thick silverblack hair, eyes seriously alive, hue from some ancient kiln. The rest of them are in profile; that face of hers I see full focus

One by one they went out through a dim doorway to meet whoever they'd been expecting. I write it down from memory. Couldn't find the house later   yet

—*No illusions at this table.*   Spoken from her time back into mine.   I'm the dreaming ghost, guest, waitress, watcher, wanting the words to be true.

Whatever the weapons may come to mean

2009

III

FROM SICKBED SHORES

From shores of sickness: skin of the globe stretches and snakes
out and in   room sound of the universe bearing
undulant wavelengths to an exhausted ear

(sick body in a sick country: can it get well?

what is it anyway to exist as
matter   to
                matter?)

All, all is remote from here: yachts carelessly veering
tanker's beak plunging into the strut of the bridge
slicked encircling waters

wired wrists   jerked-back heads
gagged mouths   flooded lungs

All, all remote and near

Wavelengths—
whose?   mine, theirs, ours   even

yours who haven't yet put in a word?

•

So remoteness glazes sickened skin   affliction of distance   so
strangely, easily, clinging like webs spread overnight
by creatures vanished
before we caught them at work
So: to bear this state, this caul which could be hell's
airborne anaesthetic, exemption from feeling   or

hell's pure and required definition:
—surrender
to un-belonging, being-for-itself-alone, runged
behind white curtains in an emergency cubicle, taking care of its own
condition

•

All is matter, of course, matter-of-course   You could have taken
courses in matter all along attending instead of cutting the class
You knew the telephone had wires, you could see them overhead
where sparrows sat and chattered together
you alongside a window somewhere phone in hand
listening to tears thickening a throat in a city somewhere else
you muttering back your faulty formulae
ear tuned to mute vibrations from an occupied zone:
an old, enraged silence still listening for your voice
                                                    Did you then holding
the phone tongue your own lips finger your naked shoulder as
if you could liquefy touch into sound through wires   to lips or
        shoulders   lick
down an entire body in familiar mystery   irregardless laws of
        matter?

Hopeless imagination of signals not to be
received

•

From the shores of sickness you lie out on listless
waters with no boundaries   floodplain without horizon
dun skies mirroring its opaque face and nothing not

a water moccasin or floating shoe or tree root to stir interest
Somewhere else being the name of whatever once said your name
and you answered   now the only where is here   this dull
    floodplain
this body sheathed in indifference   sweat no longer letting the
    fever out
but coating it in oil   You could offer any soul-tricking oarsman
whatever coin you're still palming but there's a divide
between the shores of sickness and the legendary, purifying
river of death   You will have this tale to tell, you will have to live
to tell
this tale

2008

IV

***

Axel Avákar

[Axel Avákar: fictive poet, counter-muse, brother]

AXEL AVÁKAR

The I you know isn't me, you said, truthtelling liar
My roots are not my chains
And I to you: Whose hands have grown
through mine?   Owl-voiced I cried then: Who?

But yours was the one, the only eye assumed

Did we turn each other into liars?
holding hands with each others' chains?

At last we unhook, dissolve, secrete into islands
—neither a tender place—
yours surf-wrung, kelp-strung
mine locked in black ice on a mute lake

I dug my firepit, built a windbreak,
spread a sheepskin, zoned my telescope lens
to the far ledge of the Milky Way
lay down to sleep out the cold

Daybreak's liquid dreambook:
lines of a long poem pouring down a page
Had I come so far, did I fend so well
only to read your name there, Axel Avákar?

AXEL: BACKSTORY

Steam from a melting glacier

your profile hovering
there   Axel as if we'd lain prone at fifteen

on my attic bedroom floor   elbow to elbow reading
in Baltimorean August-
blotted air

                         Axel I'm back to you
brother of strewn books   of late
hours drinking poetry scooped in both hands

Dreamt you into existence, did I, boy-
comrade who would love
                         everything I loved

Without my eyelash glittering piercing
sidewise in your eye
where would you have begun, Axel   how
would the wheel-spoke have whirled
your mind?   What word
stirred in your mouth without my
nipples' fierce erection?   our
twixt-and-between

                         Between us   yet
my part belonged to me
                         and when we parted

I left no part behind   I knew
how to make poetry happen

Back to you Axel through the crackling heavy
salvaged telephone

AXEL, IN THUNDER

Axel, the air's beaten
   like a drumhead here where it seldom thunders

dolphin
        lightning
                leaps

over the bay   surfers flee

    crouching to trucks

climbers hanging
    from pitons in their night hammocks
        off the granite face

wait out an unforetold storm

while somewhere in all weathers you're
    crawling exposed   not by choice   extremist
hell-bent searching your soul

    —O my terrified   my obdurate
my wanderer   keep the trail

I WAS THERE, AXEL

> Pain made her conservative.
> Where the matches touched her flesh, she wears a scar.
>
> —"The Blue Ghazals"

Pain taught her the language
root of *radical*

she walked on knives to gain a voice
fished the lake of lost

messages gulping up
from far below and long ago

needed both arms to haul them in
one arm was tied behind her

the other worked to get it free
it hurt itself because

work hurts   I was there Axel
with her in that boat

working alongside

and my decision was
to be in no other way

a woman

AXEL, DARKLY SEEN, IN A GLASS HOUSE

1

And could it be I saw you
under a roof of glass
in trance

could it be   was passing
by and would translate

too late the strained flicker
of your pupils   your
inert gait   the dark

garb of your reflection
in that translucent place

could be I might have
saved you   still
could   or would   ?

2

Laid my ear to your letter trying to hear
Tongue on your words to taste you there
Couldn't   read what you
                    had never written there

Played your message over
                    feeling bad
Played your message over it was all I had
To tell me what and wherefore
                    this is what it said:

I'm tired of you asking me why
I'm tired of words like the chatter of birds

Give me a pass, let me just get by

3

Back to back our shadows
stalk each other Axel but

not only yours and mine   Thickly lies
the impasto

scrape down far enough you get
the early brushwork   emblems

intimate detail

and scratched lines underneath
—a pictograph

one figure leaning forward
to speak or listen

one figure   backed away
unspeakable

(If that one moved—)

　　　but the I you knew who made

you once can't save you

my blood won't even match yours

4

"The dead" we say   as if speaking
of "the people" who

gave up on making history
simply to get through

Something dense and null   groan
without echo   underground

and owl-voiced I cry Who
are these dead these people these

lovers who if ever did
listen no longer answer

: We :

5

Called in to the dead: *why didn't you write?*
What should I have asked you?

—what would have been the true
unlocking code

if all of them failed—
I've questioned the Book of Questions

studied gyres of steam
twisting from a hot cup
in a cold sunbeam

turned the cards over   lifted the spider's foot
from the mangled hexagon

netted the beaked eel from the river's mouth
asked   and let it go

2007–2008

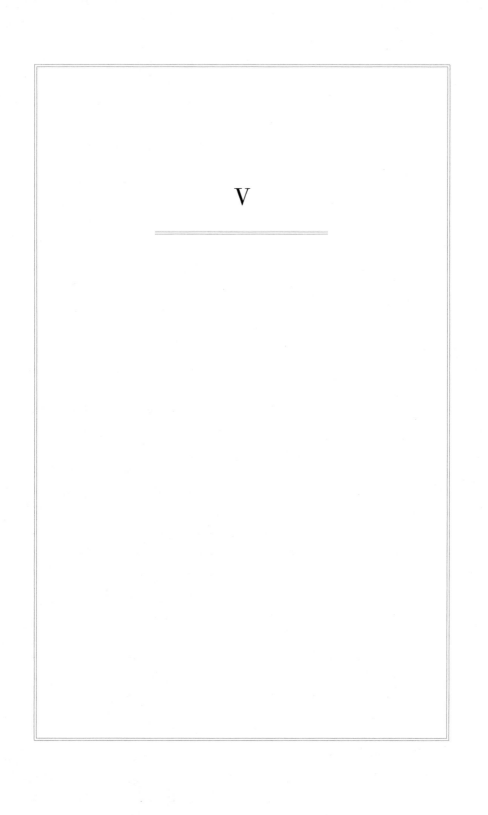

V

BALLADE OF THE POVERTIES

There's the poverty of the cockroach kingdom and the rusted
    toilet bowl
The poverty of to steal food for the first time
The poverty of to mouth a penis for a paycheck
The poverty of sweet charity ladling
Soup for the poor who must always be there for that
There's poverty of theory poverty of swollen belly shamed
Poverty of the diploma or ballot that goes nowhere
Princes of predation let me tell you
There are poverties and there are poverties

There's the poverty of cheap luggage bursted open at immigration
Poverty of the turned head averted eye
The poverty of bored sex of tormented sex
The poverty of the bounced check poverty of the dumpster dive
The poverty of the pawned horn of the smashed reading glasses
The poverty pushing the sheeted gurney the poverty cleaning up
    the puke
The poverty of the pavement artist the poverty passed out on
    pavement
Princes of finance you who have not lain there
There are poverties and there are poverties

There is the poverty of hand-to-mouth and door-to-door
And the poverty of stories patched up to sell there
There's the poverty of the child thumbing the Interstate
And the poverty of the bride enlisting for war
There is the poverty of stones fisted in pocket
And the poverty of the village bulldozed to rubble
There's the poverty of coming home not as you left it
And the poverty of how would you ever end it
Princes of weaponry who have not ever tasted war
There are poverties and there are poverties

There's the poverty of wages wired for the funeral you
Can't get to the poverty of bodies lying unburied
There's the poverty of labor offered silently on the curb
The poverty of the no-contact prison visit
There's the poverty of yard-sale scrapings spread
And rejected the poverty of eviction, wedding bed out on street
Prince let me tell you who will never learn through words
There are poverties and there are poverties

You who travel by private jet like a housefly
Buzzing with the other flies of plundered poverties
Princes and courtiers who will never learn through words
Here's a mirror you can look into: take it: it's yours.

For James and Arlene Scully

2009

EMERGENCY CLINIC

Caustic implacable
poem   unto and contra:

I do not soothe minor
injuries   I do
not offer   I require
                    close history
of the case   apprentice-
ship in past and fresh catastrophe

The skin too quickly scabbed
mutters for my debriding

For every bandaged wound
I'll scrape another   open

I won't smile
                while wiping
your tears
              I do not give
simplehearted   love and nor
allow you simply love me

if you accept   regardless
this will be different

Iodine-dark
poem walking to and fro all night

un-gainly
unreconciled

unto and contra

2008

CONFRONTATIONS

It's not new, this condition, just for awhile
      kept deep
in the cortex of things imagined

Now the imagination comes of age

I see ourselves, full-lipped, blood-flushed
in cold air, still conflicted, still
        embraced

boarding the uncharter'd bus of vanishment

backward glances over and done
afterimages
swirl and dissolve along a shoal of footprints

Simple ghouls flitter already among our leavings
fixing labels in their strange language
                                        But
        up to now we're not debris
(only to their fascinated eyes)

2009

CIRCUM/STANCES

A crime of nostalgia
—is it—to say

the "objective conditions"
seemed a favoring wind

and we younger then
                        —objective fact—

also a kind of subjectivity

Sails unwrapped to the breeze
no chart

•

Slowly repetitiously to prise
up the leaden lid where the forensic
evidence was sealed

cross-section of a slave ship
diagram of a humiliated
mind   high-resolution image
of a shredded lung

color slides of refugee camps

Elsewhere
                    (in some calm room far from pain)
bedsprings   a trunk empty
but for a scorched
                          length of electrical cord

how these got here from where
what would have beheld

Migrant assemblage: in its aura
immense details writhe, uprise

•

To imagine what   Become
present thén

within the monster
nerveless and giggling

(our familiar   our kin)
who did the scutwork

To differentiate
the common hell
the coils inside the brain

•

Scratchy cassette ribbon
history's lamentation song:

> *Gone, friend I tore at*
> *time after time*
> *in anger*
>
> *gone, love I could*
> *time upon time*
> *nor live nor leave*
>
> *gone, city*
> *of spies and squatters*
> *tongues and genitals*

All violence is not equal

(I write this
with a clawed hand

2008

WINTERFACE

i. hers

Mute it utters ravage   guernican
mouth in bleak December

Busted-up lines of Poe:

> —*each separate dying ember*
> *wreaks its ghost upon the floor*

January moon-mouth
phosphorescence purged in dark to
swallow up the gone

Too soon

Dawn, twilight, wailing
newsprint, breakfast, trains

all must run their inter-
ruptured course

—So was the girl moving too fast   she was moving fast
across an icy web

Was ice a mirror   well the mirror was icy

And did she see herself in there

ii. his

Someone writes asking about your use
of Bayesian inference

in the history of slavery

What flares now from our burnt-up
furniture

You left your stricken briefcase here
no annotations

phantom frequencies stammer
trying to fathom

how it was inside alone where you were dying

2009

QUARTO

1

Call me Sebastian, arrows sticking all over
The map of my battlefields.   Marathon.
Wounded Knee.   Vicksburg.   Jericho.
Battle of the Overpass.
Victories turned inside out
But no surrender

Cemeteries of remorse
The beaten champion sobbing
Ghosts move in to shield his tears

2

No one writes lyric on a battlefield
On a map stuck with arrows
But I think I can do it if I just lurk

In my tent pretending to
Refeather my arrows

I'll be right there! I yell
When they come with their crossbows and white phosphorus
To recruit me

Crouching over my drafts
Lest they find me out
And shoot me

3

Press your cheek against my medals, listen through them to my heart
Doctor, can you see me if I'm naked?

Spent longer in this place than in the war
No one comes but rarely and I don't know what for

Went to that desert as many did before
Farewell and believing and hope not to die

Hope not to die and what was the life
Did we think was awaiting after

Lay down your stethoscope back off on your skills
Doctor can you see me when I'm naked?

4

I'll tell you about the mermaid
Sheds swimmable tail   Gets legs for dancing
Sings like the sea with a choked throat

Knives straight up her spine
Lancing every step
There is a price
There is a price
For every gift
And all advice

2009

DON'T FLINCH

Lichen-green lines of shingle pulsate and waver
when you lift your eyes.   It's the glare.   Don't flinch
The news you were reading
(who tramples whom) is antique and on the death pages you've seen already
worms doing their normal work
on the life that was: the chewers chewing
at a sensuality that wrestled doom
an anger steeped in love they can't
even taste.   How could this still
shock or sicken you?   Friends go missing, mute
nameless.   Toss
the paper.   Reach again
for the *Iliad*.   The lines
pulse into sense.   Turn up the music
Now do you hear it?   can you smell smoke
under the near shingles?

2009

BLACK LOCKET

It lies in "the way of seeing the world": in the technical sacredness of seeing that world.

—Pier Paolo Pasolini, of his film *Accatone*

The ornament hung from my neck is a black locket
with a chain barely felt for years   clasp I couldn't open
Inside: photographs of the condemned
                                                                    Two

mystery planets
invaded from within

•

Pitcher of ice water thrown in a punched-in face
Eyes burnt back in their sockets
Negative archaeology

•

Driving the blind curve trapped in the blind alley
my blind spot blots the blinding
beauty of your face

•

I hear the colors of your voice

2009

GENEROSITY

Death, goodlooking as only a skeleton can get
(good looks of keen intelligence)
sits poised at the typewriter, her locale, her pedestal
two books, one called *Raging Beauty*
another *Lettera Amorosa,* on this table
of drafts arguments letters
Her fine bony fingers go on calmly typing
the years at her turquoise-blue machine
(I say her but who knows death's gender
as in life there are possible variations)
Anyway he or she sat on your desk in Tucson
in the apartment where you lived then and fed me
champagne, frybread, hominy soup and gave me
her or him   Later at the 7-Eleven we bought
a plastic sack of cotton to pack Death safe for travel
vagabond poet who can work anywhere
now here and of course still working
but startled by something or someone
turns her head   fingers lifted in midair

For Joy Harjo

2009

VI

YOU, AGAIN

Some nights I think you want too much. From me. I didn't ask
to parse again your idioms of littered
parking lots your chain-linked crane-hung sites
limp once more your crime-scene-festooned streets
to buildings I used to live in.   Lose my nerve
at a wrong door on the wrong floor
in search of a time.   The precision of dream is not
such a privilege. I know those hallways tiled in patterns
of oriental rugs those accordion-pleated
elevator gates. Know by heart the chipped
edges on some of those tiles. You who require this
heart-squandering want me wandering you, craving
to press a doorbell hear a lock turn, a bolt slide back
—always too much, over and over back
to the old apartment, wrong again, the key maybe
left with a super in charge of the dream who will not be found

2010

POWERS OF RECUPERATION

i

A woman of the citizen party—*what's that*—
is writing history backward

her body   the chair she sits in
to be abandoned   repossessed

The old, crusading, raping, civil, great, phony, holy, world,
    second world, third world,
    cold, dirty, lost, on drugs,

infectious, maiming, class
war lives on

A done matter she might have thought
ever undone though   plucked

from before her birthyear
and that hyphen coming after

She's old, old, the incendiary
woman

endless beginner

whose warped wraps you shall find in graves
and behind glass   plundered

ii

Streets empty now   citizen rises   shrugging off
her figured shirt   pulls on her dark generic garment   sheds
identity inklings   watch, rings, ear studs
now to pocket her flashlight   her tiny magnet
shut down heater   finger a sleeping cat
lock inner, outer door   insert
key in crevice   listen once twice
to the breath of the neighborhood
take temperature of the signs   a bird
scuffling   a frost settling

. . . you left that meeting around two a.m.   I thought
someone should walk with you

Didn't think then I needed that

years ravel out   and now

who'd be protecting whom

I left the key in the old place
in case

iii

Spooky those streets of minds
shuttered against shatter

articulate those walls
pronouncing rage and need

fuck the cops   come jesus
blow me again

Citizen walking catwise
close to the walls

heat of her lungs leaving
its trace upon the air

fingers her tiny magnet
which for the purpose of drawing

particles together will have to do
when as they say the chips are down

iv

Citizen at riverbank   seven bridges
Ministers-in-exile with their aides
limb to limb dreaming underneath

conspiring by definition

Bridges   trajectories arched
in shelter   rendezvous

two banks to every river   two directions
to every bridge
twenty-eight chances

every built thing has its unmeant purpose

v

Every built thing with its unmeant
meaning   unmet purpose

every unbuilt thing

child squatting   civil
engineer   devising

by kerosene flare   in mud
possible tunnels

carves in cornmeal mush   irrigation
canals by index finger

all new learning looks at first
like chaos

the tiny magnet throbs
in citizen's pocket

vi

Bends under the arc walks bent listening for chords and codes
bat-radar-pitched or twanging
off rubber bands and wires tin-can telephony

to scribble testimony by fingernail and echo
her documentary alphabet still evolving

Walks up on the bridge   windwhipped   roof and trajectory
shuddering under her catpaw tread
one of seven

built things holds her suspended
between desolation

and the massive figure on unrest's verge
pondering the unbuilt city

cheek on hand and glowing eyes and
skirted knees apart

2007

LATER POEMS

(2010–2012)

ITINERARY

i.

Burnt by lightning   nevertheless
she'll walk this terra infinita

lashes singed on her third eye
searching definite shadows   for an indefinite future

Old shed-boards beaten silvery hang
askew as sheltering
some delicate indefensible existence

Long grasses shiver in a vanished doorway's draft
a place of origins   as yet unclosured and unclaimed

Writing cursive instructions on abounding air

If you arrive with ripe pears, bring a sharpened knife
Bring cyanide with the honeycomb

　　　　　call before you come

ii.

Let the face of the bay be violet   black the tumbled torn
kelp necklaces strewn alongshore

Stealthily over time arrives the chokehold
stifling ocean's guttural chorales
　　　　　　　　　　　　　a tangle
of tattered plastic rags

iii.

In a physical world the great poverty would be
to live insensate   shuttered against the fresh

slash of urine on a wall
low-tidal rumor of a river's yellowed mouth
a tumor-ridden face asleep on a subway train

What would it mean to not possess
a permeable skin
explicit veil to wander in

iv.

A cracked shell crumbles.
Sun moon and salt dissect the faint
last grains

An electrical impulse zings
out   ricochets
in meta-galactic orbits

a streak of nervous energy rejoins the crucible
where origins and endings meld

There was this honey-laden question mark
this thread extracted from the open
throat of existence—Lick it clean!
—let it evaporate—

2011

FOR THE YOUNG ANARCHISTS

Whatever we hunger for
we're not seagulls, to drop things
smash on the rocks   hurtling beak-down
Think instead the oysterman's
gauging eyes, torqued wrist
hand sliding the knife into
and away from the valve hinge—
astuteness honed through
generations to extract
the meat   Cut out it can slip
through your fingers   Kicked in the sand
forget it   Only every so often will
diver rise up from stalking grounds
lifting this creature into daylight and
everyone standing around
shrinks   or think they want some   We've
fumbled at this before   trammeled
in fury, in hunger   Begin there, yes
—only fury knowing its ground
has staying power—
Then go dead calm remembering
what this operation calls for—
eye, hand, mind   Don't
listen to chatter, ignore all yells
of haphazard instruction   And
when you taste it don't
get too elated   There'll be grit
to swallow   Or spit to the side

2010

FRAGMENTS OF AN OPERA

Scene One: Ales, Sardinia, 19——

Child's voice (Antonio):

from this beam

the doctors think

I can hang straight

in this har

ness dang

ling

dai

ly

grow how

I

should be

Explicator's voice:

Village doctor on a southern island
Treating one of seven

Children of a
Father in prison
For smalltime
Pecuniary
Crimes, maybe
Framed

Mother's
Heroic measures:
Knee presses, releases
Presses again the lever
Of a machine

Fingers push
Cloth
Under the needle

A woman stitches
Years months weeks days pass
In this way

Six children
Run and scream
Antonio must hang
From a beam

Recitativo: Neurosurgeon's voice:

It would have been a kind of traction.   Who knows how
it might have been done differently, elsewhere, in another
era of medical intervention?   Another country?   Other
family?   It was a kind of childhood.   Perhaps rickets?   spina
bifida? scoliosis?

Explicator's voice:

A kind of mind
That would address
Duress
Outward in larger terms

A mind inhaling exigency
From first breath
Knows poverty
Of mind
As death

Whose body must
Find its own mind

Recitativo: Prosecutor's voice: from the future:

We must prevent this mind from functioning for twenty years.

Scene Two: Turin, Northern Italy

Industrialist's voice:

Turin, Turin makes tractors for FIAT
Makes armored cars and planes
We're making, we're taking,
We're raising our goals
We can use immigrants
We can use women
Illiterate peasants from the South
There's a war out there

A World War and it's buying
Who's crying?

LIBERTÉ

Ankles shackled
metalled and islanded
holding aloft a mirror, feral
lipstick, eye-liner

                              She's
a celebrity   a star attraction

A glare effacing
the French Revolution's
risen juices   vintage taste

the Paris Commune's
fierce inscriptions
lost in translation

2011

TEETHSUCKING BIRD

Doves bleat, crows repeat
ancient scandals
mockingbird's flown to mock
some otherwhere

Listen, that teethsucking bird's
back up on the telephone wire

talking times and customs
naming the dead to the half-alive
hardship to lyric and back again
to the open road of the toll-taker's
booth at the last exit
to skateboarding boys of body bags
to the breaker of hearts of the old-age motel
to the would-be weird of the scalded woman's
escarpment of a face

And this is the now the then the gone
the means and ends the far and near
the news we hear
from the teethsucking bird

2010

UNDESIGNED

i.

It wasn't as if our lives depended on it—
a torrential cloudburst scattering
mirrors of light : : sunset's prismatics
in a Tucson parking lot
then the desert's mute inscrutable
way of going on
but it was like that between us : : those
moments of confrontation caught in dread
of time's long requirements

●   ·

What's more dreadful than safety
you're told your life depends on
a helmet through whose eyeholes
your gun is seeing
only what guns can see

—a mask that wove itself without your
having designed it

ii.

On video : : a man exploding
about being sick for no reason
though he knows he knows the reason
: : a video that will travel
around the world
while the man sickens and sickens

●

You say we live in freedom
Have you watched the ceiling overhead
descending like Poe's pendulum
moving down slow and soundless
lower and closer for longer
than we'd thought

The last word in freedom
The first word

2011

SUSPENDED LINES

Scrape a toxic field with a broken hoe

Found legacies turn up in splinters   blood-codes, secret sharings

Cracks of light in a sky intent on rain

   Reading our words from a time
   when to write a line was to know it true

   Today your voice : : *you can make from this*

One-string / blue / speaking / guitar

suspended here

2011

TRACINGS

This chair delivered yesterday

built for a large heavy man

left me from his estate

lies sidewise legs upturned

He would sit in the chair spooked by his own thoughts

He would say to himself *As the fabric shrinks*

the pattern changes

and forget to write it

He would want to say *The drug that ekes out*

life disenlivens life

I would see words float in the mirror

behind his heaped desk

as thought were smoke

•

The friends I can trust are those who will let me have my death
—traced on a rafter salvaged
from a house marked for demolition

Sky's a mottled marble slab
webs drift off a railing
There were voices here
once, a defiance that still doesn't falter
Imagine a mind overhearing language
split open, uncodified as
yet or never
Imagine a mind sprung open to music
—not the pitiless worm of a tune that won't let you forget it
but a scoreless haunting

2011

FROM STRATA

1

Under this blue
immune unfissured autumn
urbs et orbis   pivot and axis   thrashing

upthrust from strata
deep under : silences
pressed each against

another : sharpened flints
pulverized coral   stoneware crumblings
rusted musket muzzles

chips of China-trade
porcelain   shackled bone
no death unchained

Here at eye-level the new
news new season new
moment's momentary flare :

floodlit abstractions
root-riven   scrambling
for adulation

Yes, we lived here long and hard
on surfaces stunned by the wrecking ball
where time's thought's creature only

and when all's fallen   even
our remnant renegade selves
—let this too sleep in strata :

the nerve-ends of my footsole
still crave your touch as when
my earlobes glowed between

your quiet teeth

2

Say a pen must write underground   underwater   so be it

The students gather at the site :

Come over here and look at this
Looks like writing   yes   that's how they did it   thought it

into marks they thought
would outlast them

it would take patience to do that   Anyone
                                        recognize the script?

Could it be music?   a manifesto?

3

Rescuers back off   hands lifted open as in guilt
for the ancestors no one is rescued from :

curated galleried faces staring
off   from behind long-stiffened bandages

but who would meet those lookaway eyes
maybe they're metal   blind reflectors

maybe only who choose to look can see :
thought finding itself in act

violet olive brush strokes speaking of flesh
leaps diagonals pauses : a long conversation

with others living and dead
palpable and strange

4

Viscous stealth, brutal calm : subterfugal, churning
encrypted in tar   sending expendable

bodies to underworlds unseen   until
catastrophe blows apart

the premises   a spectacle hits
the TV channels   then in a blink

a dense cloth wipes history clean :

but never in beds never to warm again
with the pulsing of arrival   shudder of wordless welcome

the body heat of breadwinners and lovers

5

My hands under your buttocks   your fingers numbering my ribs
how a bow scrapes, a string holds the after-pluck

astonishing variations   hours, bodies without boundaries

Back into that erotic autumn I search my way defiant

through passages of long neglect

6

Throw the handwritten scraps of paper
into the toilet bowl

to work their way spiraling down
the open gullet of advanced barbarism

So : if you thought no good came from any of this
not the resistance nor its penalties

not our younger moments nor the continuing on
then, I say, trash the evidence

So : a scrap of paper   a loved bitter scrawl
swirls under into the confluence

of bodily waste and wasted bodies :
—a shred   absorbed, belonging

7

Weathers drag down and claw up the will :
yellowdust wind   asphalt fog   a green slash
of aurora borealis   or :

a surveillance helicopter's high-intensity beam
impaling solitudes   ransacking solidarities

In the end no pleas no bargains :

it's your own humanity you'll have to drag
over and over, piece by piece
            page after page
                    out of the dark

2010–2011

ENDPAPERS

i.

If the road's a frayed ribbon strung through dunes
continually drifting over
if the night grew green as sun and moon
changed faces and the sea became
its own unlit unlikely sound
consider yourself lucky to have come
this far   Consider yourself
a trombone blowing unheard
tones   a bass string plucked or locked
down by a hand its face articulated
in shadow, pressed against
a chain-link fence   Consider yourself
inside or outside, where-
ever you were when knotted steel
stopped you short   You can't flow through
as music or
as air

ii.

What holds what binds is breath   is
primal vision in a cloud's eye
is gauze around a wounded head
is bearing a downed comrade out beyond
the numerology of vital signs
into predictless space

iii.

The signature to a life requires
the search for a method
rejection of posturing
trust in the witnesses
a vial of invisible ink
a sheet of paper held steady
after the end-stroke
above a deciphering flame

2011

NOTES ON THE POEMS

The following section compiles all of the notes appearing in Adrienne Rich's published books, beginning with *Snapshots of a Daughter-in-Law* in 1963. Her first two books (*A Change of World* and *The Diamond Cutters*) appeared without explanatory notes—as did *The Will to Change* in 1971 and *Diving into the Wreck* in 1973. A year later, when putting together the 1974 volume *Poems Selected and New, 1950–1974*, she provided notes for three poems selected from *The Diamond Cutters*. After that, with the exception of *The Dream of a Common Language* in 1978, all of her other volumes included some explanatory notes on sources for passages or on works that informed her writing and thinking.

In preparing the contents of *The Fact of a Doorframe: Poems Selected and New 1950–1984*, Rich added two new notes that appear here with the date in parentheses. In *The Fact of a Doorframe* and in *Collected Early Poems* (1993), she also revised, expanded, or updated some notes, and cut others (she made no changes or provisions for notes for her last book, *Later Poems: Selected and New, 1971–2012*).

For the present volume I have brought together everything from the original books, using the updated versions where possible and restoring some notes she cut from the volumes of selected poems. Typography and format of the notes is made uniform without omitting any of the information they provided at the ends of the volumes where they first appeared. Where the note on one poem makes reference to another poem in the volume, the updated page reference is given.

The notes created especially for this volume are few, and where they occur, they are given in parentheses. For example, where information on a quoted passage was provided on the copyright page in one of the books, it appears here as a note. In rare instances I added an editor's note to give publishing information about a particular poem. Finally, rather than reprinting the full text of Adrienne Rich's original forewords for *Poems Selected and New, 1950–1974*, *The Fact of a Doorframe*, or *Collected Early Poems*, relevant information is briefly quoted in note form.

A CHANGE OF WORLD

Storm Warnings
(In *Collected Early Poems 1950–1970*, this poem is dated 1949.)

POEMS 1950–1951

(In *The Fact of a Doorframe: Poems Selected and New 1950–1984*, Rich noted: ["The Prisoners" and "At the Jewish New Year"] "were 'lost' for a long time; I had even forgotten their existence.")

THE DIAMOND CUTTERS

The Tourist and the Town   The pronouns in the third section were originally masculine. But the tourist was a woman—myself—and I never saw her as anything else. In 1953, when the poem was written, a notion of male experience as universal prevailed which made the feminine pronoun suspect or merely "personal." In this poem, as in "Afterward" (page 16), I later altered the pronouns because they alter, for me, the dimensions of the poem. (1984)

Villa Adriana   The summer palace built by the Emperor Hadrian for his favorite boy lover, Antinoüs. In "Antinoüs: The Diaries" (page 125) I let the young man speak for me. (1974)

The Snow Queen   Hans Christian Andersen's tale was the point of departure.

The Diamond Cutters   Thirty years later I have trouble with the informing metaphor of this poem. I was trying, in my twenties, to write about the craft of poetry. But I was drawing, quite ignorantly, on the long tradition of domination, according to which the precious resource is yielded up into the hands of the dominator as if by a natural event. The enforced and exploited labor of actual Africans in actual diamond mines was invisible to me and, therefore, invisible in the poem, which does not take responsibility for its own metaphor. I note this here because this kind of metaphor is still widely accepted, and I still have to struggle against it in my work. (1984)

SNAPSHOTS OF A DAUGHTER-IN-LAW

Euryclea's Tale Euryclea was the old nurse of Odysseus and the first person to recognize him when he returned home from his wanderings. (1974)

Snapshots of a Daughter-in-Law Part 4: "My Life had stood—a Loaded Gun," Emily Dickinson, *Complete Poems*, ed. T. H. Johnson, 1960, p. 369.

Part 7: The lines in Part 7 beginning "To have in this uncertain world some stay" were written by Mary Wollstonecraft in *Thoughts on the Education of Daughters* (London, 1787).

Part 8: "Vous mourez toutes à quinze ans," from Diderot's *Lettres à Sophie Volland*, quoted by Simone de Beauvoir in *Le Deuxième Sexe*, vol. II, pp. 123–24.

Part 10: Cf. *Le Deuxième Sexe*, vol. II, p. 574: ". . . elle arrive du fond des ages, de Thèbes, de Minos, de Chichen Itza; et elle est aussi le totem planté au coeur de la brousse africaine; c'est un helicoptère et c'est un oiseau; et voilà la plus grande merveille: sous ses cheveux peints le bruissement des feuillages devient une pensée et des paroles s'échappent de ses seins."

("She comes from the remotest ages, from Thebes, Minos, Chichén Itzá; and she is also a totem planted in the heart of the African jungle; she is a helicopter and she is a bird; and here is the greatest wonder: beneath her painted hair, the rustling of leaves becomes a thought and words escape from her breasts." *The Second Sex*, translated by Constance Borde and Sheila Malovany-Chevallier, Vintage Feminism Short Edition.)

Artificial Intelligence See Herbert Simon, *The New Science of Management Decision* (New York: Harper & Row, 1960), p. 26. "*A General*

Problem-Solving Program: Computer programs have been written that enable computers to discover proofs for theorems in logic or geometry, to play chess, to design motors . . . to compose music. . . . From almost all of them, whether intended as simulations [of human processes] or not, we learn something about human problem solving, thinking, and learning.

"The first thing we learn . . . is that we can explain these human processes *without* postulating mechanisms at subconscious levels that are different from those that are partly conscious and partly verbalized. . . . The secret of problem solving is that there is no secret."

Always the Same The last line is quoted from D. H. Lawrence, letter to Henry Savage, in *The Collected Letters of D. H. Lawrence,* ed. Harry T. Moore, vol. 1 (New York: Viking, 1962), p. 258.

POEMS 1962–1965

(The epigraph from Montaigne on page 165 is from the *Essays,* Book 1, Chapter 20: "Shall I change, just for you, this beautiful interwoven structure! Death is one of the attributes you were created with; death is a part of you; you are running away from yourself." Translation by M.A. Screech [Penguin/Allen Lane].)

NECESSITIES OF LIFE

In the Woods The first line is borrowed and translated from the Dutch poet J. C. Bloem.

Mourning Picture Effie is the painter's daughter, who died young, and the speaker of the poem.

"I Am in Danger—Sir—" See Thomas Johnson and Theodora Ward, eds., *The Letters of Emily Dickinson,* vol. 2 (Cambridge, Mass.: Harvard University Press, 1958), p. 409. (The poem was first published as an epigraph to *Emily Dickinson: The Mind of the Poet* by Albert J. Gelpi [Cambridge, Mass.: Harvard University Press, 1965] under the title "E.")

Any Husband to Any Wife The title is, of course, a reversal of Browning's, and the epigraph comes from his poem.

Translations from the Dutch (In *Necessities of Life* Rich provided two notes for these poems: "These translations are from a group commissioned by the Bollingen Foundation. For criticism and linguistic advice my thanks go to Judith Herzberg, Marjan DeWolff, and Leo Vroman; the final responsibility is of course my own."

"Anyone who will compare the Dutch poems with my translations will see that I have, deliberately, refrained from imitating rhyme patterns and have in some instances altered metres. I have tried to be faithful first of all to the images and the emotional tone of the poems, and have been unwilling to introduce distortions in order to reproduce formal structure. Much of the onomatopoeic music of the Nijhoff poem is thus necessarily lost. Possibly I have made Hendrik de Vries sound more modern than he actually sounds in Dutch: in 'Brother' for instance he uses an old form of the second person singular which corresponds to the English 'thou.' But I believe that the inner structure of these poems remains in the translations, and as a poet-translator I have tried to do as I would be done by.")

LEAFLETS

Orion One or two phrases suggested by Gottfried Benn's essay "Artists and Old Age," in *Primal Vision: Selected Writings*, ed. E. B. Ashton (New York: New Directions, 1960).

Dwingelo The site of an astronomical observatory in Holland.

Charleston in the 1860's See Ben Ames Williams, ed., *A Diary from Dixie* (Boston: Houghton Mifflin, 1963).

For a Russian Poet Part 3: This poem is based on an account by the poet Natalya Gorbanevskaya of a protest action against the Soviet invasion of Czechoslovakia. Gorbanevskaya was later held, and bore a child, in a "penal mental institution" for her political activities.

Two Poems (adapted from Anna Akhmatova) Based on literal prose versions in Dimitri Obolensky, ed., *The Penguin Book of Russian Verse* (London: Penguin, 1962).

Implosions The first three lines are stolen, by permission, from Abbott Small.

To Frantz Fanon Revolutionary philosopher; studied medicine at the Sorbonne; worked as a psychiatrist in Algeria during the Franco-Algerian war; died of cancer at thirty-six. Author of *The Wretched of the Earth*; *Toward the African Revolution*; *Black Skin, White Masks*; *A Dying Colonialism*.

The Observer Suggested by a brief newspaper account of the field-work of Dian Fossey. She more recently wrote of her observations in *Gorillas in the Mist* (Boston: Houghton Mifflin, 1983).

Leaflets Part 2: "The love of a fellow-creature in all its fullness consists simply in the ability to say to him: 'What are you going through?'" (Simone Weil, *Waiting for God*).

Ghazals (Homage to Ghalib) This poem began to be written after I read Aijaz Ahmad's literal English versions of the Urdu poetry of Mirza Ghalib (1797–1869). While the structure and metrics of the classical *ghazal* form used by Ghalib are much stricter than mine, I adhered to his use of a minimum five couplets to a *ghazal*, each couplet being autonomous and independent of the others. The continuity and unity flow from the associations and images playing back and forth among the couplets in any single *ghazal*. The poems are dated as I wrote them, during a month in the summer of 1968. Although I was a contributor to Ahmad's *The Ghazals of Ghalib* (New York: Columbia University Press, 1971), the *ghazals* here are not translations, but original poems.

My *ghazals* are personal and public, American and twentieth-century; but they owe much to the presence of Ghalib in my mind: a poet self-educated and profoundly learned, who owned no property and borrowed his books, writing in an age of political and cultural break-up (1993).

Translations from the Dutch, Russian, and Yiddish (Rich wrote in *Leaflets* that "The Dutch poems in this book ['City' and 'Dwingelo'] are translations, in the sense that they were derived by me directly from their originals. The Russian poems ['Two Poems, adapted from Anna Akhmatova'] are adaptations of literal prose versions in the *Penguin Book of Russian Verse*, and will appear in *Poets on Street Corners*, an anthology of Russian poetry edited by Olga Carlisle, to be published by Random House in 1969. The Yiddish poem ['There Are Such Springlike Nights'] is, similarly, an adaptation from a literal version furnished by Eliezer Greenberg and Irving Howe, and will be included in their forthcoming anthology of Yiddish poetry in translation. It appears here with their permission and that of Kadia Maldovsky [*sic*].")

(The poem "Postcard" on page 289 was first published by W. W. Norton in *Poems Selected and New, 1950–1974* in a section titled "Uncollected Poems 1957–1969." In the *Collected Early Poems* it was grouped with the poems of *Leaflets*.)

White Night   This poem and "There Are Such Springlike Nights" (page 244) were adapted from the Yiddish with the aid of transliterated versions and prose translations provided by Eliezer Greenberg and Irving Howe, in whose anthology, *A Treasury of Yiddish Poetry* (New York: Holt, Rinehart and Winston, 1969), these first appeared.

POEMS 1973–1974

From an Old House in America   Part 4: The first line is borrowed from Emily Brontë's poem "Stanzas."

Part 7: Many African women went into labor and gave birth on the slave-ships of the Middle Passage, chained for the duration of the voyage to the dying or the dead.

Part 11: *Datura* is a poisonous hallucinogenic weed with a spiky green pod and a white flower; also known as jimson-weed, or deadly nightshade.

THE DREAM OF A COMMON LANGUAGE

(*Twenty-One Love Poems* was first published in 1976 in a limited edition, designed and hand-printed by Bonnie Carpenter at Effie's Press, Emeryville, California.)

Paula Becker to Clara Westhoff   Some phrases in this poem are quoted from actual diaries and letters of Paula Modersohn Becker, which were shown to me in unpublished translations by Liselotte Glozer. Since then, an annotated translation of the manuscripts has been published by Diane Radycki: *The Letters and Journals of Paula Modersohn-Becker* (Metuchen, N.J.: Scarecrow Press, 1980). (1984)

A WILD PATIENCE HAS TAKEN ME THIS FAR

The Images   The phrase "moral and ordinary" is echoed from Blanche Wiesen Cook's essay "Female Support Networks and Political

Activism" in her pamphlet *Women and Support Networks* (Brooklyn, N.Y.: Out & Out Books, 1979).

Integrity   To my knowledge, this word was first introduced in a feminist context by Janice Raymond in her essay "The Illusion of Androgyny," *Quest: A Feminist Quarterly* 2, no. 1 (Summer 1975).

Culture and Anarchy   The title is stolen from Matthew Arnold's collection of essays by the same name, first published in London, 1869. The sources for the voices of nineteenth-century women heard in this poem are as follows: diaries of Susan B. Anthony, 1861, and letter from Anthony to her sister, 1883, both from Ida Husted Harper, *The Life and Work of Susan B. Anthony* (Indianapolis and Kansas City: Bowen-Merrill, 1899); Jane Addams, *Twenty Years at Hull House* (New York: Macmillan, 1926); Elizabeth Barrett Browning, letter to Anna Brownell Jameson, 1852, in Frederick Kenyon, ed., *The Letters of Elizabeth Barrett Browning*, vol. 2 (New York: Macmillan, 1898); Ida Husted Harper, introduction to Susan B. Anthony and Ida Husted Harper, *The History of Woman Suffrage*, vol. 4 (1902); Elizabeth Cady Stanton, speech "On Solitude of Self," in Anthony and Harper, *The History of Woman Suffrage*, vol. 4; Elizabeth Cady Stanton, letter to Susan B. Anthony, in Harper, *The Life and Work of Susan B. Anthony*, vol. 1.

For Julia in Nebraska   Epigraph quoted from the Willa Cather Educational Foundation, Historical Landmark Council, marker at the intersection of Highways 281 and 4, fourteen miles north of Red Cloud, Nebraska.

For Ethel Rosenberg   Phrases italicized in Part 3, line 6, are from Robert Coover's novel *The Public Burning* (New York: Viking, 1977).

Mother-in-Law   It has been suggested to me that the lines "I am trying to tell you, I envy / the people in mental hospitals their freedom" add to a stockpile of false images of mental patients' incarceration—images that help perpetuate their pain and the system which routinely drugs, curbs, "constrains," electroshocks, and surgically experiments on them. The woman speaking in the poem speaks, of course, out of her own frustration and despair, the lines are bitterly ironic; but I agree with my critics that in a world eager both to romanticize and to torture mental patients, such cliches must be used, if at all, with utmost concern for the realities underlying them. (1984)

Heroines See Gerda Lerner: "The history of notable women is the history of exceptional, even deviant women, and does not describe the experience and history of the mass of women." ("Placing Women in History: Definitions and Challenges," in Gerda Lerner, *The Majority Finds Its Past* [New York: Oxford University Press, 1979].)

Grandmothers Part 3: Italicized lines are quoted from Lillian Smith's *Killers of the Dream* (New York: Norton, 1961), p. 39.

The Spirit of Place Part III: Italicized passages are from Thomas Johnson and Theodora Ward, eds., *The Letters of Emily Dickinson* (Cambridge, Mass.: Harvard University Press, 1958), specifically, from Letter 154 to Susan Gilbert (June 1854) and Letter 203 to Catherine Scott Anthon Turner (March 1859).

Turning the Wheel Part 3: The Hohokam were a prehistoric farming culture who developed irrigation canals in southern Arizona and southwestern New Mexico between about 300 B.C. and A.D. 1400. The word *Hohokam* is Pima and is translated variously as "those who have ceased" or "those who were used up." See Emil W. Haury, *The Hohokam, Desert Farmers and Craftsmen (sic)* (Tucson: University of Arizona Press, 1976).

Part 7: The letter is a poetic fiction, based on a reading of Virginia Grattan, *Mary Colter, Builder upon the Red Earth* (Flagstaff, Ariz.: Northland Press, 1980). Mary E. J. Colter (1869–1958) studied design and architecture in order to support her mother and younger sister upon her father's death. She taught art in a St. Paul, Minnesota, high school for fifteen years before starting to work as a decorator for the Fred Harvey Company and the Santa Fe Railroad. Soon she was completely in charge of both exterior and interior design of hotels and restaurants from Chicago westward. Her work advanced the movement away from Victorian style toward a more indigenous southwestern and western architecture. At the height of her career she designed eight major buildings at the Grand Canyon, all of which are still standing. She never married. She drew consistently on Native American arts and design in her work, and her collection of Hopi and Navaho art can be seen at Mesa Verde Museum. Colter's lifework—a remarkable accomplishment for a woman architect—was thus inextricable from the violation and expropriation of Native culture by white entrepreneurs. Yet her love for that culture was lifelong.

YOUR NATIVE LAND, YOUR LIFE

(The poem "Sources" was first published in 1983 as a chapbook by the Heyeck Press, Woodside, California.)

Sources   The phrase "an end to suffering" was evoked by a sentence in Nadine Gordimer's *Burger's Daughter*: "No one knows where the end of suffering will begin."

North American Time   Section IX: Julia de Burgos (1914–1953), Puerto Rican poet and revolutionary who died on the streets of New York City.

Dreams Before Waking   "Hasta tu país cambió. Lo has cambiado tú mismo" ("Even your country has changed. You yourself have changed it"). These lines, from Morejón's "Elogio de la Dialéctica," and Georgina Herrera's poem "Como Presentaciön, Como Disculpa" can be found in Margaret Randall, ed., *Breaking the Silences: 20th Century Poetry by Cuban Women* (1982). Pulp Press, 3868 MPO, Vancouver, Canada V6B 3Z3.

One Kind of Terror: A Love Poem   Section 6: "Now you have touched the women, you have struck a rock, you have dislodged a boulder, you will be crushed." Freedom song sung by African women in mass demonstration in Pretoria, 1956, in which 20,000 women gathered to protest the issue of passes to women. See Hilda Bernstein, *For Their Triumphs and for Their Tears*, International Defence and Aid Fund for Southern Africa, 1975.

In the Wake of Home   Section 6: The Jodensavanne is an abandoned Jewish settlement in Surinam whose ruins exist in a jungle on the Cassipoera River.

Emily Carr   Canadian painter (1871–1945). At the height of her powers she painted, with deep respect, the disappearing totem poles of the Northwest Coast Indians. See Doris Shadbolt, *The Art of Emily Carr* (Seattle: University of Washington Press, 1979).

Yom Kippur 1984   The epigraph and quoted lines from Robinson

Jeffers come from *The Women at Point Sur and Other Poems* (New York: Liveright, 1977).

Contradictions Section 16: See Elizabeth Bishop, *The Complete Poems 1927–1979* (New York: Farrar, Straus & Giroux, 1983), p. 173.

Section 26: See Cynthia Ozick, *Art and Ardor* (New York: Farrar, Straus & Giroux, 1984), p. 255: "the glorious So What: the life-cry."

Section 27: Ding Ling, leading Chinese novelist and major literary figure in the Revolutionary government under Mao. Exiled in 1957 for writing too critically and independently. Imprisoned as a counter-revolutionary in 1970; cleared of all charges in 1976 at the end of the Cultural Revolution.

TIME'S POWER

Sleepwalking Title and opening words ("next to death") from "Slaapwandelen (naast de dood)" by Chr. J. van Geel, Dutch poet and painter. For the original and my translation, see page 214.

Letters in the Family Section 11, Yugoslavia, 1944: See *Hannah Senesh: Her Life and Diary* (New York: Schocken, 1973). Born in Budapest, 1921, Hannah Senesh became a Zionist and immigrated to Palestine at the age of eighteen; her mother and brother remained in Europe. In 1943, she joined an expedition of Jews who trained under the British to parachute behind Nazi lines in Europe and connect with the partisan underground, to rescue Jews in Hungary, Romania, and Czechoslovakia. She was arrested by the Nazis, imprisoned, tortured, and executed in November 1944. Like the other letter-writers, "Esther" is an imagined person. See also Ruth Whitman's long poem *The Testing of Hannah Senesh* (Detroit, Mich.: Wayne State University Press, 1986).

The Desert as Garden of Paradise Section 2: Chavela Vargas, a Mexican popular and traditional singer.

Section 3: Malintzin/La Malinche/Marina are names for an Aztec woman given as a slave to Hernán Cortés on his arrival in Mexico in 1519. Her historical reality has undergone many layerings of legend and symbolism; more recently she has become a frequent presence in Chicana feminist literature. See, for example, Norma Alarcón, "Chicana's Feminist Literature: A Revision through Malintzin," in *This Bridge Called My Back: Writings by Radical Women of Color*, ed. Gloria

Anzaldua and Cherrie Moraga (Watertown, Mass.: Persephone, 1981; distributed by Kitchen Table / Women of Color Press, P.O. Box 908, Latham, NY 12110). See also Lucha Corpi's "Marina" poems, and the author's note, in *Fireflight: Three Latin American Poets*, trans. Catherine Rodriguez-Nieto (Oakland, Calif.: Oyez Books, 1975); and Gloria Anzaldua, *Borderlands / La Frontera: The New Mestiza* (San Francisco: Spinsters / Aunt Lute Books, 1987).

Section 7: See Peter Masten Dunne, S.J., *Black Robes in Lower California* (Berkeley: University of California Press, 1968); Antonine Tibeson, O.F.M., ed., *The Writings of Junipero Serra*, vol. 1 (Washington, D.C.: Academy of American Franciscan History, 1955); Robert F. Heizer, ed., *The Destruction of California Indians* (Santa Barbara and Salt Lake City: Peregrine Smith, 1974); Van H. Garner, *The Broken Ring: The Destruction of the California Indians* (Tucson, Ariz.: Westernlore Press, 1982).

Sections 10, 11: Italicized phrases from John C. van Dyke, *The Desert* (1901) (Salt Lake City: Peregrine Smith, 1980).

The Slides Thanks to Janis Kelly for her keen eye on the medical details.

Harpers Ferry In 1859, the white abolitionist John Brown rented a farm near Harpers Ferry, Virginia (now West Virginia), as a base for slave insurrections. On October 16 of that year, he and his men raided and captured the federal arsenal, but found their escape blocked by local militia; the U.S. marines then seized the arsenal. Ten of Brown's men were killed in this conflict, and Brown himself was later tried and hanged. Harriet Tubman (1820–1913), Black antislavery activist and strategist, led more than 300 people from slavery to freedom via the Underground Railroad. She was known as "General Moses." Though in contact with John Brown, she withdrew from participation before the raid. Tubman never actually came to Harpers Ferry; her appearance in this poem is a fiction.

Living Memory "it was pick and shovel work . . .": quoted from *Wally Hunt's Vermont* (Brownington, Vt.: Orleans County Historical Society, 1983).

An Atlas of the Difficult World Part V: "over the chained bay waters": From Hart Crane, "To Brooklyn Bridge," in *The Poems of Hart Crane*, ed. Marc Simon (New York and London: Liveright, 1989; poem originally published in 1930).

"There are roads to take when you think of your country": From Muriel Rukeyser, *U.S. 1* (New York: Covici Friede, 1938); see also Muriel Rukeyser, *The Collected Poems* (New York: McGraw-Hill, 1978).

"I don't want to know how he tracked them": On May 13, 1988, Stephen Roy Carr shot and killed Rebecca Wight, one of two lesbians camping on the Appalachian Trail in Pennsylvania. Her lover, Claudia Brenner, suffered five bullet wounds. She dragged herself two miles along the trail to a road, where she flagged a car to take her to the police. In October of that year, Carr was found guilty of first-degree murder and sentenced to life in prison without parole. During the legal proceedings, it became clear that Carr had attacked the women because they were lesbians. See *Gay Community News* (August 7 and November 11, 1988).

Part VI: "Hatred of England smouldering like a turf-fire": See Nella Braddy, *Anne Sullivan Macy: The Story behind Helen Keller* (Garden City, N.Y.: Doubleday, Doran & Company, 1933), p. 13.

"Meat three times a day": See Frank Murray, "The Irish and Afro-Americans in U.S. History," *Freedomways: A Quarterly Review of the Freedom Movement* 22, no. 1 (1982): 22.

Part X: The passages in italics are quoted from *Soledad Brother: The Prison Letters of George Jackson* (New York: Bantam, 1970), pp. 24, 26, 93, 245.

Eastern War Time Part 2: Text of a telegram sent through the American legation in Bern, Switzerland, August 11, 1942, to the U.S. State Department in Washington, and transmitted after several weeks' delay to Rabbi Stephen Wise in New York. See David S. Wyman, *The Abandonment of the Jews* (New York: Pantheon, 1984), pp. 42–45.

Part 4: Charged with the murder of a fourteen-year-old girl employed in his uncle's pencil factory in Atlanta, Leo Max Frank (1884–1915), a mechanical engineer, was tried and found guilty, and the decision appealed, in a climate of intense anti-Semitism. When his sentence was commuted from death to life by the governor of Georgia, he was dragged by a mob from prison and lynched.

Part 10: "A coat is not a piece of cloth only": See Barbara Myerhoff, *Number Our Days* (New York: Simon & Schuster, 1978), p. 44. Myerhoff quotes Shmuel Goldman, immigrant Socialist garment-worker: "It is not the way of a Jew to make his work like there was no human being to suffer when it's done badly. A coat is not a piece of cloth only. The tailor is connected to the one who wears it and he should not forget it."

Tattered Kaddish "The Reapers of the Field are the Comrades, masters of this wisdom, because Malkhut is called the Apple Field, and She grows sprouts of secrets and new meanings of Torah. Those who constantly create new interpretations of Torah are the ones who reap Her" (Moses Cordovero, Or ha-Hammah on Zohar III, 106a). See Barry W. Holtz, ed., *Back to the Sources: Reading the Classic Jewish Texts* (New York: Summit, 1984), p. 305.

For a Friend in Travail "The love of our neighbor in all its fullness simply means being able to say to him, 'What are you going through?'" Simone Weil, *Waiting for God* (New York: Putnam, 1951), p. 115.

DARK FIELDS OF THE REPUBLIC

What Kind of Times Are These The title is from Bertolt Brecht's poem "An Die Nachgeborenen" ("For Those Born Later"): "What kind of times are these / When it's almost a crime to talk about trees / Because it means keeping still about so many evil deeds?" (For the complete poem, in a different translation, see John Willett and Ralph Manheim, eds., *Bertolt Brecht, Poems 1913–1956* [New York: Methuen, 1976], pp. 318–20.)

"our country moving closer to its own truth and dread . . .": echoes Osip Mandelstam's 1921 poem that begins "I was washing outside in the darkness" and ends "The earth's moving closer to truth and to dread." (Clarence Brown and W. S. Merwin, trans., *Osip Mandelstam: Selected Poems* [New York: Atheneum, 1974], p. 40.) Mandelstam was forbidden to publish, then exiled and sentenced to five years of hard labor for a poem caricaturing Stalin; he died in a transit camp in 1938.

"To be human, said Rosa . . .": Rosa Luxemberg (1871–1919) was a Polish-born middle-class Jew. Early in her abbreviated life she entered the currents of European socialist revolutionary thinking and action. She became one of the most influential and controversial figures in the social-democratic movements of Eastern Europe and Germany. Besides her political essays, she left hundreds of vivid letters to friends and comrades. Imprisoned during World War I for her strongly internationalist and anticapitalist beliefs, she was murdered in Berlin in 1919 by right-wing soldiers, with the passive collusion of a faction from her own party. Her body was thrown into a canal.

On December 28, 1916, from prison, she wrote a New Year letter to friends she feared were both backsliding and complaining: "Then see to it that you remain a *Mensch*! [Yiddish/German for human being] . . . Being a *Mensch* means happily throwing one's life 'on fate's great scale' if necessary, but, at the same time, enjoying every bright day and every beautiful cloud. Oh, I can't write you a prescription for being a *Mensch*. I only know how one is a *Mensch*, and you used to know it too when we went walking for a few hours in the Südende fields with the sunset's red light falling on the wheat. The world is so beautiful even with all its horrors." (*The Letters of Rosa Luxemburg*, ed., trans., and with an introduction by Stephen Eric Bronner [Atlantic Highlands, N.J.: Humanities Press, 1993], p. 173.)

Calle Visión   Calle Visión is the name of a road in the southwestern United States—literally, "Vision Street."

"that tells the coming of the railroad": "With the coming of the railroad, new materials and pictorial designs and motifs, including trains themselves, appeared in Navaho weaving (ca. 1880)." (From the Museum of Indian Arts and Culture, Museum of New Mexico, Santa Fe.)

"a place not to live but to die in": See Sir Thomas Browne, *Religio Medici* (1635): "For the World, I count it not an Inn, but an Hospital; and a place not to live, but to dye in." (*Religio Medici and Other Writings by Sir Thomas Browne* [London: Everyman's Library, J. M. Dent, 1947], p. 83.)

"Have you ever worked around metal? . . .": From a questionnaire filled out before undergoing a magnetic resonance imaging (MRI) scan.

"The world is falling down. . . .": From the song "The World Is Falling Down," composed by Abbey Lincoln, sung by her on the Verve recording of the same title, 1990 (Moseka Music BMI).

"And the fire shall try. . . .": I Corinthians 3:13: "Every man's work shall be made manifest . . . and the fire shall try every man's work of what sort it is." Used by Studs Terkel as an epigraph to his *Working* (New York: Pantheon, 1974).

Reversion   This poem is for Nina Menkes and her film *The Great Sadness of Zohara*.

Revolution in Permanence (1953, 1993)   The phrase "revolution in permanence" is Marx's, referring to his concept that the creation of a just society does not end with the uprooting of the old order, "but must continue to the new, so you begin to feel this presence of the future in the present." (Raya Dunayevskaya, *Marxism and Freedom* [New York: Columbia University Press, 1988], p. 12.)

In the poem, Ethel Rosenberg is a secular vision. But she was, of course, a real woman, electrocuted in 1953 with her husband, Julius, on charges of conspiracy to commit espionage. The original charges were rapidly translated by the presiding judge and the media into "selling the secret of the atomic bomb" to agents of the Soviet Union. After the Rosenbergs' conviction, "twenty-three motions and appeals for new trial, reduction of sentence, stay of execution, and presidential clemency were made on the basis of perjury; unfair trial; cruel, excessive, inapplicable, and unprecedented sentencing; newly discovered evidence; subornation of perjury by the prosecution; application of incorrect law; and justice, mercy, or both. All appeals were denied. . . . [The day after the electrocution] Justice Hugo Black's majority opinion was published, noting that the Supreme Court 'had never reviewed the record of this trial and therefore never affirmed the fairness of this trial.' " (Virginia Carmichael, *Framing History: The Rosenberg Story and the Cold War* [Minneapolis: University of Minnesota Press, 1993], pp. 63–64. See also Walter and Miriam Schneir, *Invitation to an Inquest*

[New York: Pantheon, 1983]; Robert and Michael Meeropol, *We Are Your Sons: The Legacy of Ethel and Julius Rosenberg* [Urbana and Chicago: University of Illinois Press, 1986]; and Michael Meeropol, ed., *The Rosenberg Letters: A Complete Edition of the Prison Correspondence of Julius and Ethel Rosenberg* [New York: Garland, 1994].

Then or Now   This sequence of poems derives in part from *Hannah Arendt and Karl Jaspers, Correspondence 1926–1969*, ed. Lotte and Hans Saner, trans. Robert and Rita Kimbel (New York: Harcourt Brace Jovanovich, 1992). While reading these letters, I had been reflecting on concepts of "guilt" and "innocence" among artists and intellectuals like myself in the United States. The poems owe much also to the continuing pressure of events.

Late Ghazal   See "Ghazals (Homage to Ghalib)" on pages 275–85 and "The Blue Ghazals" on pages 307–12. See also Aijaz Ahmad, ed., *Ghazals of Ghalib* (New York: Columbia University Press, 1971).

Six Narratives   The narratives are spoken by different voices.

"Vigil for boy of responding kisses, . . .": See Walt Whitman, "Vigil strange I kept on the field one night," in *The Essential Whitman*, selected and ed. Galway Kinnell (New York: Ecco Press, 1987), pp. 123–24.

Inscriptions   "I need to live each day through. . . .": These two lines are quoted from an earlier poem of mine ("8/8/68: I") in "Ghazals (Homage to Ghalib)"; see above.

"When shall we learn, what should be clear as day, . . . ?": These two lines are from W. H. Auden's "Canzone," in *The Collected Poetry of W. H. Auden* (New York: Random House, 1945), p. 161.

"Medbh's postcard from Belfast": I thank the Northern Irish poet Medbh McGuckian for permission to quote her words from a postcard received in August 1994.

"suffused / by what it works in, 'like the dyer's hand.' ": I had written "suffused," later began looking up the line I was quoting from memory: was it Coleridge? Keats? Shakespeare? My friend Barbara Gelpi confirmed it was Shakespeare, in his Sonnet III: "Thence comes it that my name receives a brand / And almost thence my nature is subdued / To what it works in, like the dyer's hand." I have kept "suffused" here because to feel suffused by the materials that one has perforce to work in is not necessarily to be subdued, though some might think so.

MIDNIGHT SALVAGE

Char   Italicized phrases and some images from *Leaves of Hypnos*, the journal kept in 1942–1943 by the poet René Char while he was a commander in the French Resistance, and from some of Char's poems. I have drawn on both Jackson Mathew's and Cid Corman's translations of Char's journal in integrating his words into my poem. Char joined the Surrealist movement late and broke with it prior to World War II. It was André Breton who said, "The simplest surrealist act consists of going down into the street, revolver in hand, and shooting at random."

Modotti.   Tina Modotti (1896–1942): photographer, political activist, revolutionary. Her most significant artistic work was done in Mexico in the 1920s, including a study of the typewriter belonging to her lover, the Cuban revolutionary Julio Antonio Mella. Framed for his murder by the fascists in 1929, she was expelled from Mexico in 1930. After some years of political activity in Berlin, the Soviet Union, and Spain, she returned incognito to Mexico, where she died in 1942. In my search for Modotti I had to follow clues she left; I did not want to iconize her but to imagine critically the traps and opportunities of her life and choices.

Camino Real   "Can you afford not to make / the magical study / which happiness is?": From Charles Olson, "Variations Done for Gerald Van der Wiele," in *Charles Olson, Selected Poems*, ed. Robert Creeley (Berkeley: University of California Press, 1997), p. 83.

"George Oppen to June Degnan: . . .": See George Oppen, *The Selected Letters of George Oppen*, ed. Rachel Blau DuPlessis (Durham, N.C.: Duke University Press, 1990), p. 212.

"*The Night Has a Thousand Eyes*"   The title of the poem is that of a composition played by John Coltrane on the album *Coltrane's Sound*, Atlantic Jazz, 1964.

Section 5, lines 10–12: ". . . the Lordly Hudson / . . . which has no peer / in Europe or the East": From Paul Goodman, "The Lordly Hudson," in *The Lordly Hudson* (New York: Macmillan, 1962), p. 7.

Section 6, lines 9–10: "—Where do you come from?— / —Como

tú, like you, from nothing—": See Jack Agüeros, Introduction, *Song of the Simple Truth: The Complete Poems of Julia de Burgos*, comp. and trans. Jack Agüeros (Willimantic, Conn.: Curbstone Press, 1997), p. xxv.

Section 8, line 4: "through interboro fissures of the mind": From Hart Crane's "The Bridge," Part VII: "The Tunnel," line 71.

Section 8, line 9. In "The Bridge," Crane hallucinated Edgar Allan Poe in the New York subway; I conjure Crane, Miles Davis, Muriel Rukeyser, Julia de Burgos, and Paul Goodman, or their descendants.

A Long Conversation "energy: Eternal Delight": See William Blake, The Marriage of Heaven and Hell, plate 4: "The Voice of the Devil."

"Maybe this is the beginning of madness . . .": See *Osip Mandelstam: Selected Poems*, trans. Clarence Brown and W. S. Merwin (New York: Atheneum, 1974), p. 95.

"The bourgeoisie cannot exist . . . its own image": See Karl Marx, "Manifesto of the Communist Party" (1848), in *The Portable Karl Marx*, ed. Eugene Kamenka (New York: Penguin, 1983), pp. 207–8. "In proportion as the bourgeoisie, i.e., capital. . . ." Ibid., p. 211. See also Karl Marx and Frederick Engels, *The Communist Manifesto: A Modern Edition*, intro. Eric Hobsbawm (London and New York: Verso, 1998).

"—It isn't nations anymore . . .": Suggested by Hans Magnus Enzensberger, *Civil Wars: From L.A. to Bosnia* (New York: New Press, 1993).

"What is the use of studying philosophy . . .": See Norman Malcolm, *Ludwig Wittgenstein: A Memoir* (London: Oxford University Press, 1958), p. 39.

"small tradespeople . . . of the population": See Marx, p. 212.

"At the risk of appearing ridiculous": See Che Guevara, *Che Guevara Reader: Writings on Guerrilla Strategy, Politics and Revolution*, ed. David Deutschmann (Melbourne and New York: Ocean Press, 1997), p. 211: "At the risk of seeming ridiculous, let me say that the true revolutionary is guided by great feelings of love" ("Socialism and Man in Cuba," 1965).

"the memory of traditions of mercy . . .": See interview with Aijaz

Ahmad, in *In Defense of History: Marxism and the Postmodern Agenda*, ed. Ellen Meiksins Wood and John Bellamy Foster (New York: Monthly Review Press, 1997), p. 111: ". . . we certainly need the most rigorous of theories but we also need to have memories of the traditions of mercy and the struggles for justice. It is only there that any true reconciliation of the universal and the particular is really possible."

"the eye has become a human eye . . .": Marx, p. 151.

"the Arts, you know . . .": Richard M. Nixon, taped in 1972, quoted in Robert Penn Warren, *Democracy and Poetry* (Cambridge, Mass.: Harvard University Press, 1975), p. 36.

" 'This is for you . . .' ": After Georges Brassens's "Chanson pour l'Auvergnat," recorded by Juliette Greco on her album *10 Ans de Chansons*, Phillips, 1962.

FOX

The lines in Spanish in the dedication are from Violeta Parra's "Gracias a la Vida".

Nora's Gaze Alludes to works by the painter Nora Jaffe (1928–1994). See Clayton Eshleman, "Nora's Roar," in his *From Scratch* (Santa Rosa, Calif.: Black Sparrow Press, 1998), pp. 31–49.

Messages Blaise Pascal (1623–1662): *Le silence éternel de ces espaces m'affraye* ("The eternal silence of these infinite spaces frightens me"). See *Pensées of Blaise Pascal*, trans. W. F. Trotter, Everyman's Library, no. 874 (London: Dent, 1948), p. 61.

Manzanar Site of the first War Relocation Center activated in World War II for the internment of Japanese Americans, Manzanar is located east of the Sierra Nevada range and northeast of Death Valley.

Twilight Brownington, Vermont, is the site of the "Old Stone House" completed in 1836 as a dormitory for the Orleans County Grammar School. Its architect and builder, African American Alexander Lucius Twilight, served as principal of the school for most of its existence ("The Old Stone House Museum" [Orleans, Vt.: Orleans County Historical Society, 1996]). A working granite quarry still operates in Barre, Vermont.

Noctilucent Clouds "Several times in the last few months, observers in the lower 48 have seen 'noctilucent clouds,' which develop about

50 miles above the earth's surface—clouds so high that they reflect the sun's rays long after nightfall. . . . [G]lobal warming seems to be driving them toward the equator. . . . In retrospect it will be clear." Bill McKibben, "Indifferent to a Planet in Pain," *New York Times*, September 4, 1999, sec. A.

"Usonian:" The term used by Frank Lloyd Wright for his prairie-inspired American architecture.

Terza Rima Section 3: *Vivo nel non volare* . . . : "I live in the failed will / of the post-war time / loving the world I hate"—Pier Paolo Pasolini, "Le Ceneri di Gramsci," in Lawrence R. Smith, ed. and trans., *The New Italian Poetry, 1945 to the Present* (Berkeley: University of California Press, 1981), pp. 80–81. See also Pier Paolo Pasolini, *Poems*, selected and trans. Norman MacAfee and Luciano Martinengo (London: John Calder, 1982), pp. 10–11.

Waiting for You at the Mystery Spot " 'The *mystai* streamed' toward [the Telestrion]." C. Kerényi, *Eleusis*, trans. Ralph Manheim, Bollingen series 65, vol. 4 (New York: Bollingen Foundation/Pantheon, 1967), p. 82.

THE SCHOOL AMONG THE RUINS

Tell Me "remembered if outlived / as freezing": Emily Dickinson, *The Complete Poems*, ed. Thomas H. Johnson (Boston: Little, Brown, 1960), no. 341.

"harrowed in defeats of language": Michael Heller, "Sag Harbor, Whitman, As If an Ode," in *Wordflow: New and Selected Poems* (Jersey City, N.J.: Talisman House, 1997), p. 129.

"in history to my barest marrow": *Black Salt: Poems by Édouard Glissant*, trans. Betsy Wing (Ann Arbor: University of Michigan Press, 1998), p. 33.

This evening let's "friendship is not a tragedy": See June Jordan, "Civil Wars" (1980), in *Some of Us Did Not Die: New and Selected Essays* (New York: Basic Books, 2002), p. 267.

Delivered Clean "Delivered vacant" is a developer's phrase for a building for sale whose tenants have already been evicted. See Rebecca Solnit, *Hollow City: The Siege of San Francisco and the Crisis of American Urbanism* (New York: Verso, 2000), p. 158.

Transparencies   "we are truely sorry . . .": Clyde Haberman, "Palestinians Reclaim Their Town after Israelis Withdraw," *New York Times*, August 31, 2001, p. A6.

Collaborations   *dimdumim*: Hebrew for "dawn," "dusk," "twilight."

"what thou lovest well . . .": See Ezra Pound, *The Pisan Cantos* (London: Faber & Faber, 1959), p. 112: "what thou lovest well remains . . . cannot be reft from thee."

"what does not change . . .": See Charles Olson, "The Kingfishers," in his *Selected Poems* (Berkeley: University of California Press, 1997), p. 5: "What does not change / is the will to change."

"the fascination with what's easiest . . .": See W. B. Yeats, "The Fascination of What's Difficult," in his *Collected Poems*, 2nd ed. (New York: Macmillan, 1950), p. 104.

Alternating Current   The Villa Grimaldi outside Santiago, formerly a military officers' club, was converted to a detention and torture facility during the Pinochet regime in Chile. It is now a memorial park honoring the victims of torture.

V   "If some long unborn friend . . .": Muriel Rukeyser, "Tree of Days," in *Muriel Rukeyser, Selected Poems*, ed. Adrienne Rich (New York: Library of America, 2004), p. 69.

After Apollinaire & Brassens   Derived from Guillaume Apollinaire's poem "Le Pont Mirabeau" and Georges Brassens's song "Le Pont des Arts."

Slashes   "October '17 / May '68 / September '73": October 1917 marked the beginning of the Bolshevik Revolution in Russia, a determinative event in twentieth-century history. May 1968 saw massive popular U.S. opposition to the war in Vietnam, linked with the movement for Black civil rights and with anticolonial struggles abroad; in France there were uprisings of workers and students. On September 11, 1973, in Chile, a military coup under General Augusto Pinochet backed by the CIA violently seized power from the elected Socialist government of Salvador Allende.

"*In wolf-tree, see the former field*": See Anne Whiston Spirn, *The Language of Landscape* (New Haven: Yale University Press, 1998), pp. 18–19: "A 'wolf' tree is a tree within a woods, its size and form, large trunk and horizontal branches, anomalous to the environs of slim-trunked trees with upright branches . . . a clue to the open field in which it once grew alone, branches reaching laterally to the light and up."

Dislocations: Seven Scenarios   Section 5: "You thought you were inno-cent . . .": See Paul Nizan, *Aden Arabie* (New York: Monthly Review Press, 1968), p. 131.

Five O'Clock, January 2003   "most glorious creature on earth": See Robinson Jeffers, "Ninth Anniversary," in *The Wild God of the World: An Anthology of Robinson Jeffers*, ed. Albert Gelpi (Stanford, Calif.: Stanford University Press, 2003), p. 52: "there the most glorious / Creature on earth shines in the nights or glitters in the suns, / Or feels of its stone in the blind fog."

TELEPHONE RINGING IN THE LABYRINTH

Epigraphs on page 972 from Alan Davies, review of Brenda Iijima's *Around Sea* (Oakland, Calif.: O Books, 2004), in *St. Mark's in the Bowery Poetry Newsletter* (April/May 2004), used by permission of Alan Davies; and from Michael S. Harper, *Songlines in Michaeltree: New and Collected Poems* (Urbana: University of Illinois Press, 2000).

Calibrations   Landstuhl: American military hospital in Germany.

"You go to war with the army you have." U.S. Secretary of Defense Donald Rumsfeld, December 2004.

Melancholy Piano (extracts)   This translation was published as part of an international poetry project by the Quebec literary magazine *Estuaire* and the *New Review of Literature* (Otis College of Art and Design, Los Angeles) with Quebecois and Anglophone-American poets trans-lating poems by their counterparts.

Élise Turcotte's works include *Sombre Ménagerie* (Montreal: Éditions du Noroît, 2002) and *Diligence* (Longueuil: Les Petits Villages, 2004). Her novel *The Alien House* (Toronto: Cormorant Books, 2004), trans-lated into English by Sheila Fischman, received the Canadian Gover-nor General's Prize.

Improvisation on Lines from Edwin Muir's "Variations on a Time Theme"   See Edwin Muir, *Collected Poems, 1921–1951* (London: Faber

& Faber, 1952), and John C. Weston, ed., *Collected Poems of Hugh MacDiarmid*, rev. ed. (New York: Macmillan, 1967).

Hubble Photographs: After Sappho   For Sappho, see *Greek Lyric, I: Sappho, Alcaeus,* trans. David A. Campbell, Loeb Classical Library 142 (Cambridge, Mass.: Harvard University Press, 1982–), fragment 16, pp. 66–67: "Some say a host of cavalry, others of infantry, and others of ships, is the most beautiful thing on the black earth, but I say it is whatsoever a person loves. . . . I would rather see her lovely walk and the bright sparkle of her face than the Lydians' chariots and armed infantry."

This Is Not the Room   U.S. Vice President Richard Cheney, on NBC's *Meet the Press*, September 16, 2001: "we also have to work, though, sort of, the dark side . . . use any means at our disposal, basically, to achieve our objective."

Rereading The Dead Lecturer   See LeRoi Jones (Amiri Baraka), *The Dead Lecturer: Poems* (New York: Grove, 1967).

Letters Censored, Shredded, Returned to Sender, or Judged Unfit to Send   Passages in quotes are from Giuseppe Fiori, *Antonio Gramsci: Life of a Revolutionary*, trans. Tom Nairn (New York: Verso, 1990), pp. 31, 239; Antonio Gramsci, *Prison Letters*, ed. and trans. Hamish Henderson (London: Pluto Press, 1996), p. 135; and Antonio Gramsci, *Prison Notebooks*, ed. Joseph A. Buttigeig, trans. Joseph A. Buttigeig and Antonio Callari, vol. 1 (New York: Columbia University Press, 1992), p. 213.

Draft #2006   Part vi: "Out of sight, out of mind": See Carolyn Jones, "Battle of the Beds," *San Francisco Chronicle*, December 19, 2005, p. A-I.

TONIGHT NO POETRY WILL SERVE

Waiting for Rain, for Music   "*Send my roots rain*": Gerard Manley Hopkins, *Gerard Manley Hopkins: Selections*, ed. Catherine Phillips, The Oxford Authors (New York: Oxford University Press, 1986), p. 183.

"A struggle at the roots of the mind": Raymond Williams, *Marxism and Literature* (Oxford, UK: Oxford University Press, 1977), p. 212.

Reading the Iliad *(As If) for the First Time*   "For those dreamers who considered that force, thanks to progress, would soon be a thing of the past, the *Iliad* could appear as an historical document; for others, whose powers of recognition are more acute and who perceive force, today as yesterday, at the very center of human history, the *Iliad* is the purest and the loveliest of mirrors": Simone Weil, *The Iliad; or, The Poem of Force* (1940), trans. Mary McCarthy (Wallingford, Pa.: Pendle Hill, 1956), p. 3.

"Delusion / a daughter": See Homer, *The Iliad*, trans. Richmond Lattimore (Chicago: University of Chicago Press, 1951), pp. 394–95, bk. 19, lines 91–130.

"Horses turn away their heads / weeping": Homer, pp. 365–66, bk. 17, lines 426–40.

Fracture "it would be strange not to forgive": "Essentially all this is crude and meaningless . . . as an avalanche which involuntarily rolls down a mountain and overwhelms people. But when one listens to music, all this is: that some people lie in their graves and sleep, and that one woman is alive . . . and the avalanche seems no longer meaningless, since in nature everything has a meaning. And everything is forgiven, and it would be strange not to forgive": Anton Chekhov, *Notebook of Anton Chekhov*, trans. S. S. Koteliansky and Leonard Woolf (New York: B. W. Huebsch, 1921).

Turbulence "O the mind, mind has mountains, cliffs of fall / Frightful, sheer . . . Hold them cheap / May he who ne'er hung there": Gerard Manley Hopkins, *Gerard Manley Hopkins: Selections*, ed. Catherine Phillips, The Oxford Authors (New York: Oxford University Press, 1986), p. 167.

I was there, Axel "The Blue Ghazals." See "The Blue Ghazals," pages 307–12.

Ballade of the Poverties This revival of an old form owes inspiration to François Villon, *The Poems of François Villon*, ed. and trans. Galway Kinnell (Boston: Houghton Mifflin, 1977).

Black Locket "It lies in 'the way of seeing the world'. . .": Laura Betti, ed., *Pier Paolo Pasolini: A Future Life* (Italy: Associazione "Fondo Pier Paolo Pasolini," 1989), pp. 19–20.

Generosity The books mentioned are James Scully, *Raging Beauty: Selected Poems* (Washington, D.C.: Azul Editions, 1994), and René Char,

Lettera Amorosa (Paris: Gallimard, 1953), with illustrations by Georges Braque and Jean Arp.

Powers of Recuperation   "the massive figure on unrest's verge." See *Melencolia I*, a 1514 engraving by Albrecht Dürer. The "I" is thought to refer to "Melencolia Imaginativa," one of three types of melancholy described by Heinrich Cornelius Agrippa (1486–1535).

INDEX OF TITLES AND
FIRST LINES

3 1333 04606 0883